English Past and Present

Bamberger Beiträge zur Englischen Sprachwissenschaft

Bamberg Studies in English Linguistics

Begründet von / founded by Wolfgang Viereck

Herausgegeben von / edited by Manfred Krug,
Heinrich Ramisch und / and Wolfgang Viereck

Bd./Vol. 55

PETER LANG

Frankfurt am Main · Berlin · Bern · Bruxelles · New York · Oxford · Wien

Wolfgang Viereck
(ed.)

English
Past and Present

**Selected Papers
from the IAUPE Malta Conference
in 2010**

PETER LANG
Internationaler Verlag der Wissenschaften

Bibliographic Information published by the Deutsche Nationalbibliothek
The Deutsche Nationalbibliothek lists this publication in the Deutsche Nationalbibliografie; detailed bibliographic data is available in the internet at http://dnb.d-nb.de.

ISSN 0721-281X
ISBN 978-3-631-63895-8

© Peter Lang GmbH
Internationaler Verlag der Wissenschaften
Frankfurt am Main 2012
All rights reserved.

www.peterlang.de

Table of Contents

Preface

Ian Kirby
University of Lausanne

The present collection of articles represents for the most part papers given at the 21st Triennial Conference of the International Association of University Professors of English, which was held at the Valletta Campus of the University of Malta during the week beginning 19 July 2010 under the presidency of Professor Peter Vassallo. A few papers were given at the Association's Medieval Symposium which immediately preceded the main conference and which also took place in Malta.

The Conference, like its predecessors, offered a wide range of sections in the field of English studies. Most periods of world-wide literature in English from Anglo-Saxon to the present day were represented as well as many aspects of language and linguistics, and there was one subject of particular local interest, 'Writers and the Mediterranean'. Following IAUPE's regular practice, the conference week also included cultural activities and visits to some of the many ancient monuments of Malta and Gozo. Of these latter, a number were included in a one-day post-Conference tour of the islands.

The Association is open to all full professors of English and other scholars of distinction, and welcomes applications for membership. Information may be obtained from the undersigned, currently Secretary-General of the Association, at ian.kirby@bluewin.ch The Association's website may also be consulted, at www.iaupe.net

Editor's Note

Papers 1-19 were delivered in various sections at the main conference in Malta, paper no. 20 was given at the Malta Medieval Symposium and the final paper was presented at the IAUPE conference in Lund in 2007.

Supplementary Evidence and the Manuscript Text of *Beowulf*: A Survey of Sources

J. R. Hall
University of Mississippi

The text of *Beowulf* is part of London, British Library, MS. Cotton Vitellius A. xv, a volume composed of two originally separate manuscripts bound together presumably by a bookbinder in the employ of Sir Robert Cotton. The first of the two originally separate manuscripts is now called the Southwick Codex; the second, the Nowell Codex.[1]

Robert Cotton, born in 1571, began collecting manuscripts as a teenager, evidently inspired by William Camden, his former teacher at Westminster School and a noted antiquary. By the time he died, in 1631, Cotton had amassed some nine hundred manuscripts, among them the Southwick Codex and the Nowell Codex.[2]

The Southwick Codex, named from the location of its first known owner, St. Mary's Priory, in Southwick, Hampshire, consists of 90 leaves of parchment and dates from the mid-twelfth century. The codex contains four works translated into Old English: St. Augustine's *Soliloquies*, the *Gospel of Nicodemus*, the prose *Solomon and Saturn*, and eleven scribal lines remaining from a homily on St. Quintin, a Roman Christian martyred in Gaul in 287.

---

1   Kemp Malone popularized the terms Southwick Codex and Nowell Codex in his facsimile edition, *The Nowell Codex: British Museum Cotton Vitellius A. xv. Second MS*, Early English Manuscripts in Facsimile, 12 (Copenhagen, 1963). For a succinct description of Cotton Vitellius A. xv and its contents, see Malone, pp. 11-17; and N. R. Ker, *Catalogue of Manuscripts containing Anglo-Saxon* (Oxford, 1957), no. 215 (Southwick Codex) and no. 216 (Nowell Codex), pp. 279-83. (Ker does not use the terms Southwick Codex and Nowell Codex.) A valuable digitized color facsimile of Cotton Vitellius A. xv as a whole has been done by Kevin Kiernan, with Andrew Prescott et al., *Electronic 'Beowulf'*, 2 CDs (London and Ann Arbor, 1999). Steven E. Smith, 'The Provenance of the *Beowulf* Manuscript', *ANQ* 13.1 (2000), 3-7, speculates that the two codices may have been from Southwick and that the custodians of the Cotton library may have wanted to keep together two manuscripts of the same provenance. In '*Beowulf*' *and the 'Beowulf' Manuscript*, rev. ed. (Ann Arbor, 1996), pp. 73-79, Kiernan cites a table of contents made by Richard James, Cotton librarian, showing that the two codices were associated no later than c. 1628-1638.

2   For a survey of Cotton's life and library, see Graham Parry, 'Sir Robert Cotton', *The Trophies of Time: English Antiquarians of the Seventeenth Century* (Oxford, 1995), pp. 70-94; and Thomas N. Hall, 'Sir Robert Bruce Cotton', *Pre-Nineteenth-Century British Book Collectors and Bibliographers*, ed. William Baker and Kenneth Womack, *Dictionary of Literary Biography*, 213 (Detroit, 1999), pp. 57-69.

The second manuscript that makes up Cotton Vitellius A. xv, the Nowell Codex, is named after Laurence Nowell, who apparently owned it and who, in any
case, wrote his name and the date 1563 on the first extant leaf, folio 91r.[3] The
codex consists of 116 leaves of parchment and dates from perhaps the first quar-
ter of the eleventh century.[4] It contains five articles in Old English: a fragment of
the *Life of St. Christopher*, *Alexander's Letter to Aristotle*, *Wonders of the East*,
the poem called *Beowulf*, and part of another poem called *Judith*.

In 1622 Robert Cotton, a sometime Member of Parliament, purchased a
house adjoining the House of Commons within the confines of Westminster
Palace, and there, in what came to be called Cotton House, he lived and main-
tained his library. The library continued to be kept at Cotton House for a century.
In 1722 the Cotton Library was relocated from Cotton House to Essex House in
the Strand because Cotton House had fallen into disrepair.[5] A decade later Essex
House came to be considered a firetrap, and in 1730 the collection was moved to
Ashburnham House in Little Dean's Yard, Westminster.[6]

Unlike Essex House, Ashburnham House proved to be a firetrap not merely
in thought but in deed: a chimney on the floor below the library caught fire on 23
October 1731, Saturday, in the young hours of the morning, little more than a
century after the death of Robert Cotton. Some two hundred manuscripts were
destroyed or damaged, including Cotton Vitellius A. xv. Both portions of the
Cotton Vitellius A. xv – the Southwick Codex and the Nowell Codex – sustained
loss as flames ate inward at the folio edges, but the loss to the Nowell Codex was
worse because the width of the writing area is greater.[7] Although reclamation
work soon began on the damaged manuscripts, it was attenuated, and the brittle

---

3   The date 1563 is what is routinely reported as legible in Nowell's hand at the top of the folio.
     When I studied the leaf, I found the putative '3' unreadable, lost to a tear in the parchment. A
     later hand has penciled '1563' above Nowell's date on the paper frame in which the folio is set. I
     suspect that when readers report that that Nowell wrote '1563' they are depending on the pen-
     ciled annotation for the '3' rather than on what they can read in ink on the parchment itself. In
     citing folios, I follow Kiernan and others and use the older foliation. (In the alternate foliation,
     employed by Malone, the leaf is cited as 94r.)

4   The dating of the Nowell Codex as well as the dating of the composition of *Beowulf* is fraught
     with controversy. See, for example, Kiernan, '*Beowulf* and the '*Beowulf*' *Manuscript*, pp. xv-xxi.

5   Two decades before that, in 1702, Sir John Cotton, grandson of Robert Cotton, bestowed the
     Cotton Library on the English people, an act of generosity that contributed to the founding of the
     British Museum in 1753. See Thomas Hall, p. 68.

6   On the establishment of the library at Cotton House, its location within the precincts of West-
     minster Palace, its physical organization, its donation to the public, its movement from one site
     to another, and its partial burning, see Colin G. C. Tite, *The Manuscript Library of Sir Robert
     Cotton* (London, 1994), pp. 19-39, 79-99.

7   Ker, *Catalogue*, p. 281.

leaves remained imperiled for more than a century until Sir Frederic Madden, Manuscript Librarian of the British Library (1837-66), designed a method for restoring and conserving the Cotton manuscripts and personally directed the project.[8]

As first pointed out by Kevin Kiernan, August 1845 is crucial to *Beowulf* studies because it was then that Madden saw to the preservation of Cotton Vitellius A. xv.[9] Madden commissioned a craftsman, Henry Gough, to mount each leaf on a stiff paper frame of which the interior edge was cut to contour the leaf's uneven edges and leave all or most of the script visible to the naked eye. Each leaf was affixed to the frame by glue on the verso and by transparent goldbeater's skin (thin animal membrane) on the recto.[10] Some letters in the text of *Beowulf* and of the other works in the Nowell Codex crumbled off in the process of preparing and mounting the folios; other letters or letter fragments were hidden under the stiff paper frame where the frame overlaps the writing on the verso of the leaves. Today the Nowell codex is virtually the same as it was in 1845 after restoration. But many letters along the folio margins were lost between October 1731, the month and year of the fire, and August 1845. This means that any records we have of manuscript readings before August 1845, when the text of *Beowulf* was more nearly complete than now, claim value.

There are seven chief records, two from the latter part of the eighteenth century and five from the earlier part of the nineteenth century.

The first and the most important record is a copy of *Beowulf* usually known as Thorkelin A written by an anonymous scribe. We do not know exactly when the transcript was written. The prevailing assumption is that it was done some time in or after late 1786 under the direction of Grímur Thorkelin, an Icelandic scholar employed by the king of Denmark to investigate Danish antiquities in England and the first editor of *Beowulf*.[11] I prefer to call the document transcript A rather than Thorkelin A because I am uncertain that Thorkelin commissioned

---

8 Madden's work is chronicled and celebrated by Andrew Prescott, ' "Their Present Miser- able State of Cremation": The Restoration of the Cotton Library', *Sir Robert Cotton as Collector*, ed. C. J. Wright (London, 1997), 391-454.

9 *'Beowulf' and the 'Beowulf' Manuscript*, pp. 68-70.

10 For more details on the manner of preservation see Kiernan, *'Beowulf' and the 'Beowulf' Manuscript*, p. 69; Prescott, "'Their Present Miserable State of Cremation'", pp. 416-17, 426; and Prescott, *'The Electronic Beowulf* and Digital Restoration', *Literary and Linguistic Computing*, 12.3 (1997), 189.

11 On Thorkelin and his trip to England, see Kiernan, *The Thorkelin Transcripts of 'Beowulf'* (Copenhagen, 1986), pp. 1-41. On Thorkelin's edition see my essay, 'The First Two Editions of *Beowulf*: Thorkelin's (1815) and Kemble's (1833)', *The Editing of Old English: Papers from the 1990 Manchester Conference*, ed. D. G. Scragg and Paul E. Szarmach (Woodbridge, 1994), pp 239-50. The two Thorkelin transcripts, brought back to Denmark by Thorkelin in 1791, are held by the Kongelige Bibliotek, Copenhagen.

the transcript.[12] For one thing Thorkelin complains in a letter home that hiring people to make transcripts at the British Museum is very costly.[13] Further, when Thorkelin himself copies the text of *Beowulf* in transcript B, he copies it line for line, whereas the copyist of transcript A does not. In Cotton Vitellius A. xv, the text of *Beowulf* occupies 70 leaves or 140 pages; the transcript A scribe, using a wider writing area, fits the text of *Beowulf* into 89 pages plus two lines. A third reason for doubting that Thorkelin himself commissioned the transcript is that it is so inaccurately executed, especially the first third of the work, that Thorkelin found it necessary to make his own transcript. If Thorkelin were paying a handsome price for the transcription, one would think that he would be closely checking on the accuracy of his hired hand from the outset.

If Thorkelin did not commission the transcript A scribe to copy the text of *Beowulf*, who did? I do not know. However, Reading Room Registers in the British Library record that Cotton Vitellius A. xv was requested by five borrowers – Barrington, Astle, Topham, Strutt, and Milman – sometimes for long periods in 1772, 1773, 1774, and 1776.[14] Daines Barrington, Thomas Astle, and John Topham were antiquaries with whom Grímur Thorkelin became acquainted during his extended stay in England (1786-91).[15] One of them may have commissioned a copy in the 1770s for an antiquarian purpose and later, on learning of Thorkelin's deep interest in Danish history, may have donated the transcript to him.[16]

---

12 In 'The First Two Editions of *Beowulf*', p. 240, I endorse Kiernan's identification of the transcript A copyist as James Matthews, an employee of the British Museum (*The Thorkelin Transcripts*, pp. 21-25). I now find the identification unpersuasive for the reasons given in the present essay.

13 After quoting Thorkelin's complaint to his patron, Johan Bülow, that copying costs are high, Kiernan, *The Thorkelin Transcripts*, pp. 15-16, contends that this is the reason that only one copy of a British Museum document commissioned by Thorkelin – transcript A – has come to light. I would reverse the argument: the high cost of hiring a copyist is reason to doubt that Thorkelin commissioned transcript A.

14 British Library, Reading Room Registers, Add. MS. 46509 (fols. 148v, 149r, 150v, 151r, 153v, 154r) and Add. MS. 46510 (fols. 7v, 8r, 9v, 11r, 19v, 21r, 39v, 40r, 101v, 102r, 118v, 119r). (Milman requested the manuscript on behalf of Topham.) To request Cotton Vitellius A. xv need not indicate interest in *Beowulf*. A reader may have wished to study any of the nine pieces in the manuscript.

15 In his edition, *De Danorum Rebus Gestis Secul. III & IV. Poëma danicum dialecto anglossaxonica* (Copenhagen, 1815), p. xvii, Thorkelin refers to the late Thomas Astle as a dear friend (*amicissimus*). In 'Letters to an Antiquary: The Literary Correspondence of G. J. Thorkelin (1752-1829)', Ph.D. Thesis, University of Edinburgh, 1972, E. H. Harvey Wood in her index lists six letters from Astle to Thorkelin (p. 506), two from Barrington (p. 507), and one from Topham (p. 547).

16 This idea was suggested to me some years ago by Dr. Andrew Prescott (then on the staff of the Department of Manuscripts, British Library) soon after I discovered the evidence for the use of Cotton Vitellius A. xv in the 1770s in the Reading Room Registers. See also Prescott, '*The Electronic Beowulf* and Digital Restoration', p. 188.

In any case the transcript A scribe, like nearly everyone else in England at the time, did not know Old English and was unacquainted with Insular minuscule. This makes him a more literal copyist than a scholar, like Thorkelin, with perhaps an edition in mind.[17] Thanks to transcript A, we have evidence for more than 115 letters in the text of *Beowulf* for which otherwise we would otherwise have questionable evidence or no evidence. For example, transcript A is the only witness to record *wit* 589b, *um* of *mærþum* 828a, and *h* of *dyhttig* 1287a.[18]

The transcript is, however, rife with errata. For the first nine hundred lines or so the A copyist repeatedly confuses three similar but separate graphemes – wynn, thorn, and *p*.[19] To judge by the text of *Beowulf* as it now stands in the manuscript, A commits more than a thousand letter errors, including some seventy times in which he fails to record an individual letter that can be read today and several instances in which he fails to copy extant syllables, words, scribal lines, and even longer passages.[20]

Transcript B was executed by Thorkelin himself in perhaps 1789.[21] Thorkelin made his own transcript when he already had transcript A probably because (as earlier noted) transcript A has so many errors and because transcript A, not following the lineation of *Beowulf* in Cotton Vitellius A. xv, is very difficult to collate with the text of *Beowulf*.[22] But transcript B itself is rife with errata: Thor-

---

17 A reason for thinking that Thorkelin, in making his own transcript (transcript B), had an edition in mind is that he silently expanded abbreviations and introduced capital letters as he copied when he recognized – or thought he recognized – proper names.

18 Citation of the poem is from R. D. Fulk, Robert E. Bjork, and John D. Niles, eds., *Klaeber's Beowulf and the Fight at Finnsburg*, 4th ed. (Toronto, 2008).

19 In *The Thorkelin Transcripts of Beowulf in Facsimile,* Early English Manuscripts in Facsimile, 1 (Copenhagen, 1951), p. 5, Kemp Malone calls line 917 of *Beowulf* 'a dividing line' in transcript A. After transcribing this line from the poem, the scribe is generally much more accurate in distinguishing wynn, thorn, and *p*.

20 The count of letter errors for transcript A and (later) for transcript B is mine, derived from the folio-by-folio inventory of copying errors in Kiernan's *The Thorkelin Transcripts of 'Beowulf'*, pp. 47-95. I define a letter error as a letter miscopied as another letter, an abbreviation incorrectly expanded, a letter extant in the manuscript text but omitted by the copyist, or a letter added to the original text. For detailed discussion on the surviving readings omitted by the transcript A scribe, see Malone, *The Thorkelin Transcripts of Beowulf in Facsimile*, pp. 18-20.

21 For the date 1789 see Kiernan, 'Madden, Thorkelin, and MS Vitellius/Vespasian A XV', *The Library*, 6th ser., 8.2 (1986), 127-32. The date has been challenged by Johan Gerritsen, 'The Thorkelin Transcripts of *Beowulf*: A Codicological Description, with Notes on their Genesis and History', *The Library*, 6th ser., 13.1 (1991), 15-18. The evidence seems to favor Kiernan's argument.

22 Locating readings in transcript A corresponding to readings in the manuscript text of *Beowulf* is so irksome that in April 1983 folio numbers and slashes indicating folio changes in Cotton Vitellius A. xv were inserted into transcript A to facilitate reference. (For the date of the insertions, see the inside back cover of transcript A.) A drawback of the insertions is that they distort historical experience,

kelin commits more than 1,500 letter errors.[23] More than 600 of these letter errors, however, are occasioned by Thorkelin's failure to cross *d* to make *ð* (eth),[24] a natural error for an Icelander educated in Denmark to make since in Danish and in the Icelandic of Thorkelin's day the single letter *d* represents both the voiced alveolar stop [d] and the voiced interdental fricative [ð]. Subtract his eth errors, and Thorkelin seems about as accurate – or about as inaccurate – a copyist as A.

Nonetheless, Kiernan, calling transcript B 'an edition-in-progress', contends that 'we cannot depend on B as a primary source for lost readings in *Beowulf*' because the transcript contains a 'mysterious mixture of emendation and restoration, and of conflation and collation with A'.[25] Kiernan's conclusion is, I believe, mistaken. Thorkelin's transcript, as we have it, shows (like transcript A) much editorial alteration of the original text. We can identify the editorial alteration as such because (like the editorial alteration in transcript A) it is written in ink different from the original ink in which Thorkelin copied *Beowulf* from the manuscript. If we discount all readings in transcript B not in the original ink, we are left with a transcript not conflated with readings in A or contaminated by speculative emendation.[26]

Further, Kiernan's argument is inconsistent. 'With a few exceptions', he says, 'Thorkelin obliges us to relinquish B as a textual authority for the poem'.[27] But if transcript B is 'a mysterious mixture of emendation and restoration', how does one justify exceptions? Why should a scholar trust *any* readings from Thorkelin's copy of the poem? I find that, rather than emendations, Thorkelin's substantive departures from the manuscript text of the poem *as he copied* are, like the departures in transcript A, scribal errors.[28] If we evaluate transcript B by the same standards by which we evaluate transcript A, we have evidence for more than a hundred letters lost from the text of *Beowulf* for which transcript A either

---

rendering transcript A easier to use than it had been for Thorkelin. Cf. Gerritsen, 'The Thorkelin Transcripts of *Beowulf*: A Codicological Description', p. 6, n. 7.

23 I do not consider as letter errors the hundreds of times that Thorkelin copies a capital letter for a small letter (e.g., B for b) or a small letter for a capital letter (e.g., s for S). These changes misrepresent the visual, but not phonological, nature of the text copied. See also n. 17 above.

24 In *The Thorkelin Transcripts of 'Beowulf'*, p. 131, Kiernan reports that Thorkelin erroneously transcribes ð as d 620 times.

25 *The Thorkelin Transcripts of 'Beowulf'*, pp. 97, 117.

26 My conclusion agrees in substance with Gerritsen's in '*Beowulf*: The Foundations of the Text', *NSES Bulletin* 1.1 (1991), 27-28; and 'What use are the Thorkelin transcripts of *Beowulf*?' *Anglo-Saxon England* 28 (Cambridge, 1999), pp. 28, 37-8.

27 *The Thorkelin Transcripts of 'Beowulf'*, p. 97.

28 By substantive departures I mean changes in letter values. Substantive departures do not include the introduction of capital letters or changes in spacing or the accurate expansion of abbreviations. See also n. 17 above.

gives no reading or for which A's reading is questionable.[29] For example, transcript B is the only witness to record *ða com* 1802b, *r* in *fær[e]* 2009a, and *se* in *eorðse[le]* 2232a.[30] As I hope to show elsewhere, evidence from nineteenth-century witnesses to the text of *Beowulf* support the majority of the more than one hundred letters for which I think we may confidently depend on transcript B. To the five nineteenth-century witnesses we now turn.

In 1815 Thorkelin published his edition of *Beowulf* under the title *De Danorum Rebus Gestis Secul. III & IV. Poëma danicum dialecto anglo- saxonica.* In the next fifteen years three scholars took their copies of Thorkelin's edition and collated his text against the text of *Beowulf* in Cotton Vitellius A. xv: John J. Conybeare in 1817, Frederic Madden in 1824, and Benjamin Thorpe in 1830. Further, in 1829 N. F. S. Grundtvig, a Dane, brought to London a handwritten text of *Beowulf* to collate with the manuscript. A fifth and final witness to the manuscript text of *Beowulf* is John M. Kemble, who published the first English edition of the poem in 1833. A word about each man and his work.

In 1809 Conybeare, Oxford's Professor of Anglo-Saxon, called for an edition of what he termed the 'Saxon Romance' known today as *Beowulf.*[31] Eight years later he collated Thorkelin's text against the manuscript, finding countless errors.[32] Conybeare was not a dependable collator, however. By my count Thorkelin's

---

29 In *The Thorkelin Transcripts of 'Beowulf'*, pp. 144-45, Kiernan finds 72 potentially genuine letters in B not found in A. However, he questions or rejects more than half of the letters and makes it clear that other letters among the 72 could be questioned as well. We are left, finally, with 16 letters that Kiernan expressly accepts. In his edition of the poem in *Electronic 'Beowulf'*, Kiernan increases the number of letters he expressly accepts from B but places the letters in square brackets (e.g., *sea[ro]net* 406a) in contrast to the letters he accepts from A alone or from A and B together, which he places in parentheses (e.g., *wear(ð)* 6b). Nowhere does Kiernan abrogate his conclusion, 'we cannot depend on B as a primary source for lost readings in *Beowulf*'.

30 In line 2009a the letter *e* in *fær[e]* is a modern editorial restoration not found in transcript A or B. But we can be reasonably certain of the rest of the restoration on the basis of A and B's *f*, A's *æ*, and B's *r*. See my essay, '*Beowulf* 2009a: *f... bifongen*', *JEGP* 106:04 (2007), 417-27. In line 2232a the letters *le* in *eorð-se[le]* are a modern editorial restoration not found in transcript A or B. We are able to restore the letters with near certitude only because Thorkelin preserved se in his transcript. See my essay, 'Three Studies on the Manuscript Text of *Beowulf*: Lines 47b, 747b, and 2232a', *Beatus Vir: Studies in Early English and Norse Manuscripts in Memory of Phillip Pulsiano*, ed. A. N. Doane and Kirsten Wolf (Tempe, 2006), 458-67.

31 John J. Conybeare, *The Romance of Octavian, Emperor of Rome* (Oxford, 1809), p. 49.

32 A selection of these corrected errors was posthumously published as 'Collation of the Copenhagen Edition of Beowulf with the Original Manuscript Preserved in the British Museum' in John J. Conybeare's *Illustrations of Anglo-Saxon Poetry*, ed. William Daniel Conybeare (London, 1826), 137-55. The existence of Conybeare's original collation did not come to light until W. F. Bolton acquired Conybeare's copy of Thorkelin from a book dealer. See Bolton's 'The Conybeare Copy of Thorkelin', *English Studies*, 55 (1974), 97-107. I am grateful to Professor Bolton for lending me the book for private study before he donated it to the British Library in January 1994.

edition contains more than 1,900 letter errors. In his collation Conybeare failed
to correct more than a third of them. This does not mean, however, that Conybeare's transcript has little value as a witness to letters now lost from the manuscript text of *Beowulf*. Most of his collational errors are errors of omission, instances in which Thorkelin's text has an error that Conybeare fails to correct.
When there is evidence in Conybeare's collation that he actually worked on a
particular reading, his work – to judge by the comparative evidence of transcripts
A and B and of the later nineteenth-century witnesses – is reasonably reliable.

Conybeare's most valuable reading comes at line 1741a, in which he provides
the only solid evidence we have for a letter. At this place the manuscript today
preserves only *wet*.[33] Transcripts A and B read *weaxed*, a reading Thorkelin
incorporated in his edition as *Weaxed*. In collating Thorkelin's *Weaxed* with the
manuscript text of *Beowulf*, Conybeare crossed the ascender of *d* to make *ð*.
There are two things to note about these readings. First, transcripts A and B often
neglect to add the cross stroke to make *d* into *ð* even when the cross stroke is
clear in manuscript. Second, in collating Thorkelin's text with the manuscript
Conybeare never crosses *d* to make *ð* unless the manuscript itself has *ð*. In short,
line 1741a appears to be an instance in which transcripts A and B are careless (as
they often are) and in which Conybeare is careful (as he sometimes is). Conybeare
alone preserves for us the final letter in the expected reading *weaxeð*.[34]

When Conybeare collated Thorkelin's edition of *Beowulf* with the manuscript
text in 1817, he was no longer Professor of Anglo-Saxon at Oxford but Vicar of
Batheaston, a village three miles northeast of Bath, in Somerset. The circumstance
was fortunate for Frederic Madden – the same Frederic Madden whose leadership
and ingenuity later led to the restoration of Cotton Vitellius A. xv in 1845 – who
happened to be visiting his brother at Batheaston in January 1824. Conybeare
befriended Madden, then twenty-three, and introduced him to Old English, even
to the point of allowing him to copy his collation of *Beowulf* in his (Madden's)
copy of Thorkelin's edition. In June and July of 1824, after Conybeare's sudden
death, Madden made his own collation of Thorkelin's text with the manuscript.[35]

---

33   Here and hereafter I use a double dagger, ‡, to represent an ambiguous letter fragment.

34   For further details see my essay, '*Beowulf* 1741a: *we‡*... and the Supplementary Evidence', *ANQ*
     21.1 (2008), 3-9.

35   Details on Conybeare's and Madden's friendship and on Madden's collation are recorded in
     Madden's journal for 1824 (Oxford, Bodleian Library, MSS. Eng. hist. c. 145 and 146), as I dis-
     cussed in my unpublished paper, 'Madden's Collation of *Beowulf*: Some Preliminary Findings',
     Tenth Annual Conference of the Southeastern Medieval Association, Eastern Kentucky University,
     6 October 1984. I discovered the existence of Madden's collation in June 1984 in Harvard's
     Houghton Library. See my essay, 'Some Additional Books at Harvard Annotated by Sir Frederic
     Madden', *Notes and Queries*, 32.3 (1985), 313-15.

Meticulous by nature, Madden corrected more than ninety percent of Thorkelin's letter errors, a much higher percentage than Conybeare.

Madden's collation is valuable in various ways. For example, at line 1754b the manuscript today preserves only an ambiguous fragment that may be the remains of *e* or the right side of *æ*. Transcript A reads *lane*; transcript B, *læne*. Madden's reading, *læne*, confirms B's reading and, along with other nineteenth-century witnesses, supports the expected spelling of the word in *Beowulf*. Again, at line 2094b the manuscript now has only *hon*. For this place A reads *hondlean*; B, *hondlan*. For Madden six letters were left: *hondle*. His reading supports A that there was once an *e* immediately following *l* in the manuscript. Finally, on rare occasion Madden preserves a letter or two no one else records. The best example comes at line 2268b, in which A reads *hpeir* (which makes little sense), B gives no reading, and the manuscript today has *hʒeʒ*. Madden's reading, *hwear*, plus a vertical stroke, shows that we may confidently restore the damaged form as *hwearf*, a word well suited to the context.[36]

In May 1829, nearly five years after Madden collated Thorkelin's text, N. F. S. Grundtvig, a controversial Danish churchman and man of letters, arrived at the British Museum to collate a handwritten text of *Beowulf*, which he composed mainly from Thorkelin's edition, transcript A and transcript B (then, as now, housed in the Kongelige Bibliotek, Copenhagen), and his own conjectures.[37] Grundtvig had long been intrigued by the text of *Beowulf*. Fourteen years earlier in an extended book review he had severely faulted Thorkelin's edition,[38] and in an appendix to his paraphrase of *Beowulf* published in 1820 he had furnished forty-six pages of learned textual notes.[39]

Grundtvig proved to be a more acute critic and philologist than collator. Although he recorded more than two thousand annotations and may have spent two weeks on the project (28 May-15 June), his overall collation is not as accurate as Madden's: Grundtvig's testimony, like Conybeare's, is reliable only when there

---

36 The examples of Madden's evidence at lines 1754b, 2094b, and 2268b come from my unpublished paper, 'Madden's Collation of *Beowulf*' (n. 35 above).

37 Grundtvig's collated handwritten text (Grundtvig-Arkivet Fasc. 307, Kongelige Bibliotek) was brought to light by Birte Kelly, 'The Formative Stages of Modern *Beowulf* Scholarship, Textual, Historical and Literary, Seen in the Work of Scholars of the Earlier Nineteenth Century', Ph.D. Thesis, University of London, 1979, pp. 90-110. For an informative summary of Grundtvig's life and work, see Niels Lyhne Jensen, 'Grundtvig, Nikolaj Frederik Severin', *Dictionary of Scandinavian Literature*, ed. Virpi Zuck (New York, 1990), pp. 187-90.

38 'Et Par Ord om det nys udkomne angelsaxiske Digt', *Nyeste Skilderie af Kjøbenhavn* (1815): no. 60, cols. 945-52; no. 63, cols. 998-1002; no. 64, cols. 1009-15; no. 65, cols. 1025-30; no. 66, cols. 1045-7.

39 *Bjowulfs Drape. Et Gothisk Helte-Digt fra forrige Aar-Tusinde af Angel-Saxisk paa Danske Riim* (Copenhagen, 1820), 267-312.

is direct evidence in his collation that he evaluated a reading. The direct evidence usually consists of his using the label O – standing for Original – in one of two circumstances. First, he simply inserts O after a difficult reading or a half-line in his handwritten edition when the difficult reading or half-line agrees with the manuscript text of *Beowulf*. (The insertion of O after a half-line is sometimes ambiguous: Does it refer to the entire half-line or to a particular word in it?) Second, he inserts O together with the letter or letters surviving from a word in the manuscript. For example, the handwritten text that Grundtvig took to London has the reading *wynn* at line 5448 (line 2727a in more recent editions). In actually comparing *wynn* of his handwritten text against the manuscript, Grundtvig wrote in the right margin 'wynn. O', which would indicate that the manuscript reading is *wynn* with a letter evidently lost after the second *n*.

I have chosen this particular reading because it exemplifies a difficulty in working with the supplementary textual evidence of *Beowulf*. Today the manuscript text of *Beowulf* has only *wy* followed by three minims. Transcript A reads *wym*; transcript B, *wyni*; Conybeare, *wynne*; and Madden, *wyn*. The expected reading is *wynne*, and that indeed is what Conybeare implicitly reads in accepting without note *wynne* in Thorkelin's edition. In collating Thorkelin's edition, however, Madden deletes *ne* of *wynne*. We can set aside Conybeare's testimony in that he gives no evidence of having worked on the word, but Grundtvig's reading – 'wynn. O' – is explicit and precise. It is difficult to accept Grundtvig's second *n*, however, in view of transcript A's reading, transcript B's reading, and Madden's finding no evidence for a second *n* five years before Grundtvig's collation. The earlier readings may be incorrect (the readings of transcripts A and B make no sense as such), but so may be Grundtvig's despite his labeling the reading in his collation O. Years later Grundtvig used the reading in his edition of the poem.[40] In his facsimile edition of *Beowulf*, Julius Zupitza, reading *wynn[e]*, cites Grundtvig's edition as evidence that the form in question once had a second *n*.[41] Should we, like Zupitza, accept Grundtvig's evidence? There is no certain answer.

The summer after Grundtvig did his work, Benjamin Thorpe, an Irish businessman who became an Anglo-Saxonist after studying under Rasmus Rask in Denmark, arrived in England to collate Thorkelin's text against the manuscript.[42] We

---

40 *Beowulfes Beorh eller Bjovulfs-Drapen, det Old-Angelske Heltedigt* (Copenhagen and London, 1861), line 5446.

41 Julius Zupitza, ed., *Beowulf Reproduced in Facsimile from the Unique Manuscript British Museum MS. Cotton Vitellius A. xv.* 2d ed., ed. Norman Davis (London, 1959), p. 126.

42 For background on Thorpe see Phillip Pulsiano, 'Benjamin Thorpe (1782-1870)', *Medieval Scholarship: Biographical Studies on the Formation of a Discipline*, ed. Helen Damico, with Donald Fennema and Karmen Lenz (New York, 1998), II, 75-92. For background on Rask, see Kirsten Wolf, 'Rasmus Rask (1787-1832)', in the same volume, pp. 109-24.

know exactly when Thorpe finished because he tells us on the front flyleaf recto of his copy of Thorkelin that it was 13 August 1830.[43] When Thorpe collated Thorkelin's text, he did not work with a tabula rasa. While still in Denmark, he had copied many textual notes in the appendix to Grundtvig's paraphrase of *Beowulf*, notes on which Grundtvig and Rask had collaborated to some extent when they planned on a new edition of the poem.[44] But Thorpe did not commingle Grundtvig's and Rask's notes with his own. In a memo dated 'Elsinore 5 June 1830', written on the inside front cover of his copy of Thorkelin's edition, Thorpe specifies that the annotations recorded in the left margin in pencil are taken from Rask and Grundtvig.[45] This implies that Thorpe planned to write his own annotations in ink in the right margin, and so he did some two months later.

In the first five hundred lines of *Beowulf*, Thorkelin's text contains more than five hundred departures from the manuscript text of the poem. Thorpe corrected more than eighty-five percent of the departures and introduced only a few of his own. Of Thorpe's 72 missed letter corrections in these lines, however, 51 occur in places in which he failed to replace one of Thorkelin's 220 *þ*'s with *ð*, a kind of correction not attempted by Conybeare, Madden, and Grundtvig.[46] If, for the sake of comparison, the category be excluded, Thorpe's accuracy looks more impressive. His 21 missed letter corrections are comparable to Madden's and Grundtvig's for the first five hundred lines of the poem and many fewer than Conybeare's. Ironically, among the most valuable readings in Thorpe's collation are four places in

---

43 Thorpe's collated copy of Thorkelin, owned by the Universitätsbibliothek Freiburg im Breisgau, was brought to light by Tilman Westphalen, *Beowulf* 3150-55: *Textkritik und Editionsgeschichte* (Munich, 1967), pp. 109-24. For Thorpe's statement (in Latin) that he has completed the collation, see table IC, following p. 116.

44 The collaboration ended when Rask went to Sweden, where he published a pioneering Old English grammar, *Angelsaksisk Sproglære tilligemed en kort Læsebog* (Stockholm, 1817). In the same year in which he collated Thorkelin's Beowulf, Thorpe published an English translation of Rask's revised edition of his grammar: *A Grammar of the Anglo-Saxon Tongue, with a Praxis* (Copenhagen, 1830).

45 Westphalen reproduces Thorpe's memo in table IB, following p. 116.

46 In most Old English manuscripts written in Insular minuscule the characters *ð* and *þ* are interchangeable, each standing for both the voiced and voiceless interdental fricatives (today spelled <th> as in *the* or as in *thin*), depending on phonological context. The *Beowulf* scribes also appear to use the two characters interchangeably. In his edition Thorkelin intentionally replaced the *ð*'s he found in the manuscript text of *Beowulf* (as recorded in transcript A or B) with *þ*'s. In their collations Conybeare, Madden, and Grundtvig do not attempt to replace the *þ*'s in the texts before them with *ð*'s to conform with the manuscript text of the poem. Thorpe, however, tries to restore the original *ð*'s. I include Thorkelin's systematic substitution of *þ*'s for *ð*'s in the category of departures from the manuscript text but not in the category of letter errors.

which he supports *ð* in transcript A as against original *d* in transcript B: *hroðgar* 407a, *maðþum*s*weord* 1023a, *guð[um]* 2178a, and *bealonið[e]* 2714b.[47]

Thorpe's 1855 edition of *Beowulf* supposedly reflects his 1830 collation.[48] I say *supposedly* because throughout his edition he often implicitly claims to have seen letters in the manuscript that he had expunged as no longer present twenty-five years earlier. For example, in collating the first five hundred lines of *Beowulf* in 1830, he underpoints 109 letters in Thorkelin's text as no longer in the manuscript. In his 1855 edition he preserves all but nine of the letters without indicating his dependence on Thorkelin's edition for the remaining hundred. It is difficult to excuse Thorpe's cavalier treatment of the textual record. By 1830 the manuscript had born many more losses than his edition acknowledges.

The fifth and final nineteenth-century witness to the text of *Beowulf* before 1845 is John M. Kemble, a graduate of Trinity College, Cambridge, who published the first English edition of the poem in 1833.[49] In late September 1832 Kemble, at age twenty-five, wrote his philological hero, Jakob Grimm, to say that he had made Grimm a transcript of *Beowulf* but that his friends persuaded him to edit the poem himself.[50] Although dependent on Thorkelin's text in ways that Kemble fails to acknowledge, Kemble's text is much more accurate than Thorkelin's: in the first five hundred lines of the poem, Thorkelin has about three hundred letter errors; Kemble has twenty-one (not counting his misprinting *þes* for *þæs* at line 108b, an error he corrected in his *corrigenda*).[51]

---

47   For the sake of simplicity I omit many details. For example, at line 407a only *hr‡* remains in the manuscript at the end of a scribal line, with *gar* beginning the next scribal line. Further, *o* in *hroðgar* (printed by editors as *Hroðgar* since it is a proper name) is supported by transcript A, transcript B, Madden, Grundtvig, Thorpe, and Kemble much as °ð is supported by transcript A and Thorpe. At line 1023a the letter in question is the one after *ma* (*ð* as in transcript A or d as originally in transcript B?).

48   *The Anglo-Saxon Poems of Beowulf, The Scôp or Gleeman's Tale, and The Fight at Finnesburg* (Oxford, 1855), p. xii.

49   For biographical detail on Kemble, see John D. Haigh, 'Kemble, John Mitchell (1807-1857)', *Oxford Dictionary of National Biography* (Oxford, 2004), 31:153-5.

50   *John Mitchell Kemble and Jakob Grimm: A Correspondence 1832-1852*, ed. and trans. Raymond A. Wiley (Leiden, 1971), pp. 23-31 (letter of September 1832).

51   This count of Thorkelin's letter errors does not include his departure from the manuscript by replacing *ð*'s with *þ*'s; see n. 46. If we include all of Thorkelin's departures, the literal reliability of Kemble's text is more impressive: he departed from the manuscript text of *Beowulf* only twenty-one times in the first five hundred lines of the poem as opposed to Thorkelin's more than five hundred times. Thorpe had failed to correct some seventy-two letter errors in Thorkelin, including fifty-one times in which he did not correct *þ* to *ð* (as above). Kemble failed to correct *þ* to *ð* just twice in 220 instances. (On the other hand, Kemble mistakenly replaced *ð* in the manuscript with *þ* three times.) Kemble's edition was published as *The Anglo-Saxon Poems of Beowulf, The Travellers Song and The Battle of Finnes-burh* (London, 1833).

Only a hundred copies of Kemble's edition were published, and demand soon arose for a second edition. The second edition appeared in two volumes: the first contains a somewhat revised text (1835); the second, a lengthy postscript to the introduction, a translation, detailed philological notes, and a comprehensive glossary (1837).[52] On the matter of accuracy, Kemble's somewhat revised text is somewhat a disappointment, containing only one fewer letter error in the first five hundred lines of the poem than the first edition.[53] However, in the list of *corrigenda* printed in the second volume, Kemble reduced the number of letter errors in these lines by seven, leaving but thirteen. The main reason that Kemble's second edition is more accurate is that it is based in part on a collation of Kemble's earlier text with the manuscript text of *Beowulf*. Evidence for the collation, probably begun in 1834, is found in London, British Library, Add. MS. 36531, a copy of Kemble's first edition interleaved with blank pages on which he then wrote a variety of textual, philological, historical, and literary notes, many of which made their way in Kemble's second edition.[54]

Thirteen errors in the first five hundred lines of *Beowulf* are thirteen too many by today's standards, but the number is not too surprising in view of Kemble's low esteem for medieval scribes. 'A modern edition, made by a person really conversant with the language which he illustrates,' he asserts, 'will in all probability be much more like the original than the MS. copy, which, even in the earliest times, was made by an ignorant or indolent transcriber' (p. xxiv), a statement that appears unaltered in the first volume of Kemble's second edition (p. xxiv).

Even so, he had some readings right that other early scholars had wrong. At *Beowulf* 469a, for example, the manuscript today reads *ꝥealfdanes*. Transcript A reads *healfdanes*; transcript B, *Healfdanes*. (The capital *H* in transcript B is editorial, showing that Thorkelin recognized a proper name as he copied.) Although the two transcripts agree on the spelling of the word, Thorkelin in his 1815 edition erroneously prints *Halfdenes*. In collating Thorkelin's text with the manuscript text of *Beowulf*, Conybeare, Madden, and Thorpe all inaccurately accept *Halfdenes* as the manuscript reading, and Grundtvig, in collating his handwritten text with the manuscript, also inaccurately accepts *Halfdenes* (probably based on

---

52　*The Anglo-Saxon Poems of Beowulf, The Travellers Song, and The Battle of Finnesburh.* 2nd ed., vol. 1 (London, 1835), vol. 2 (London, 1837).

53　This letter error occurs in line 628 (line 315b in modern editions), in which Kemble in 1833 printed *cwaeð* (*a* and *e* as separate letters) instead of *cwæð*, a correction for which Kemble in preparing his 1835 text did not need to consult the manuscript text of *Beowulf*.

54　Add. MS. 36531, mentioned by Westphalen, pp. 121-22, n. 177, was first studied in illuminating detail by Kelly, pp. 125-40.

Thorkelin's text). Among the early nineteenth-century scholars, only Kemble, in reading *Healf-denes*, spells the word as the manuscript has it.[55]

Again, at *Beowulf* 2335b the manuscript reads *guð* at the end of one manuscript line and *kyning* at the beginning of the next. The *k* of *kyning* is obscure, however; most of the vertical stroke is gone.[56] The letter is so obscure, in fact, that transcript A, transcript B, Conybeare, Madden, Grundtvig, and Thorpe – noticing only the curved stroke of the grapheme – record the letter as *c*. Of the early witnesses, only Kemble correctly reads *k*.[57]

Transcript A, transcript B, Conybeare, Madden, Grundtvig, Thorpe, and Kemble: these are the main witnesses to the manuscript text of *Beowulf* before 1845, when Madden took steps to preserve the manuscript in the state in which we now have it. Of the seven witnesses the most important are the two eighteenth-century transcripts, executed when fewer letters had crumbled from the brittle manuscript. The chief value of the five nineteen-century witnesses is to give additional firsthand evidence when one transcript has a reading where the other transcript has no reading and to help us decide which transcript to follow when the two transcripts have different readings for the same place. I would like to detail an instance, however, in which the nineteenth-century evidence claims unanimous independent value. It occurs on folio 184v13-14 in line 2464a of the poem.

The context is the *sorge weal / ‡‡‡de*, 'welling sorrow', that King Hrethel of the Geats feels because of the accidental death of his firstborn son, Herebeald, at the hands of his second son, Hæthcyn. The textual question is whether we should read *weallende*, with *e* as the fourth to last letter, or *weallinde*, with *i* as the fourth to last letter. This is no idle question. After acknowledging that transcripts A and B record the *i*-spelling, Elliott Van Kirk Dobbie nonetheless noted some sixty years ago, 'A present participle in *-inde* would be surprising in Beowulf.'[58] Dobbie's observation is reasonable. Elsewhere I have not found a present participle in the poem with *i* as the first vowel of the suffix. Further, the four times in which the verb *weallan* elsewhere occurs as a present participle in *Beowulf* the vowel before *n* is *e*: *weallende* 546a and 847b, *weallendu* 581a, and *hioroweall-ende* 2781b. Finally, I have been unable to find an instance of the present partici-

---

55 Line 469a in modern editions of *Beowulf* corresponds to line 932 in Kemble's edition. Like the capitalization of H, Kemble's hyphen in *Healf-denes* is editorial, marking the division of a compound noun.

56 Backlighting in the enlarged image in *Electronic 'Beowulf'* is so strong that what survives of the vertical stroke is difficult to discern. Other facsimiles, however, are less revealing. The manuscript is best studied in person.

57 Line 2335b in modern editions of *Beowulf* corresponds to line 4665 in Kemble's edition. Kemble's precise reading is *guð-kyning*; the accent mark is editorial, marking a long vowel.

58 Elliott Van Kirk Dobbie, ed., *Beowulf and Judith* (New York, 1953), p. 244.

ple of the verb *w(e)allan* in the extant body of Old English in which the vowel preceding *n* is *i*.[59]

However, the last two editions of the poem – Kiernan's *Electronic 'Beowulf'* (1999) and Fulk, Bjork, Niles's edition of *Klaeber's Beowulf* (2008) – read *weallinde* at 2464a, with *i* as the fourth to last letter. Fulk, Bjork, and Niles give the *i*-spelling because that is what transcript A, transcript B, and Kiernan read. Kiernan comments in 1984 and again in 1999, "*lin* torn through the middle, but not much missing from any of the letters, though *li* and part of *n* are covered (the base of *l* obscured by the shine-through of *ð*).'[60] What do other scholars think?

On folio 184v the morpheme *weal* is well preserved at the end of scribal line 13. What survives of the rest of the word comes at the beginning of line 14. Eugen Kölbing, Richard Paul Wülcker, Alfred Holder, and Kemp Malone all report that at the beginning of line 14 they can discern no letter to the immediate left of *n* in the manuscript.[61] Besides Kiernan, the only scholar who reports seeing *i* to the left of *n* is Zupitza, who says, 'the lower part of *l*, almost the whole of *i*, and a small part of *n* gone; and part of what is left of *li* covered.'[62]

Of the six scholars cited, only Zupitza and Kiernan claim to see *i*, and Zupitza reports that 'almost the whole' of the letter is lost. Both Kiernan and Zupitza knew the readings of transcripts A and B when they studied the manuscript. (So did Malone. Kölbing, Wülcker, Holder did not know the readings.) If the two eighteenth-century transcripts had attested *len* as the first three letters of 184v14, I suspect that Kiernan and Zupitza would have said that a fragment of *e* survives as the second letter.

My own reading is *‡‡‡de*. The folio is ripped apart at the beginning of line 14, and the folio edge is reinforced with heavy paper that covers most of the remains of the first two letters and parts of the third and fourth. Of the first letter I see only the upper part of a perpendicular stroke that could be the remains of various letters with a tall ascender. To the right come ambiguous bits of ink: above the top edge of the heavy paper I discern a small curve like an inverted breve; under the paper are a point at the baseline and another above it, the two points looking a bit like a colon.

---

59 My finding is based on a hundred occurrences of the participle in Dictionary of *Old English Corpus on the World Wide Web* <http://tapor.library.utoronto.ca/doecorpus/>.

60 'The state of the *Beowulf* manuscript 1882-1983', *Anglo-Saxon England* 13 (1984), 37. Kiernan repeats his analysis in the note to folio 184v14 in *Electronic 'Beowulf'*.

61 Kölbing, 'Zur Beóvulf-handschrift', *Archiv für das Studium der neueren Sprachen und Literaturen*, 56 (1876), 113; Wülcker, ed., *Bibliothek der angelsächsischen Poesie* (Kassel 1881), I.1.117; Holder, ed., *Beowulf. I. Abdruck der Handschrift im British Museum, Cotton. Vitellius A. XV.* (Freiburg im Breisgau [1881], p. 56; Malone, *The Nowell Codex*, p. 91:2.

62 *Beowulf Reproduced in Facsimile*, p. 115.

To the right of the two points are two minims not ligated at the top. Farther to the right is *d*, the upper part of its ascender gone. Last comes *e*, intact.[63]

Granted that the first and third letters in line 14 once were *l* and *n*, as transcripts A and B report, what I see in the manuscript between the two letters better comports with *e* than *i*: *e* would fill the intervening space better than *i* would, and *e* would better explain the small curve I see above the top border of the heavy paper. But I cannot say that I see the remains of *e* in the manuscript. The evidence is too scant.

The early nineteenth-century witnesses, however, unanimously support *e* as the letter between *l* and *n*. In his edition Thorkelin gives the reading as *Weal-linde* (p. 184:6). In their collation of Thorkelin's text, Conybeare, Madden, and Thorpe all alter Thorkelin's *i* in *Weal-linde* to *e*. Further, Grundtvig underlines *weallende* in his text and inserts 'O' after it to specify that the Original manuscript reading has *e* where Thorkelin has *i* (line 4922). Finally, in his 1833 edition of *Beowulf* Kemble gives the reading as *weallende* (line 4923). It is more likely that here, as sometimes elsewhere, the A and B transcribers misread what Dobbie characterizes as the second *Beowulf* scribe's 'heavy vertical stroke of *e*' as *i* than that five of five nineteenth-century scholars who studied the manuscript before 1845 mistakenly recorded *i* as *e*.[64]

The nineteenth-century evidence supplementing the manuscript text of *Beowulf* cannot claim as much value as the eighteenth-century evidence. We are fortunate, however, to possess records from both the eighteenth century and the nineteenth century that help us restore readings otherwise lost from the sole manuscript of the central poem in Old English.[65]

---

63 The enlarged image of the crux in *Electronic 'Beowulf'* is so suffused with backlighting and (inevitably) with shine-through that I can distinguish in it none of the finer points I here report. Only a firsthand study of the manuscript suffices. See also n. 56 above.

64 For other instances in which transcripts A and B miscopy the second *Beowulf* scribe's *e* as *i*, see Dobbie, p. 244.

65 I am indebted to various libraries for permission to study and quote from original documents: British Library, London (Cotton Vitellius A. xv, Conybeare's collation, Kemble's collation of 1834); Kongelige Bibliothek, Copenhagen (transcript A, transcript B, Grundtvig's collation); Universitätsbibliothek Freiburg im Breisgau (Thorpe's collation); Houghton Library, Harvard University (Madden's collation); Bodleian Library, Oxford (Madden's journal). I read a shorter version of this paper at the Medieval Symposium, IAUPE, Malta, on 16 July 2010. I am grateful to Professor Ian Kirby, organizer of the symposium, and other participants for their kind suggestions.

The Barnaby Googe Experiment: Readings and Misreadings

Manfred Malzahn
Al-Ain, United Arab Emirates

This paper grows out of experience gathered, methods tried and perspectives formed in well over twenty years of teaching English literature. The main concern of the argument is with the dialectic of reading and misreading in and out of the literature classroom, and in particular, with the option of making creative use of misreading in the expansion and refinement of reading or readings. Countermeasures amounting to a didactic of misreading are submitted as a possible antidote to three forces that militate against inductive understanding of literary texts: the assumed 'authority' of authors, critics and teachers; the corresponding diffidence and anxiety of learners; and the ever easier access to assumedly 'authoritative' readings as a convenient bypass around the trials and errors involved in the individual encounter with literature. The case presented here for the didactic of misreading as a subversion of the three abovementioned forces is based on readings and misreadings of a 'minor' sixteenth-century poem by the 'minor poet' Barnaby Googe.

Anyone who has been teaching EngLit for the abovementioned period can be expected to have formed a fairly comprehensive view of the benefits as well as of the difficulties inherent in this enterprise. Much has changed during that time, in a curriculum whose content and delivery have moved along with "the shift from the informative to the formative paradigm of teaching and learning" (Pieper et al. 2007: 16) that characterises modern pedagogical practice at all levels of education. To teach or be taught literature in such enlightened ways, however, does not put anyone on an easy shortcut to enlightenment. On the contrary, it makes greater demands in terms of basic reading skills and processes that were underused within the traditional framework of teaching students about literature, rather than teaching them how to read it. The difference between the two is like the one between teaching someone about swimming, and teaching someone to swim. For the latter, immersion in water is the essential ingredient; and the equivalent in literary didactics is surely the individual first-hand and hands-on experience of literary works, an experience that involves the challenge "to engage with choices of meaning in a text" (Birch 1996: 88)

Purely informative teaching tends to bypass individual attempts at making sense of given texts, often by a jump from background knowledge to readymade exegesis or evaluation. In contrast, the formative teaching of literature should foster what Peter Stockwell calls "the pro- cess of arriving at a sense of the text that is personally acceptable" (2007: 8). In his *Introduction to Cognitive Poetics*, Stockwell uses the term 'interpretation' for such a successive build-up of meaning as readers move through texts, and the term 'reading' for the understanding that is thus formed. He suggests that in the field of Cognitive Poetics, no actual reading should be regarded as worthless or wrong merely because it is idiosyncratic and personal, or because the interpretation that produced it involved "mistakes, errors, miscues" along the way (ibd.).

If interpretations engender readings, then errors seem not only pardonable, but vital to a sequential comprehension effected through falsification as well as verification of assumed meanings. For many students, though, the potential gains do clearly not outweigh the disadvantages of a procedure perceived as laborious and hazardous, while in the electronic information age that we all inhabit, accessing authoritative 'information' is easier than ever before. This shortcut, however, unduly favours the opposite of a better understanding, namely, a lack of personal understanding: a lack that is involuntarily highlighted in virtually any effort to mask it by adopted insight or opinion.

The greater students' anxiety about the painstaking and error-prone nature of individual efforts at comprehending literary texts, the more likely they are to take refuge in the treacherous ease and safety of borrowed wisdom. Though convenience often plays a part, this effective return to the aforementioned, outdated paradigm is bound to be primarily fear-driven. Especially in teaching English literature to learners of English as a foreign language, one can hardly overestimate the students' dread of immersion in a literary text with only their wits and their dictionaries to decide whether they will sink or swim. The lower the students' language competence or their confidence in it, the greater their temptation to skip reading primary texts altogether, and to leap to prefabricated conclusions or judgments.

In these circumstances, teachers need to find means of subverting a tendency that is in turn threatening to subvert the favoured pedagogical model. In contemplating forms of defensive action, I believe that a crucial first step is to get a clearer picture of what really happens when students read literary texts without the facility of recourse to secondary sources. In the following, I shall hence summarise the findings of a small-scale experiment in which students in the UAE, Taiwan and Germany were exposed to an unprepared and unaided confrontation with a short piece of literature; I shall briefly identify patterns of reading or misreading that may be indicative of practices, beliefs or values held by "the reader's interpretative community" (Stockwell 2007: 8); and I shall then try to demonstrate that if clusters of systematic misreadings – as opposed to isolated instances of individual or accidental non- or miscomprehension – are indeed taken seriously, they can be used to illuminate the nature of the interpretative process as well as the multiplicity of possible meanings that can be perceived in a text.

The poem I chose for my experiment is given in Figure 1 below; it is a lesser known work by one of the lesser known poets of the English Renaissance. It seemed suitable first of all because of its relative obscurity, which virtually precluded the chance that any of the students in the targeted groups would have come across the text by accident, let alone on a course syllabus. Then, in spite of being written in what students who have not seen any Old English tend to call 'old English', "Of Money" presents relatively few lexical difficulties. Many of its key nouns, adjectives, verbs and adverbs can be taken as known; and as is common in Elizabethan poetry, there is enough redundancy to ensure that the gist of the speaker's statement is not lost even if single words are not understood. Finally, the topic could hardly be perceived as alien or esoteric by any imaginable reader.

Figure 1: Featured primary text

> "Of Money"
> Give money me, take friendship who so list,
> For friends are gone come once adversity,
> When money yet remaineth safe in chest,
> That quickly can thee bring from misery.
> Fair face show friends when riches do abound;
> Come time of proof, farewell, they must away;
> Believe me well, they are not to be found,
> If God but send thee once a lowering day.
> Gold never starts aside, but in distress,
> Finds ways enough to ease thine heaviness.

The instruction given to students was to select one, and only one of the ten statements shown in Figure 2 below, as the one that most accurately summarises what is said by the speaker in the poem. While the wording of the task carried a special significance for those who had learned to distinguish between authors and speakers, it essentially asked them to do what those unaccustomed to making such distinctions were going to do anyway, which was, as a common metonymy has it, to summarise 'what the poem says'.

Figure 2: Suggested summaries of the speaker's statement

1	It is good to have rich friends.
2	Friendship is the most important thing in life.
3	Money cannot buy friendship.
4	True friendship is not affected by money problems.
5	Money is more reliable than friendship.
6	A friend in need must always be taken care of.
7	Money should never be an issue between friends.
8	Rich people cannot know true friendship.
9	Money is silver, but friendship is gold.
10	A true friend will always be ready to help with money.

At a first glance, only item number 5 could be taken as a literal representation of what the speaker states. The others would appear to be propositions, judgments or maxims that have little or no relation with the point the speaker in the poem is making, or that even claim the opposite: item 3 for instance, "Money cannot buy friendship", appears to run counter to the assertion in line 5 of the poem, "Fair face show friends when riches do abound". While such offhand assessments are later to be put into perspective, I shall for the time being classify items 1 to 4 and 6 to 10 as descriptive or prescriptive utterances whose selection as the 'correct' summary may be triggered by the reader's agreement or disagreement with the judgment in the given sentence, whether or not this judgment tallies with that expressed by the poetic speaker.

The about 500 responses given by students in different locations, of different ages and at different levels, from GCSE pupils at Al-Ain English Speaking School to senior undergraduate students in Germany, show a clear correlation between language competence and the overall meaning perceived. At lower levels of competence, items 3 "Money cannot buy friendship" and 9 "Money is silver, but friendship is gold" were equally or even more popular choices than "Money is more reliable than friendship", selected by just under or just over 10% in the groups with the least proficiency in English, but by well over 90% in a group of senior students majoring in Translation at the University of Regensburg. Degrees of preferences for item 3 or 9 could be seen as degrees of preference for a culturally as well as personally acceptable reading: in other words, as evidence of readiness to settle for something that sounds like safe proverbial wisdom, rather than to acknowledge a statement that contradicts orthodox views. If this assumption were true, it would of course be interesting to know to what extent such self-censorship was conscious or unconscious, but the rather crude methods whose results I have documented in detail elsewhere (cf. Malzahn

2009) do not allow any such distinctions and should in any case rather be perceived as testing the ground for proper empirical research, than as constituting such research.

My main concern here, in any case, is not with the genesis or the avoidance of misreadings, but with their potential role in teaching practice. The simple misreadings of literary texts by students who have difficulties also with other kinds of English reading comprehension may not be quite comparable to the misreadings or strong readings made by literary authors of their precursors that Harold Bloom sees at the heart of literary history. It does, however, seem reasonable to invokes Bloom's precept for literature teaching in our day and age, phrased in A *Map of Misreading* as follows (Bloom 2003: 40):

Instruction, in our late phase, becomes an antithetical process almost in spite of itself, and for antithetical teaching you require antithetical texts, that is to say, texts antithetical to your students as well as to yourself and to other texts.

Is "Of Money" such a text then? That it is not always perceived as such is documented by two online references a Google search threw up. One of these references is a blog posting entitled "Googe on money" and starts with the remark "No, that's not a misspelling. It's Googe, not Google." (Fitzgerald 2004) The misreading preventatively conjured up here is indeed a likely one nowadays: so much so that it infiltrated the way the title of my paper was featured on the provisional programme of the IAUPE conference. The blogger Eamonn Fitzgerald obviously did not fall into this trap; and his clarification of the poet's name is matched by an equally unambiguous reading of the poem taken for a straightforward authorial statement on the topic, a statement in which Barnaby Googe "is concise and practical in a way that suggests close contact with the bitter experience of false friendship." (ibd.)

A further reference to Googe as one whom "Fame and fortune eluded" (ibd.) completes the suggestion that the authorial voice in "Of money" belongs to a disgruntled and disillusioned and hence presumably older man; a suggestion made in spite of dates cited by Fitzgerald himself that indicate Googe had composed the poem, as all the other pieces alongside which it appeared in 1563, by the time he was in his early twenties. What Fitzgerald does not mention is that the publication of the young author's poetry was apparently due to the efforts of a friend with whom Googe had left his work before going abroad (Arber 1871: 8):

1562-3? WINTER. Googe reaches home from Spain, while Blundeston is away from London [...] on whose return, he is astonished to learn that his poems are in the printer's hands, and the paper provided for the impression. Yielding at length to his friend's persuasion, he suffers them to appear [...]

This story has been suspected as mere fabrication, "a device by which Googe could avoid criticism" (Eccles 1985: 6), but even if this were so, Blundeston obviously was a friend who helped the author rather than let him down. Most of the disappointments in Googe's life seem to have come after the publication of his *Eglogs*, and to have been caused by people other than friends. All told, an autobiographical reading thus appears neither as the simplest nor as the most unproblematic choice. Among approaches to literature, the biographical ones are after all among those that most evidently ask for a mapping of textual interpretation against external evidence.

On the lookout for more straightforwardly 'correct' or convincing readings, one may consequently want to consider the kind that merely takes the speaker's statement at surface value, without any attempt at locating its conception in a biographical or historical context. Or how about going one better on the road to simplification; namely, to a kind of reference that takes the plainest of all understandings so firmly for granted that it does not even have to be made explicit? For a prime example of this, the reader is hereby referred to the website of a certain Manoj Sharma who styles himself "World Class Organization Strategist", formerly "World Class Wealth Strategist" (Sharma 2007). Here, Googe's poem is presented without any explanation: instead, visitors to Sharma's website are asked for comments, as well as for their name and e-mail address. In this context, the obvious use of the poem is to put readers in the right frame of mind for considering the merits of "The Manoj Sharma Individual True Wealth Model" or "The Manoj Sharma Organization True Wealth Model".

This, it seems to me, is the point where extremes are seen to meet: namely, where the reading that enabled the harnessing of the text for commercial purposes converges with the disinterested but perhaps equally one-dimensional reading that prevailed in the aforementioned class of German students, whose teacher sent me their responses with the comment that the chosen format of the task yielded no differentiation. I in turn am led to conclude that the respective presence or absence of self-interest need not produce differences in understanding, if the text is presented to readers with a high degree of linguistic competence and no reason or inclination to consider complexities or ambiguities in the given poetic utterance.

Teachers and students of literature, however, should always see a reason to dig a little deeper. There is the question, for instance, whether the speaker of Googe's poem subverts the terms of his own statement by claiming that true friendship does not exist, while nonetheless using the words 'friendship' and 'friends', as in "False face show friends when riches do abound". Those meant here can thus at best be so-called or fair-weather friends, just as it can only be the semblance of love that is designated by the first noun in the "Love is not love" formula of a Shakespeare sonnet, where the paradox is only partly resolved by the continuation of the phrase. For a slightly more recent instance of such verbal trickery, see Matthew Arnold's "Dover Beach", where the address "Ah, love, let us be true | To one another!" is followed by the assertion that the world really has "neither joy, nor love, nor light": and if this be true, then it seems ironic or plainly insincere to address someone as 'love'.

On such closer inspection of "Dover Beach", does its world-weary speaker not sound as if he were sad about his own sadness? And on similarly close inspection, does the defiant speaker in "Of Money" not reveal a similar kind of sadness, masked by sour-grapes rhetoric? If we opt for such a reading, we will need to reckon with the possibility that the author presents the readers with the dramatic speech of a character who is not to be believed but seen through. Consideration of such reading options will actualise dimensions of the text ignored in ostensibly correct but ultimately flat readings that treat the utterance merely as a persuasive statement asking for acceptance or rejection. An autobiographical reading of the aforementioned kind will include the speaker, and in all likelihood engender an emotional reaction by the reader: but if the reader equates speaker with author, the pity is bound to be sympathetic and not empathetic.

A somewhat fuller implication of the reader in the process of literary communication can be ensured by a view of the speaker as a fictional character deliberately set before an audience in order to elicit and manipulate emotional responses. Readers who become conscious of their own responses may realise that they feel disgust at the speaker's diatribe against something which most people hold in high regard, or they may realise that they feel self-disgust if they have allowed themselves to be even partly won over by someone who propagates such a joyless world view. These readers may, in short, recognise their own part in the linguistic game latent in all Renaissance poetry, where virtually nothing is only what it seems at first sight, and the reading experience challenges the reader to acknowledge the dazzling complexity of the world, the text and human minds, including the readers' own.

Once the existence of various possible meanings or readings has been acknowledged, it would seem proper to draw attention to a range of interpretative methods, terminologies or tools. As an example, I would like to cite the so-called Semiotic Square, particularly apt in this instance because of its spectral refraction of a simple opposition. My application of the tool, also known as the Greimas Square after its originator A.J. Greimas, follows guidelines given in an exposé by Louis Hébert (Hébert 2006). I am taking "Money" and "Friendship" as the dichotomic Terms A and B, and supplying "Friendlessness" and "Pennilessness" as the corresponding terms "Not-B" and "Not-A". These are placed at the four corners of the square, while six different combinations of these four terms then result in six metaterms, occupying positions 5 to 10 below.

Figure 3:   Semiotic Square based on key terms in "Of Money"

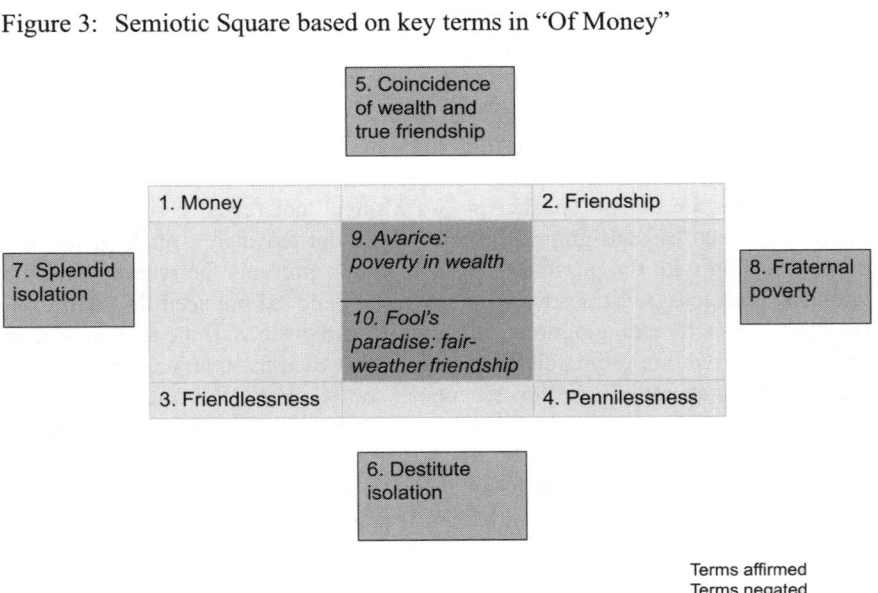

The specific nature of the speaker's statement in "Of Money" can be shown in his respective affirmation, negation and evasion of the various terms that constitute the field created by the central opposition. What should be immediately clear is that money and friendship are not in themselves opposites, a fact that contrasts with the speaker's apodictic certainty; what may become clear eventually is that as every term includes a suggestion of its opposite, so does every claim, plea or argument like that made in "Of Money" imply a previous or a subsequent utterance: a counterargument that can be actualised on the level of author-reader communication. Students may thus be encouraged to construct a dramatic or narrative context for the Googe's speaker, and this may well lead to the picture of a character resembling Charles Dickens' Ebenezer Scrooge, i.e., one meant to be perceived as a bad example.

This takes us to a stage of the didactic process where a reconsideration of the initial misreadings is indicated, since they seem to bear an uncanny resemblance to the more sophisticated reading suggested by the application of structuralist and poststructuralist concepts. Classroom discussions about the process of understanding may hence come to address questions concerning the value and the goal of the education or sophistication; if it takes us back full circle, does this not mean that it has initially lead us away from a state of innocence? Perhaps we can invoke Pope's dictum about the dangers posed by a little learning, and ask the students to reflect on how their perceptions of and responses to art and life have changed with increasing exposure to all kinds of messages, and how education and sophistication may correlate with desensibilisation. This is sure to be an interesting discussion, at some point of which, I would want to bring in another example of Renaissance art and its diverse readings.

Figure 4: Painting by Gerard ter Borch (1617-1681)

Ter Borch's painting is widely known by titles such as "Paternal Admonition". A corresponding reading clothed in vivid description is found in Johann Wolfgang von Goethe's novel *Elective Affinities* that contains the following passage (Goethe 1885):

> One foot thrown over the other, sits a noble knightly-looking father; before him stands his daughter, to whose conscience he seems to be addressing himself. She, a fine striking figure, in a folding drapery of white satin, is only to be seen from behind, but her whole bearing ap-

pears to signify that she is collecting herself. That the admonition is not too severe, that she is not being utterly put to shame, is to be gathered from the air and attitude of the father, while the mother seems as if she were trying to conceal some slight embarrassment – she is looking into a glass of wine, which she is on the point of drinking.

Compare this to the following decoding by an academic, presented in a manner no less vivid than that of the former description (Adams 1999: 229):

Seated in a lavishly appointed interior, a soldier raises his hand – and may proffer a coin – to an expensively dressed young woman, whose profile is outlined by a bed richly draped in red. A slightly older woman, a procuress seated between them, is preoccupied with the glass of wine she silently sips. The latter's presence and activity dispel any doubt about the nature of the encounter. Rather than responding to the gesture or accepting money – much less soliciting either – the object of the soldier's attention stands impassively, almost demurely, her face hidden from our view.

If students discuss the respective merits of the two readings, they are bound to face an ultimate undecidability. There is then no right and no wrong interpretation: and recent scholarship seems to agree that exactly this state of affairs was intentionally created by the painter, whose work was – pardon the German – "absichtlich mehrdeutig konzipiert" (Weber 2008: 5) or "intentionally ambiguously conceived". This, however, should not prevent us from ranking different readings as more or less convincing or refined, and it should moreover make us ask what the different readings say about different readers, including those who themselves distinguish between right and wrong readings while claiming that a blatantly wrong reading may nonetheless be dead right. According to the *Web Gallery of Art*, Goethe failed to recognise the painting as a depiction of a brothel scene mainly because he knew it through a popular engraving that showed no hint of a coin; and yet, it is claimed, the German poet was curiously right in his misreading (Kren and Marx, n.d.):

Ter Borch's psychology is so delicate that the common scenes he repeatedly painted are raised to the level of highly civilised life. That Goethe's interpretation was possible at all shows the refinement of Ter Borch's treatment. Even if he made a mistake, Goethe had the right feeling for the way Ter Borch treated his subjects. Psychologically and pictorially he retains a sensitive touch and delicacy. The young woman is seen from behind; thus her face is averted. The only flesh visible is in her neck, which is modelled with tender, silvery grey shadows. We have, however, opportunity to admire the silver-grey satin and black velvet of her gown.

Did we not suspect this all along? Someone of Goethe's status can count on being forgiven or even praised for what might be deplored or penalised if it came from a sophomore student. There is apparently a world of difference between the endearing naïveté of an enlightened reader on the one hand, and the naivety of the ignorant on the other. Or is there only a world of difference between the ways the two are likely to be judged? There are, in any case, perfectly good reasons for making such questions the topic of conversation in a literature class.

To round this off, let me get back to the question whether "Of Money" is one of the antithetical texts meant by Harold Bloom. I have already shown that it generates or provokes antithetical readings; and it is surely just as apt to consider antithetical relationships with previous works. A promising line of investigation would be to examine ways in which other early Renaissance texts treat friendship differently from those of the medieval age; this has been the subject of much recent scholarship tracing the genesis of the idea of friendship "in its narrow and distinctly modern sense of a disinterested, equal relationship between unrelated individuals" (Burke 1999: 1). Googe's poem can furthermore be contrasted with "the fatuous and insincere praises of friendship" in contemporary commonplace books (Peterson 1967: 121): it would then ask to be understood as a condemnation of hypocritical cant rather than as a cynical comment on humanity in general. In such a reading, one might be able to reconcile the use of a fictional persona in the poem with the sense of a "personal conviction that comes through in its unrelieved severity of statement" (Peterson 1967: 121).

Being directed at scholars and teachers of literature, this paper is likewise imbued with a personal conviction: namely, that one can still get students at whatever level to engage with literary texts, although the task is getting ever harder especially with regard to canonical authors, genres and periods. Giving more time and attention to 'minor poets' or "lesser lights of English Renaissance literature" (Renchler 1987: 14) such as Googe could help; but then again, widespread attention could result in a spate of publications such as this one, and this spate of publications would in turn severely damage the chances for experiments such as the one described here. I fear that by bringing my Barnaby Googe experiment to the attention of others, I may already have scuppered some other people's hopes of similarly using "Of Money" themselves. This leaves me feeling somewhat like the adventurous traveller who spreads the word of an unspoiled natural paradise, and on his next trip there, finds the beach full of backpackers and company scouts who are looking at convenient sites for tourist hotels. Perhaps I should ask my readers to keep fairly quiet about the whole thing; but if you do set up a similar experiment of your own, I would be most grateful if you let me know.

References

Adams, Ann Jensen. 1999. "Money and the Regulation of Desire. The Prostitute and the Marketplace in Seventeenth-Century Holland." In *Renaissance Culture and the Everyday*. Ed. Patricia Fumerton and Simon Hart. Philadelphia: University of Pennsylvania Press. 229-253.

Arber, Edward, ed. 1871. *Barnabe Googe. Eglogs, Epytaphes, and Sonettes. 1563. Three Copies Only at Present Known. From the Copy in Possession of Henry Huth, Esqre.* Westminster: A. Constable & Co. English Reprints.

Birch, David. 1996 (1989). *Language, Literature and Critical Practice*. London and New York: Routledge. Reprint.

Bloom, Harold. 2003 (1975). *A Map of Misreading. With a New Preface.* Oxford and New York: Oxford University Press.

Burke, Peter. 1999. "Humanism and Friendship in Sixteenth-Century Europe." In *Friendship in Early Modern Philosophy and Science*. Ed. Vanessa Smith and Richard Yeo. *Parergon* 26/2. 1-9.

Eccles, Mark. 1985. "Barnabe Googe in England, Spain, and Ireland." *English Literary Renaissance* 15/3 (Autumn). 353-370.

Fitzgerald, Eamonn. 2004. "Googe on money." *Eamonn Fitzgerald's Rainy Day*. http://www.eamonn.com/2004/11/googe_on_money. htm

Goethe, Johann Wolfgang von. 1885 (1809). *Elective Affinities*. In *Goethe's Works*, Illustrated by the Best German Artists. 5 vols. Philadelphia: G. Barrie. Vol. 5: *Wilhelm Meister's Travels*; *Elective Affinities*. http://oll.libertyfund. org/title/2275/214919.

Hébert, Louis. 2006. "The Semiotic Square." In *Signo*. Ed. Louis Hébert. Québec: Rimouski. http://www.signosemio.com/greimas/a_carresemiotique.asp

Kren, Emil and Daniel Marx. n.d. *Web Gallery of Art*. http://www.wga.hu/ index1.html

Malzahn, Manfred. 2009. "Patterns of (Mis)Reading: Student Responses to a 16th Century Poem." Paper given at The Tenth Annual UAE University Research Conference, Al-Ain.

Peterson, Douglas L. 1967. "The Early Elizabethans." In *The English Lyric from Wyatt to Donne: A History of the Plain and Eloquent Styles*. Princeton: Princeton University Press. 120-163.

Pieper, Irene, Laila Aase, Mike Fleming and Florentina Sâmihăian. November 2007. "Text, Literature and 'Bildung'". Intergovernmental Conference on 'Languages of Schooling Within a European Framework for Languages of Education: Learning, Teaching, Assessment'. Prague. www.coe.int/t/dg4/ linguistic/Source/Prague07_LS_EN.doc

Renchler, Robert. 1987. *"Goe Thou forth my Booke": Authorial Self-Assertion and Self-Representation in Printings of Renaissance Poetry*. Ph.D. Dissertation. University of Oregon.

Sharma, Manoj. 28 September 2007. "Another Perspective On Money by Barnaby Googe." Manoj Sharma. World Class Strategist. http://www.manojsharma. com/another-perspective-on-money-by-barnaby-googe

Stockwell, Peter. 2007 (2002). *Cognitive Poetics. An Introduction*. London and New York: Routledge. Reprint.

Weber, Barbara. May 2008. *Im Spannungsfeld von Subjektivität und Kommerz. Die Kopien der Rückenfigur aus Gerard Ter Borchs "Die väterliche Ermahnung"*. M.Phil. dissertation. University of Vienna. http://othes.univie.ac.at/701/1/05-26-2008_9609383.pdf

Plato, Poetic 'Praxis', and Renaissance Censorship

Richard A. McCabe
Merton College, Oxford

When Elizabeth I ascended to the throne in 1558 expectations were high, and literary expectations particularly so. The new queen was a poet and a published author with well-known interests in humanist learning, philosophy, and theology.[1] She had actively cultivated this image as a princess and continued to develop it as queen. In compiling *The Queen's Majesty's Passage through the City of London to Westminster the Day before her Coronation*, Richard Mulcaster duly records that when she approached St Paul's School, one of the boys stepped forward and addressed her (in Latin) as follows:

> The divine philosopher Plato left this observation for posterity...that a state would be most fortunate if its princes should be interested in matters favourable to wisdom and conspicuous for their virtues. And if it seems to us that he was right (and he was indeed entirely right), why should Britain not rejoice? Why should this day not be marked (as they say) with a white stone? A day when we have with us a prince whose like was never seen by our ancestors ... She is most learned in Greek and Latin literature, and outstanding in intellectual gifts. Under her rule religion will flourish, England will prosper, the Golden Age will return.[2]

The Platonic allusion is to the fifth book of the *Republic* where Socrates famously declares that 'untill philosophers rule as kings or those who are now called kings and leading men genuinely and adequately philosophize, that is, until political power and philosophy entirely coincide, cities will have no rest from evils ... nor, I think, will the human race' (473c-d).[3] The St Paul's tribute was intended to suggest that this state of affairs had now been achieved, that England had finally acquired if not exactly a philosopher king, at least the next best thing, a philosopher queen. One of Elizabeth's earliest soubriquets was Augusta and as the female Augustus she would, it was hoped, usher in a golden

---

1   *A Godly Medytacyon of the Christen Sowle* (1548) was published in Germany when the future queen was fourteen years old (the manuscript being completed when she was eleven). See Marc Shell, *Elizabeth's Glass* (Lincoln: University of Nebraska Press, 1993).

2   In *Renaissance Drama: An Anthology of Plays and Entertainments*, ed. Arthur F. Kinney (Oxford: Blackwell, 1999), pp. 29-30.

3   All quotations are from Plato, *Complete Works,* eds. John M. Cooper and D. S. Hutchinson Indianapolis: Hackett, 1887).

age of English letters. On her first visit to Cambridge in 1565, Abraham Hartnell dubbed her 'regina literata', the lettered queen.[4]

But all was not what it seemed. Augustus was as well known for the banishment of Ovid as the patronage of Virgil, and any allusion to Plato's *Republic* in the context of *literary* discussion raised the spectre of Socrates' call for the expulsion of the poets from the ideal state. In fact, the *Republic* was the foundational text in the debate on censorship, and every Early Modern defence of poetry had to address its arguments at some point.[5] Plato expressly invited such responses by having Socrates conclude that poetry might 'return from exile' if it were able to demon-strate that 'it ought to have a place in a well-governed city' (607c-d). This paper examines key aspects of the complex dialectic that emerged as Early Modern poets and commentators struggled to respond to Plato's challenge to relate poetics to politics.

The tenth book of the *Republic* could be seen to strike at the heart of Humanist claims for the utility of poetics to the polis. Julius Caesar Scaliger argued in his *Poetics* that 'Plato himself, in the *Ion*, calls [poets] the interpreters and expounders of the gods. Wherefore the dictum expressed in the *Republic*, which some crude and insensible men would construe to the exclusion of poets from the republic, should be taken less seriously, for though he condemns certain scurrilous passages in the poets, we are not on that account to ignore those other passages which Plato cites times out of mind in support of his own theories [of poetic inspiration].'[6] In the great Stephanus edition of 1578 (the first volume of which was dedicated to Elizabeth), Jean de Serres approvingly quotes Scaliger – as later would Sidney – but only compounds the problem by identifying the notion of divine inspiration, an irrational force that cannot be politically contained, as the reason for the exclusion of the poets. He hereby recognises Plato's arguments from inspiration as a double-edged weapon that deprives poets of all conscious control over their art (all sense of *techne*) while seeming to elevate them (in fact, poets are given relatively low ranking in the *Phaedrus*, 248e). So far as de Serres is concerned, attitudes toward poetic 'authority' ['Poetices authoritatem'] depend upon one's assessment of the worth of poetic inspiration. So he labours to distinguish it from insanity (as later would Puttenham) by pursuing the distinc-

---

4   See James Binns, 'Abraham Hartwell, Herald of the New Queen's Reign. The *Regina Literata* (London, 1565)', in G. Tournoy and D. Sacré, eds., *Ut Granum Sinapis: Essays on Neo-Latin Literature in Honour of Jozef Ijsewijn*, Supplementa Humanistica Lovaniensia XII (Leuven: Leuven University Press, 1997), pp. 292-304.

5   See Ramon A. Naddaff, *Exiling the Poets: The Production of Censorship in Plato's Republic* (Chicago: University of Chicago Press, 2002).

6   *Select Translations from Scaliger's Poetics*, trans. F. M. Padelford (New York: Henry Holt, 1905), pp. 14-15.

tion that Plato makes elsewhere between icastic and phantastic imitation (*Sophist*, 266d-e).[7]

The claims made by the supporters of poetry were high. In Plato's *Laws* the Athenian contends that because people, and particularly the young, come to resemble what they enjoy – because of that form of mimesis which sees life imitate art (ironically the same form that also supports arguments for the moral benefits of literature) – 'the true legislator will persuade (or, failing persuasion, compel) the man with a creative flair … to compose correctly by portraying…[only] men who are moderate, courageous and good in every way' (660a). So far the *Laws*, but poetry's defenders asked where law itself originated. According to George Puttenham, synthesizing generations of Humanist comment in *The Arte of English Poesie* (1589), poets themselves were 'the first legislators and politicians in the World'. To illustrate the point he uses the familiar myths of Amphion and Orpheus as bringers of civil life to 'rude and savage people'. The truth that he discerns behind these myths is that poets were 'the first lawmakers to the people, and the first politicians, devising all expedient means for the establishment of commonwealth, to hold and contain the people in order and duty by force and virtue of good and wholesome laws'.[8]

According to this version of events literary and social history developed symbiotically. The first poems were hymns to the gods, but the second were not, as might be expected, eulogies of princes, but reproofs of common vices through satire and comedy – and that for the simple reason that poets precede princes. As the first philosophers, prophets, lawgivers and teachers, poets held society together before the emergence of Princely government. When such government arose, the conditions for the creation of poetry altered radically – and to the public detriment. Tragedy arose in response to the excesses of princely government as the form in which '[Princes'] infamous life and tyrannies were laid open to all the world, their wickedness reproached, their follies and extreme insolencies derided, and their miserable ends painted out in plays and pageants to show the mutability of fortune and the just punishment of God in revenge of a vicious and evil life'.[9] To Juvenal's question, highly pertinent to the *Republic*, 'quis custodiet ipsos custodes?' (*Satire* VI, 347-8), Puttenham effectively answered 'the poets'. In his view poets were aboriginally the censors of princes rather than the other way around.

---

7   For De Serres' original text and a translation see S. K. Heninger, Jr.,'Sidney and Serranus' Plato' *ELR*, 13 (1983), 146-61 (pp.153-6, 160-1).

8   George Puttenham, *The Art of English Poesy*, eds. Frank Whigham and Wayne A. Rebhorn (Ithaca: Cornell University Press, 2007), pp. 96-7.

9   Ibid., p. 123.

Of particular interest in this regard is Puttenham's account of pastoral poetry. Scaliger advanced the widely accepted view that pastoral is a very early form of poetry reflecting the primitive stages of human development prior to urbanisation.[110] Puttenham refutes this view directly. 'I do deny', he asserts, 'that the eclogue should be the first and most ancient form of artificial poesy, being persuaded that the poet devised the eclogue long after the other dramatic poems, not of purpose to counterfeit or represent the rustical manner of loves and communication, but under the veil of homely persons and in rude speeches to insinuate and glance at greater matters, and such as perchance had not been safe to have been disclosed in any other sort'.[11] This is a familiar passage but so often quoted out of context that its primary purpose is habitually overlooked. What Puttenham is saying is that pastoral was invented as an oppositional mode in response to the increasing unwillingness of princes to accept poetic censure. The invention of pastoral space is poetry's protest against urbanization and cen-tralization. Pastoral provides a means of recreating the circumstances of primitive poetic liberty while simultaneously registering its disappear-ance. Its shepherds speak freely and openly within their own fictive landscapes while its readers, trapped within the repressive structures of princely government, overhear conversations in which they can no longer engage.

A perfect example would be Spenser's *Shepheardes Calender* published anonymously in 1579 at a time when England's philosopher queen had expressly forbidden all allusion, in verse or otherwise, to the political matters it handles. Just a few months previously the country had witnessed a horrifying demonstration of the sort of censorship that princely government could effect when, according to William Camden, the author and publisher of *The Discoverie of a Gaping Gulf Whereinto England is Like to be Swallowed* 'had their Right hands cut off with a Cleaver, driven through the Wrist by the force of a Mallet, upon a Scaffold in the Marketplace at Westminster. The Printer was pardoned'. 'I remember', adds Camden, '(being there present) that when Stubbs [the author], after his Right hand was cut off, put off his Hat with his Left, and said with a loud voice, 'God save the Queen'; *the Multitude standing about was deeply silent*'.[12]

The best Princes, according to Puttenham, were those who accepted poets as counsellors. Accordingly he represents Augustus as offering Horace not just the

---

10   Select Translations from Scaliger's Poetics, p. 21.

11   The Art of English Poesy, pp. 127-8.

12   William Camden, *The History of the Princess Elizabeth*, ed. by Wallace T. MacCaffrey (Chicago: University of Chicago Press, 1970), p. 138. I discuss this further in '"Little booke: thy selfe present": the Politics of Presentation in *The Shepheardes Calender*' in *Presenting Poetry*, edited by Howard Erskine-Hill and Richard A. McCabe (Cambridge: Cambridge University Press, 1995), 15-40.

post of personal secretary (as is usually stated) but of 'secretary of estate', a major public office. And he emphasises the fact that such poets as Virgil and Horace won their honours not because they were – perish the thought! – 'cunning prince-pleasures' but 'for that also they were thought for their universal knowledge to be very sufficient men for the greatest charges in their commonwealths, were it for counsel or for conduct, whereby no man need to doubt that both skills may very well concur and be most excellent in one person'.[13] This is a fine sentiment, but that 'also' is radically disconcerting. It recognises the ironic fact that political endorsement may be as hazardous to 'libertas' as political censorship. Those who find favour with princes must be 'prince-pleasers' *at some level* with all that this entails.

Puttenham characterises himself as writing an 'arte' of poetry in an age no longer conducive to that art.[14] References in the body of the text suggest that the work was originally intended for dedication to the queen, 'being already, of any that I know in our time, the most excellent poet. Forsooth, by your Princely purse, favors, and countenance, making in manner what ye list, the poor man rich, the lewd well learned, the coward courageous, and vile both noble and valiant'.[15] At first this reads like a very handsome tribute, except that 'making in *what manner you list* ' suggests the arbitrariness of royal power, and the original reading, altered by the text's modern editors, is not 'Princely purse, favors' but 'Princely pursefavours' which creates a very different impression. It is clear how the prince's 'pursefavour' might make a poor poet rich, but how could it make a 'lewd' poet 'well-learned' or a cowardly poet 'courageous'? – unless, of course, all of these qualities are defined politically rather than intellectually or ethically. Furthermore the acceptance of 'pursefavours' in any circumstances generates the sort of obligations that can be seen to compromise artistic integrity – the problem that Horace faced throughout his career as he repeatedly represented his Sabine farm as an altruistic gift rather than payment in kind for political services poetically rendered.[16]

Though aware of the author's intention in the matter of dedication, Puttenham's publisher dedicated the work not to Elizabeth but to the man with his hands on the nation's purse-strings, Lord Burghley, the Lord Treasurer. And he apologizes for doing so on the ground that the subject matter is so 'slender' that 'nothing almost could be more discrepant from the gravity of your years and honourable function, whose contemplations are every hour more seriously em-

---

13   The Art of English Poesy, pp. 107-8.
14   Ibid., p. 106.
15   Ibid., p. 95.
16   See Phebe Lowell Bowditch, *Horace and the Gift Economy of Patronage* (Berkeley: University of California Press, 2001).

ployed upon the public administration and services'.[17] The dedication thus poses the question of why a practitioner in the art of government should be interested in the art of poesy without there being some political advantage to such interest. For Spenserian scholars the wording of the dedication is highly significant. Just two years later Spenser's *Complaints* (1591) were censored for their attacks on Lord Burghely who was alleged to have grudged the poet his pension – remember the famous remark later attributed to him 'all this for a song?'[18] At the outset of the second part of *The Faerie Queene* (1596) Burghley is characterised in very similar terms to those used by Puttenham but to very different effect. In Spenser he is 'the rugged forehead that with grave foresight / Welds kingdoms causes, and affaires of state' (IV Proem 1) and who, precisely because of these political preoccupations, wishes to suppress Spenser's poem on the grounds that it corrupts the young – the same grounds that Socrates advances for state censorship in the second and third books of the *Republic* and also, very tellingly, the grounds alleged to justify the philosopher's own execution by the Athenian state. At the end of the sixth book of*The Faerie Queene*, in a passage that obliquely alludes to the censoring of the *Complaints*, Burghley is further characterised as one of those who reject the poet's right to proffer counsel or critique and demand instead only flattery: 'therefore do you my rimes keep better measure, / And seek to please, that now is counted wiseman's threasure' (VI.xii.41). 'Threasure', the last word of *The Faerie Queene* published in Spenser's lifetime, wryly reflects on the sort of 'wisdom' the country's leading politician pos- sesses. It was, of course, richly ironic that at the same time that he was complaining about the loss of artistic freedom in England Spenser was actively calling for the censorship of the Irish bards. He was calling, in other words, for the expulsion of the Bards from the ideal colonial commonwealth that he was labouring to establish in Ireland. He simultaneously opposed Platonic censorship because of poetry's power to elevate, and promoted it because of its power to corrupt.[19]

This contradiction is richly indicative of the complex problems that Early Modern censorship occasioned. Spenser's *Shepeardes Calender* was dedicated to Philip Sidney at a time when Sidney had been expelled from the court for circulating a letter opposing the queen's proposed match to Alençon, a subject that, as Blair Worden has expertly demonstrated, he would later treat covertly in the

---

17 The Art of English Poesy, p. 90.

18 *Spenser Allusions in the Sixteenth and Seventeenth Centuries*, ed. William Wells, 2 Pts. *Studies in Philology*, Texts and Studies (Chapel Hill: University of North Carolina Press, 1971-72), II, 269.

19 See Richard A. McCabe, 'Spenser, Plato, and the Poetics of State', *Spenser Studies,* 24 (2009), 433-52.

Arcadia.[20] But in that same year of 1579 Sidney received another dedication, that of Stephen Gosson's *Schoole of Abuse* which calls for the banishment of public plays and players from the common-wealth and repeatedly references Plato's call for the expulsion of the poets as its moral precedent. Gosson rejects as a mere sham the traditional defence of poetry as a morally didactic art: he urges the reader to 'pul off the visard that Poets maske in' in order to 'perceive their sharpe sayings to be placed as Pearles in Dunghills, fresh pictures on rotten walles, chaste Matrons apparel on common Curtesans ... No marveyle though Plato shut them out of his Schoole, and banished them quite from his common wealth, as effeminate writers, unprofitable members, and utter enimies to vertue'.[21] In casting about to find historical exemplars of Socrates' attitudes he not only praises Augustus for the banishment of Ovid, but even praises Tiberius for the execution of the tragedian Scaurus.[22]

Gosson was one of the first to recognise the aesthetic implications of the *Republic* when he identified the cause for the moral decline of the arts as aesthetic innovation. 'It was an old law and long kept', he writes, 'that no man should, according to his owne humor, adde or diminish, in matters concerning that Art, but walk in the pathes of their predecessors'.[23] The art in question is music but the principle applies to all the others. In Plato's *Laws* the Athenian declares that only one nation has acted prudently with regard to the effects of art on the education of the young, and that is Egypt. In Egypt, he alleges, they drew up a list of acceptable forms and modes with the result that,

modification and innovation outside this traditional framework were prohibited, and are prohibited even today, both in this field [music and movement] and the arts in general. If you examine their art on the spot, you will find that ten thousand years ago (and I'm not speaking loosely: I mean literally ten thousand), paintings and reliefs were produced that are no better and no worse than those of today, because the same artistic rules were applied in making them.

Clinias responds by crying 'fantastic!', to which the Athenian replies, 'no: simply a supreme achievement of legislators and statesman' (656d-657a). And that is the crux of the whole matter: what Gosson realised was that Socrates's political programme entails aesthetic stasis. Only hymns to the gods and eulogies of good men will be allowed in the ideal republic, a poetry as static in form and fixed in content as the institutions of the ideal state itself. The state of the arts will be state art. Patronage will petrify.

---

20 Blair Worden, The Sound of Virtue: Philip Sidney's Arcadia and the Elizabethan Politics (New Haven: Yale University Press, 1996), pp. 89-124.
21 Stephen Gosson, *The Schoole of Abuse* (1579), sigs. 2v-3r.
22 Ibid., sig. 9v.
23 Ibid., sig. 9v.

But the ethos of Elizabethan literature is profoundly innovative in form, language, content and mode. E. K. introduced Spenser to the reading public in 1579 as the 'new Poet' whose writings would inaugurate a new beginning in English poetics. In the Spenser-Harvey *Letters* of the following year, Spenser makes a point of asserting that Gosson's attempt to gain Sidney's patronage was brusquely rejected, which is an oblique way of implying that his own has been accepted *because* his aesthetic theory is more congenial. The implication is probably valid in view of Sidney's avowed appreciation in the *Apology for Poetry* of 'that high flying liberty of conceit [that is] proper to the Poet'.[24] Sidney identifies Plato's supposed opposition to poetry as one of the strongest weapons in his opponents' arsenal but rather compounds than solves the problem by emphasising the 'praxis' of poetry, its power to move and take effect in the real world. In the tenth book of the *Republic* Socrates admits a strong personal attraction to what he repudiates and argues, in effect, that poetry must be banished *precisely because of its power*. In response to this, Sidney concentrates on the power to improve, but exacerbates the central issue of censorship by responding directly to Socrates' challenge to show how mimetic poetry relates to the 'well-governed state'. This is particularly obvious when he comes to the subject of tragedy which was one of Socrates', and Gosson's, main targets. The *Apology* is often celebrated for introducing Aristotelian poetics to English readers, and one would therefore expect that Sidney's main defence of tragedy would deploy Aristotle's notion of *catharsis*, since that concept was primarily designed to respond to Plato's attack on the genre. But Sidney's formulation of the matter at this point is quite distinct from that of Aristotle in emphasising not the purgation or rebalancing of dangerous emotions (which *catharsis* was generally understood to imply in the Renaissance) but the political potency of the genre in the face of tyranny. Tragedy is defended because it is the genre that,

> openeth the greatest wounds, and sheweth forth the Ulcers that are covered with Tissue; that maketh Kinges feare to be Tyrants, and Tyrants manifest their tirannicall humors … that maketh us knowe, *Qui sceptra saevus duro imperio regit, / Timet timentes, metus in auctorem redit*' [Seneca, *Oedipus*, 705-6].[25]

This, of course, is political dynamite and is precisely the reason that Tiberius, suspecting himself to be represented as a tyrant, was believed to have executed Scaurus – to Gosson's apparent approval, as we have seen. While the moral defence of literature along the familiar Horatian lines of the *utile dulce* was common, Sidney's political inflection pits the poet squarely against the legislator. The

---

24 *Elizabethan Critical Essays*, ed. G. Gregory Smith, 2 vols (Oxford: Oxford University Press, 1904), I, 154.

25 Ibid, I, 177.

more he emphasises the power of poetry, the more it emerges as a powerful tool of political opposition, a peculiarly efficacious species of rhetoric that takes hold on its audience.

The commentator who responded perhaps most innovatively to this dilemma was not Sidney but Lodovico Castelvetro who pioneered the view that the primary goal of poetry was not moral didactism but aesthetic pleasure. He appealed to Aristotle's dictum that 'correctness in the art of poetry is not the same thing as correctness in the art of politics' (*Poetics*, 1460b). It followed that,

> The two arts [of government and poetry] have different ends: the government of a city contemplates peace and concord among its citizens to the end that their life together may be conducted with greater ease and bring them greater material and spiritual benefits; poetry contemplates no more than the pleasure and recreation of its audiences ... Yet in so far as poetry is subordinate to the art of government and is used by it as an instrument to attain its own end ... public magistrates in the cities take care to forbid the performance of tragedies and comedies and the recitation of epic poems which may not only corrupt or injure by their shows of lewdness or other means the city's severe and divinely sanctioned moral customs ... And on the assumption that it is a matter of no small consequence to the citizenry that the art of poetry be well formulated and properly practised, they offer public prizes and titles of honour to exemplary poets. Hence the laurel crowns which in modern times are conferred in solemn ceremonies by emperors and popes upon poets in recognition of the impeccable practice of their art.[26]

Whereas on one level Castelvetro establishes the independence of poetics and liberty of aesthetic innovation – a poem being good or bad solely in terms of artistic accomplishment rather than moral effect or political orientation – it concedes the primacy of politics over poetics. Within this system laureation is little more than a mark of political approval, and banishment of political disapproval. From a purely aesthetic viewpoint, it might be better to be Ovid than Virgil.

Early Modern commentators and poets were grappling with a problem that could not be resolved in the terms in which it was discussed. Those who argued, like Alberico Gentili, that poetry was important because of its utility to the state risked reducing the criteria of assessment to those of political utilitarianism – a criterion that would ultimately be decided by those who undertook to speak for, or to represent themselves as, the state.[27] Those who, like Sidney, argued for the praxis of poetry, for its effect upon human agency, inevitably configured it as a

---

26 Castelvetro on the Art of Poetry: An Abridged Translation of Lodovico Castelvetro's Poetica d'Aristotele Vulgarizzata et Sposta, by Andrew Bongiorno, Medieval and Renaissance Texts and Studies (Binghampton NY: 1984), p. 278.

27 J. W. Binn, ed. and trans., Latin Treatises on Poetry from Renaissance England: Henry Dethick, 'Oratio in laudem poeseos Alberico Gentili, 'Commentatio ad Legem III Codicis de professoribus et medicis'; Caleb Dalechamp, 'Artis poeticae et versificatoriae encomium' (Signal ountain, Tennessee: Summertown for the Library of Renaissance Humanism, 1999), pp. 95-99.

force no politician could afford to ignore or permit to pass uncontrolled. Those who, like Julius Caesar Scaliger, identified moral didacticism as the goal of poetics, necessarily subjected literary production to the sort of censorship envisaged in the second, third and tenth books of the *Republic* if only, as Socrates maintains, in the interests of the young (an argument that remains influential today). Those who, like Castelvetro, sought to dissociate aesthetics from politics effectively deprived the poet of all moral agency and lent force to the Socratic objection that the mimetic poet, in seeking only to give the maximum aesthetic pleasure to the greatest number of people, 'puts a bad constitution ['kaken politeian'] in the soul of each individual by making images that are far removed from the truth and by gratifying the irrational part' in a manner directly analogous to someone who 'destroys the better sort of citizens' by strengthening the 'vicious ones' and surrendering the city to them (605b). The mimetic poet will always be the enemy of the ideal state because that state is maintained by what Socrates calls 'noble lies' or 'magnificent myths' (382c-d; 414b-c) and is, to that extent, a fiction in itself. Mimetic poets are dangerous to the state because they produce alternative fictions that the public prefers. Writing in a later age, and with a different definition of poetry – as 'the expression of the imagination' – Shelley famously asserted that 'poets are the unacknowledged legislators of the world' and it was precisely that issue of unacknowledged power – of hidden praxis – that lay at the heart of the Early Modern debate. It is sobering to remember, particularly in the light of Camden's account of Stubbs and Page, that the only author in Elizabethan England who could neither be censored, nor aesthetically criticised with impunity, was the sovereign philosopher herself, the creator of the 'magnificent myth' of the Virgin Queen.

Paul's Cross: Context, Occasion, Significance

Mary Morrissey
University of Reading

The Paul's Cross sermons form part (perhaps a rather vague part) of the 'background' to Renaissance literature familiar to most scholars, because of the calibre of the preachers (Hugh Latimer, John Foxe, John Jewel, John Donne), and the fame of the sermons delivered there (John Jewel's 'Challenge' sermon of 1559, Richard Bancroft's anti-Puritan sermon of 1589, or John Donne's 1622 sermon on the *Directions for Preachers*). But Paul's Cross is often described in a static and rather nostalgic way, both by early modern writers like John Stow and John Strype, as well as by modern historians of the subject. Millar MacLure described the sermon series as a 'ritual, as old as a folkmoot'.[1] What follows is an attempt to create a brief narrative *history* of the Paul's Cross sermons, to show the ways in which this crucial aspect of early modern London's religious life changed in the sixteenth and early seventeenth centuries. To do this, we must consider the renovations made to the pulpit and its attendant buildings, the development of arrangements for funding the sermons, and the variations in patterns of attendance by members of the London community. Paul's Cross served several functions for its many auditors: it was a place from which 'godly' preaching was heard, from which important announcements were made, and where news and gossip circulated. In the late 1630s, Paul's Cross stopped serving these purposes, and so no-one thought to object when building work on St. Paul's cathedral closed the pulpit down.

Paul's Cross stood in the churchyard on the north-east of Old St Paul's, between the choir and St Faith-under-St Paul's to the east and the northern transept of the cathedral. This meant that it stood at the centre of the news-gathering networks of early modern London. The 'middle aisle' of the cathedral became famous for the collection of gossip in the city, as we know from Jonson's *Everyman in his Humour*.[2] The Children of St Paul's operated a commercial theatre in the cathedral precinct for much of the time between 1575 and 1606-8. Although its exact location is unknown, it was probably in the almonry, on the opposite side

---

1   Millar MacLure, *The Paul's Cross Sermons* (Toronto: University of Toronto Press, 1958), p. 167.
2   Ben Jonson, *Everyman Out of his Humour*, Act 3, in *Works*, eds C. H. Herford and Percy Simpson (Oxford: Clarendon Press, 1925–52), vol. 3.

of the cathedral to Paul's Cross.[3] Most important for our purposes were the pulpits' immediate neighbours: the north side of the Cross Yard (where the sermons were preached) had become the home of the London book trade. Peter Blayney writes that: 'other than St Paul's School, the Sermon House, and the cathedral itself, by the time of the Civil War virtually every frontage in the Cross Yard either was, or had been, a bookshop'.[4] It is not surprising, therefore, that contemporaries associated the Paul's Cross sermons with news about religious and political controversies. Many of the most significant public statements in the Reformation debates, from the penance of the 'Maid of Kent' to John Jewel's 'Challenge' sermon, were delivered from here.

The pulpit and its attendant buildings were a functional part of public life in London, and not a relic of pre-Reformation piety: the renovations made to the buildings demonstrate this. The medieval cross was replaced in 1449 by Bishop Thomas Kempe of London with the pulpit known to Elizabethan Londoners.[5] This was a substantial building made up of a pulpit with an ambulatory around it, in all forming an octagon about thirty-seven feet in diameter. The pulpit itself was roofed with open sides.[6] The ambulatory immediately surrounding the pulpit had been open until 1595. In that year a low wall was built around a section of it,[7] and this wall was extended to encompass the pulpit in 1608. These changes turned the ambulatory into an enclosed space, a 'room' where people sat for the sermons, and there was a charge for entrance into this space.[8] Other auditors could sit on benches laid out for the purpose. A dialogue about attending a Paul's Cross sermon from 1591 has one speaker say 'Let us go, for it is time, or else we shall have no place, for all the formes will be taken up.'[9] Members of the richer livery companies, such as the Merchant Taylors, made arrangements to have their benches ready for them.[10]

3   Roger Bowers, 'The Playhouse of the Choristers of Paul's, c. 1575-1608', *Theatre Notebook*, 54 (2000), 70-85; Herbert Berry, 'Where Was the Playhouse in Which the Boy Choristers of St Paul's Cathedral Performed Plays?', *Medieval and Renaissance Drama in England*, 13 (2001), 101-16, pp. 109-113.

4   Peter W. M. Blayney, *The Bookshops in Paul's Cross Churchyard* (London: The Bibliographical Society, 1990), p. 5.

5   William Dugdale, *The History of St Pauls Cathedral* (1658), p. 128.

6   F. C Penrose, 'On the Recent Discoveries of Portions of Old St Paul's Cathedral', *Archaelogia*, 47 (1883), 381-92, p. 385.

7   Stow, *Annales* (1631 [i.e. 1632]), p. 770.

8   City of London, Guildhall Manuscript 25630, Vol. 5 (Dean's Registers, 1604-14), ff. 170v-172r; I would like to thank Peter McCullough for this reference.

9   William Stepney, *The Spanish Schoole-master* (1591), p. 126.

10   City of London, Guildhall Manuscript 34048 (Merchant Taylors Company, Master and Wardens Account Books), vols 15, 16 and 17. I would like to thank Emma Rhatigan for alerting me to this source.

Arrangements for seating dignitaries became even more elaborate over the sixteenth century. Before 1483, the lord mayor and aldermen were protected from the weather by a cloth or awning; in that year a gallery was built against the wall of the north choir aisle of the cathedral.[11] This too became insufficient: in 1569, a substantial 'sermon house' was built into the buttresses of the cathedral. This provided accommodation for the lord mayor and city officers, as well as for the lady mayoress and the aldermen's wives.[12] The effect of these changes was to make the pulpit and the accommodation for London's governing elite more permanent, as well as more comfortable. But it may also have made the pulpit less accessible to those who did not have seating in the sermon houses, or who could not afford to pay the entry fee into the 'room' in the ambulatory beside the pulpit. This exclusion of ordinary hearers intensified yet further in 1634, when the outdoor pulpit was closed permanently and the sermons were transferred to the choir of the cathedral. There, seating was provided for the lord mayor and city officers, but there cannot have been as much space for ordinary auditors.

Who were these auditors of the Paul's Cross sermons? It is very difficult to reconstruct the audience at events like this: the sermons were too regular for the audience to be recorded (except on extraordinary occasions), and they were not compulsory for most people (and so there was no reason to record attendance). The sermons were free to those who did not wish to pay for seating, and so there are no paper records (in the form of accounts) for those who attended casually or as private individuals. We have no sources telling us explicitly about changes in the composition of the auditory over time. But frequent references are made in early modern sources to people attended particular sermons (diarists, for example, record going to hear sermons at Paul's Cross), and to groups who attend sermons on particular occasions annually. This allows us to build up some picture of the audience to whom the preacher spoke.

The monarch was the least regular but most prestigious auditor: Elizabeth, James I and Charles I attended one sermon each at Paul's Cross during their reigns. But the royal government was more often represented by members of the Privy Council, particularly on occasions that would emphasise the government's support for the religious authorities (on 20 August 1553, for example, the Sunday after an anti-Catholic riot). Privy Councillors may have begun to attend the sermons preached on the anniversary of the Queen's accession sometime in the

---

11   Caroline M Barron, 'London and St Paul's Cathedral in the Later Middle Ages', in *The Medieval English Cathedral: Papers in Honour of Pamela Tudor-Craig*, ed. Janet Backhouse (Donington: Shaun Tyas, 2003), p. 140, n. 77.

12   London Metropolitan Archive, Corporation of London Letter Book 5, f. 224r; LMA, Corporation of London Repertory, vol. 16, ff. 447r, 448r.

1590s: certainly, their attendance at Accession Day sermons had become expected by the middle of James I's reign; I have no evidence to say that they were still going to hear these sermons regularly in the reign of Charles I.

The presence of the bishops of London or deans of Paul's was more frequent than that of Privy Councillors, but these men were senior clerics with obligations to preach at court: it seems unlikely that they were among the auditors at Paul's Cross on a very regular basis. When they did come to Paul's Cross, bishops of London were more likely to be preaching as hearing another man preach, and at least one Paul's Cross sermon seems to have been expected of the bishop in this see. John Aylmer famously referred to it as his 'chair', suggesting that he considered it a symbol of his episcopal authority no less important than the cathedra in St Paul's.[13] Deans of St. Paul's had no obligation to preach at Paul's Cross, and there was no formal connection between the Dean and Chapter of the cathedral and the sermon series in the churchyard. Many deans did preach at Paul's Cross, however: Alexander Nowell and John Donne delivered several sermons in their time as dean. Other members of the ruling class (Members of Parliament, for example), attended sermons at Paul's Cross on an irregular basis. Members of the Inns of Court, and students like Simonds D'Ewes and John Manningham, were also occasionally in the audience at Paul's Cross, and their diaries offer us valuable clues on how the sermons were received by their hearers.

In marked contrast to these irregular auditors, the lord mayor and aldermen of London are referred to as attending the sermons weekly. This had been a custom since the fifteenth century, but Paul's Cross gained a more central role in the corporate religious observances of the civic authorities after the Reformation. There was a tendency to replace undeniably Catholic customs with sermons, a form of religious devotion that was favoured, at least in principle, by all confessional groups. For example, the elaborate Whitsunday processions through the city to the cathedral were discontinued in 1548. Rather than being censed by a chorister dressed as an angel while the '*veni creator*' was sung, the corporation listened to 'three solemn sermons' at Paul's Cross.[14] Paul's Cross became so much the focus for the religious element of civic ritual that in May 1619, when the principal officers of the city were (belatedly) given mourning cloth after the death of Queen Anne, they wore it to a sermon at Paul's Cross and the pulpit was hung with black for the occasion.[15]

---

13 LMA, Corporation of London Remembrancia, vol. 1, f. 143v.
14 Caroline Barron, 'London and St Paul's Cathedral in the Later Middle Ages', pp. 142-3; LMA, Letter Book Q, f. 94v.
15 *Letters of John Chamberlain*, ed. Norman Egbert McClure, 2 vols (Philadelphia: The American Philosophical Society, 1939), vol. 2, p. 241.

Formal attendance by the ordinary guildsmen happened on holidays and special occasions. From at least 1596, the guildsmen were present at the Easter sermons (the Good Friday 'Passion Sermon' and the Rehearsal sermon of the Sunday after Easter). This annual cycle of sermons, which began at Paul's Cross on Good Friday, was followed by three sermons at St Mary's Spital on the Monday, Tuesday and Wednesday after Easter, and ended at Paul's Cross on 'Low Sunday' with a virtuosic display of preaching at the 'Rehearsal' sermon, was the high-point in the corporation's calendar of religious observances. John Stow devotes considerable space to these sermons in the *Survey*, more than to any other aspect of the Paul's Cross sermons.[16] Not surprisingly, charitable collections were organised at these, the most well attended sermons of the year.[17] The proliferation of political anniversary sermons in the reign of James I (sermons commemorating the defeat of the Gowrie Conspiracy and the Gunpowder Plot, as well as sermons celebrating the monarch's accession to the throne) meant that there were more occasions for formal attendance by London's citizens in their guilds. In the reign of Charles I, however, sermons on the Gowrie Conspiracy were discontinued, and sermons on the Gunpowder Plot and the king's accession were preached less frequently. This probably meant that the London livery companies made fewer formal visits to the Paul's Cross sermons.

Members of the royal government, MPs, and officers of the city government attended sermons at Paul's Cross at least partly to make evident to the rest of the population their loyalty to the established reli-gion. But what of weekly, informal attendance by the rest of the population? It is very hard to get a sense of the individuals who attended the sermons as a religious devotion or out of curiosity. We do know, however, that sufficient numbers attended Paul's Cross for it to be considered a crowded place, even on ordinary Sundays: Thomas Platter, a German visitor to London in 1599, describing the auditory as 'so vast that the aforesaid big church [Paul's] will not hold it'.[18] In popular literature, Paul's Cross is described a place where crowds of people are to be expected. In Thomas Middleton's *Black Book* (1604), the devil bequeath to 'Benedick Bottomless, most deep cutpurse' the benefit of 'pageant days, great market days, ballad places' and exhorts him not to 'stick, Benedick, to give a shave of your office at Paul's Cross in the sermon time'.[19]

---

16 *A Survey of London by John Stow*, ed. Charles Lethbridge Kingsford, 2 vols (Oxford: Clarendon Press, 1908), vol. 1, pp. 167-8.
17 LMA, Rep. 23, ff. 520v, 594v.
18 *Thomas Platter's Travels in England*, 1599, translated and introduced by Clare Williams (London: Jonathan Cape, 1937), p. 177.
19 Thomas Middleton, *The Black Book* (1604), ed. G. B. Shand, *Thomas Middleton: The Complete Works*, gen. eds Taylor and Lavagnino (Oxford University Press, 2007), p. 217.

This large and heterogeneous audience, which included members of the national and civic governments, gentlemen and citizens, men and women, may not have been a feature of the Paul's Cross sermons by the end of their history: it seems likely that audiences dwindled in the 1620s. The reasons for this are partly to do with the changing role that Paul's Cross played in the religious life of the city. In the early years of Elizabeth's reign, with many non-preaching and barely conformable ministers still in benefices around the city, Paul's Cross was one of the few pulpits that was open to the public and where the bishop of London had an uncontested right to appoint the preacher. Not surprisingly, efforts were made to ensure that as many Londoners as possible could attend the sermons there. An episcopal injunction of 1579 ordered that Morning Prayer in London parishes be over in time for the parishioners to attend the sermons at Paul's Cross; the policy may have been in place earlier in the Queen's reign.[20] Preaching provision in the city expanded greatly thereafter, and there must have been some competition for auditors. The Inns of Court appointed their own preachers, mostly in the 1580s, and there was also a great increase in the number of parish lectureships in London. Even within the cathedral, the number of sermons being delivered every week increased. Londoners had a far greater choice of sermons in 1600 than they had in 1560. But why did the 'sermon-gadders' not choose Paul's Cross? After the 1622 *Directions for Preachers* and with the elevation of William Laud to the See of London in 1628, there was far greater regulation of the sermons at Paul's Cross. It seems that as they became more predictable, the sermons became less newsworthy, and so there were fewer private auditors willing to attend.

Even though the audience was contracting, however, the prestige of Paul's Cross among the clergy was undiminished. The appointment of Paul's Cross preachers lay with the bishops of London, and for much of the sixteenth century, they had to rely on the good will of their peers and clients to fill the rota. Before the Reformation, the Paul's Cross sermons were funded by bequests left by those wishing to be included in the 'bead roll' read at the end of the sermons, and by gifts from religious gilds or fraternities.[21] The end of prayers for the dead meant the end of the bead roll; the end of the fraternities meant the end of those gifts. Quite soon, it seems that there were no longer funds to pay the preachers, and preachers became reluctance to undertake such an arduous task without compen-

---

20 *Narratives of the Days of the Reformation*, ed. John Gough Nichols (London: Camden Society, 1859), p. 23.

21 *Registrum Statutorum et Consuetudinum Ecclesiae Cathedralis Sancti Pauli Londiniensis* (1873), ed. W. Sparrow Simpson, pp. 446-452, p. 451, See also Susan Bridgen, 'Religion and Social Obligation in Early Sixteenth-Century London', *Past and Present* 103, (1984), 67-112, p. 100; Susan Wabuda, *Preaching during the English Reformation* (Cambridge University Press, 2002), pp. 52-3.

sation. Edmond Bonner was the first to complain of a shortage of preachers: he asked a correspondent in Cambridge to 'exhorte suche as ye knowe apte and mete for that purpose' to preach at the Cross, because 'of late' there 'hath not been many here at paules crosse to preche the word of God'.[22] The early years of Elizabeth's reign did not see any improvement in the funding of the sermons, but the sermons continued because of the assiduousness of the returning Marian exiles. There was also a small but growing supply of scholars from Cambridge and Oxford.[23] Finding preachers able and willing to preach a two-hour sermon before an exacting audience was no small problem for the Elizabethan bishops of London. The solution came only when John Aylmer, Bishop of London between 1577 and 1594, bequeathed a fund to ensure a stipend for the Paul's Cross preachers. Aylmer's gift (which arrived into the Chamber of London in 1606) amounted to £480 (including interest), but it was also important because it spurred other bequests, which allowed the Corporation to pay the preachers more generously. In 1606, the Corporation could give 26s 8d to all unbeneficed preachers appointed to Paul's Cross.[24] This went up in 1612 (to 33s 4d), and again in 1616 (40s) and 1640 (£2 9s). A comparison with Paul Seaver's estimates for the average salary of London lecturers shows that in James I's reign, one Paul's Cross sermon was worth about 7% of the annual income of a parish lecturer.[25]

By the end of James I's reign, a Paul's Cross sermon was an attractive proposition for a young minister: John Earle's 'bold Forward man', 'if hee bee a scholler, ... ha's commonly stept into the Pulpit before a degree; ... and his next Sermon is at *Pauls* Crosse, and that printed'.[26] The ready supply of able preachers, combined with an episcopate committed to public preaching and a civic government determined to be seen doing Protestant things, meant that the Paul's Cross sermons were a well-funded, regular event with powerful supporters. But the accession of Charles I brought several changes that would result in the decline of the Paul's Cross sermons and the demolition of the pulpit cross. As supporters of Laud took more senior positions in the church, there were fewer bishops with the same commitment to public preaching. This meant that fewer members of the senior clergy from these years appeared at Paul's Cross. The same decline in support from the bishops meant that fewer Paul's Cross sermons were printed.

---

22 Corpus Christi College Cambridge MS 119, item 14.
23 Mary Morrissey, *Politics and the Paul's Cross Sermons, 1558-1642* (Oxford University Press, 2011), pp. 28-30.
24 LMA, Rep. 28, f. 145r.
25 Paul Seaver, *The Puritan Lectureships: The Politics of Religious Dissent, 1560–1662* (California: Stanford University Press, 1970), p. 150.
26 John Earle, *Microcosmosgraphie* (1633ed), sig. Mv.

Given their stated opposition to 'sermon-centred piety', it is not surprising that the Paul's Cross sermons did not appeal to the Laudians, and two of the most powerful Laudians (Laud himself and William Juxon) were bishops of London, and therefore the men who had the right to appoint preachers to Paul's Cross, from 1628 until the Civil War. As a member of the commission for rebuilding St Paul's, Laud was also instrumental in the demolition of the pulpit cross itself.

In 1633 building work began on the cathedral and in March 1634, workmen were paid for 'a fence and making the Gates about the Crosse Churchyard'.[27] On 9 April 1634, the Court of Aldermen gave order that the sermon house where the aldermen and their wives had sat for the sermons 'be removed and carried away in regard of the Masons workeing there for the repaire of the Church'.[28] Although it disrupted their Sunday ritual, the lord mayor and aldermen still had (more comfortable) seats in the cathedral choir to hear the sermons, and the older custom must have seemed like a lost cause in the face of the King's determination to see the cathedral renovated. It is ironic, then, that blame for the demolition of the pulpit cross has (until recently) been levelled at the parliamentary Presbyterians in the Corporation: they were, in fact, the ones who recovered the endowments and used them to fund sermons in the cathedral choir throughout the 1640s and 1650s.[29]

The story of Paul's Cross is one of *ad hoc* arrangements achieving a kind of permanence while they served a function. For Londoners and visitors to the city, Paul's Cross had been a place from which learned preaching could be heard, but it had also been a place from which newsworthy things might have been said. It was the unpredictability of this pulpit that made it such an important medium for communicating religious and political controversies in the sixteenth and seventeenth centuries. Once it lost that unpredictability, Paul's Cross lost its audience, and then it matter very little what the preachers had to say. In 1634, the pulpit cross was abandoned, and then demolished, and almost nobody commented on the fact: Paul's Cross had stopped making the news.

---

27   LMA, Guildhall MS 25,473/1, f. 48r.
28   LMA, Rep. 48, f. 270v.
29   Morrissey, *Politics and the Paul's Cross Sermons*, pp. 223-6.

Mark(et)ing Differences on the Early Modern Stage: Malta's Slave Market and London's Exchange

James R. Siemon
Boston University

It is an apparent paradox that the founding instance of London City Comedy, William Haughton's innovative *English Men for My Money, or A Woman will Have her Way* (performed 1598), and one of the most popular such plays in the period, Thomas Heywood's slightly later *2 If You Know Not Me* (*Stationers Register* 1605), respond to Christopher Marlowe's Mediterranean play, *The Jew of Malta* (performed 1592).[1] All three concern themselves with trans-national commerce, a central merchant figure, and a symbolic market site. While the Merchant Jew Barabas and the Maltese Slave market focus Marlowe's play; London's Royal Exchange and two figures (linked to its founding and its function) ground Haughton's and Heywood's. Heywood dramatizes the founding of the Royal Exchange (1566-71) by Thomas Gresham, who sometimes sounds like Marlowe's Tamburlaine in a play with scenes that revise *The Jew of Malta*; Haughton dramatizes the function of the Exchange in trans-national trade involving a 'Portingale' usurer, Pisaro, who frequently echoes Marlowe's Barabas.

These plays might appear to offer opposing views of the Exchange and its economic processes. Haughton's Exchange appears to be a confusing, threatening place of exotic foreigners, barely concealed animosities, tricky negotiations, extreme financial risk, and the exploitation of naïve English gentlemen by a hypocritical Merchant-usurer who traffics in the sexuality of his daughters. Haughton's Exchange could be seen as offering a London equivalent of Malta's slave market where Marlowe's Machiavellian protagonist wheels and deals amid exotic foreigners, against a backdrop of global ventures, while he negotiates Christian

---

1   William Haughton, *Englishmen for My Money,* ed. A. C. Baugh (Philadelphia: University of Pennsylvania Press, 1909); Thomas Heywood, *If You Know Not Me You Know Nobody, Part II,* ed. Madeleine Doran (1935; rpt. New York: AMS Press, 1985); Christopher Marlowe, *The Jew of Malta,* ed. James R. Siemon (London: Methuen, 2009). These editions quoted throughout. On the popularity of Heywood's play, see Dieter Mehl, 'The Late Queen on the Public Stage: Thomas Heywood's *If You Know Not Me You Know Nobody, Parts I and II*' in *Queen Elizabeth I: Past and Present,* ed. Christa Jansohn (Münster: Lit Verlag, 2004), 153-72.

gentlemen into a trap baited with his daughter. Heywood's Exchange, by contrast, appears to be a site that encourages piety and community: 'a parish for good Cittizens / And their faire wiues to dwell' that 'hides not heauen from vs' and will encourage 'euery honest man [to] warme one another' in winter (1218-1231). However, Haughton's and Heywood's London comedies are both more complex than these summaries grant, and they offer to complicate recent critical clichés about early modern anxieties concerning the forces of the market and the threat of foreign infection to English identity. This essay will examine some of the intertextual connections between Haughton and Heywood's London plays and Marlowe's drama symbolically centered in the Mediterranean's notorious slave market.

Marlowe's slave market furnishes a symbol for recent criticism exploring connections between the Mediterranean and London's stage. Daniel Vitkus enlists the major terms: 'The Mediterranean, with its Barbary pirates, Turkish galleys, and slave markets, must have seemed to Londoners to be a place where everything was up for sale and subject to exchange, a place like Marlowe's Maltese slave market where "Every one's price is written on his back" (2.3.3). Piracy and slavery were the most sensational aspects of this mercenary mercantilism, but in a more general way, what disturbed and titillated English culture was simply … multicultural mixing.'[2]

Stephen Greenblatt and Lawrence Danson, also enlist Marlowe's slave market as an emblem for Elizabethan anxieties about threats to identity posed by the alienating forces of market exchange and 'multicultural mixing'.[3] These interpretations parallel Jean-Christophe Agnew's argument that early modern English people were 'perplexed' by a new 'fluidity of social relations' and that 'as London's Exchange enforced an ideal of financial liquidity, so London's theaters enacted a vision of this new sociological and psychological fluidity'.[4] Such readings cite contemporary comparisons linking the Exchange and the theatres, such as Thomas Dekker's claim that 'The Theater is your Poets Royal Exchange, vpon which their Muses ([that] are now turnd Merchants) meeting, barter away that light commodity of words for a lighter ware then words, *Plaudities*, and the Breath of

---

2   Daniel Vitkus, *Turning Turk: English Theater and the Multicultural Mediterranean, 1570-1630* (NY: Palgrave Macmillan, 2003), 196.

3   See Stephen J. Greenblatt, 'The Will to Absolute Play: *The Jew of Malta*', in *Staging the Renaissance: Reinterpretations of Elizabethan and Jacobean Drama*, ed. David Scott Kastan and Peter Stallybrass (London: Routledge, 1991), 114-21, esp. 117; Lawrence Danson, 'England, Islam, and the Mediterranean Drama: Othello and Others', *Journal for Early Modern Cultural Studies* 2 (2002), 1-25; esp. 15.

4   Agnew, *Worlds Apart: The Market and the Theater in Anglo-American Thought, 1550-1750* (Cambridge: Cambridge University Press, 1989), 97-98.

the great Beast'.[5] This familiar linkage has been complicated by Aaron Kitch's contrary claim that: 'Unlike theater ... the Royal Exchange was a symbol of political and religious stability'.[6] Kitch cites John Payne's 1597 exhortation against divisive sectaries, *The Royal Exchange* (London, 1597), which treats the Exchange as an emblem of the proper alliance of the English state with trade and a model of religious and civic order to argue that, instead of threatening England with foreigners, fluidity and destabilization, the Exchange actually '[formalized] domestic and international commercial relationships, [and] embodied the significance of trade to the political stability of the nation.' However, Kitch adds a significant qualifier, noting that Gresham's Exchange 'was also the site of contestation and negotiation in which commerce could both undermine and uphold structures of power' (4). I think this double view of the Exchange may be right in both ways.

The re-working of Marlovian themes in Haughton and Heywood's plays supports this mixed interpretation of the Exchange as both stabilizing and contestatory. The very titles of the plays invoke price, value and identity, choosing Englishmen for my money and knowing true identity. Further understanding of Gresham's London home for trans-national marketing could profitably begin by considering Marlowe's Malta. Surveying Malta's international slave market, Marlowe's Barabas inquires, implausibly, about price disparities, 'Why should this Turk be dearer than that Moor?' (2.3.109). Comically, Barabas first wonders if the Turk might weigh more than the Moor. This poundage to price ratio is meant to be ridiculously reductive, of course, performing another Marlovian mockery of the 'unseen hypocrisy' of Christian idealism (1.2.293) that is wonderfully compounded by the scene's simultaneous negotiations by the Christians, as Don Matthias's mother, debates whether this Moor or that is 'comeliest' (2.3.144), and buys a human being while berating her son for even speaking with a Jew 'cast off from heaven' (2.3.157). Meanwhile, Matthias's Christian rival for Barabas's daughter negotiates the 'price' of a night with her, discussing her as a costly gem (2.3.48-135). As this extended episode ends, the Maltese Officers dispassionately sum up the day's transactions as 'a reasonable market' (2.3.161). Marlowe's satiric point, with his mash-up of overlapping discourses and transactions, is that the slave market is anything but 'reasonable,' even in material economic terms.

Marlowe's market initially suggests that all relationships are subject to material definition by bringing together Christian slaving with all these other transactions, but any single standard of value seems utterly inadequate to the com-

---

5   Thomas Dekker, *The Guls Hornbook* (London, 1609), 27.
6   Aaron Kitch, *Political Economy and the States of Literature in Early Modern England* (Farnham, Surrey: Ashgate, 2009), 1.

plexity of the situation. After all, in this very scene, Barabas jauntily dismisses his own costly defrauding with 'I have wealth enough' (2.3.244), and chooses to pursue the personal rather than financial revenges that, often to his economic cost, dominate his attention – except when they do not, and he suddenly decides to grant minimal credit to Christian truisms about the value of kingship (1.1.130-33) and commit his fate to the very Christians who have repeatedly victimized him (5.2).[7]

The Jew of Malta does not portray a trans-national world where gold drives everything and other values or identities mean nothing; rather, the play overlays so many layers of pricing and identity on one another that characters, even the arch-Machiavels and the resident Merchant-Usurer all make mistakes, misjudging the overlapping and sometimes contradictory political, economic, religious and erotic interests that intersect in Malta. It is not that Malta represents *the* market but that Malta represents the interpenetration of different sorts of evaluation that permit mis-evaluations and mis-alliances. For one example, the Turks themselves bizarrely represent 'the least treacherous of the three religious groups' (Vitkus, 184) in Malta, despite familiar early modern European denunciations of Turks as 'the most barbarous, couetous, & cruel nation of the world ... in whom there is neither truth nor fidelity, neuer observing the one half of that they promise, and yet men must always be giuing to them'.[8] Marlowe's Calymath remarkably (and stupidly) even renounces the use of force on the grounds that it is 'more kingly to obtain by peace / Than to enforce conditions by constraint' (1.2.25-6), and with fatal naïveté he credits Barabas's word (5.1.93). All Marlowe's characters make serious mistakes, but their mis-evaluations are, as in this case, enabled by supporting social languages. Without a discourse ascribing value to true kingliness, Calymath would hardly have made his mistake.[9]

What does this Mediterranean confusion have to do with the London Exchange? Elizabethan associations of the Exchange with the Mediterranean, with aggressive marketing, with luxury goods and with heterogeneity of persons, values, and languages are frequent. Although the Exchange was modeled on the New Burse of Antwerp, its courtyard where foreign traders conducted their dealings was called 'New Venice,' and one play calls Gresham himself 'Rialto'.[10] Thomas

7   For Barabas's generalization, see Innocent Gentillet, *A Discourse Upon the Meanes of Well Governing* (London, 1602), 13, 200, 216.

8   Nicholas Nicolay, *Nauigations, Peregrinations and Voyages made into Turkie* (London, 1585), 27v.

9   Nor, for another example, would Barabas's daughter convert to Christianity without a sustaining language invoking holiness that she mistakenly presumes in the play's corrupt priests.

10 See Ceri Sullivan, *The Rhetoric of Credit: Merchants in Early Modern Writing* (Cranbury, NJ: Associated University Presses, 2002), 177-8.

Coryat termed the Rialto 'the Exchange of Venice.'[11] The London Exchange also had a commercial area called 'The Pawne,' housing shops with fine wares; Thomas Middleton's *Chaste Maid in Cheapside* refers to these goods as 'spanglings' from 'the gaudy-shops in Gresham's Burse' (1.2.32-4). The Pawne was notorious for attracting and employing women reputed to be sexually available, and it replaced St. Paul's as the chief site for payments by debtors.[12] Furthermore, what happened at the Exchange, famously, did not stay at the Exchange, for its vaulted canopies were represented as echo chambers where gossip about sex and debt, and misinformation could proliferate instantly, allowing eavesdroppers to 'take vppe a little newes at interest' as 'Eccho' then 'multiplies euery worde that is spoken by Arithmaticke, [inflating] a thousand of one ... with all speede into euery corner of the Realme.'[13] Thus, there were ample reasons to associate the Exchange with 'destabilizing' economic activity, as well as with the commodified sexuality, hard bargains, and deceptive misinformation of Marlowe's Malta.

The verbal and structural connections between Haughton's Exchange play and Marlowe's Malta play are strong: their alien (one a Jew, one a 'Portingale') protagonists, each sporting an enormous stage nose, open their respective plays with similarly grandiose boasts about their self-interested villainy and their transnational trading empires employing far-flung trading vessels; each will profess false 'love' for gentlemen suitors they subsequently kill, and each will exploit the beauty of his offspring.[14] Both frequently indulge in parenthetical asides that register a 'Judas-like' (Haughton, 28) deviousness. As alien merchants, both endure insults and general prejudice, both suffer enormous losses, and lose control over their families. However, the origin of the prejudice against each is significantly different, and the treatments of their losses differ radically.

When Barabas's wealth is brutally expropriated by Malta's Christians very early in his play, his lamentable state seems at first calculated to awaken audience sympathy. But no sooner does he finish lamenting his ruin as worse than that of Job than, left alone onstage, he rises, laughing. He then mocks his onstage Jewish sympathizers and, by implication, any sympathizers among the theatre audience, as fools and 'slaves', and to affirm his own superiority as being 'framed of finer mold than common men' by virtue of his deep wit and cunning foresight into the 'time to come' (1.2.216-25). When the tables turn on him yet again with further losses, it is surely highly unlikely that any audience would feel inclined to pity him a second time around.

11 Thomas Coryat, *Coryat's Crudities* (1611) (Glasgow: University Press, 1905), 1.312.
12 See John Payne, *The Royall Exchange* (1597), 15; for payment, see John Stow, *A Survey of London*, ed. C. L. Kingsford (Oxford: Clarendon Press, 1905), 1.225.
13 *The Works of Thomas Nashe*, ed. R. B. McKerrow (London: Sidgwick & Jackson, 1904-10), 1.82.
14 For jokes about noses, see Marlowe, 2.3.172 and Haughton, 243-4.

Compare this Marlovian sequence of abuse, loss, misplaced pity and mockery to the treatment Haughton's play gives Pisaro and his financial disasters in the central Exchange scene of *Englishmen for My Money*. Among the various 'nations, sects, and faction' (704) present at the scene, those who sympathize with Pisaro's plight are the citizens of London like Master Moore, who recognizes his financial pain as communal: 'twentie Marchants will be sorry for it', Moore says, since they share Pisaro as 'partners … in losse' (588-9). By contrast with these ordinary Englishmen who care about the Stranger merchant's pain the play represents the completely uncomprehending and offensively condescending gentlemen suitors for Pisaro's daughters as behaving like ignorant louts. They wonder what all the fuss is about, ask impatiently about dinner, mock the 'busy' traders, pick fights with laborers, and insufferably proclaim their own superiority to mere business men in values and behavior. To the gentlemen the traders' reactions to a messenger appear to be savagery, infection and madness: 'Sure, yonder fellow will be torne in peeces' one says, while the other marvels that Pisaro seems 'tainted with this madness,' till the third figures it out: 'Upon my life, tis some body bringes newes' (479-82). Haughton's scene de-familiarizes the Exchange by presenting it through an alien, un-businesslike consciousness, but the aliens being mocked are the gentle English not the alien or English traders.

The play memorably condenses this genteel offensiveness in the gentlemen's lecture to Pisaro, whom they denigrate as a 'slave' behind his back, about the differences between social ranks. Sounding exactly like Marlowe's hypocritical Christians lecturing Barabas about their own religious superiority over the Jews, the gentlemen announce that 'Gentlemen, you know, must want no Coyne, / Nor are they slaues vnto it, when they haue [it]' (447-8). The fact that they are actually pursuing marriage with Pisaro's daughters as the means to erase their debts at precisely the time they lecture Pisaro about their superiority to mere economic means and necessities, renders them structurally equivalent to Marlowe's Christian hypocrites in *Jew of Malta*. In this case, however, social rank rather than religion defines the identity of the group that would appropriate the merchant's profits while pronouncing him contemptible. 'What a pox care I', says one gentleman in responding callously to Pisaro's enormous losses, 'S'wounds tis dinner time' (525-32). Pisaro's daughters may choose to love these English suitors rather than the foreign merchants with funny accents who seek their hands, but their choice seems no more validated than the love of Barabas's daughter – or that of Shylock's daughter, for that matter – for the Christians who exploit and mock their fathers.[15] The daughters make fun of the 'base slavering French' (1795) and their

---

15   The gentlemen mock others, even the lowly Postman, whom they admonish: 'yee patch, cannot you suffer Gentlemen Iest with you?' (582).

'Pigges language' and they joke about being 'infect[ed] with 'the French *et cetera*' (823-4). Nevertheless, it is hard to endorse the affection of these outspoken, half-English/half-Portuguese young women for the same English gentlemen who crudely joke about using sex to cancel their debts, defraud, and insult their father. 'Weele worke our landes out of *Pisaros* Daughters: / And cansell all our bondes in their great Bellies, / When the slaue knowes it, how the Roge will curse,' boasts Walgreave (1862-4). He threatens Pisaro with the spectacle of sexually humiliating his daughter, 'Hearst thou, Ile lie with her before thy face, / Against the Crosse in Cheape' (1895-6), and jokes about transnational miscegenation as 'A *Spanish* Iennet and an *English* Mare, / A Mongrill, halfe a Dogge and halfe a Bitch' (1795-6).

Haughton's Exchange brings diverse, potentially violent and clearly aggressive groups together in a series of tension-filled interactions, but to some degree it also offers to civilize them. Frenchmen, Italians, Dutchmen, Portuguese, traders, factors, minor functionaries and even landed English gentlemen do not have to like one another, but outright violence is prevented by the laws of the Exchange (see 583-4). Its defined codes of behavior enable lowly messengers to criticize the great, for dealing that 'fits not one of your account' (519). The merchant lectures gentle 'Unthrifts' to 'Learne to be thriftie, learne to keepe your Lands / And learne to pay your debts' (1883-4); the gentlemen lecture the usurer about illegal rates of return, about taking 'Tenn in the hundred more then Law' (1889). Time itself appears organized, not according to hungers and whims, but by the clock, which defines when it is time for dinner – even for traders and gentlemen.

Furthermore, the vicissitudes of merchants teach a moral that Pisaro admits: 'Gentlemen, as I haue regard to you, / So doe I wish you'll haue respect to mee: / You know that all of vs are mortall men, / Subiect to change and mutabilitie' (455-8). Trade offers lessons about 'patience' and 'equitie' (461) that Pisaro may appreciate but that he fails to live by and, like all fathers, has trouble applying at home. However, as overseas trading is a hard teacher, so domestically speaking is parenthood, which offers to teach him 'sooner may one day the Sea lie still / Then once restraine a Woman of her will' (2160-1).

Payne's *Royall Exchange* calls the sea 'the Lord's great schoule houwse' (Payne, 32-3), and he defines its lessons as the mutability of the world and the merchant's debt of gratitude. 'Marchants,' he writes, 'must bothe pray the more earnestly / and say with Job / I did feare all my worcks: and not to forget that you be subiect to change and casualties: and next to be thankfull for your daylie gettings' (Payne, 15). Payne's religious values are so deeply inflected by commercial attitudes that his denunciation of Anabaptists, a standard target of abuse in the period for their religious and social beliefs, attacks them for their attitude toward commerce as 'deny[ing] marchandise to be Gods ordinans/seinge buyenge and

sellinge is one of the leggs / whereupon every comm. Welthe dothe stande / for
the better helpe of Prynce/ nobles and contrey' (15). This juncture of state and religion is where Heywood's portrayal of Thomas Gresham comes into the picture.

In contrast to Marlowe's Barabas and Haughton's Pisaro with their vexed or
conflicted relationships to authority as alien merchants out for a profit, Heywood's Gresham in *If You Know Not Me* is outspokenly English and directly
linked to English state authority. Furthermore, he is never overtly villainous, and
his definition of profit needs some examination. Nevertheless, Heywood's play
responds to themes and issues raised by the other plays while adding one crucial
ingredient to the mix: credit. Credit, the master term of early modern social
economy, never figures in Marlowe and Haughton's plays. Although he boasts of
his internationally acknowledged credit before the Maltese seize his possessions,
by the time Barabas gets to the market he cannot even purchase the cut-rate slave
Ithamore without possessing 'present money' for the transaction (1.1.57; 2.3.6).
Thus, Marlowe's slave market is precisely *not* like the early modern market. In
fact, participation in early modern commerce crucially depended on one's being
recognized as credit-worthy; it was all about whom you knew and who knew
you. Robert Greene even claimed the superiority of the London Exchange to the
Venetian Rialto lay not in 'riches' but in the extent to which 'our Merchants and
other Cittizens' are prepared to 'stand so much vppon their credits, as they
grudge not to disburse any sum, eyther necessarie to their priuate Poluteia, or
helpfull to the common profit of theyr Countrey'.[16] Heywood's title directly
concerns Gresham and how one might get to know him, and his play opens with
a discussion of Gresham's 'credite' (8) between Gresham's agent and a 'Barbary
Merchant', and follows with a demonstration of his credit when he gives his
word for an enormous sum to buy 'all' Barbary's sugar (28). Before the play
concludes, Gresham's credit gets further definition by two spectacularly contrasting means: he successfully founds the Exchange and he also grandly loses
this Barbary investment. These actions, though superficially opposed to one
another as apparent success and failure, actually constitute the twin pillars that
support his attainment of new titles redolent of social advancement: 'royall citizen'
(1397), 'noble citizen' (1504), and, proudest of all, 'London Merchant' (1561). He
acquires this supreme title not by his successes but by grandly losing a fortune.

---

16 Robert Greene, *The Royal Exchange* (London, 1590), sig. ¶2v. Discussion of credit in early
    modern England and English literature has been extensive, especially since Craig Muldrew's
    groundbreaking *The Economy of Obligation: The Culture of Credit and Social Relations in Early
    Modern England* (New York: St. Martin's Press, 1998). For one useful summary, see Sullivan,
    The Rhetoric of Credit.

The Exchange itself is presented by Heywood as taking its initial impetus from Gresham's inspired reaction to a 'cruell storme' (542). Subsequently, it reaches its physical realization through his careful supervision of its construction, with not a moment lost, since 'neglect' of time 'is a sinne' (1181). In its completed form it surpasses any building in 'Christendome' or in 'Turkies great *Constantinople*,' in Rome, '*Franckeford*, and *Emden* ... the greatest Marts'; even Venice's '*Realto* ... / T'is but a bable if compar'd to this' (1352-1370). Despite this impressive monumentality, the Exchange is represented as a product of an environment permeated by complex intersections of economic, social, political and religious discourses that suggest volatility. These discourses appear in the play as invocations of the words 'raise' or 'rise.'

The play represents characters insulting one another by making insinuations about their modes of 'rising' in the world (452). These incendiary accusations tar even Gresham himself, as he and an adversary, Sir John Ramsey, a knight, whom Gresham calls '*Ramsie* the rich' (425), trade insults in a dispute over a piece of land:

> RAMSEY Doe not I know thy rising?
> GRESHAM I, and I know thine.
> RAMSEY Why, mine was honestly.
> GRESHAM And so was mine. (452-3)

Forced to listen to this war on one another's credit, Old Hobson, a comical character and Gresham's smalltime retail double, lectures these prominent Londoners that it is 'Gods blessing, that hath rais'd them both' (457). Hobson's attribution of success to 'Gods blessing' repeats the sentiments of Gresham himself, who admits that 'wealthy men' are 'by Gods blessing onely rais'd' (846-7). Yet the formula is heavily ironized when Hobson explains his own blessing, introducing further notions of dubious practice as he justifies his own rise to wealth in highly-loaded terms, asking:

> Am I worse because in *Edwards* dayes,
> When Poperie went downe, I did ingrosse
> Most of the Beades that were within the Kingdome,
> That when Queene *Marie* had renewed that Church,
> They that would pray on Beades were forc't to me:
> I made them stretch their purse-strings, grew rich thereby;
> Beads were to me a good commoditie. (458-64)

Hobson shamelessly defends the providential nature of his own economic rising in the very terms reserved for grievous offenses in Tudor-Stuart social and religious polemic: engrossing, monopolization and abetting ritual Catholicism.

Thus, two means of 'rising' socially and financially are sharp practice and religious profiteering, but the play's other two ways to rise are supposedly better alternatives. One is notable achievement which occasions Gresham's knighting, with its traditional kneeling to 'Arise' a knight (2107). This recognition is but one instance of traditional royal bounty; 'gracious' Queen Elizabeth, we are told, 'raiseth' many, 'wisheth none should fall' (2258). The second means to rise is remedial charity, London's civic care has generously 'rais'd many falling' (2128). But the means for rising socially and economically that is most emphatically endorsed by the play appears embodied in the Exchange itself.

Gresham expects the Exchange to elevate London wives, shop girls and apprentices, by offering a venue where 'shops, with faire wiues'

Sit to attend the profit of their husbands: 'Young maides brought vp, yong men as prentises. / Some shall prooue masters, and speake in *Greshams* praise, / In *Greshams* worke, we did our fortunes raise' (1155-58). Without God, Queen, charity or even heroic achievement, the commerce enabled by the Exchange will facilitate rising by self-advancement, though even here we find the remarkable double consciousness of Heywood's drama. While Gresham envisions the Exchange as enlisting 'both Countrey and the Court' as 'beholding' to it for provision of wares (1159-60), the vision of economic self-advancement and mutual obligation is compounded with oddly insistent notes of social antagonism. Gresham foresees his Exchange as 'like a parish for good Cittizens' where 'their faire wiues' will wear such 'neat attire' that

> when our Courtiers
> Shall come in traines to pace old *Greshams* Burse,
> They shall haue such a girdle of chaste eyes,
> And such a globe of beautie round about:
> Ladies shall blush to turne their vizards off,
> And Courtiers sweare they ly'd when they did scoffe. (1231-39)

Gresham imagines that the City's rise will socially impoverish the Court, robbing female courtiers of confidence in their beauty and male courtiers of condescending superiority.

This competitive social context informs Gresham's spectacular failure, granting it major resonance. His Barbary venture fails because the royal order is intrinsically less dependable than the civic. While 'London Merchants' pride themselves on honoring their word, when the Barbary king dies, his word is no longer taken to be binding: end of Gresham's contract, loss of his £60,000. But this is where credit is key, for Gres-ham's response is not to revenge his honor, to rant, to kill himself or even, one would think appropriately, to cut his losses. Taking the joking present from the Barbary King of a dagger and slippers, instead of stabbing himself with the dagger in imitation of Tamburlaine's own deadly gift (see *1 Tamburlaine* 3.2), Gresham performs a vivid demonstration of his own independence from royal fiat. First, he laughs at his loss, then he dances in the King's slippers, before drinking off a cup of wine containing a dissolved pearl so expensive that 'the French King / And many other Dukes,' lords, and ambassadors have been unable to afford purchasing it (1464-5). His actions, he proclaims, are not evidence of actual waste: 'I doe not this as prodigall of my wealth,' he insists, but 'Rather to shew how I esteeme that losse / Which cannot be regain'd. A London Marchant / Thus tread on a kings present' (1559-62). This spectacular act, which Jean Howard calls merchant *sprezzatura* and witnesses claim to be 'as royall ... as his buildings' (1540), Gresham explains as something nearer to London virtues than an appropriation of a courtly value like *sprezzatura*.[17] Instead of imitating a courtier, Gresham demonstrates the credit specific to a merchant, proclaiming his resources vast enough to withstand even such losses. He also witnesses to moral, social resources that go deeper still, for Gresham repeatedly devalues his financial and material goods: the Exchange, he dismisses as a 'pretie bable' (1433), a ship gone to wreck 'but wealth' (1500). His true capital is the credit he commands as a person.[18]

This last point suggests an unreasonable alternative to the 'reasonable market.' The early modern market may have its reasons, but it turns on factors scarcely quantifiable. Witness Hobson, Gresham's alter ego. Hobson participates in a scene that strangely reverses the prostitution scenes of Marlowe's *Jew of Malta*. Hobson's ne'er do well gentleman prentice, who may or may not have been done out of his inheritance by Gresham, appears with a French 'Curtezan'.[19] But instead of defrauding Jack the way Bellamira defrauds Marlowe's Ithamore, Heywood's prostitute is wheedled out of her own jewelry by the apprentice merchant (1846-51). But such irrational transactions implicating credit extended to the unmeriting are not safely cordoned off within the erotic sphere; a similarly oddly uneconomic transaction occurs in Hobson's treatment of his own debtors.

Having pursued an embezzler with capital prosecution, Hobson is enjoined by friends to mercy for the sake of his credit:

Oh, sir, the loue I beare you makes me charie
Of your good name, your credit's deere to me;
You neuer were condemn'd for any thing,

---

17 Jean E. Howard, 'Competing Ideologies of Commerce in Thomas Heywoood's *If you Know not Me You Know Nobody, Part II*' in *The Culture of Capital: Property, Cities and Knowledge in Early Modern England*, ed. Henry S. Turner (NY and London, 2002), 163-82; cf. Sullivan, *Rhetoric of Credit*, 91.

18 On the darker view of Gresham evident in the sources and traceable in the play's references to land deals, see Charles W. Crupi, 'Reading Nascent Capitalism in Part II of Thomas Heywood's *If You Know Not Me, You Know Nobody*', *Texas Studies in Literature and Language* 46 (2004), 296-323.

19 On the possible significance of Heywood's 'seemingly gratuitous' hints about Gresham's chicanery, see Theodore Leinwand, *Theatre, Finance and Society in Early Modern England* (Cambridge: Cambridge University Press, 1999), 25.

> Since I had first acquaintance with your name;
> As now you are, you haue done a deed this day,
> That hath from you tane all good thoughts away. (2157-62)

By having 'pursued the law seuerely' (2164), Hobson has risked damage to his credit. The realization that getting justice and his money will come at such a cost, prompts Hobson's proclamation of an alternative economy: 'Men are more worth then monie' (2181). Maybe so, but Hobson's panic about his credit going down even as his cash goes up underlines Heywood's exploration of an aspect of the early modern market. 'Few are found', an observer comments, 'To saue a man would loose a hundred pound' (2190-91) as Hobson hurries off to forgive his monetary loss, but his extravagant embrace of his own losses, like the similar action of Gresham, enacts an aspect of early modern credit that helps to constitute it as a notion far more complicated than comparisons with the slave market of Marlowe's Malta suggest.

Standing for and Standing in for: Metonymy in *Henry V*

Ann Thompson and John O. Thompson
King's College London

It is not unreasonable to read *Henry V* backwards, not least because in the experience of the forward arc of the play on stage we may be a bit weary when we
come to the verbal elaborations of 5.2. Henry is throughout the play a 'man of
parts', and nowhere more than in the play's long concluding scene; equally, his
Europe is a space of contested boundaries. The climax of his courtship of Katherine as the play draws to its close operates on the boundaries of language. Earlier
in the play, Princess Katherine has been learning some English language words
for body parts, not without some doubleness of entendre.

A word about how we use the term 'metonymy' in what follows may be helpful.
Just as metaphor is the figure of similarity, metonymy is the figure of contiguity, of
next-to-ness. We allow ourselves to group together, as metonymic, several relationships which are distinguishable from one another, notably next-to-ness in
space, physical part-wholes, and conceptual part-wholes (species, genus). This
risks broadening the field of metonymy unduly, but the wide use, we find, illuminates features of Shakespeare's language and thought in a particular way.

One challenge for a metonymic mode of reading and commenting on Shakespeare (or any text) is that it makes the reader slow down, almost to the point of
'freeze framing'. On the one hand, a sort of swamping by detail threatens, against
which the critic's craft must be itself a 'part for the whole' exercise, the choice of
examples. Which larger, richer verbal forces can the example stand in for, illuminate? On the other hand, if the metonymic approach is not simply to amount to a
selective version of a concordance, a broader argument about the relationship of
sets of relationships amongst each other needs to be advanced. And in this particular play, we must attend to the ways in which, theatrically, parts are quite
self-consciously made to stand in for wholes.

For present purposes, terms for parts, as possessions, of a person or of a
bounded area, may be treated as one set of issues. The other set, which clearly
intertwines with the former in the language of *Henry V*, is that of boundaries,
lines dividing territories, possibilities for such lines being redrawn or abolished,

along with the vital human need *for* them.[1] Parts and boundaries in *Henry V* are both, and very directly, brought together meta-linguistically through Henry and Katherine's negotiation of their imperfect grasp of each other's languages ('tongues'). ['Tongues' and 'dead metonymy'; L&J, why tongues not mouths?]

But we do, as we have said, want to begin at the end, while we are still fresh enough to attend to some of the details in Burgundy's powerful speech in favour of peace when the Kings of France and England meet to conclude a treaty in the final scene of the play:

> Let it not disgrace me
> If I demand before this royal view
> What rub or what impediment there is
> Why that the naked, poor and mangled peace,
> Dear nurse of arts, plenties and joyful births,
> Should not in this best garden of the world,
> Our fertile France, put up her lovely visage?
> Alas, she hath from France too long been chased,
> And all her husbandry doth lie on heaps,
> Corrupting in it own fertility.
> Her vine, the merry cheerer of the heart,
> Unpruned dies; her hedges even-pleached,
> Like prisoners wildly overgrown with hair,
> Put forth disordered twigs; her fallow leas
> The darnel, hemlock and rank fumitory
> Doth root upon, while that the coulter rusts
> That should deracinate such savagery.
> The even mead, that erst brought sweetly forth
> The freckled cowslip, burnet and green clover,
> Wanting the scythe, all uncorrected, rank,
> Conceives by idleness, and nothing teems
> But hateful docks, rough thistles, kecksies, burrs,
> Losing both beauty and utility.
> And as our vineyards, fallows, meads and hedges,
> Defective in their natures, grow to wildness,
> Even so our houses and our selves and children
> Have lost, or do not learn for want of time,
> The sciences that should become our country,
> But grow like savages, as soldiers will
> That nothing do but meditate on blood,
> To swearing and stern looks, diffused attire,
> And everything that seems unnatural.
> Which to reduce into our former favour

---

1   We have elaborated on the issue of boundaries in our chapter, 'Making Mistakes: Shakespeare, Metonymy, and *Hamlet*' in Christa Jansohn and Lena Cowen Orlin (eds.), *Shakespeare without Boundaries?* (Newark, DE: University of Delaware Press, 2010), 123-37.

> You are assembled; and my speech entreats
> That I may know the let why gentle peace
> Should not expel these inconveniences
> And bless us with her former qualities. (5.2.31-67)[2]

To call France a garden is to speak metaphorically. France is not literally a garden. It is *like* a garden in various respects. It is bounded, for one thing, and it includes botanical contents, for another. In both these respects, metonymy is in play. The garden that is France has gone badly wrong, through war:

> ... all her husbandry doth lie on heaps,
> Corrupting in it own fertility. (5.2.39-40)

Its hedges, defining its boundaries, in particular are out of order. 'Like prisoners wildly overgrown with hair', they 'put forth disordered twigs' (43-44). If the borders of the garden are in bad shape, its contents are even worse, the good plants ('freckled cowslip, burnet, and green clover') having given way to weeds ('darnel, hemlock and rank fumitory', 'hateful docks, rough thistles, kecksies, burrs') (45-52).[3] [See similar list of weeds in *King Lear* 4.4.3-6]. The garden's contents express, and constitute, its disorder.

Burgundy's speech clearly anticipates Ulysses' better-known 'degree' speech (*Troilus and Cressida* 1.3.75-137). What in the rich semantics of the passage is especially striking, however, is the hair of the prisoners. A particular part of the human body, hair, grown in a specific condition of that body, captivity (with what particular background of violence is left unspecified) is made to stand for how the mis-ruled garden has grown, the garden that 'is' France, the country over which Henry and his opponents have fought. Henry's achievement, the Chorus reiterates eight lines before the end of the play, was to have gained the possession of 'the world's best garden', and to have done so by his sword. (His literal sword – for which the actor's stage sword, 'vile and ragged foil', stands in – itself represents a 'greater sword', military force wielded on behalf of the nation, which is the sword 'by Fortune made'. Fortune does not literally make literal swords.)

Henry's sword is an appurtenance which – bended as it is, like his bruised helmet – he gets credit for not showing off during his triumphal return to London (5.0,19). War's own 'bleeding sword' is banned from being in future 'advanced' between England and 'fair France' by the defeated French King Charles (5.2.348-9). Swords are metonymic for war, as spectacular props; even today, training in

---

2   Except where stated, all quotations from *Henry V* are from the Arden text edited by T. W. Craik (London: Routledge, 1995).

3   Shakespeare has Cordelia give a similar list of weeds in *King Lear* 4.4.3-6. Again we quote from the Arden text, edited by R. A. Foakes (Walton-on-Thames: Thomas Nelson, 1997).

sword-fighting is a part of the classical actor's technique. The ways in which men are related to their weapons is another area in which metonymy is in play.

If we list the characters of *Henry V* in order of appearance, as Andrew Gurr does in his New Cambridge edition,[4] Burgundy is the last speaking character to appear, immediately preceded by Isabel, Queen of France; neither character appears or is mentioned before this final scene (and both are usually subjected to cuts on stage and screen). Moving back from his speech to hers, we find another metonymic trope which is very characteristic of this play. She says she is glad to behold the eyes of her 'brother England', Henry:

> Your eyes which hitherto have borne in them
> Against the French that met them in their bent
> The fatal balls of murdering basilisks. (5.2.15-17)

The trope here is that parts of people become parts of murderous animals or weapons of warfare. As editors point out, the word 'bent' can mean 'aim', as in archery, 'balls' are cannon balls as well as eyeballs, and 'basilisks' are large cannon as well as mythical beasts that can kill with a glance of their eyes. The men/animals/weapons combination has occurred previously in the Constable's comparison of the English soldiers with mastiffs – 'give them great meals of beef and iron and steel, they will eat like wolves and fight like devils' (3.7.148-50) – but also in a much more famous passage from the play, Henry's 'Once more unto the breach' speech before the assault on Harfleur. He tells his men:

> But when the blast of war blows in our ears,
> Then imitate the action of the tiger:
> Stiffen the sinews, conjure up the blood,
> Disguise fair nature with hard-favoured rage.
> Then lend the eye a terrible aspect;
> Let it pry through the portage of the head
> Like the brass cannon. (3.1.5-11)

Human beings turn first into animals here and then into weapons, while in the immediately preceding Chorus, the reverse has happened with the guns turning into people (or perhaps animals):

> Behold the ordnance on their carriages
> With fatal mouths gaping on girded Harfleur (26-7)

The Folio text of the Harfleur speech actually has Henry say 'commune up the blood' which does not make much sense. Some editors adopt Rowe's emendation to 'summon', but Gary Taylor (1982), Andrew Gurr (1992) and T. W. Craik (1995) all prefer the suggestion of the 1954 Arden editor J. H. Walter, 'conjure',

---

4   Cambridge: Cambridge University Press, 1992.

partly because F's reading could result from minim error ('coniure') but also because Galenist physiological theory maintained that the blood contained the vital spirits and 'to conjure up the spirits' was a common expression.[5] Gurr adds that 'conjure' 'has the advantage of connecting warfare with sex', citing the 'bawdy magic' of Mercutio's conjuration of Romeo in *Romeo and Juliet* (2.1.17 and 26). In *Henry V* the attack on Harfleur is graphically presented as a rape in 3.4, and when it is all over the French King talks of Henry conjuring up the spirits of love in Katherine and describes his cities as being like virgins, 'girdled with maiden walls that no war hath entered' (5.2.285-6, 318). The walls of cities are physical boundaries vital to the defence of the less material boundaries defining a country.

The broad metaphorical structures evoked here seem to be reversible: 'war is sexual assault', but 'sexual assault is war'; 'men are animals/weapons', but 'animals/weapons are men'. Moreover, the play repeatedly focuses on specific body parts: eyes are like cannons because they both have balls (the modern idiom 'to have balls' is much more recent); cannons are like men (or animals) because they both have mouths. Mouths take us to appetite: Henry offers free pass to him 'which hath no stomach to this fight' (4.3.35). Hand, heart and head are frequently named body parts here. We have been told 'While that the armed head doth fight abroad / Th'advised head defends itself at home' (1.2.178-9) and Exeter, speaking for Henry, has warned the French 'if you hide the crown / Even in your hearts, there will he rake for it', inviting them to take mercy 'On the poor souls for whom this hungry war / Opens his vasty jaws' (2.4.97-8, 104-5). War is personified again in 3.3 when Henry asks the representatives of Harfleur:

> What is it then to me if impious war,
> Arrayed in flames like to the prince of fiends
> Do with his smirched complexion all fell feats
> Enlinked to waste and desolation? (3.3.15-18)

Personified War becomes 'The blind and bloody soldier with foul hand' (34) who commits rape and murder on the citizens; later, the French King reflects in a message to Henry 'Tell him we could have rebuked him at Harfleur, but we thought not good to bruise an injury till it were full ripe' (3.6.119-22), imaging the entire conflict as a kind of sore or boil on the body of France. [One entailment of personification, as distinguished from metaphor and metonymy, is that the 'person' has 'parts'.]

While they are in contrast to the play's generally military subject-matter, the two scenes involving Princess Katherine make use of the same metonymic re-

---

5   Gary Taylor edited *Henry V* for the Oxford Shakespeare series, Oxford: Oxford University Press, 1982.

sources. The latter of these scenes follows on from Burgundy's speech, as Henry seals the peace by wooing and winning Katherine. But in the middle of the play (3.4), Katherine begins to learn English, from her lady-in-waiting Alice.

The words she learns are, with one exception, those for body parts. She starts with *main* (hand), proceeding to *doigts* (fingers), then to *ongles* (nails). Note that fingers are themselves parts of hands, and nails parts of fingers; the effect might remind one of a cinematic zoom. Then come *bras* (arm – which Alice mispronounces 'arma') and *coude* (elbow – which Katherine will further on twice mispronounce, as 'bilbow' and 'ilbow'). Again, a basic body part is succeeded by a part of that part. Here there are two added twists. The more likely of two contemporary meanings for 'bilbo' is a particular type of sword (the *OED* cites Michael Drayton's own annotation for the word in his *Battaile of Agincourt*, published in 1627, and the word had appeared earlier in his 'Ballad of Agincourt' published around 1605), so swords once again enter the picture.[6] Gary Taylor remarks in his commentary, 'This is the first time that a mispronunciation results in an unintended meaning, and alerts us to subsequent puns (nick, sin, foot, cown)' (26n). That is to say neck, chin, foot, gown, the final four words of the lesson, with the last being the one word that is not for a body part; 'gown' is, though, a garment, so related to the body by contiguity rather than by part-whole relations but still part of metonymy's domain. It is around the last four items that the scene's famous double entendres congregate, and by this point Catherine's second 'elbow' mispronunciation, 'ilbow', occurs; Taylor is inclined to read this as 'ill-bow', concurring with E. A. M. Colman (*The Dramatic Use of Shakespeare's Bawdy*) that '*bow* could, in suggestive contexts, carry the sense *vulva*' (42n).

A broad question arises about the English lesson. Of all the words Katherine might choose to ask Alice about, why choose this particular semantic field, rather than other (perhaps more 'courtly' or practical) terms? One answer is that the scene is being set up as a progression to the bawdy jokes, and these parts are well suited for this. But in the light of what emerges in the play more generally, the word choices are clearly part of the play's larger metonymic operations.

This might be confirmed in what could be called either 'Henry's wooing scene' or 'Katherine's second English lesson'. No sooner does Henry embark upon his courtship than he makes reference to Katherine's 'lady's ear' and 'gentle heart'; he moves swiftly on to an elegant chiasmus, '... if you will love me soundly with your French heart I will be glad to hear you confess it brokenly with your English

---

6   The other meaning of 'bilbo' or 'bilboes' (fetters) occurs in *Hamlet* at 5.2.6: our reference is to the Arden text edited by Ann Thompson and Neil Taylor (London: Thomson Learning, 2006). Both swords and fetters were named after Bilbao in Spain, from whence various iron artefacts were imported.

tongue' (5.2.103-6). He carefully balances his terms – 'Love / confess', 'soundly
/ brokenly', 'French / English' – Henry demonstrates his bluff, soldierly distance
from rhetoric with all the craft of Othello declaring 'Rude am I in my speech'
(*Othello* 1.3.82).

Much more in the scene deserves attention, but from the body-part perspective, one bravura passage stands out:

> What, a speaker is but a prater, a rhyme is but a ballad; a good leg will fall, a straight back
> will stoop, a black beard will turn white, a curled pate will grow bald, a fair face will wither,
> a full eye will wax hollow, but a good heart, Kate, is the sun and the moon, or rather the sun
> and not the moon, for it shines bright and never changes, but keeps his course truly. (158-65)

After two instances which deprecate artful words (prose, then verse), Henry
settles into the aging prospects for, in turn, leg, back, beard, hair ('curled pate',
head for its hair), face, eye. All these are subject to aging, but not the true heart.
The heart's constancy is likened to that of celestial entities (sun and moon –
recalling, perhaps, another Kate's testing by Petruchio as to her willingness to
use those names interchangeably (in *The Taming of the Shrew* 4.5), but implicitly
the contrast between 'heart' and the other parts is also one of interior to exterior.
It is one of spiritual to physical as well, for the physical heart is hardly immune
from aging. Hovering over all this as dramatic irony is our knowledge, as an
audience, that Henry himself will not live long enough for the physical changes
he speaks of to occur in his case.

We will now turn to a different, but we think related, aspect of the play, one
more directly theatrical. While body-parts stand in for whole bodies, those whole
bodies have to stand in for larger entities on stage. The opening Chorus of *Henry
V* famously asks the audience to 'Piece out our imperfections with your thoughts' (23), [Add Gurr's point that the Chorus consistently mis-describes what the
audience sees.] using their imaginations to allow actors to stand in for monarchs
and 'this wooden O': (theatre is like the printed letter in shape (metaphor) but
also in so far as the two share the shape of their boundary) for 'the vasty fields of
France', a trope which is repeated in the Chorus to Act 4:

> And so our scene must to the battle fly,
> Where – oh for pity! – we shall much disgrace
> With four or five most vile and ragged foils
> Right ill-disposed in brawl ridiculous
> The name of Agincourt. Yet sit and see,
> Minding true things by what their mockeries be. (48-53)

The audience must, paradoxically, both divide and multiply what they see: 'Into
a thousand parts divide one man / And make imaginary puissance' (Prologue 24-5).
In the theatre, we must accept that half a dozen men constitute an army, though
as the Boy points out, some of those men do not even amount to one individual:

'I am boy to them all three, but all they three, though they would serve me, could not be man to me, for indeed three such antics do not amount to a man' (3.2.29-31).

The notion of a man being literally split into his component parts is a grim reality for soldiers. Williams tells the disguised Henry 'If the cause be not good, the King himself hath a heavy reckoning to make when all those legs and arms and heads chopped off in a battle shall join together at the latter day and cry all "We died at such a place"' (4.1.134-8). Soon after this, Westmoreland wants to multiply his forces in the same way as the audience:

> O that we now had here
> But one ten thousand of those men in England
> That do no work today. (4.3.16-18)

This evokes Henry's response, 'What's he that wishes so? / My cousin Westmorland?' (18-19) leading into his famous speech before Agincourt. In the Quarto text however, he says 'What's he that wishes so? My cousin Warwick?' Gary Taylor also adopts this reading in his 1982 Oxford edition. If you check Shakespeare's chronicle sources, you find that the person who actually asked this question was one Walter Hungerford. There is in fact a curious instability of personnel in this scene, given Henry's fierce refusal of 'one man more' and his insistence that those present will be remembered 'From this day to the ending of the world'. He imagines a soldier remembering them in old age:

> Then shall our names,
> Familiar in his mouth as household words,
> Harry the King, Bedford and Exeter,
> Warwick and Talbot, Salisbury and Gloucester,
> Be in their flowing cups freshly remembered. (4.3.51-5)

This is the Folio version; the Quarto however gives rather a different list:

> Then shall we in their flowing bowls
> Be newly remembered. Harry the King,
> Bedford and Exeter, Clarence and Gloucester,
> Warwick and York,
> Familiar in their mouths as household words.[7]

Apart from the reflection that we don't in fact recall these men on the anniversary of Agincourt (25 October) today, Henry seems a bit vague as to who exactly was included in 'We few, we happy few, we band of brothers', even in 1415. Editors point out that Warwick and Talbot do not appear and are not otherwise mentioned in the Folio text (nor were they historically present at Agincourt), while York, who died at Agincourt, is not listed in the Folio, though he is in the

---

7   Craik includes a facsimile text of the Quarto in his edition (as cited in footnote X above); this passage is on p. 390. We have modernised the spelling.

Quarto. His death is described later in both texts, as is that of Suffolk whom both texts omit from these lists. Finally, the Quarto has Clarence where the Folio has Salisbury. Does this matter? On one level, Henry is saying precisely that it doesn't: 'For he today that sheds his blood with me / Shall be my brother' (61-2). One cousin or brother can stand in for another: York can stand in for Talbot, Clarence for Gloucester; these noblemen are more generic than individualised. As Taylor points out, 'Shakespeare surrounds Henry – particularly in difficult moments – with people he can quietly turn to and call 'uncle' or 'brother'.[8] (In a possibly misguided attempt to clarify some of these relationships, Terry Hands, directing the play for the Royal Shakespeare Company in 1975, made Henry's actual blood-brothers redheaded, but critics and audiences failed to notice this.)[9]

These substitutions may not matter very much and editors have not worked very hard to find reasons for them: compression of casting (either for the London stage or for a touring company) has been suggested, or possibly just an imprecise recollection of the names of characters and who spoke which lines on the part of the scribes who compiled the Quarto. One other substitution which is even more striking *has* been felt to matter and to require explanation: in the Quarto text, the Duke of Bourbon stands in for the Dauphin in the scenes at Agincourt (3.7 and 4.5). This seems surprising to those of us familiar with productions and films in which the Dauphin is caricatured as the effete prince who epitomizes French arrogance and writes sonnets to his horse, but it is in fact historically accurate: he was not present at Agincourt. In both Q and F, the French King forbids his son from going to Agincourt (3.5.63-6), but in the Folio he nevertheless appears there just two scenes later. Most editors (apart from Taylor and Gurr) and most productions follow the Folio, but some directors feel obliged to invent a piece of business to signal that the Dauphin intends to disobey his father.[10] It can be argued that substituting Bourbon for the Dauphin was a deliberate decision on the part of Shakespeare, perhaps to build up Bourbon for his role in the latter part of the play; the Dauphin disappears from both texts after Agincourt and Shakespeare thus avoids the humiliating aspect of the final treaty whereby the French King disinherited his son in favour of Henry. This is staged in the source-play, *The Famous Victories of Henry the Fifth*,[11] where the Dauphin is present in the

---

8   Introduction to Taylor's Oxford edition (as cited in footnote X above), p.61.
9   See Sally Beauman, *The RSC's Production of 'Henry V' for the Centenary Season of the Royal Shakespeare Theatre* (Oxford: Oxford University Press, 1976), p.89.
10   See examples of this cited in Emma Smith (ed.), *Shakespeare in Production: 'Henry V'* (Cambridge: Cambridge University Press, 2002), 158.
11   Our references, including scene numbers, are to the version of this text printed in Geoffrey Bullough (ed.), *Narrative and Dramatic Sources of Shakespeare,* 7 vols. (London: Rout-ledge), vol. 4.

last scene and swears fealty to Henry, but Shakespeare makes the political set-
tlement seem less brutal.

All modern scholars agree that, although it was printed first, the 1600 Quarto
represents a later stage of the text than the 1623 Folio, so it is curious that tradition has favoured the Folio's choice in this instance. A reason may be found in
one of the play's most iconic moments of substitution, of one thing standing in
for another, namely the Dauphin's mocking gift of a 'tun of treasure' (1.2.256)
that turns out to contain tennis balls (the balls mockingly standing in for gold or
other valuables) and that evokes Henry's long speech in which of course he de-
velops the metaphor:

> When we have matched our rackets to these balls
> We will in France, by God's grace, play a set
> Shall strike his father's crown into the hazard.
> Tell him he hath made a match with such a wrangler
> That all the courts of France shall be disturbed
> With chases. And we understand him well,
> How he comes o'er us with our wilder days,
> Not measuring what use we made of them ....
> But tell the Dauphin I will keep my state,
> Be like a king and show my sail of greatness,
> When I do rouse me in my throne of France.
> For that have I laid by my majesty
> And plodded like a man for working-days,
> But I will rise there with so full a glory
> That I will dazzle all the eyes of France,
> Yes, strike the Dauphin blind to look on us.
> And tell the pleasant Prince this mock of his
> Hath turned his balls to gun-stones, and his soul
> Shall stand sore charged for the wasteful vengeance
> That shall fly with them; for many a thousand widows
> Shall this his mock mock out of their dear husbands,
> Mock mothers from their sons, mock castles down,
> And some are yet ungotten and unborn
> That shall have cause to curse the Dauphin's scorn.
> (1.2.262-69, 274-89)

This moment must have been familiar to at least some members of the early
audiences from *The Famous Victories,* where it is not only enacted in scene ix
but referred back to in Henry's messages via the herald in scene xii and scene xiv
(scene numbers from Bullough). It provides the first occasion on which Henry
can assert his authority and demonstrate to audiences both on and off stage that
he has matured and become a force to be reckoned with. To continue to represent
the Dauphin as Henry's leading antagonist in the Agincourt scenes is understandable, even though it is unhistorical and inconsistent with Shakespeare's

ending of the play. Perhaps curiously, in this context, on the Dauphin's first appearance in the play in 2.4, he does not reveal himself at first, telling Exeter 'For the Dauphin, / I stand for him' (2.4.115-6), anticipating how Bourbon will in fact stand in for him in the later text.

Be this as it may, the *general* randomness of the names of those 'remembered' as the heroes of Agincourt suggests a perfectly conscious irony on Shakespeare's part, given that the audience won't remember them enough to know the difference, as well as his realistic theatrical sense that it is the roll-call of names here that is doing the work, not the particular historical figures behind the names.

In conclusion, we would suggest that the intertwined metonymic (and metaphoric) strategies we have been looking at combine to further an overall Shakespearean project. This is the heightening of the sense of presence (albeit 'virtual' as we might put it today) of the characters presented to the audience on the Globe stage. Heightening itself has intertwined motives. There is heightening for its own sake (heightened language, rhetoric, poetry). But there is also the heightening of the reality of the fictional character, specifically the 'body' of that character, given that it is being 'stood in for' by a 'mere' player. Heightening also strives to overcome the audience's physical distance from the stage (bare but for minimal props), as well as to accomplish the necessary task of all theatre dealing with crowds – here the cinema is different – in allowing a few to stand in for many. We hope that our use of the concept of metonymy makes the relationships amongst these poetic and theatrical aims and achievements more visible.

Voicing Criticism in Eighteenth-Century Novels by Women: Narrative Attempts at Claiming Authority

Vera Nünning
University of Heidelberg

To combine the topics of criticism and authority in eighteenth-century novels by women may seem surprising; after all, someone in a position of authority does not have to worry about voicing criticism. For female novelists of the eighteenth century, however, the mere attempt at claiming authority was anything but un-problematic. Denied access to grammar schools and universities, they were as a rule less educated than their male counterparts, and they were certainly not ex-pected to express their opinions in public. Even though the situation slightly improved during the course of the eighteenth century,[1] women had difficulties laying claim to a position of authority. They were supposed to be modest, chaste and inexperienced as far as the important facts of life are concerned; and this, of course, clashed with the writing of literary works, which were expected to both instruct and delight their readers. On the one hand, the brazenness of the assump-tion of the 'Amazons of the Pen', whom Samuel Johnson criticised for entering a male dominion,[2] was meliorated by the fact that they chose to write novels. This new genre had a bad reputation anyway, and since there were no established classical rules which writers had to follow, the lack of education did not matter so much. On the other hand, this lack of acceptance posed a problem for authors who wanted their work to be read (and sold); the repeated claims in prefaces that this particular work was an exception in so far as it really did teach moral values and good behaviour had to be borne up by the content at least superficially. Any

---

1   See Vera Nünning. "Changes in the Representation of Men and Women in the Second Half of the Eighteenth Century." *REAL: The Yearbook of Research in English and American Literature* 20 (2004): 183-207.

2   See Samuel Johnson's unfavourable opinion in "The Adventurer." *The Yale Edition of the Works of Samuel Johnson.* Ed. Donald J. Greene. Vol. 2. New Haven, CT: Yale University Press, 1963, 339-498. No. 115. 11.12.1753. 456-61, 457f., where he denigrates the "generation of Amazons of the pen, who [...] have set masculine tyranny at defiance, asserted their claim to the regions of science, and seem resolved to contest the usurpations of virility". At the same time, however, Johnson helped a number of young female writers.

kind of fiction that was meant to be taken seriously by the majority of literary critics and readers had to be didactic.

Moreover, at the beginning of the eighteenth century, female authors suffered from a poor reputation: the suspect morals of a few successful female writers rendered the writing of novels a morally dubious endeavour. Admitting to publishing novels was equivalent to throwing one's chastity into doubt. Aphra Behn had famously written juicy Restoration Comedies as well as love poetry and the notorious *Love-Letters Between a Nobleman and His Sister* (1684-87). Even worse, Mary Delarivière Manley had styled herself as a very alluring, sexually attractive persona in her novels *The New Atalantis* (1709) and *The Adventures of Rivella* (1714); and Eliza Haywood had established a reputation as a writer of amorous novels – in her stories, she had even created an 'authorial' narrator who assumed the role of an 'expert on love' and commented knowingly on the affairs he or she was delivering.[3] While such novels could find interested readers during the 1710s and the 1720s, the situation got more difficult in the 1730s, when the growing moralisation of society led to a sharp decline in their readership, and when women who wanted to preserve a good reputation refrained from writing novels. It was only in the 1740s that a new generation of women writers published morally unexceptionable works which slowly changed the image of female authors. During the second half of the eighteenth century, therefore, women had to make doubly sure to adhere to existing moral standards and to teach the socially sanctioned values in their works. There are thus a whole number of reasons why we should not expect any criticism of established norms in works written by women; the restrictions of the newly emerging market place, the danger of a threat to one's own reputation, the lack of acceptance of the genre of the novel, the necessity to conform to the didactic function of literature: all these aspects made it obligatory to adhere to cultural values. Similar to historical works, novels had to teach by way of example; they had to depict models of good behaviour and make quite sure that villains were not only duly punished but also painted in the darkest colours in order to appear as unattractive as possible.[4]

---

3   Even Haywood's first novel, *Love in Excess* (1719), features an overt narrator who extensively comments on the nature of love in a way that does not conform to the alleged sexual reticence and chastity of women, which was held to be so important at the time; see, for instance "and tho' all those kinds of desire, which the difference of sex creates, bear in general, the name of love, yet they are as vastly wide as heaven and hell; [...] love *there* is a divinity indeed, because he is immortal and unchangeable, and if our earthy part partake the bliss, and the craving nature is in all obeyed, possession thus desired, and thus obtained, is far from satiating [...] the different powers [sense and reason] become pure alike." *Love in Excess*. Ed. David Oakleaf. 2nd ed. Peterborough, Ontario: Broadview Press, 2000, 33-266, 224; see also ibid. 225.

4   See, for instance, Samuel Richardson's "Preface" to *Pamela* (1740), where he refers to the doctrine of the just distribution of sympathy.

It has often been observed, however, that, in spite of these expectations and restrictions, female novelists did not conform as strictly to the social rules as we should expect. There are, of course, any number of novels which embody and teach established values, which confirm the subordination of women and subscribe to the newly established image of women as weak, pure, pious, tender, docile, obedient, dependent and inefficient creatures who passively waited to be married to the right man. Quite often, however, there is an implicit criticism of social norms: the experiences of women are foregrounded, we are led to see society and their inability to act as they want to from their eyes, and we concur with their, partly rebellious, thoughts and feelings. As Jane Spencer asserted as early as the 1980s, the ending is sometimes undercut by the bulk of the work, which deeply involves us in the plight and the critical attitudes of heroines, who are then briefly 'reformed' and rewarded at the end of the book.[5] Spencer, however, focuses mainly on the content of novels, and although some later critics take into account some formal features, they do not do so in a pronounced or coherent, let alone systematic way.

In this paper, I will concentrate on the modes of writing novels and try to show that implicit criticism of social conventions was possible by the skilful use of narrative techniques. Female novelists did not only meekly conform to public opinion; they also tried to enlarge the horizon of readers by making them aware of the tensions and difficulties inherent in female life, by alerting them to the problematic situation of women, to the impediments they had to contend with, and to their feelings with regard to a society dominated by masculine values. At the same time, they tried to establish a position of authority, which lends weight to their point of view and the implicit criticism they voice. Why, after all, should anyone but a young, inexperienced girl listen to a more or less uneducated and fallible woman writing about other women? Female novelists who wanted their work to be taken seriously were therefore faced with the task to search for strategies which might help them to establish a position of authority.

---

5   Cf. Jane Spencer. *The Rise of the Female Novelist: From Aphra Behn to Jane Austen.* Oxford: Blackwell, 1986, 140-180. The impact of presenting the female point of view in eighteenth-century fiction by women is also emphasised by Ansgar Nünning. "Mimesis und Poiesis im englischen Roman des 18. Jahrhunderts: Überlegungen zum Zusammenhang zwischen narrativer Form und Wirklichkeitserfahrung." *Neue Lesarten, neue Wirklichkeiten: Zur Wiederentdeckung des 18. Jahrhunderts durch die Anglistik.* Ed. Gerd Strat-mann and Manfred Buschmeier. Trier: Wissenschaftlicher Verlag Trier, 1992, 46-69.

Female narrators and 'authorial narrators' in the eighteenth century

There are, of course, a whole number of ways to lay claim to a position of authority. Popular strategies in the eighteenth century included the use of prefaces or titles which illustrate the seriousness or morality of a work, or the shaping of a 'private' persona which embodies values like chastity or self-restraint. In the following, however, I will focus on the texts themselves and concentrate on the choice of narrators and the use of narrative strategies.

Susan Sniader Lanser, who was very aware of the problem female writers had with regard to establishing a position of authority (for her, the mere attempt at publication implies such a claim to authority which had to be dealt with in some way), assumes that most female authors tried at least in so far to conform to prevailing opinions that they employed a 'personal voice', that is autodiegetic narration, in which the hero/ines tell their own story, or the epistolary style.[6] This way of writing can be related to social norms and values, according to which the 'personal sphere' was held to be the proper place of women; mothers were accepted in their role of teaching their children, and women were encouraged to write (spiritual) diaries and letters.

At least with regard to the British novel, the assumption that the majority of women adhered to expectations by using the 'personal voice' is not true; apparently women were more daring and put in a more pronounced claim to authority than has been realized before. Only about thirty-five percent of the roughly 500 British novels by women published in the eighteenth century (which have survived today) employ these modes; if one discounts the use of letters, which was very popular in most non-fictional genres and used by any number of male authors as well, one finds that only about 10% of British novels written by women during the eighteenth century had 'autodiegetic' female narrators. Instead, a vast majority of female novelists employed heterodiegetic narration in their novels, thereby assuming a position of authority generally not conceded to women in the eighteenth century:[7]

---

6   Cf. Susan Sniader Lanser. *Fictions of Authority: Women Writers and Narrative Voice.* Ithaca: Cornell University Press, 1992, 45f. See also "the project of self-authorization [...] is implicit in the very act of authorship", ibid., 7. Judith Lowder Newton. *Women, Power and Subversion: Social Strategies in British Fiction, 1778-1860.* 1981. New York; London: Methuen, 1985, 45, also assumes that letter writing is "traditionally feminine".

7   I owe this important number to Irina Bauder-Begerow, whose book on this subject is to appear in 2011; its working title is *Weibliches Erzählen im 18. Jahrhundert (1680-1800): Eine diachrone Betrachtung des Wandels von Erzählformen im englischen Roman.* I have reflected on the reasons for the use of heterodiegetic narrators in: "Gender, Authority and Female Experience in British Novels

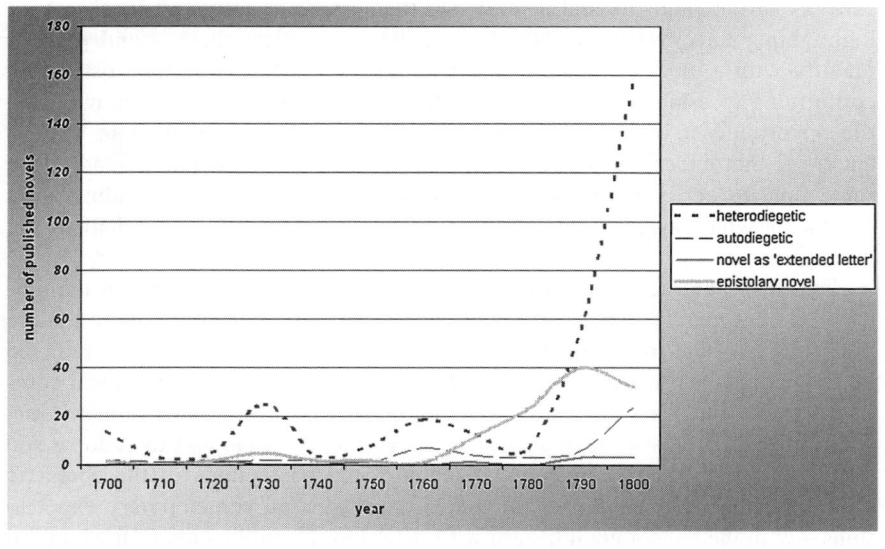

To present such a chart which suggests that we are dealing with exact numbers is, of course, tricky, given many uncertainties: we have to bear in mind that we do not know how many novels got lost, we do not know whether male authors used female names for some works (or vice versa), and the identity of the authors of some novels which were published anonymously have not been ascertained as yet. But even if one allows for 10% or 20% variation, the numbers are still impressive and the result seems to be valid: women did prefer the 'public' voice of 'authorial' narration. I would like to argue that this can be explained with recourse to the necessity of acquiring – and establishing – a position of authority, which female authors had to achieve in order to validate their demand to be listened to and popularise modes of female experience. But let me first point out the advantages of 'autodiegetic narration', which made this mode of writing a favourite mode of expression for many male writers.

As Daniel Defoe demonstrated at the beginning of the eighteenth century, the use of the autodiegetic narrator had the great advantage of allowing the author to fulfil contradictory expectations: On the one hand, one could show a character who deviates from conventional norms and leads an exciting, adventurous life that generates suspense and captures the reader's interest. On the other hand, it allows the mature, reformed narrator to comment on his youthful self, and cen-

from the Eighteenth to the Nineteenth Century: A Narratological Perspective." *Theorizing Narrative Genres and Gender*. Ed. Suzan van Dijk and Liselotte Steinbrügge. Leuven: Peters, 2010.

sure his earlier thoughts and actions. On the surface, it seems an ideal way of highlighting unconventional experiences, making readers share – and perhaps identify with – unusual thoughts and feelings, and at the same time ostensibly conforming to established moral rules. In Great Britain, however, women used this opportunity to both privilege an unconventional view by positing an 'experiencing I' that experiences uncommon, but understandable emotions and at the same time to act in accordance with contemporary norms by providing short comments which criticise this stance only rarely before the second half of the nineteenth century.[8]

This may have several reasons. If the female experience transgresses the limits of the acceptably female, it would have to be criticised by the more mature 'narrating I' – and in this case the story would not only have been contradicted by the ending, but in addition have been undercut continuously by critical comments of the older and allegedly wiser narrator, who would have to admit that her former emotions were 'wrong'. To forego this criticism and to endorse and sympathise with the unconventional feelings and perceptions of the character would, on the other hand, run the risk of contradicting contemporary expectations – with the concomitant hazard with regard to the publication of the book. It was therefore nearly impossible at the time for a female author to use this narrative device in order to evoke sympathy for an unconventional point of view.

But there may be a much more simple reason than this: I think that women mostly shunned autodiegetic narration or a 'personal voice' until the nineteenth century because they needed a more authoritative way of fostering understanding for an unconventional perspective than the use of a narrator telling the story of her own life could provide. After all, a female voice had no authority in the eighteenth century, and its support of the female perspective would have carried only little weight.[9] If authors wanted to make sure that an unconventional view on female experiences would be taken seriously, they had better not have recourse to autodiegetic narration. I would like to argue that female novelists preferred the use of the heterodiegetic ('omniscient') narrator, because he could implicitly claim a position of authority – an important aspect of lending credibility to the female perspective which will be analysed in greater detail later on.

---

8   Two earlier examples of works which use the 'private voice' and project a narrator who comments on her earlier experiences are Sarah Fielding's *Ophelia* (1760), who is, however, a perfect embodiment of the ideals of womanhood, and Mary Brunton's *Discipline* (1815).

9   Susan Sniader Lanser also agrees that a personal voice is less formidable for women "than authorial voice, since an authorial narrator claims broad powers of knowledge and judgement, while a personal narrator claims only the validity of one person's right to interpret her experience" (1992, 19).

By convention, a heterodiegetic narrator is not involved in the fate of his characters; he stands aloof, knowing everything about them in the present, past and future; as Catherine Belsey states, he does "not re-quire verification", but rather "verifies all other statements"[10]. A hetero-diegetic narrator could therefore be put to good use by women in the eighteenth century. But women novelists as a rule did not follow the example of Henry Fielding, who had introduced the full range of functions the 'overt' heterodiegetic narrator could fulfil. Fielding had self-confidently attempted to imbue the novel with dignity, describing it as a "comic epic-poem in prose"[11] and linking it to the genre of history, then thought to be the 'mistress of wisdom'. His definition of his alleged "new province of writing"[12], however, implicitly excluded female writers, for he claimed that a good novelist had to bring with him a background that was more or less outside the range of women in the eighteenth century: according to him, a competent novelist had to have a thorough classical education, very good knowledge of literature, and widespread experiences with members of all social groups.[13] The narrators in Henry Fielding's fictions make ample use of their prerogative and act according to their elevated position by commenting extensively on the status and worth of the narrative, evaluating and explaining the motives and fates of the characters, addressing the narratee numerous times, making generalisations that include the state of the world at large, showing off their learning by quoting from – preferably classic – authors in the original (but providing a translation for his less knowledgeable readers) and commenting on the act of narrative.[14]

From the 1740s onwards, the stance of the 'overt' heterodiegetic narrator was therefore well known – but to my knowledge the full extent of its use and the implied claim to authority is only very rarely found in the works of British women novelists. In a society in which the mere fact of publishing was thought to be 'unwomanly', it was probably flying in the face of providence to claim such a pronounced 'omniscient' position. In addition, an overt narrator provides

---

10 See Catherine Belsey. *Critical Practice.* London: Methuen, 1980, 70-72.
11 Henry Fielding. *Joseph Andrews.* 1742. Ed. Martin C. Battestin. Middletown, CT: Wesleyan University Press, 1967, 4. Susan Staves. *A Literary History of Women's Writing in Britain, 1660-1789.* Cambridge: CUP, 2006, 250, regards this as a display of the "tactics of a male writer struggling to create a hierarchy of writers that elevates male writers like himself".
12 Henry Fielding. *The History of Tom Jones, A Foundling.* 1749. Ed. Martin C. Battestin. 2 vols. Middletown, CT: Wesleyan University Press, 1975, 77.
13 Cf. Fielding, *Tom Jones,* 1975 [1749], 487ff., 523-26, 567, 739ff., 832. Laura L. Runge. *Gender and Language in British Literary Criticism 1660-1790.* Cambridge: Cambridge University Press, 1997, 115, stresses that Fielding's claim to build on classical traditions was not as new as he would like to have us believe.
14 All of these speech acts are also recognised as ways to claim a position of authority by Sniader Lanser (1992, 48).

information about his opinion and standards of judgement – thereby also endangering his position of authority, since his evaluations or generalisations might be objected to by the reader.[15] This risk becomes especially pertinent when an unconventional view on female experience is to be advanced and supported by the narrator. An added drawback was that authors could not rely on their anonymity.[16] A pronounced claim to authority with the full use of extra-representational privileges might therefore prove to be a double-edged sword.

In the second half of the eighteenth century, female authors preferred a more unobtrusive way of exploring female experience: Instead of making full use of the range of opportunities open to the 'overt' narrator, they employed various degrees of 'covert' heterodiegetic narrators, who mainly restrict themselves to the task of narration and use their additional privileges either only sparingly or make sure that their judgements are in accordance with contemporary values.[17] An extensive female use of the privileges of the 'overt' narrator in Great Britain that dares to utter unconventional opinions – or at least tries to change the reader's point of view – is mainly a feature of the nineteenth century and can be found quite extensively from the 1840s onwards, in the novels of Elizabeth Gaskell, George Eliot, Mary Braddon or in Charlotte Brontë's *Shirley*. Though the degree to which heterodiegetic narrators in works by women overtly take charge of the story and use the full range of their possibilities varies, one can safely conclude that, compared to Henry Fielding, they decline a pronounced position of authority.[18] This, how-ever, is only to be expected, since the mere use of 'omniscient' narrators was in itself a subversive act which did not conform to general expectations concerning 'proper' female behaviour.

---

15 Shlomith Rimmon-Kenan. *Narrative Fiction: Contemporary Poetics*. London: Methuen, 1983, 103, also stresses that when a narrator "becomes more overt, his chances of being fully reliable are diminished, since his interpretations, judgements, generalizations are not always compatible with the norms of the implied author."

16 Especially after the publication of successful novels, authors were often identified – and as late as the nineteenth century, some critics changed their formerly favourable opinion of a novel when they found out that the book was really written by a woman.

17 See, for instance, a typical comment by the narrator in Penelope Aubin's *The Life of Charlotta DuPont* (1723): "I wish Mankind would but reflect how barbarous a deed it is, how much below a Man, nay how like the Devil 'tis, to debauch a young unexperienc'd Virgin, and expose to Ruin and an endless train of Miseries, the Person whom his Persuasions hath drawn to gratify his Desire" (quoted after Staves 2006, 194). Haywood's narrator, who in her amatory early novels pronounces on the 'irresistibility' of true love, may be held to be an exception – but within the context of the genre, readers had to accept this position.

18 A notable exception is Sarah Fielding's *Countess Dellwyn*. It has to be taken into account, however, that the heterodiegetic narrators of other female authors do use quite a number of generalisations and evaluations, particularly with regard to the behaviour of the heroine.

Moreover, from the 1740s onwards, the rather rare and interspersed judgements or evaluations by heterodiegetic narrators usually do not deviate from commonly accepted sentiments. Female misconduct is not explicitly condoned; on the contrary, narrators make sure that they overtly censure it – mostly, however, reserving that blame for minor characters who serve as a foil to enhance the real heroine's innate virtue. The authority of the 'authorial' narrator is thus not employed in order to bolster up deviating female views; on the contrary, the voice of narrative authority concurs with social authorities in upholding prevalent norms and values.

The fact that female authors did not make full use of the possibilities of an 'overt' narrator does not preclude their more covert attempts at establishing authority and voicing at least subdued criticism. This is quite often done by the gentle use of irony. In her novel *Belinda* (1801), for instance, Maria Edgeworth manages the tricky business of establishing her heroine as a good and benevolent character, who, however, is influenced by self-serving ladies who have no claim to virtue. When Mr Hervey, who is admired by Belinda and the ladies, is first introduced, the narrator employs irony in order to ridicule this 'hero'. At first sight, the description of Hervey seems to be quite neutral, for the narrator summarizes the topics of his conversation and his mimicking and ridiculing another (absent) character only very briefly. He talks about

> the nature of ladies' promises – on fashionable bracelets – on the size of the arm of the Venus de Medici – on Lady Delacour's and Miss Portman's – on the thick legs of ancient statues – and on the various defects and absurdities of Mrs. Luttridge and her wig. On all of these topics Mr. Hervey displayed much wit, gallantry, and satire, with so happy an effect, that Belinda [...] was precisely of her aunt's opinion, that he was a most uncommonly pleasant young man.[19]

The staccato mentioning of the topics is seemingly neutral, but, considering their obvious banality, which is only surpassed by the arrogance and malevolence towards Mrs Luttridge, who is syntactically set on a par with her wig, the implicit criticism of the narrator is easy to detect. The praise of the "happy effect" of Hervey's talk therefore already shows an ironic stance, a stance that is even more pronounced in the following sentence, in which the criticism is rather explicit: "Clarence Hervey might have been more than a pleasant young man, if he had not been smitten with the desire of being thought superior in every thing"[20]. Here the detached handling of the characters' affairs is quite obvious; after the reader has been allowed to form his own judgement of the character on the basis of the topics of his discussion, his opinion is reinforced by the comment of the

---

19   Maria Edgeworth. *Belinda*. Ed. Eva Figes, London: Pandora, 1986, 7f.
20   Ibid., 8.

narrator, who can therefore be trusted to act as a competent guide through the narrative. This mode is brought to perfection by Jane Austen, but she had many (if more clumsy) predecessors in the eighteenth century.

There is no rule without exceptions, however, and in a stylistically very puzzling and complex novel, Eliza Haywood does employ a very outspoken and explicit heterodiegetic narrator who seems to delight in criticising female behaviour and uphold current standards of morality. In her novel *The History of Miss Betsy Thoughtless* (1751), the narrator establishes himself as a persona who does not mince words and employs his heightened position in order to hold up the mirror to the wrongdoings of women. One reason for this firm and overt establishment of a position of moral authority may be that Haywood was already very well known and had to get rid of her reputation as the writer of – commercially very successful – amatory romances and miscellaneous writings in the 1720s and early 1730s, in which the narrator had loudly proclaimed the irresistibility of '*Love*'.[21] Because of the changed expectations of an audience which set more and more store by virtue and morality, she fell into disgrace, remained silent for nearly a decade and staged her 'comeback' as a didactic novelist in the early 1740s. In *Betsy Thoughtless* she affirmed this new self-image – which, given her former fame and ongoing notoriety, may have called for rather drastic means. The text begins with two sentences which serve to distance the narrator from "the ladies", thus by implication suggesting that the narrator is a man:

> It was always my opinion, that fewer women were undone by love than vanity; and that those mistakes the sex are sometimes guilty of, proceed, for the most part, rather ftrom inad-vertency, than a vicious inclination. The ladies, however, I am sorry to observe, are apt to make too little allowances to each other on this score, […] and it is not above one, in a greater number than I will presume to mention, who, while she passes the severest censure on the conduct of her friend, will be at the trouble of taking a retrospect on her own.[22]

The narrator begins very confidently with a generalisation that may deviate from the individual opinion of readers (though misdemeanours due to both love and vanity were at the core of many stories from antiquity onwards, which makes it quite safe to rank them) and thus explicitly renounces – and at the same time

---

21 See, for instance, "till *Love*, that sweet Destroyer, that stealing Poyson of a Woman's Peace […]. That litte Regard which *Love*, especially in a young Heart, leaves for Reputation". Eliza Haywood. *The Tea-Table; or, a Conversation between Some Polite Persons of Both Sexes*. 1725. *Fantomima and Other Works*. Ed. Alexander Pettit, Margaret C. Croskery and Anna C. Patchias: Broadview Press, 2004, 73-106, 88f. See also Eliza Haywood. *Lasselia. The Injur'd Husband* and *Lasselia*. Ed. Jerry C. Beasley. Kentucky: University of Kentucky Press, 1999, 103-150, 119.

22 Eliza Haywood. *Miss Betsy Thoughtless*. 1751. Oxford; New York: Oxford University Press, 1997, 9.

alludes to! – the opinion the author voiced in her earlier popular romances. The narrator then goes on to criticise the female sex at large, claiming that they are, on the whole, censorious, prone to misconduct themselves, but devoid of self-criticism. This rather harsh judgement establishes him as a judge of the whole sex and makes it quite clear from the beginning that the history of his heroine should teach ladies to be more benevolent towards other women. This is a double-edged device, because while it fosters the authority of the narrator and, by implication, the author, it demeans the female sex as a whole. It is, moreover, very unusual with respect to the practices of other narrators of novels by women, which refrain from criticising women in general, and the heroine in particular. Moreover, such passages, uttered by the authority of the 'omniscient' narrator, contradict instances of social criticism which can be found in this novel.

The narrator, however, seems to fully endorse prevailing opinions on morality in general and on women in particular, and even subscribes to the double standard. Thus he harshly criticises the young friend of Betsy, who lures the heroine into dangerous situations even while they are both at school. Later on, the aptly named 'Miss Forward' slips into prostitution because of economic necessity;[23] but instead of trying to raise the reader's pity or sympathy for this young woman, the narrator takes great pains to lay the blame for her fate entirely on her:

> [A]s few women who have once lost the sense of honour, ever recover it again, but [...] devote themselves to vice [...]; Miss Forward could not content herself with the embraces nor allowances of her keeper, but received both the presents and caresses of as many as she had charms to attract.[24]

Instead of economic reasons, moral faults are put in the limelight and current prejudices are confirmed. The men, in contrast, get off scot-free; when the good Mr. Trueworth, for instance, seduces and ruins another woman, this is only mentioned in passing; he is not even criticised for what he has done. Instead, the narrator shows understanding for his position; after all, he has to overcome his former love for Betsy, and "the amour with this fond girl [Flora] afforded him a

---

23 Cf. Nestor, Deborah J. "Virtue Rarely Rewarded: Ideological Subversion and Narrative Form in Haywood's Later Fiction." *Studies in English Literature* 34.3 (1994): 579-598, 583.

24 Haywood (1997 [1751], 191f.). Mary Anne Schofield. "'Descending Angels': Salubrious Sluts and Pretty Prostitutes in Haywood's Fiction." *Fettered or free? British Women Novelists, 1670-1815*. Ed. Mary Anne Schofield and Cecilia Macheski. Athens, OH: Ohio UP, 1986, 186-200, 189, argues that Haywood's prostitutes "become healthier figures than the docile, pale heroines [...] They 'tell' women that it is all right to be angry, that it is right to sell out for the female self." None of the three types of prostitutes Schofield discusses seems to fit the prostitutes in *Betsy Thoughtless,* a novel which is not mentioned in the article.

pleasing amusement for a time"[25]. However, even Haywood's narrator is not consistently critical of women in general and of his heroine in particular. In spite of some rather harsh judgements about Betsy, which establish a distance to his protagonist, he sometimes tries to engage the reader's sympathy for her and stresses that she has a good heart.[26] Moreover, there are some implicit self-characterisations which show that he does not approve of all the cultural norms concerning the behaviour of women. Thus he implies that wives have to behave in ways that run counter to reason and morality in some instances – why should he otherwise make that distinction in the following praise of Betsy, when the heroine, for once, is "not uttering a single word unbecoming of her character, either as the woman of good understanding, or the wife"[27].

Strategies for privileging female experiences at the level of the story

Even though most female authors from the 1740s onwards refrained from an extensive use of the functions of overt narrators, they employed a number of more unobtrusive strategies on the level of the fictional world in order to highlight female experience. In the following, I want to introduce ten strategies which were quite common in female texts and served to subtly criticise general mores. The strategies themselves are not specifically female; they are used – albeit to different ends – by male authors as well, and they can be found in British novels from the last four centuries. In the eighteenth century, however, they were often employed by women in order to voice subdued criticism; a form which might just as well be employed with the aim of confirming the established social hierarchy is here used to different ends.[28]

---

25 Haywood (1997 [1751], 272). Andrea Austin. "Shooting Blanks." *The Passionate Fictions of Eliza Haywood*. Ed. Kirsten Saxton and Rebecca Bocchicchio. Lexington, KY: University of Kentucky Press, 2000, 259-82, 266, however, stresses that there is a lot of evidence in "a miscellany of episodes, heaped up in insistent detail, that undercut Trueworth's role by subtly contradicting the narrator's view of him", see also ibid. 267, 276-277. Austin gives a few examples, some of which may not have been as averse to contemporaries as to modern readers.

26 See, for instance, "Miss Betsy, who had a great deal of good-nature, and somewhat extremely engaging in her manner of behaviour [...]" (Haywood 1997 [1751], 4). See also Paula R Backscheider. "Literary Culture as Immediate Reality." *A Companion to the Eighteenth-Century English Novel*. Ed. Paula Backscheider and Catherine Ingrassia. Oxford: Blackwell, 2005, 504-38, 514f.

27 Haywood (1997 [1751], 448).

28 I owe my reflection on the relation between these narratives forms and gender to a suggestion from Cindy Hall, who commented on a lecture in which I gave this paper in June 2010. I intro-

Even Eliza Haywood employs these strategies, which serve to counteract the voice of the narrator. I will refer to her novel in my attempt to illustrate the use of the narrative conventions I want to introduce; I hope that this will illustrate the fruitfulness of looking closely at narrative strategies and working with the tools that narratology provides. After all, it has often been said that Haywood's novel is somehow critical of social mores, but I know of no detailed analysis of her ways of writing; what we are faced with are either scattered statements by critics who do not argue how they have arrived at their opinion, or detailed analyses of the content. In an article concerned with a more abstract topic, for instance, Paula Backscheider emphasises that the narrator criticises Betsy, and postulates that the novel is nonetheless ambivalent, partly criticising social hierarchies. She claims, however, that this criticism is voiced by a kind of 'author-function' which allegedly establishes a dialogue with the narrator. What this author-function is, how we can recognize it and the way in which it speaks to the narrator is not explained.[29]

In the following I will argue that there are at least ten strategies, which are used to highlight female experience and justify the female point of view on the diegetic level: (1) quantity of female perspective(s), (2) explaining the reasons for deviant behaviour; (3) presenting (nearly) perfect heroines, (4) the use of ideal characters (whom readers should identify with), who admire and understand the heroine, (5) presenting criticism of the heroine and pejorative opinions about women by way of unattractive, unworthy characters (the reader cannot identify with), (6) focussing on the heroine's feelings, and not on those of her 'victims', (7) appealing to the reader's pity and sense of justice by punishing the heroine to an unwarranted degree; (8) staging conflicts between the sexes and emphasising female powerlessness, (9) highlighting the narrow range of choices by the use of contrasts and mirrors, which includes the constellation of characters and stock characters, (10) the choice of focalisors and the depiction of con-

---

duced these ten strategies in an earlier article, in which, however, I restricted myself to more general remarks and did not tackle the ambivalent strategies in Haywood's novel.

29 See Backscheider (2005, 514-515). In some statements, Backscheider seems to equate the narrator with the author; some remarks are very astute, emphasising the intertextual parody of Haywood's style in her earlier novels in that of *Betsy Thoughtless* or her reworking of well-known scenes of literature. It does not become clear, however, how this serves to establish an author function that is set in "diagolized relationships" with author and narrator. Nonetheless, Backscheider's approach seems to be rather similar to the one pursued here. For a detailed analysis of the implied criticism inherent in the content of the novel (as seen against the background of conduct literature), see Shea Stuart. "Subversive Didacticism in Eliza Haywood's *Betsy Thoughtless*." *Studies in English Literature* 42 (2002): 559-75.

sciousness. Usually, many of these techniques are to be found in one novel – albeit in varying degrees – and more often than not they reinforce one another.

(1) As in many other novels subtly criticising patriarchal values, the female perspective dominates the story in *Miss Betsy Thoughtless*. Though there are a host of characters, both male and female, the fate, actions and opinions of the heroine are at the centre of the story. The protagonist mostly serves as the main focalisor, which means that we get more insight into her thoughts and feelings than into those of the other characters – thus privileging a particular female point of view in a quantitative and a qualitative way. Betsy's thoughts are quite often rendered as direct quotations in her own words or via free indirect discourse, she is present in nearly every scene and given ample opportunity to explain her motives and reasons in dialogues with her relatives, her friends and suitors. Even though the narrator is at best ambivalent as far as his comments on Betsy are concerned, the heroine's thoughts and feelings are the centre of attention throughout the book.

(2) Moreover, the narrator presents the story in such a way that the reasons for Betsy's behaviour become quite clear, thus inducing understanding for her strange behaviour. The heroines' misconceptions or slips of behaviour are explained by the circumstances and, while not explicitly condoned and often criticised by the overt narrator, are presented in a mode which invites empathy with the heroine. We are given a reason which is often used to explain female foibles: the death of her mother. This left Betsy prone to bad influences first at school, and then at the house of her guardian, Mr. Goodman, who has unfortunately married the wrong woman, the scheming, avaricious, hypocritical and deceiving Lady Mellasin.

(3) As just about every other heroine at the time, Betsy's character traits are basically in accordance with current values: she is innocent, benevolent and beautiful; she has good intentions and wants to help others. Apart from her one (minor) fault, she can be held up as a model of female behaviour. She wants to do well, has a good heart, is an expert in the art of polite behaviour, is graceful as well as witty, if just a bit too lively and adventurous. Her only faults are her desire to prolong the period of courtship and her tendency to play the coquette. But since the main focus is on Betsy, we see how innocent her desires are; and when we see how badly she is treated when she has finally been forced to marry, we can see that it was quite reasonable to postpone this period and to prolong the only phase in the life of a young (middle class and wealthy) woman in which she enjoys a modicum of power. Other heroines differ from Betsy in many ways, but all of them are beautiful, innocent and good-natured – even though they are sometimes wilful and naïve, providing easy prey for false friends or evil councillors. But the good qualities dominate, ensuring that the characters are allowed sentiments and

feelings that contradict current values and broaden the understanding of readers. Concomitantly, any negative characteristics which would impair this good image and render the heroine unsuitable for the reader's sympathy are conspicuous by their absence.

(4) One of the most important implicit devices of fostering sympathy and understanding for the heroine's feelings is the use of positively depicted characters who are in full accordance with social norms and who think well of the heroine. Quite often, ideal characters excuse her blunders and her misbehaviour. In *Betsy Thoughtless,* the heroine is esteemed and loved by the ideal Mr. Trueworth, whose very name indicates that he deserves the respect and admiration that is accorded to him by the other characters; he is the descendant of an old family, has a large estate "unincumbered with debts, mortgages, or poor relations" (67), and, above all, he is reasonable and good natured. He only agrees to fight a duel because of his sense of honour, for instance, but then refrains from killing his opponent twice.[30] As in other novels – i.e. Orville in *Evelina,* or Glanville in *Arabella* – the character who commands the respect of all the other characters provides a model for the reader's supposed reaction to the heroine: rather than align him- or herself with the negatively portrayed characters who censure the heroine, the suggested mode of reacting to the protagonist is that of this character.[31]

(5) The counterpart to this strategy is introduced in one of the first novels by women, in Mary Davys' *The Accomplish'd Rake: or, Modern Fine Gentleman* (1727), in which this author, as Susan Staves has recognised, "inaugurates a tactic of women's fiction: characterizing undesirable male characters by allowing them to pontificate foolishly on their mistaken ideas about women's nature".[32] This tactic presents the other side of the coin and achieves more than just the kind of negative characterisation already mentioned by Staves: These unattractive, unworthy characters and their opinion about the negative features of women provide models readers are meant to disagree with. This 'tactic' therefore serves to render their (often exaggerated) truisms and criticism of the heroine suspect.

(6) In order not to impair the positive image of the protagonist, the focus of the narrative remains firmly on the heroine; possible negative consequences of her behaviour on others are played down. The only one who is shown to be endangered by her actions is Betsy herself: When she kindly visits her old friend, Miss Forward, for instance, she falls prey to a 'gentleman' who said he would drive her home; when he lets on that he is about to abduct and rape her, she feels

---

30 Haywood (1997 [1751], 67, 142f.).
31 This strategy is quite common, but it was used with some discretion even at the beginning of the eighteenth century in Mary Delarivière Manley's *The Adventures of Rivella* (1714).
32 See Staves (2006, 186).

sheer terror and is barely able to escape.[33] The havoc that Betsy might have caused in her partly less than kind behaviour to her suitors, the unfulfilled hopes or the adjustment of financial expectations, are not even mentioned in passing. Usually, the story focuses on the heroines and the negative results their actions have for themselves; whatever consequences there are for other characters lies in obscurity. Even when Arabella realizes that others were inconvenienced by her actions, she is shown to be 'mortified' by feelings of regret; what the others feel is passed over.[34] The ideal characters may understand and defend the heroines' actions, but the protagonists usually solely blame themselves.

(7) Though many novels provide a happy ending for the heroines, most of them are punished in a most unwarranted and harsh way during the course of the story. As far as the plot is concerned, many novels run counter to the principle of refraining from "cruel and unusual punishments".[35] *Betsy Thoughtless* is a case in point; not only is she wrongly suspected of a lack of virtue by Trueworth, who temporarily rejects her, she is also forced to marry a cruel and despotic husband, who mistreats her in any number of ways. The years of marriage to him can surely be judged to be 'excessive punishment' for her minor faults. From the 1720s onwards, female novelists presented heroines who are ruined by their seducers, or who begin life in a comfortable position but are impoverished and have to endure extreme poverty, or even wake up in an asylum for the insane, like the heroine in Mary Brunton's *Discipline* (1815). Since the heroines have to repent and get rid of their (minor) faults, their 'correction' – induced by society or fate – is justified and conforms to contemporary values. But the punishment often by far transgresses the faults and the misbehaviour of the heroine, which invites readers to feel pity for her – and even to distance themselves from those characters who harshly punish the protagonist, or who bring about or welcome this harsh treatment. Therefore it becomes possible for readers to distance themselves from social norms and officially sanctioned behaviour that they may endorse in reality, but that appears heartless and narrow-minded in the context of the novel.

(8) Conflicts between male and female characters often focus on innocent and quite understandable wishes of the heroine – like Betsy's desire to prolong courtship or the more serious desire of Maggie Tulliver to get a better education.

---

33 This scene does not only illustrate the courage and power of Betsy, who convinces the gentleman that she is "of a family of some consideration in the world", it also teaches readers which kind of women are truly respected, because even the libertine admits that "I love my pleasures, and think it no crime to indulge the appetites of nature. I am charmed with the kind free woman, but I honour and revere the truly virtuous" (Haywood, 1997 [1751], 205).

34 Charlotte Lennox. *The Female Quixote, or the Adventures of Arabella*. 1752. Ed. Margaret Dalziel. Oxford: OUP, 1989, 15.

35 British 'Declaration of Rights'; the phrase is taken up in the American Bill of Rights.

Differences of opinion with regard to parents or other male characters highlight the dependence and powerlessness of female characters, who, in contrast to their male counterparts, either cannot realise their dreams or rely on male support. If it comes to a pinch, male characters do not hesitate to insist on an unwanted marriage, such as Miss Betsy Thoughtless' relatives, who force her to marry Mr. Munden, who shows in many conflicts with his wife that he is mean, dishonourable, faithless and unscrupulous; he even asks Betsy to have an affair with a nobleman, because he expects a preferment in exchange for the caresses of his wife. Such staging of conflicts, which the women are doomed to lose (though Betsy draws a line at having sex with the nobleman), emphasises both female experiences and emotional reactions to a crisis as well as the unjust distribution of power in society. Even if women reject proposals of marriage – which they do at their own peril – the men (mis)use their position of power by telling them that they have to marry and will not get a better offer, such as Mr Collins does with regard to Elizabeth in *Pride and Prejudice*, or the lower (middle) class characters Mr Branghton and Mr Smith when they propose to Evelina in Burney's novel.

(9) The range of experiences open (or closed) to women is highlighted by the means of mirroring or contrasting the heroine's experiences with the fate of other characters in roughly the same position.[36] Betsy, for instance, is contrasted with her cousin Flora, a woman with far less goodwill and attractions than Betsy, and both are set in relation to Miss Forward, whose social position – in conjunction with her 'forwardness' – leads her into prostitution. The only character clearly more virtuous and perfect than Betsy is Miss Harriot, who marries Trueworth but dies conveniently early. However, she is introduced very late in the novel, and not described in any detail – and Betsy acquires this character's perfections in the end. On the other end of the scale are some stock characters like young prostitutes or 'mistresses', and it does not seem to be a coincidence that two of these are French. These women, who have obviously erred in fatal ways, invite comparison with the married women; the less than perfect, superficial and self-serving Lady Mellasin, who has to leave her husband Goodman in the end, and the perfect (but powerless) Lady Trusty, whose good advice during Betsy's difficulties in her first marriage turns out to be utterly useless. The choice, or rather the lack of choices, and the punishment for swaying from the way of chastity are therefore illustrated by the character constellation and relations of contrast and similarity.

---

36   The importance of this strategy for Haywood is rightly emphasised by Sabine Augustin. *Eighteenth-Century Female Voices. Education and the Novel*. Frankfurt a.M.: Peter Lang, 2005, 48. This device is also mentioned by Austin (2000, 270), who sees it as a part of Haywood's technique of repetition, which allegedly "undercut[s] Betsy's supposed final reformation". Austin is one of the few authors who is concerned with formal features.

Quite a lot of novels use this device of describing the fate of other characters that are in a similar situation in order to highlight the particular characteristics that distinguish the heroine from others, to broaden the reader's understanding of the heroine's predicaments, and to widen his horizon with regard to the options and dangers of female behaviour. In the eighteenth century, those characters are sometimes introduced in a more didactic, isolated manner, when they meet the heroine accidentally and tell her the tale of their lives.[37] The constellation of characters is therefore an important ingredient of enlarging the point of view while at the same time privileging the female perspective.

Stock characters, however, mostly confirm existing prejudices. There seems to be a pattern of privileging female experiences in order to highlight the differences and similarities between the main characters and thus induce understanding for the heroine, but to conform to existing prejudices with regard to more unimportant characters. Perhaps this made the books more palatable to the contemporary audience, since it gave them something to recognise and hold on to; perhaps it was even reassuring for the authors themselves. The female adventuress is only (and then moderately) successful in Victorian melodrama, otherwise she ends up as a damsel in distress; the coquette has to be reformed (or ends up as a prostitute, as many 'mirror' characters show); mentors are male (though not always entirely trustworthy), while female mentors (apart from mothers, who are often conspicuously absent) play a rather negative role. It seems as if female novelists made their bid for respectability by the use of – more or less unimportant – stock characters, whom readers could recognise and (dis)approve of.

As John Richetti has demonstrated, eighteenth-century heroines were in no position to give longish explanations of their views and feelings, since this would have contradicted the ideal image of girls: voluble women were suspect; often their use of speech is criticised or ridiculed.[38] It is therefore rarely, and in moments of great emotion, that Betsy defends herself, either against 'gentlemen' that are too forward with her, or against Mr. Munden, who asks her to pay household expenses with her pin money. At first, Betsy is speechless, giving him room to utter a few more insults, but then "[t]he innate rage which [...] swelled her breast to almost bursting, would now no longer be confined. 'Good Heavens,' cried she, 'to what have I reduced myself! Is this to be a wife! [...] Call it rather an Egyptian bondage!'"[39]. This is, however, only barely acceptable in moments of

---

37 In Sarah Scott's novel *Millenium Hall*, the embedded stories of several women even form the bulk of the novel; and Sarah Fielding's *Cleopatra and Octavia* (1757) uses the juxtaposition of two voices as a major narrative device.

38 See John Richetti. "Voice and Gender in Eighteenth-Century Fiction: Haywood to Burney." *Studies in the Novel* 19.3 (1987): 263-272, esp. 268-270.

39 Haywood (1997 [1751], 442).

extreme emotion; Lady Mellasin, by contrast, is denigrated by her passionate outbursts in front of the servants which illustrate her lack of self-restraint.

Given the problems of letting the heroine speak for herself, it became important at least to depict her consciousness. The develop-ment of free indirect discourse is often attributed to Jane Austen, though many scholars have drawn attention to the fact that we can also find it in Behn's *Love-Letters* (1684-87) and many other novels of the eighteenth century. Though, in comparison to Austen, the rendering of con-sciousness more often than not seems to be a little clumsy, there are many instances of quoted or narrated thought in eighteenth century novels by women. When Mr Munden shows his cruelty, unfairness and despotism once again, Betsy's thoughts are rendered by means of free indirect discourse. The narrator uses some of Betsy's alleged words and punctuates them with exclamation and interrogation marks, in order to illustrate that, in spite of her good intentions, and in spite of the good council of Lady Trusty, Betsy does not see any way out of her predic-aments any more:

> How utterly impossible was it for her now to observe the rules laid down to her by Lady Trusty! Could she, after this, submit to put in practice any softening arts she had been ad-vised, to win her lordly tyrant into temper? Could she, I say, have done this, without being guilty of a meanness, which all wives must have condemned her for?[40]

Passages such as these reduce the distance between narrator and protagonist as well as that between her and the reader. The merging of the character's and the narrator's speech and thought are quite pronounced here – they both concur, and it might even be the narrator alone who is responsible for the last question. The insertion 'I say' emphasises the weight of Betsy's thoughts, and shows that the narrator is, for once, definitely on her side.

After such attempts at raising understanding and sympathy for Betsy, her conversion to docility and obedience comes as a surprise. Suddenly, we are faced with a long quoted monologue which shows us a completely different Betsy, who realises that she has been wrong all along: "'Good God!' cried she, 'what infatuation possessed me! Am I not married? Is not all I am the property of Mr. Munden?'"[41] The long monologue of two pages, in which Betsy gives vent to her new insights into the rights of husbands over their wives is not only formally less convincing than the earlier attempts at depicting her consciousness; it is also dubious as far as its content is concerned. After all, few Englishmen, who prided themselves on their liberty as well as on that of Englishwomen during the eight-eenth century, would agree with the statement that Betsy is the property of Mr. Munden. She is, of course, a *femme coverte*, is no legal person and represented in

---

40   Ibid., 448.
41   Haywood (1997 [1751], 495).

all legal, public and political matters by her husband – but she is not his property
and his 'slave', even though he tries to treat her as such.[42]

Even without making use of the full range of functions that an overt heterodiegetic narrator can fulfil, female authors succeeded in writing works which
ostensibly met the requirements of didacticism, but conveyed subdued criticism
of the position of women at the same time. Though the techniques of rendering
consciousness were not as refined as those employed by later novelists, many of
the strategies in use seemed to be 'natural' and 'realistic'; they were less obtrusive and perhaps even more effective than explicit statements by a narrator might
have been.

Claims to authority: Overt narrators in the nine-teenth century

In order to highlight the particularities of eighteenth-century novels, I want to
provide a brief glimpse of the changes which occurred during the nineteenth
century. It is important to recognise, however, that the use of the ten strategies
outlined above continued to be an important means of conveying criticism and
emphasising the perspectives of young women. In Charlotte Brontë's novel *Jane
Eyre: An Autobiography* (1847) and in George Eliot's *Mill on the Floss* (1860),
for instance, each and every strategy can be found. A very brief sketch of the
features of *Jane Eyre* may serve to illustrate this:

Jane is at the centre of the story, the female perspective predominates (1), and
her deviant behaviour is explained, once again, with the death of her parents and
the bad treatment she receives at the hands of her relatives (as well as her love of
liberty and fairness) (2). Although Jane desires independence and admits to being plain, she is nearly perfect: good-natured, forgiving, tender-hearted, upright,
just, and, ultimately, worshipping domesticity in her little home with her cousins
and, later, with Rochester (3). Moreover, the characters which are unanimously
admired respect and love Jane: both the angelic Helen Burns, who dies of tuber-
culosis in Lowood, and Rochester are cases in point (4). Criticism of Jane is
voiced by her despotic and cruel young cousin John Reed, who beats her in the

---

42 For the legal definition of wives, see William Blackstone. *Commentaries on the Law of England.*
4 vols. London: Murray, 1857. The strong prejudice against slavery was used by feminists, who
compared wives to slaves in order to achieve an improvement of their situation; see, for instance,
Mary Wollstonecraft. *A Vindication of the Rights of Woman. With Strictures on Political and
Moral Subjects.* 1791. Ed. Ulrich H. Hardt. Troy, NY: Whitston, 1982, 23, "[uneducated wives]
may be convenient slaves, but slavery will have its constant effect, degrading the master and the
abject dependent."

very first scene, as well as by the hypocritical, hard-hearted and self-serving schoolmaster of Lowood and by many other figures characterised by unattractive traits (5). In addition, the focus firmly remains on Jane's feelings; when she leaves Rochester (or later on St. John), we do not come to know anything about the grief she causes (6). Like many other heroines, Jane is punished cruelly; her minor faults do not call for such suffering, neither when she is put in the 'red room', nor when she nearly dies of thirst and hunger after days without shelter (7). Conflicts with males end with Jane being beaten and punished (as in the beginning of the book), or having to run away: winning is impossible (8). The lack of choices available to women is highlighted by female characters like Jane's female cousins or the housekeeper Mrs Fairfax as well as by Jane's longing for experiences and travels that she can never get (9). Our understanding of the heroine's motives and feelings is enhanced by the fact that Jane is the only focalisor and that we get detailed access to her processes of consciousness (10).

In that respect, nothing has changed. There is a huge difference however, with regard to the persona of the narrator, as far as both heterodiegetic and homodiegetic narrators are concerned. In Eliot's *Mill on the Floss*, for instance, the techniques regarding the level of the story are given additional weight by the persona of the narrator, who takes great care to show that he is to be taken seriously as a judge of what is going on. His wide education and learnedness is indicated not only by his use of words and grammar, but also by a host of intertextual references to classical works of literature and science from a whole range of languages and centuries.[43] This illustrates the writer's erudition and is one strategy to ensure that 'mere' female experience is taken seriously; it could also serve to persuade (conservative) readers to identify with thoughts and feelings that are connected 'only' to the domestic sphere. It also suggests that reading such a work was a profitable endeavour and that the one who was telling it knew what he or she was doing. Eliot's narrator arguably projects a 'male' persona, self-confidently using strategies which are typical of male writers, who, in contrast to females, had access to a classical education. Bolstered up by this confident claim to authority, the narrator in Eliot's novel is so sure of himself that he even dares to criticise well established ideals of womanhood. He thus openly criticises the heroine's mother, who is fond of complaining that her daughter does not match her standards of womanhood and, in particular, that she has hair that refuses to curl properly:

> [F]rom the cradle upwards [Mrs Tulliver] had been healthy, fair, plump, and dull-witted; in
> short, the flower of her family for beauty and amiability. But milk and mildness are not the
> best things for keeping [...]. I have often wondered whether those early Madonnas of Raph-

---

43   This convention was already used in the eighteenth century in some novels by Sarah Fielding.

ael, with the blond faces and somewhat stupid expression, kept their placidity undisturbed
[…]. I think they must have been […] getting more and more peevish as it became more and
more ineffectual.[44]

This acid criticism of prevalent ideals of womanhood, provided by an 'authorial narrator' who often refers to himself in the first person singular, shows that the narrator in this novel is quite confident with regard to his position. The use of irony ("in short, the flower […] for beauty and amiability") shows his detached, censorious stance, and the reference to works of art by Raphael illustrates the extent of his education. This runs counter to important cultural values – and it would have been unthinkable a mere century earlier.[45]

The authority of the narrator can also be witnessed in more or less explicit appeals for sympathy with the (blundering) heroine. Eliot, for instance, employs an intertextual allusion in order to raise sympathy for "poor Maggie", for whom the harmless ride home with the mercenary gypsies is a nightmare: "Not Leonore, in that preternatural midnight excursion with her phantom lover, was more terrified than poor Maggie in this entirely natural ride on a short-paced donkey."[46] Novels by far less adept writers demonstrate how difficult it still is in the nineteenth century to evoke pity for a heroine who does not conform to the expectations of society. As Virginia Woolf said, the elegance with which problems are solved in masterpieces can be appreciated by looking at less worthy predecessors; and Mary Braddon's *The Doctor's Wife*, a reworking of Flaubert's *Madame Bovary*, is a case in point. In this novel, the narrator tries to retain respectability and demonstrate that he himself is in full accordance with current values, while at the same time win the reader's understanding and sympathy for the heroine:

> I know that [the heroine] was alike wicked and silly; I know that it must be difficult to win
> sympathy for a grief so foolish, an anguish so self-engendered; but her sorrow was none the
> less real to her […]. It was not so long since she had lain awake for many weary nights
> weeping for the death of a pet spaniel; […]. All the sterner business of life lay before her as
> yet, all the harder lessons yet remained to be learned.[47]

---

44 George Eliot. *The Mill on the Floss*. 1860. Ed. Gordon S. Haight. Oxford: Clarendon, 1980, 13.

45 It is a matter of contention whether Eliot's heterodiegetic narrators project a male or a female persona. Ansgar Nünning argues with reference to the change of the respecting functions and (implicitly) self-characterising remarks of the narrator that a crucial change occurred when it became public knowledge that a woman, Mary Ann Evans, was the author of these novels. Before that point, Eliot projected a male persona, afterwards, a female one. Cf. Ansgar Nünning. *Grundzüge eines kommunikationstheoretischen Modells der erzählerischen Vermittlung: Die Funktion der Erzählinstanz in den Romanen George Eliots*. Trier: WVT, 1989.

46 Eliot (1980 [1860], 99). See also "[Tom] left poor Maggie to that bitter sense of the irrevocable which was almost an everyday experience of her small soul." (121)

47 Mary Braddon. *The Doctor's Wife*. 1864. Ed. Lyn Pykett. Oxford: OUP, 1998, 223.

The extent to which the position of female authors changed can also be exempli-fied with regard to *Jane Eyre*, which makes full use of the privileges of an autodiegetic narrator: On the one hand, Brontë employs the perspective of the 'experiencing I' in order to render Jane's sufferings in a very immediate way. On the other hand, there are a host of interspersed comments by the older Jane, who supposedly writes this book when she is in her thirties. Though Jane has many longings and character traits that were held to be 'unwomanly' at the time, the narrator does not distance herself from these desires; she rather justifies and explains them – thus showing that a female voice by then held enough authority to contradict social rules and conventional opinions. In a very famous passage, Jane describes how she longed for the "busy world, towns, regions full of life I had heard of but never seen" and repeatedly asks the question "Who blames me?"[48] – knowing full well that this was exactly what most readers could be expected to do. What is interesting here is the way in which the 'narrating I' becomes indistinguishable from the 'experiencing I' and results in a 'merging' of two voices, which enhances the importance of the generalisations.[49]

Jane's very unconventional opinion on the liberty of women is not only bol-stered by the harmony between 'narrating' and 'experiencing I', but also by another privilege of overt narrators: that of addressing the reader, which is used in the rather conventional way of trying to establish common ground between narrator and audience. She also uses generalisations and employs her privileged narrative position to give voice to female experience in general.[50] At least for a daring author it was possible in 1847 to use the 'personal voice' of a woman in order to criticise society. Apparently, the opinion of women had gathered weight over the preceding decades.

---

48 Charlotte Brontë. *Jane Eyre.* 1847. Ed. Margaret Smith. London: OUP, 1973, 110; in the follow-ing sentence, Jane answers this rhetorical question: "Many, no doubt; and I shall be called dis-contented." (Ibid.)

49 S. Lanser (1992, 182) also states that Jane's discourse mingles past and present tense, as if "what the one did the other still supports" (Ibid., 183).

50 See, for instance: "Women are supposed to be very calm generally: but women feel just as men feel; they need exercise for their faculties, and a field for their efforts as much as their brothers do; they suffer from too rigid a restraint, too absolute a stagnation, precisely as men would suf-fer; and it is narrow-minded in their more privileged fellow-creatures to say that they ought to confine themselves to making puddings and knitting stockings, to playing on the piano and em-broidering bags." (Brontë 1973 [1847], 110f.).

Changes in female writing from the eighteenth to the nineteenth century

Looking at the differences between the modes of narration in Haywood and Eliot or Brontë, it is not difficult to detect a significant development in English female writing. On the one hand, there is – apart from the refinement with regard to the presentation of consciousness – little change. Strategies pertaining to the diegetic level, which were meant to ensure the identification with more or less unconventional heroines and their female point of view, were in full use by the middle of the century and continued to be employed throughout the following decades. Even though such conventions seem, in some respects, to be quite basic, they can arguably be held to be more subtle – and possibly more convincing – than explicit comments on the level of narrative transmission. After all, it is impossible to argue with a story or with a complex web of different narrative means, while it seems fairly easy to flatly contradict evaluations or generalisations by a heterodiegetic narrator. The strategies on the diegetic level may therefore serve to lead readers to disagree with characters who pronounce misogynistic truisms which they themselves would support in their daily life, and to confirm the opinion of more unconventional characters, who are idealised within the context of the story. What is presented by means of narrative techniques may change not only the way we think, but the way we feel about female experience or the (mis)use of power.[51]

On the other hand, there is a huge change with regard to women's ways of claiming authority as narrators. The self-confidence which female narrators developed from the beginning of the nineteenth century onwards is rather astonishing. In the eighteenth century, female novelists had shied away from the full use of 'overt' narrators, which imply both self-assertion and self-confidence. Even though they had not quite given in to the public expectation concerning 'female writings' by taking recourse to the 'personal voice', they restricted themselves to the use of rather covert heterodiegetic narrators, which seems to be the most unobtrusive and efficient way to establish a 'superior', 'omniscient' and gender-neutral position. From the early nineteenth century onwards, this reticence towards overt narration diminished: By the middle of the century, authors like Charlotte Brontë and George Eliot could make extensive use of the privileges of overt narrators and thus lay claim to a position of authority.

The more modest attempts at becoming heard and listened to in the eighteenth century therefore prepared the ground for an improved position of narrators created by female authors in the nineteenth century. This development is, at least in Great

---

51   A similar view is held by Newton (1985, 6).

Britain, not related to a corresponding improvement of the legal or cultural position of women. On the contrary, one might even argue that the enhanced status women had gained in the second half of the eighteenth century declined after the French Revolution, when radical ideas were relentlessly repressed and it became even more important to conform to social norms.[52] It also has to be stressed that the heightened position of women as narrators does not become visible if one looks at the content of the stories and the image of the heroine; it is only manifested in the narrative ways of exploring female experience and asserting female authority. Neither George Eliot's Maggie, nor Mary Braddon's 'doctor's wife' gain more authority, independence or freedom than the heroines of the eighteenth century. On the contrary, the latter sometimes enjoy a wider range of experience than their successors in the nineteenth century. Even Charlotte Brontë's Jane Eyre, who is an exception in many ways, is safely and happily married in the end, when her urgent desire for independence seems to have vanished. There is thus, I would like to argue, an important change in the development of women's writing from the mid-eighteenth to the mid-nineteenth century; but this change only becomes visible when one looks closely at the formal features and the style, both of which testify to the increased power and self-confidence of female narrators who focus on the representation of female life.

Bibliography

Augustin, Sabine. *Eighteenth-Century Female Voices. Education and the Novel.* Frankfurt a.M.: Peter Lang, 2005.

Austin, Andrea. "Shooting Blanks." *The Passionate Fictions of Eliza Haywood.* Ed. Kirsten Saxton and Rebecca Bocchicchio. Lexington, KY: University of Kentucky Press, 2000. 259-82.

Backscheider, Paula R. "Literary Culture as Immediate Reality." *A Companion to the Eighteenth-Century English Novel.* Ed. Paula Backscheider and Catherine Ingrassia. Oxford: Blackwell, 2005. 504-38.

Belsey, Catherine. *Critical Practice.* London: Methuen, 1980.

Blackstone, William. *Commentaries on the Law of England.* 4 vols. London: Murray, 1857.

Braddon, Mary. *The Doctor's Wife.* 1864. Ed. Lyn Pykett. Oxford: OUP, 1998.

Brontë, Charlotte. *Jane Eyre.* 1847. Ed. Margaret Smith. London: OUP, 1973.

---

52 See V. Nünning (2004). It is no coincidence that there is only one author like George Eliot in comparison to numerous intellectual women in the eighteenth century with a high reputation, who excelled in fields like translations from the classics, historiography, political writing.

Edgeworth, Maria. *Belinda*. Ed. Eva Figes, London: Pandora, 1986.

Eliot, George. *The Mill on the Floss*. 1860. Ed. Gordon S. Haight. Oxford: Clarendon, 1980.

Fielding, Henry. *The History of Tom Jones, A Foundling*. 1749. Ed. Martin C. Battestin. 2 vols. Middletown, CT: Wesleyan University Press, 1975.

—. *Joseph Andrews*. 1742. Ed. Martin C. Battestin. Middletown, CT: Wesleyan University Press, 1967.

Haywood, Eliza. *The Tea-Table; or, a Conversation between Some Polite Persons of Both Sexes*. 1725. *Fantomima and Other Works*. Ed. By Alexander Pettit, Margaret C. Croskery and Anna C. Patchias: Broadview Press, 2004.

—. *Love in Excess*. Ed. David Oakleaf. 2nd ed. Peterborough, Ontario: Broadview Press, 2000.

—. *Lasselia. The Injur'd Husband* and *Lasselia*. Ed. Jerry C. Beasley. Kentucky: University of Kentucky Press, 1999.

—. *Miss Betsy Thoughtless*. 1751. Oxford; New York: Oxford University Press, 1997.

Johnson, Samuel. "The Adventurer." *The Yale Edition of the Works of Samuel Johnson*. Ed. Donald J. Greene. Vol. 2. New Haven, CT: Yale Univ. Press, 1963.

Lanser, Susan Sniader. *Fictions of Authority: Women Writers and Narrative Voice*. Ithaca: Cornell University Press, 1992.

Lennox, Charlotte. *The Female Quixote, or the Adventures of Arabella*. 1752. Ed. Margaret Dalziel. Oxford: OUP, 1989.

Nestor, Deborah J. "Virtue Rarely Rewarded: Ideological Subversion and Narrative Form in Haywood's Later Fiction." *Studies in English Literature* 34.3 (1994): 579-598.

Newton, Judith Lowder. *Women, Power and Subversion: Social Strategies in British Fiction, 1778-1860*. 1981. New York; London: Methuen, 1985.

Nünning, Ansgar. "Mimesis und Poiesis im englischen Roman des 18. Jahrhunderts: Überlegungen zum Zusammenhang zwischen narrativer Form und Wirklichkeitserfahrung." *Neue Lesarten, neue Wirklichkeiten: Zur Wiederentdeckung des 18. Jahrhunderts durch die Anglistik*. Ed. Gerd Stratmann, Manfred Buschmeier. Trier: Wissenschaftlicher Verlag Trier, 1992.

— *Grundzüge eines kommunikationstheoretischen Modells der erzählerischen Vermittlung: Die Funktion der Erzählinstanz in den Romanen George Eliots*. Trier: WVT, 1989.

Nünning, Vera. "Gender, Authority and Female Experience in British Novels from the Eighteenth to the Nineteenth Century. A Narratological Perspective." *Theorizing Narrative Genres and Gender*. Ed. Suzan van Dijk and Liselotte Steinbrügge. Leuven: Peters, 2010.

–. "Changes in the Representation of Men and Women in the Second Half of the Eighteenth Century." *REAL: The Yearbook of Research in English and American Literature* 20 (2004):183-207.

Richetti, John. "Voice and Gender in Eighteenth-Century Fiction. Haywood to Burney." *Studies in the Novel* 19.3 (1987): 263-272.

Rimmon-Kenan, Shlomith. *Narrative Fiction: Contemporary Poetics.* London: Methuen, 1983.

Runge, Laura L. *Gender and Language in British Literary Criticism 1660-1790.* Cambridge: Cambridge University Press, 1997.

Schofield, Mary Anne. "'Descending Angels'. Salubrious Sluts and Pretty Prostitutes in Haywood's Fiction." *Fettered or free? British Women Novelists, 1670-1815.* Ed. Mary Anne Schofield and Cecilia Macheski. Athens, OH: Ohio UP, 1986. 186-200.

Spencer, Jane. *The Rise of the Female Novelist: From Aphra Behn to Jane Austen.* Oxford: Blackwell, 1986.

Staves, Susan. *A Literary History of Women's Writing in Britain, 1660-1789.* Cambridge: CUP, 2006.

Stuart, Shea. "Subversive Didacticism in Eliza Haywood's *Betsy Thoughtless.*" *Studies in English Literature* 42 (2002): 559-75.

Wollstonecraft, Mary. *A Vindication of the Rights of Woman. With Strictures on Political and Moral Subjects.* 1791. Ed. Ulrich H. Hardt. Troy, NY: Whitston, 1982.

Constructions of Identity in Romanticism: The Case of William Wordsworth

Christoph Bode
LMU Munich

1. Introduction

This paper is part of a larger research project on discursive constructions of identity in British Romanticism.[1] Today, my topic is the paradigmatic, but also unique case of William Wordsworth and my reference text is the *Prelude*. In talking about the *Prelude*, I will not only focus what is arguable its most interesting aspect with regard to life writing or identity formation, viz. the two movements in time that it displays in all its different versions: the time span of 1770-1798/99, which is the period covered by that long autobiographical epos, *plus* the period during which William Wordsworth worked on the *Prelude*. For it is true that there is this temporal double movement in Wordsworth's ongoing project – one is layered upon the other, or copied onto the other, so that the trace of that work in progress signifies the subject that produces the discourse, but is also produced by the discourse.

The Prelude is, of course, also the prime example and piece of evidence for the impossibility of ever ending and of the complementary necessity to continually re-write one's own life (even if the period covered remains constant). This process of continual re-writing of the self finds its only logical ending in the ontological fact of the death of its author; which, in turn, means that this kind of discursive identity formation can never be finished – the subject will always remain, and inevitably so, fragmentary, incomplete, in addition to being, arguably, the non-presence of that something that left a trace behind.

But, as indicated, this will not be my sole topic. I will also (and primarily) talk about a certain movement that can be regarded as characteristic of William Wordsworth, a kind of signature of his way of relating subject to object, of relating himself to the world – a fingerprint, if you will, that identifies William Wordsworth, but that is also paradigmatic for the period, because it is itself the result of a negotiation of difficulties that are essentially Romantic (not that I believe in

---

1 Cf. Christoph Bode, Selbst-Begründungen: Diskursive Konstruktion von Identität in der britischen Romantik I: Subjektive Identität, Trier: wvt, 2008.

any sort of essentialism – but these difficulties become virulent in the period that we call the Romantic Age – and Wordsworth has a very special way of dealing with them).

In reading *The Prelude*, I will focus on a few selected episodes only, episodes that illustrate the kind of processing of experience for which Wordsworth was known or notorious, even by his contemporaries – which makes my case, I hope, all the more stronger, since the *Prelude*-passages I refer to were, of course, unknown to his contemporaries.

Before I begin, I should like to give at least a sketch of the theoretical framework for my engagement with William Wordsworth, a sketch of how I *generally* approach the matter of self-modelling, or the discursive construction of subjective identity; because what I say here about Wordsworth is, as I remarked before, part of a larger project on discursive constructions of subjective identity in the Romantic Age.

In my larger project, I work form three premises: My first premiss is that in the 18th century, we witness the formation of what Niklas Luhmann calls a fully-fledged functionally differentiated modern society with a variety of different social sub-systems. This coincides with the event of new, discursive practices of identity construction that are dynamic, flexible and open-ended. These new discursive practices allow the different social sub-systems to operate with variable and fluid identity designs and thereby to avoid the counterproductive and dysfunctional rigidity of identity concepts that are prematurely fixed by 'substantialist' parameters or content-defined entities.

My second premise is that such discursive constructions of identity are always prone to paradox and self-contradiction. But this fact must be masked or veiled in ordinary communication, because a systematic unmasking or ostentatious exhibition of these paradoxes would be counterproductive in virtually all social sub-systems.

There is, however, and that is my third premise, *one arena* in which the contingency and the very 'impossibility' of discursive self-grounding can be displayed conspicuously and without any sanction, and that is exactly the designated field of texts that are freed from fulfilling any *specific* function: *literature*. The conspicuous foregrounding and thematization of the *immensely varied* and paradoxical ways in which identities are discursively constructed becomes the true province of literature – it can indulge in practices that elsewhere would lead to the breaking down of any communication, but which, in this field, are the defining trait, the *differentia specifica,* of this particular kind of communication, viz. enhanced and foregrounded auto-referentiality.

Therefore, the defining trait of modern literature, viz. that it speaks about itself and directs our attention to the text *as text* and to the processes of meaning production themselves, structurally coincides with that which, by definition, has no other subject but itself and has, as its own telos and reason for being, the proof of its own meaningful coherence, of its own necessity, i.e. the discursive production (*Hervorbringung*) of identity. The discursive construction of identity can only be self-referential, as are modern art and literature in their most characteristic manifestations.

In separate studies I have already traced the ways in which the paradoxicality of discursive self-constitution shows itself in John Keats, Lord Byron, P.B. Shelley, Samuel Taylor Coleridge and Charlotte Smith. For the decisive point is *not* that any attempt at deriving the subject from itself or at grounding the subject in itself can only end in paradox, contradiction, or infinite regress; the decisive point is that these paradoxes and contradictions come out differently in different poets. Here, we shall look at how they come out in William Wordsworth.

2. Boat Stealing

In the early passage commonly referred to as the "Fair seed-time had my soul" section of the *Prelude* (I, 305f.), Wordsworth mentions two powers that predominatly formed his personality, beauty and fear.

> Fair seed-time had my soul, and I grew up
> Fostered alike by beauty and by fear
> (I, 305/306)[2]

Beauty and fear are a duality that is of prime importance, a fact that is even underlined when later on he mentions other influences as well:

> Nor, sedulous as I have been to trace
> How nature by extrinsic passion first
> Peopled my mind with beauteous forms or grand
> And made me love them, may I well forget
> How other pleasures have been mine, and joys
> Of subtler origin [...]
> (I, 571-576)

In the following, I will trace how the fear that was once experienced by the little boy is later re-interpreted as a beneficial power that "fostered" him. 'What is good about fear?' is not only structurally akin to the question, 'What is pleasing about the sublime?' Beauty does not stand in need of such a re-interpretation.

---

2   Unless mentioned otherwise, I refer to the 1805 version of *The Prelude* throughout. My edition is William Wordsworth, *The Prelude: The Four Texts (1798, 1799, 1805, 1850)*, ed. Jonathan Wordsworth, Harmondsworth: Penguin, 1995.

Beauty is always taken as a matter of course. But that which inspires fear has to be processed – psychologically, rationally, imaginatively, by way of interpretation.

One of Wordsworth's most impressive childhood memories – possibly also his most terrifying experience – in any case, more so than the fatalities of the "dead man" and "the boy of Winander", and also, in spite of its Gothic elements, more scary than the encounter with the "discharged soldier" – is the "boat stealing episode" of Book I (I, 372f.). One night during his school holidays, Wordsworth took a skiff to row on Ullswater. The introduction to this episode makes it very clear that this tale is meant to be an exemplum – an example of how Nature, sometimes through "gentlest visitations", but sometimes employing "severer interventions", educates a "favoured being" – "and so she dealt with me".

When we read lines I, 362-371, we can't help feeling that this idea of being used, being tricked by Nature is underscored by Wordsworth's particular choice of words:

> I believe
> That nature, oftentimes, when she would frame
> A favoured being, from his earliest dawn
> Of infancy doth open out the clouds
> As at the touch of lightning, seeking him
> With gentlest visitation; not the less,
> Though haply aiming at the self-same end,
> Does it delight her sometimes to employ
> Severer interventions, ministry
> More palpable – and so she dealt with me.
> (I, 362-371)

Of course, 'frame' has a positive, constructive meaning, but 'to frame sb.' also means 'to deliberately make someone seem guilty of a crime when they are not guilty' (DCE), to lure somebody into a compromising situation. And this is, I would argue, what happens here, because it is personified Nature herself that seduces him:

> One evening (surely I was led by her)
> I went alone into a shepherd's boat,
> A skiff that to a willow-tree was tied
> Within a rocky cave, its usual home.
> 'Twas by the shores of Patterdale, a vale
> Wherein I was a stranger, thither come
> A schoolboy-traveller at the holidays.
> Forth rambled from the village inn alone
> No sooner had I sight of this small skiff,
> Discovered thus by unexpected chance,
> Than I unloosed her tether and embarked.
> (I, 372-382)

The nocturnal scene is beautifully evoked:

> The moon was up, the lake was shining clear
> Among the hoary mountains; from the shore
> I pushed, and struck the oars, and struck again
> In cadence, and my little boat moved on
> Even like a man who walks with stately step
> Though bent on speed. It was an act of stealth
> And troubled pleasure, nor without the voice
> Of mountain-echoes did my boat move on,
> Leaving behind her still on either side
> Small circles glittering idly in the moon
> Until they melted all into one track
> Of sparkling light.
> (I, 383-394)

"Stealth", of course, indicates that the nocturnal silence is broken by a breach of social and moral law – for "stealth" is not only "the act or characteristic of moving with extreme care and quietness, especially so as to avoid detection", archaically it also means "the act of stealing" (*Collins English Dictionary*). And the detail that the sides of the mountain are purportedly echoing the soft sounds of rowing can either be read as an indicator of the "extreme silentness" (cf. S.T. Coleridge, "Frost at Midnight") of the scene or as the projection of an extremely guilty conscience, like the ones we later encounter in Edgar Allan Poe (*The Tell-Tale Heart, The Black Cat,* with a different drift in *The Fall of the House of Usher*) – prolepsis of imminent nemesis.

The rowing boy has now, so as not to lose direction, fixed his eyes upon the top of a mountain ridge, when, all of a sudden, as he rows away and the smaller ridge no longer hides what lies behind it, a huge black cliff appears, growing bigger and bigger:

> And as I rose upon the stroke my boat
> Went heaving through the water like a swan –
> When, from behind that craggy steep (till then
> The bound of the horizon) a huge cliff,
> As if with voluntary power instinct,
> Upreared its head. I struck and struck again,
> And, growing still in stature, the huge cliff
> Rose up between me and the stars, and still,
> With measured motion, like a living thing
> Strode after me.
> (I, 403-412)

Psychologically, it is easy to understand that the boy, feeling guilty, believes the mountain is after him. What is more remarkable is that this confrontation with what is "big beyond all measure" (Kant) *and* seems alive and is moving at the same time – so that it combines Kant's mathematically-sublime with his dynamically-sublime in *one* object – has all the aspects of a truly *traumatic* experience:

> and after I had seen
> That spectacle, for many days my brain
> Worked with a dim and undetermined sense
> Of unknown modes of being. In my thoughts
> There was a darkness – call it solitude
> Or blank desertion. No familiar shapes
> Of hourly objects, images of trees,
> Of sea or sky, no colours of green fields,
> But huge and mighty forms that do not live
> Like living men moved slowly through my mind
> By day, and were the trouble of my dreams.
> (I, 417-427)

Obviously, the child is incapable of coping with this experience, because the boy does not have the strategies at his disposal that would allow him to rationally convert the fearful experience into something meaningful and constructive – in other words, to sublimate it. It is the grown-up narrator who frames the childrens' story of crime and imminent punishment by making Nature herself the power that both first seduces and then (seemingly) punishes – and both for a higher purpose, a greater good. Because of the conspicuous ambivalence of Nature and the gendered set-up of seduction, stealth, and traumatic threat of punishment, it is easy to engage in psychoanalytical readings of the episode. But what others have done, I do not have to repeat.

Instead, let me focus not on that first obvious mountain ridge, but on the second one, the one that appears behind it, or rather on the triangulation of the two ridges and the moving boy in the rowing boat. The boy has mistaken the effect of his own subjective movement for the objective motion of an object that in reality is perfectly static. This misunderstanding, which treats as independent life and autonomous power what is only an effect of my own activity – a classic case of what Karl Marx called fetishism – leads to an absurdly inappropriate response and to uncontrolled escalation: the further I move away, the more becomes visible of what was hidden, the more I am afraid, the more I row, the more becomes visible etc. I create what haunts me through my own activity, through my own fear – and it gets bigger and bigger. In fleeing the scene, I create my own pursuer and persecutor. Experiencing an effect of which I am the sole cause, I believe I am hunted by something outside myself. The mere change of an optical or visual angle results in the illusionary exchange of subject and object positions.

This, it seems to me, is emblematic of the narrative logic of the *Prelude* as a whole – and doubly so. First, the movement of the rowing boy can evidently be seen as analogous to that of Wordsworth writing the *Prelude*. As he moves away from the period of time that he deals with (which remains objectively constant: 1770-1798/99), this period of time does not get smaller and smaller and more and more insignificant, but, quite the contrary, it gains more and more importance. The steady change of angle through subjective motion (Wordsworth growing older) guarantees that Wordsworth will never come to an end, trying to arrest and interpret definitively what he remembers of those early years. The movement, his leaving of the scene, guarantees that more and more will appear, more and more will surface, which then has to be interpreted and processed in the attempt to bring it under control. That in turn guarantees that the relevance of those first 28, 29 years of his life can only increase in the course of his lifetime. That is no poststructuralist paradox – you learn it by rowing.

But if what steadily increases and what inspires fear demands constant processing and interpretive control and if the answer of the boy is the same as that of the author ("Row harder!"), then this explains not only the urgency of the *Prelude* project but also the *selbstaufklärerischer* impuls behind it: the grown-up subject has to re-assert himself time and again and to reassure himself that it was he himself who acted – nothing external; it was *me* who moved; no fear: *I* was the only cause.

But the second lesson of the boat stealing episode, if we regard it as emblematical of the narrative logic of the *Prelude* as a whole, is slightly at odds with this first. Let me explain: the boy was a victim of his own imagination when he felt persecuted by the mountain as if it were a living thing of huge and mighty form, all the more when these ideas even followed him into his dreams. The *moral lesson* of the boat stealing episode is based upon a delusion that the grown up person can see through. That Nature sanctions social offences and misdemeanours is a *childish* idea, which an adult person knows to be a naïve error – but it is the same adult person who introduces this tale with the statement that sometimes Nature employs "severer interventions" to educate "a favoured being". The implied conclusion is: sometimes Nature uses an overheated imagination for higher ends, in order to make someone believe that sometimes Nature uses an overheated imagination for higher ends. In other words: 'I believe this, but, of course, I don't believe this.' Or in a temporal triple jump: When I was a boy I took this as a moral lesson. Of course, I was mistaken in that. But now I believe it again.

Possibly, the two lessons of the boat stealing episode coincide in this: the Nature in question here has to be put into heavy quotation marks, because it is the paradoxical product of what can easily be identified as a characteristic interpretive move: sometimes, the intentionality of a living, animate thing is attributed to this product; sometimes, the product is denied this intentionality. In case of doubt, Nature does what Wordsworth wants. No, that is not quite correct. Nature *always* does what Wordsworth wants. It's the revenge of a "favoured being": she is by the grace of WW.

To be more fair: Wordsworth accepts the limits of interpretation, because he so ostentatiously parades his interpretation as a (paradoxical) *interpretation*. But that doesn't alter the fact that one of the greatest passages in the *Prelude* – and not only this one! – is based on the shaky foundation of a conspicuous 'as if':

> The mind of man is framed even like the breath
> And harmony of music; there is a dark
> Invisible workmanship that reconciles
> Discordant elements, and makes them move
> In one society. Ah me, that all
> The terrors, all the early miseries,
> Regrets, vexations, lassitudes, that all
> The thoughts and feelings which have been infused
> Into my mind, should ever have made up
> The calm existence that is mine when I
> Am worthy of myself. Praise to the end –
> Thanks likewise for the means!
> (I, 351-362)

"The calm existence that is mine when I / Am worthy of myself" not only thematizes the tension between norm and reality, which biographically can hardly be imagined without a presupposed telos, it also postulates in retrospect the logic of an evolution in which even the worst was good for something. The problem is: the example that follows for the meaning of it all – viz. the boat stealing episode – doesn't prove this at all. You *can* imagine such a totality of meaning. But that is (if the schoolboy is to be regarded as an exemplum) nothing but a delusion. Undeniably, you *can* do this. "Praise to the end – / Thanks likewise for the means!"?

In this case it's not only that the end justifies the means – trickery for your own good – , but also that the idea of an agent is pure projection – and projection that knows itself to be projection. The only thing that is certain is: I know what I am meant to be ("The calm existence that is mine when I / Am worthy of myself") and that I'm moving in that direction.

For it is true, whichever way you turn it: in this picture of the boy rowing in Nature, there is only one thing that is stable and reliable: *his steady motion, the movement of the subject*, as it tries to get away from here to there; the subject, which feels impotent when it understands the motion of the world as an *objective* one, but which feels empowered, almost omnipotent, if it reads the motion of the world as the mere result of its own *subjective* movement. Wordsworth's attempt at tracing how he became what he became is an attempt at self-empowerment also in the sense that he appropriates his story as *his* own story. "The growth of a poet's mind" presupposes the realization – *Verwirklichung* – of an inner, preferably organic plan; for this, one needs imagined patterns of meaning, which cannot help but reflect the mind of the poet.

3. Refusing to be impressed: the Wordsworthian Sublime

The trace of this reversion – that the external and what is big, huge, majestic and grand are only an effect of the motion of the subject – can be found everywhere in the *Prelude*. It is most conspicuous in a systematic exchange of the point of view and of the position of the subject in space. Whenever it is possible, it will be placed *above* and will look *down upon* the world and subject it to its look. Even before the boat stealing episode, *Prelude* I, 332ff. gives a great illustration of this boy's marked inclination to hang suspended and look down on the earth (I, 332-350).

In Book IV we encounter familiar elements in a new combination: the gliding boat, the hanging boy, the fusion of subject and object in his own mind (cf. IV, 247-268) It is an ingenious picture, because it emblematically combines the basic problem of the *Prelude*, viz. that often when you look into the depths of time, you cannot tell the shadow from the substance, an object from a mere reflection and from what fancy adds (cf. III, 644-648), with Wordsworth's other problem, viz. that, if it can be arranged, everything that is above him should be below him: when you lean over the side of a slow-moving boat and look on and into the water, you can see everything that is above you reflected down there, below you, but with the resulting problem that you cannot always tell real objects in the water from objects that are reflected on the surface of the water. The passage has the stringent logic of an allegory: of course, you can declare that everything is only within your consciousness, within your mind (= water, inclusive of its reflecting surface), and you turn your back on "rocks and sky / mountains and clouds", but in exchange you will then get a problem of differentiation, since the contents of this mind – facts and their interpretations – will be become indifferent against each other. What's so intriguing about the *Prelude* is that it does not run away from this consequence, but that it faces it and that it acts out this predicament: the *Prelude* displays the effects of what happens if a subject that constitutes itself out of itself and can only be understood *in process*, understands external, objective reality as a reflex of its own movement. It must not be understood as mere psychologizing when I say: never would Wordsworth allow again that he'd be scared by the effect of a subjective movement. From now on, even the movements of objects will be read as subjective ones, as perspectival changes in the position of the observer. And when it is not possible for him to practice what psychologists call identification with the aggressor, then he simply refuses to acknowledge whatever is great, huge, big, grand etc. outside himself. This is not about the identification of a personal oddity of his, but about the internal logic of a processing of experience which shows in the *Prelude* and which is epistemologically and ontologically compelling and consistent, whatever may have been the initial triggering in the empirical being William Wordsworth (1770-1850) and however grotesque some of the consequences of such a redefinition of the subject-object relationship may seem.

The most outstanding instance of this self-empowerment of the subject in the *Prelude* must be its highly idiosyncratic treatment of the encounter with *the* epitome of the natural sublime, i.e. Wordsworth's non-encounter with Mont Blanc. In Book VI, Wordsworth has only five lines for the view that every British Alpine tourist *knew* had to move him deeply. But these five lines speak volumes:

> That day we first
> Beheld the summit of Mont Blanc, and grieved
> To have a soulless image on the eye
> Which had usurped upon a living thought
> That never more could be. (VI, 453-457)

Mere reality is no match for Wordsworth's imagination. So much the worse for reality, Hegel would say. But it is kind of sad that the view of *real* Mont Blanc has spoilt the idea, and the choice of "usurped" indicates that something has taken a position illegally – it shouldn't be there. The image of the real mountain should not have replaced the "living thought" of the idea of what Mont Blanc is like. Reality can only provide a "soulless image". But tellingly the valley of the Arve, into which you can look from above, reconciles them to realities:

> The wondrous Vale
> Of Chamouny did on the following dawn,
> With its dumb cataracts and streams of ice,
> A motionless array of mighty waves,
> Five rivers broad and vast, make rich amends,
> And reconciled us to realities.
> (VI, 457-461)

In contrast to P.B. Shelley's "Mont Blanc", any productive engagement with or negotiation of the traditional topos of the sublime is simply missing. Wordsworth persists in pure negation, and the very brevity of the passage expresses his dismay, or even total disregard. But it also nourishes the suspicion that Wordsworth simply refuses to be impressed, that he cannot allow himself an experience that, as a rule, overpowers others.

The episode of the crossing of the Simplon Pass, which immediately follows this, is further proof that Wordsworth has a most idiosyncratic way of handling up and down, upwards and downwards. As you all know, the passage describes how Wordsworth and his friend Robert Jones, having lost contact with a group of travelers they had joined, cross the Alps without realizing it. They find it hard to believe that from now on they have to *descend*, that their way is *downward*. It is easy to read this allegorically, for the text had stated explicitly before (VI, 469ff.) how the magnificent Alpine landscape had inspired their revolutionary hopes – it is the year after the fall of the Bastille – and that in Nature's open book they "could not choose but read / A frequent lesson of sound tenderness, / The universal reason of mankind, / The truth of young and old." VI, 474-477), if even if sometimes a fashionable melancholy mood took hold of them (l. 482: "Dejection taken up for pleasures sake"). The young political enthusiasts believe that things will march to their perfection and that the liberation of mankind will continuously progress – but in reality, the apex of the revolution is already behind them and from now on it's only downwards. The Alpine landscape, semiotically charged in the first place, is turned into a regular *paysage moralisé*, and the *1850 Prelude* makes this point even stronger in motivating the incredulity of the wanderers with "For still we had hopes that pointed to the clouds" (587) and by putting the final "that we had crossed the Alps" in emphatic italics.

For me, the intriguing thing about this passage is that the companions' disappointment fails to convince because it is only stated, but not in the least dramatized or elaborated. Because immediately following the depressing piece of news "that we had crossed the Alps", we find one of the most impressive apotheoses of the imagination in Wordsworth's entire œuvre. It is almost as if, contrary to what the preceding lines say, Wordsworth is *immensely relieved* to know that from now on it will be downhill – it's a relief that finds issue in this glorious, incomparable outpouring:

Imagination – lifting up itself
Before the eye and progress of my song
Like an unfathered vapour, here that power,
In all the might of its endowments, came
Athwart me! I was lost as in a cloud,
Halted without a struggle to break through;
And now, recovering, to my soul I say
'I recognize thy glory.' In such strength
Of usurpation, in such visitings
Of awful promise, when the light of sense
Goes out in flashes that have shown to us
The invisible world, does greatness make abode,
There harbours whether we be young or old.
Our destiny, our nature, and our home,

Is with infinitude, and only there –
With hope it is, hope that can never die,
Effort, and expectation, and desire,
And something evermore about to be.
(VI, 524-542)

All of a sudden, all the standard elements of the eighteenth-century discourse of the sublime, so conspicuously missing from the account of his encounter with Mount Blanc, are assembled here, in curious displacement. What is more: the text is ambiguously evasive about when this onslaught of the imagination (1850: "Like an unfathered vapour that enwraps, / At once, some lonely traveller." VI, 595-596) took place: was it then, when they had crossed the Alps? Or was it at the point of writing about this experience? The evidence is inconclusive because it points in different directions: "[L]ifting up itself / Before the eye and progress of my song" suggests that this is now, during the writing of the *Prelude*. But "came / Athwart me!" insinuates that it was then. This is corroborated by the contrastive "and *now*, recovering to my soul I say" etc. (even stronger in 1850: "but to my conscious soul I now can say –" VI, 598), although this could also be construed to be a case of epic present tense.

The difference is anything but trivial, for the question is: when was the mind seized by the imagination as by some external power and when did it realize and recognize this power in all its glory? Then, or now? This is the key question of so many political scandals, adapted to subjectivity: when did the mind know what?

For the second time within the span of only 70 lines we encounter a "usurpation", but this time, and in contrast to Mont Blanc, it is welcomed, for in these "visitings" we get a glimpse of what we really are: beings whose destiny is with infinitude. But the question *when* exactly this happened remains undecideable: all we know is that this hymnic incantation of the imagination – if it is not totally out of context – must somehow be related to what went on before, that is, to the unconscious crossing of the Alps and to the overcoming of this disappointment.

And this disappointment is overcome by a re-coding of the experience, so that the all too real disappointment is presented as the outcome of a *misreading* of the Alpine landscape. Being relatively inexperienced, the young students had projected meanings onto the landscape

Whate'er in this wide circuit we beheld
Or heard was fitted to our unripe state
Of intellect and heart.
(VI, 469-71)

and they had misinterpreted ascent as progress ("For still we had hopes that pointed to the clouds"). It was the delusive power of the imagination that led to their disappointment. But it is the very same power of the imagination – now

'good' – that allows Wordsworth to see the 'real' truth, this time: that the highest
point of revolutionary change lies behind them, only that they find it hard to
accept this. The trick, of course, is that the narrator of the *Prelude* uses the very
same *paysage moralisé* which had caused his characters so much pain and disappointment. Exactly like in the boat stealing episode the delusionary power of the
imagination is exposed – but at the same time, it is presented as the saving grace.
Twice – in a kind of double gesture – is the Alpine landscape given a significa-
tion. But exactly because this ascription is so obvious and because its attribution
so conspicuously fabricated, is it so bold that in the replay the same line is taken
('the "real" symbolism of this space is an illusion, but I handle it as if it weren't'),
and it is truly astoninshing, I believe, that such an unqualified apostrophe is directed to this deeply ambivalent and high-ly questionable power of the imagination. It was totally *wrong* to read the Alpine landscape as a confirmation of revolutionary hopes; but it is totally *correct* to read the aspiration of those who want
to go further as emblematical of the destination of mankind:

> With hope it is, hope that can never die,
> Effort, and expectation, and desire,
> And something evermore about to be.
> The mind beneath such banners militant
> Thinks not of spoils or trophies, nor of aught
> That may attest its prowess, blest in thoughts
> That are their own perfection and reward –
> Strong in itself, and in the access of joy
> Which hides it like the overflowing Nile.
> (VI, 540-548)

The *Prelude* does not deny physical space – it denies that physical space *as such*
has any meaning. But in clarifying that when the human mind's imagination
attributes meanings to the external world, or to aspects of it, it projects its ideas
onto a neutral and ultimately meaningless reality, the *Prelude* can no longer
differentiate and distinguish between the transcendental destination of man, on
the one hand, and the self-delusions of young students. Both are based on the
same operations; both are only ideas; both are products of the imagination – a
luring, seductive, deluding and cruel mistress, and yet, or so says Wordworth, an
"awful Power" (1850, VI, 594) that deserves our adoration. It is the human
imagination that is sublime, not the Alpine landscape.

    In this, Wordsworth follows the Kantian turn in the theory of the sublime, in
all but terminology. But there is another, more crucial point in which the
Wordsworthian or egotistical sublime breaks away from other manifestations of
the eighteenth-century discourse of the sublime. Since Edmund Burke's *Philosophical Enquiry into the Origin of Our Ideas of the Sublime and Beautiful* (1757)
the experience of the sublime is not only seen as a mixed feeling ("delightful

horror", "terrible joy"), but as a temporally differentiated two-phase phenomenon: a first phase in which you feel dwarfed and threatened and overpowered is followed by a second one in which you are de-lighted, relieved, relaxed, in which you feel sublime. Evidently, this intense feeling of delight derives from the second phase, not from the initial encounter with that which is big beyond all measure or with powerful Nature (the mathematically sublime and the dynamically sublime, respectively). Burke explains this positive feeling as the effect of a physiological relaxation of the nerves and vessels of the body once you realize that you are not really threatened; Kant says you feel sublime when, although you feel overpowered as a sensual being, you realize that as a rational being you can form an idea of infinity, or, in the case of the dynamically sublime, when you realize that even if you as an individual, biological being were annihilated, the idea of mankind could not be killed in you.

What is idiosyncratic about the Wordsworthian sublime is not that, like Kant, he ascribes it to a human faculty (in his case, to the imagination) rather than to an object, but that in his case the phase of humiliation and the feeling of being overpowered is simply missing. Remember his (non-)encounter with Mont Blanc: he simply refuses to be impressed. The praises of the imagination correspond to phase two, but what is lacking in the text is the threat or overpowering or at least the questioning of man and his faculties. Wordsworth sings the praises of the powers of the human mind – but without any provocation or preceding crisis that would have fundamentally put these powers in question; for, the mere fact that somebody was wrong about their position on a hike can hardly, even in a symbolical reading, be taken as an existential threat or questioning of human capacities in principle, which, in turn, would have to be reinstalled, put into their rights again, with extraordinary fanfare. No, this is an unprovoked display of power, a preventive or pre-emptive strike, in order to make absolutely clear who is in command, even here in this sublime Alpine landscape. For what follows is Wordsworth's most classic depiction of the natural sublime (cf. VI, 556-572). Now that it is going downhill and now that there can be no doubt any longer where the sublime really resides, the infinite grandeur of the mountains can be mentioned for the first time! Now that they are identified as the external representation of something internal, they are no longer terrifying, but downright uplifting. This landscape does not praise God, it praises Mind.

In Wordsworth, and in Wordsworth alone, the sublime appears when you descend and when you look down, not, as usual, when you look up. And this positioning in space is correlated to a temporal idiosyncrasy: curiously enough, in Wordsworth phase two comes first. But since usually phase one contains an experience of impotence and near annihilation, this changes everything – it is a game changer. If the sublime rule of subjective consciousness, of the imagination, is established right from the beginning, then fear and terror are preventively fore-stalled. The Wordsworthian sublime, a characteristically one-phase phenomenon, is analogous to a counter-revolution without a preceding revolution.

4. Mount Snowdon, once more

For reasons of space, I cannot go into what is arguably the most pertinent in-stance of Wordsworth's projective, allegorizing technique of presenting external reality as an emblem of mind, viz. the ascent of Mount Snowdon in the last Book of the *Prelude*. If you check it again, you will find that all the familiar elements are there: the downward gaze, the *paysage moralisé*, the apotheosis of the secon-dary shine of the moon over the primary light of the sun etc. etc. But my final point will not be the repetition of that Wordsworthian signature. Instead, I would like to come back to sth. we have encountered in the boat stealing episode as well as in the Simplon Pass episode: *when* exactly is *which* meaning super-imposed upon a scenery? When exactly is an 'erroneous' reading of Nature re-placed with a 'correct' one, that is not just presented as 'another' reading, but as *the* ultimate reading, the *ultimate* truth? When did the subject know what?

And this is the interesting thing about the Mount Snowdon episode: in both major versions, 1805 and 1850, the moment of recognition is presented as *then*, "in one of these excursions" (XIII,1), during that night, not during the writing of it. *Then* he understood (not immediately, but in the same night) that – wherever the imagination and this particular idea may have come from – it is (self-)reflecting consciousness, the highest power of the human mind, the capacity to see 'this as that', that transforms the moonlit landscape into an emblem, "the type of a ma-jestic intellect"; even then he understood how and why spirit transcends matter; why this is enough and why one does not have to speculate about the *primary* source of light; and why to watch the sunrise on top of Mount Snowdon, the purpose of their hike, is no longer of any importance. Because it is human con-sciousness, the light of the imagination, that bathes the world in meaning. Con-sequently, the *Prelude* ends with this emblematical episode that is taken out of the chronological sequence – the unreserved apotheosis of human consciousness, of the human subject. The poetical reconstruction of the ontogenesis of the poet's mind is a lesson for others, as the epic itself demonstrates and dramatizes its theme: the self-realization of subjectivity in reflection:

What we have loved
Others will love, and we may teach them how –
Instruct them how the mind of man becomes
A thousand times more beautiful than the earth

On which he dwells, above this frame of things
(Which, mid all revolutions in the hopes
And fears of men, does still remain unchanged)
In beauty exalted, as it is itself
Of substance and of fabric more divine.
(XIII, 444-452)

In Wordsworth, the self-grounding of the subject leads to the apotheosis of Mind, of consciousness in its most exalted form, the imagination. "The mind of man" illuminates the earth, "as it is itself / Of substance and of fabric more divine". The story of this realization is the story of the story of the epic that in an exemplary way wanted to trace the "growth of a poet's mind" and that wanted to tell the tale, retrospectively, of course, of how everything began and how it happened that 'now' we have reached this point. Is it just another variation on Hegel's *Phenomenology of Spirit*, a tale that produces the inevitability of its own coming about? With a compelling ending that you cannot possibly top?

Not quite. There is something wrong with the narrative logic of the *Prelude* at its very core. And again it has to do with the old question, 'When did I know what?' The *grand récit* that Wordsworth wants to tell is that of the early fostering of his talents ("fair seed-time had my soul"), how his imagination was then impaired and almost submerged in the events of the French Revolution and afterwards, only to be restored in his native Lake District (Books XII and XIII of the *1850 Prelude*, "Imagination and Taste, How Impaired and Restored"). The only problem is that the climax of it all, his vision on Mount Snowdon – which from the narrative logic of the whole *has* to stand at the end of the epic – really happened in the summer of 1791, and even in the text itself it is clearly marked as an event that happened *before* the horrors of the French Revolution ("in one of these excursions"). From a chronological point of view, Wordsworth had the solution before there was any problem; there was rescue and salvation before there was any danger.

To be sure: any narrator may change the order of events in telling them. The order of events in a narrative is a matter of the discourse, which means, there is absolute freedom in the arrangement of the events I narrate – a freedom of which Wordsworth makes full use in the overall architecture of the *Prelude*. But this here is something different, because Wordsworth creates an impossibility on the level of *histoire*, or story: "I can mar a curious tale by telling it", as Kent says in Shakespeare's *King Lear*. Was ever the whole meaning of a story more radically undercut than in Wordsworth's *The Prelude*, where the protagonist knows the answer *before* he even meets with the problem? The theme of the *Prelude* is the discursive construction and thematization of self-grounding, self-foundation (*Selbstbegründung*), but one thing at least is absolutely certain: whatever may be the truth of the matter, it's not in the story he tells. The truth of the story resides in this, and in this alone: in the ongoing *process* in which a subject tries to understand itself; in the endeavour to narrate the self and its story, to come to terms with what was, and is, and will be. The only reliable data is the *movement* of the subject as it moves from A to B, and then from C to D, as it records this first movement and copies itself onto it. "The Form remains, the Function never dies." (Wordsworth, "After-thought" to *The River Duddon: A Series of Sonnets*).

If the subject is thrown back upon itself, it has no absolute standpoint from which it could tell its own story 'objectively'. What it can do is to tell and re-tell its own story from the series of points that it occupies as it moves along in time. Such a project has no natural ending except the death of its author. If the *Prelude* is the first really modern epic, one of the reasons is that it demonstrates that all we can ever know about ourselves can only be provisional; and that when we try to arrest a meaning, let alone *the* meaning of it all, we produce narrative para-doxes and contradictions, like: children believe that Nature teaches moral les-sons; of course, that's absurd; but I do believe that Nature teaches moral lessons. Or: in our youthful enthusiasm we believed that the Alpine landscape confirmed our convictions and hopes; of course, the Alpine landscape does no such thing; it confirms the convictions I have now. Or, more covert: I was saved even before I was imperilled. Although, when you ponder this last one, it may not be totally absurd. The Wordsworthian subject remains sublimely egotistical, even if it ruins the story.

The Pictorial Turn in the Contemporary Novel

Danuta Fjellestad
Uppsala University

> It is raining images outside …
> Barbara Maria Stafford, *GoodLooking* (87)

In 2004 *The New Yorker* published a cartoon by Bruce Eric Kaplan that shows two people passing by a bookstore, one of them complaining "Now I have to start pretending I like graphic novels too?" The cartoon captures well one of the recent developments in literary studies: a turn to the so-called graphic fiction. The type of novels that are the subject matter of my examination share with graphic fiction one important feature: they all weave the visual into a verbal narrative. To describe what I see as an emerging aesthetic dominant in contemporary literature I appropriate, as must be clear, W.J.T. Mitchell's term "the pictorial turn," introduced first in an article published in *ArtForum* in 1992 and reprinted in the collection of essays *Picture Theory*, published two years later. According to Mitchell, at the beginning of the 1990s, the picture was "emerging as a central topic of discussions in the human sciences, in the way that language [previously] did" (13).

The concept of the pictorial turn has gained wide currency to postulate a shift from language to image-saturated culture. So we hear, for instance, that "Western philosophy and science now use a pictorial, rather than textual, model of the world, marking a significant challenge to the notion of the world as a written text" (Mirzoeff 5) or that images are "fast replacing words as our primary language" (Stephens 11). I find such claims both captivating and quite wrong. What I want to insist on is that it is *combinations* of words and images (and seeing words themselves as images) that is our time's central trend. Think of film, television, newspapers and magazines, posters, Internet sites, or indeed graphic novels that the cartoon refers to as our time's hype phenomenon. Yet there is little doubt that the pictorial plays a very important role today even in the areas that for a long time were the domain of the verbal, that is, in fictional narratives.

My project has its roots in my reading experiences of the past decade or so. As my shelves were getting filled with new fictions, I was struck by how commonplace it became to include a wide range of pictorial material. What is the relation between the verbal text and the pictorial image, I wondered? What is the specific contribution of images to the story told in words? How can we make sense of and describe the braiding of the pictorial and the verbal? How does the presence of images in a novel affect our reading of that novel? Most importantly: Why this intensification of the pictorial in contemporary novels? How different is the use of images in contemporary novels from the uses in earlier periods? These are some of the questions that inform what follows, although of course the length of the article does not allow for an in-depth treatment of these questions. Thus I will indicate some of the *visual registers* that I find of interest in a couple of novels in which interactions between the verbal and the visual are of central importance.

Let me start by listing some novels that I see as ushering the pictorial turn in literature and that seem to me to be paradigmatically *post-postmodern*. Perhaps the most widely known is Jonathan Safran Foer's *Extremely Loud and Incredibly Close* (2005), while Mark Z. Danielewski's *House of Leaves* (2000), though perhaps less known to broad audiences, has reached a cult status and can boast of an active group of aficionados. Salvador Plascencia's novel *The People of Paper* (2005) resonates in interesting ways with *The House of Leaves*. Umberto Eco's, *The Mysterious Flame of Queen Loan* (2004), Mark Haddon's *The Curious Incident of the Dog in the Night* (2003), W.G. Sebald's *Vertigo* (2000), Steven Hall's *Raw Shark Texts* (2007), and Mark Zusak's *The Book Thief* (2005) are some further examples.

At this point two caveats are in place. First, my use of the "pictorial," "picture," or, interchangeably, "image," in this paper corresponds roughly to what W.J.T. Mitchell calls the "graphic image" in *Iconology* (1986), that is, any recognizable figure and likeness, pictogram, geometrical shape, drawing, photograph, musical notation, doodles. It also covers those graphic devices and layout that address the eye through alternations or disruptions of the conventional look of the page. Mental or verbal images (ekphrasis) are not of interest to me here. Second, I do not claim novelty for the use of the visual in fiction. Images in fictional narratives are by no means a new phenomenon; we are all aware of the long tradition of illustrations in children's books or of experimentations with layout and fonts in, say, *Tristram Shandy* or the postmodern novel. But I do claim novelty as regards the variety, type, intensity, and tonality with which images are woven into verbal narratives today. The image-to-word ratio may vary from novel to novel, but in all the texts I am interested in images are used *strategically* and have important *semantic* functions, that is, the interdependency between word and image is central to all of them.[1]

---

[1]   The interweaving of words and images in contemporary novels is very different from the traditional use of images for decoration of the text, decoration that has no semantic function (cf. ornamentation of some letters). It also differs from the tradition of narrative illustration, in which the pictorial is meant to "mirror" what is expressed in words (a practice common in children's books). Nor is the combination of words and images in these novels similar to that which is central to the so-called graphic novel. While the graphic novel simultaneously mobilizes the visual and linguistic codes that constitute it, it is, as Thierry Groensteen argues, a *"predominantly visual*

In what follows I discuss two examples of the verbal – visual interactions. I'd like to begin with Gordon Sheppard's *HA! A Self-Murder Mystery* (2003). *HA!* tells a story of the life and death of Hubert Aquin (1929-1977), a Québécois separatist intellectual, novelist, and film-maker. Or, to be more correct, it is a story of Gordon Sheppard's quest to understand the 1977 suicide of Aquin. Called a novel by its publishers, this gargantuan text (it is close to 900-pages long) draws heavily on the genre of biography, but it also borrows from a wide range of other genres (a detective novel, a play, a psychological study, a film script, etc.) Most importantly for my discussion, even at first glance *HA!* presents itself as an aggressively–perhaps even *oppressively*–visual book. Apart from an unconventional layout, it makes use of a variety of fonts; its pages are crowded with maps, diagrams, postcards, reproductions of hand-written letters and notes, reproductions of classical paintings, music notations, film stills, cartoons, and numerous photographs. Indeed, it is easy to understand why one of the reviewers has called *HA!* "the wildest scrapbook" (David Homel, n.pag).

I want to focus on the use of photographs in the novel-cum-biography, or, to be more specific, on the sequence of nine photographs of Aquin in the order in which they appear in the text, with the emphasis on the final portrait.[2] That there are quite a few photographs of Aquin is in line with the biographical dimension of the novel. Each photograph interacts with the immediate verbal context in which it is placed, sometimes echoing it, sometimes contradicting, subverting, or complementing the verbal narrative. But the photographs interact with each other and the whole of the story as well. So what can be said about the sequence of Aquin's images? We see a progress from snapshots that reveal few individualizing features of Aquin and occupy but a portion of the page to a fully-fledged distinct and most traditional facial portrait.[3] The sequence resonates – not to say mimics – the verbal narrative's non-chronological organization. One reading of the sequence would be that the images take us on a seemingly teleological journey toward some kind of knowledge of Aquin. When the photographs are looked

---

narrative form" (12; italics in the original). Groensteen argues against a common assumption that the text and image are two equal components of comics and, by extension, of the graphic novel. The most known advocate of the equality of the two codes is Scott McCloud.

2   The practice of inserting photographs into an imaginary text is not new, but until the last decade it was very rare. André Breton's surrealist novel *Nadja*, published in 1928, contains 44 photographs within its 158 pages. In the same year, Virginia Woolf's *Orlando* was published by her own Hogarth Press. The first edition contained a number of illustrations including photographs of (the real) Vita Sackville-West as (the imaginary) Orlando. Many subsequent editions were published without the photographs but in the 1973 (American) edition, the photographs returned.

3   Analyzing the significance of the placement of the photographs on the pages is a challenge in itself; I am currently looking into methodologies that would help me analyze what – if any – diegetic function such spatial arrangements may have.

at as a sequence, they seem to echo the verbal narrative's quest to understand – to piece together – a portrait of Aquin. The sense of temporal and thematic closure and finality is reinforced by the final full-page frontal portrait of Aquin: dressed in a suit with a tie, smiling slightly, Aquin stares straight at the reader. The photograph's placement in the series of photo-images and in the book, its size, and the caption that provides the dates of Aquin's birth and death work together to consolidate the feeling that the narrative has achieved its goal of capturing Aquin's singularity.

Undoubtedly, this reading is invited and justified. At the same time, it is undercut and even slightly ridiculed if we take into consideration what comes linearly before the photo-image. On the left-hand page we see the word "end" in big block letters crossed over and a seemingly hand-written word "home" placed above it. At the bottom of the page in a small-size font we read "*Montréal-Hollywood-Toronto-Montréal 1977-2003* " (italics in the original). A full exploration of the complexities of the interplay of the verbal and the visual is beyond the scope of this presentation, but let me mention a few points. We may notice the multiplication of the signs of closure: the words "end" and "home" as well as the dates seem to parallel the finality that the portrait evokes. But of course what stands out is the word "end" crossed-out and the handwritten word "home" given as its substitute. Both words function as images. (I leave uncommented the resonances with Derrida's "under erasure" argument.) We will notice that the date of Aquin's death, 1977, is given as the date of a beginning – well, of what exactly? The dates coincide with Sheppard's first interview and the ultimate publication of *HA!* But there is an interesting merge of time and space, as the dates are attached to Montréal – Holly-wood – Toronto – Montréal. We will observe that the references to geographical spaces evoke both linear and circular movement: the place of departure is the same as the place of arrival. We will also notice that the end of the narrative does *not* coincide with the end of the book, since several sections are placed after the portrait: a coda, a list of characters, "authorized comments," contents, credits, and, finally, a painting by Rembrandt. Thus endings, literal as well as metaphoric deaths, lose their sense of finality and closure. Other issues may be teased out: the relation of endings to homes (as places of arrival, rest, and safety), the book / narrative as a home securing a life after death, the possibility of death being the proper home for Aquin, who, as we have learned, felt out of place in life as a French Canadian intellectual.

I want to make a couple of general points at this point. First, it is important to analyze not only individual images but also their sequencing in a verbal narrative. Second, such sequences raise the question not only of inter-visuality but also of intra-visuality. Third, we do not yet have a vocabulary to adequately describe the diverse ways in which interactions between the verbal narrative and the images take place. Finally, the question must be asked how our reading conventions are being challenged by the presence of images in narratives. This is a central point in the second example of how the pictorial and the verbal are woven together.

Published in 2009, Reif Larsen's *The Selected Works of T.S. Spivet* is a first-person narrative. The titular T.S. Spivet (T standing for Tecumseh and S for Sparrow) is a twelve-year-old boy living with his family on a ranch in Montana.[4] A precocious child, T.S. is an avid map-maker. He compulsively documents small and big events: the flight-paths of bats around his house, the dynamics of his sister shucking corn cobs, his father's facial expressions, etc. The reader follows T.S. on his train travel across the country to get to Washington D.C. to collect a prize from the Smithsonian.

Yet what captures the reader's attention at first sight, what is the most striking – not to say mesmerizing – feature of the book is its lavish production. The book startles by its look: its size, the broad outer, top, and bottom margins, the double-spacing of its main text that creates a feel of a typed manuscript, the sepia coloring that gives an "antique" look to the images.[5] Most importantly, the margins of virtually every page in the book are filled with a baffling variety of images: with graphs, charts, maps, drawings, doodles, and other pictorial material as well as with chunks of text. These marginal texts are printed in a variety of typefaces, in sizes different from the one used for the main story. In addition, the notes are often surrounded by frames which set them visually apart. Most often – but far from always – dotted lines link the main text and the marginalia, making the reader's eye wander along different paths from the story to the annotations, digressions, and notes to the left or right of the text. One's attention, I would say, is immediately visually re-routed from the physical center / the verbal narrative to the margins dense with images, making the reader aware of what is usually ignored: the space that surrounds the narrative. This space is used constantly to remind the reader of T.S.'s talents as cartographer and of his compulsion to document the life around him. Crucially, Larsen puts key elements of the story in the physical space of his book's margins: these thus serve as a repository of stories triggered off by the main narrative; they provide an outlet for T.S.'s fears, se-

---

4   Tecumseh, as is well known, was a late-eighteenth-century Native American leader of the Shawnee tribe that opposed the United States during the so-called Tecumseh's war. Larsen's novel alludes to a broad variety of historical material, most of which can be linked to heroic and / or traumatic events.

5   It needs to be noted that there is a difference between the American Penguin edition and the British Harvill Secker in this respect. While in the British edition the sepia coloring is sustained throughout the book, in the American edition the images in the text are in black ink, the sepia coloring used only on the pages that frame the text.

crets, desires, anxieties, and memories; they are places of comic relief from the story of T.S.'s loneliness; they accommodate clues about what is to happen. To repeat: called back, so to speak, both literarily and metaphorically into visibility, the margins are transformed into a semantically meaningful site, a site teeming with signs to be interpreted.

It is in the margins of the book that the reader is given an indication of what spurs the narrative, what constitutes its "heart of darkness": the death of the family's youngest child, Layton.

The tragedy of Layton's death is interlaced in complex ways with T.S.'s uncertainty about the family's emotional bonds. Let us take a closer look at the drawing with the caption "Patterns of Cross-Talk Before and After." We are given two images of a rectangular table with the names of the Spivet family members placed at its four sides. Full and dotted lines, some of them straight, some slightly curved, link the various seats/names. The image of the table marked with number 1 (the "before" table) gives a "messy and "crowded" impression, while the second image (marked as number two and placed below the first drawing) has an orderly look, the number of lines reduced from nine to five. It should be noted, too, that some of the lines have arrows at both ends, while others end with one arrow only. The caption's reference to time signals a narrative that asks to be deciphered.

It is not difficult to see that the "before" and "after" refer, in an elliptical way, to Layton's death. At the same time the caption signals that this event is erased from the family discussions, that it remains unspoken. Before the accident, the pattern of talks among the Spivet family members, the first image shows, is rich and complex, both the dotted and the full lines pointing to Layton as the focus of attention at the dinner table. Conversations take place *around* as much as *across* the table. The diagram of communication *after* the accident is much more orderly, the "across" coming closer to a cross. At the same time the second drawing makes the pattern of communication of the first much more visible: as the full line indicates, the father of the family communicated only with Layton. Layton now gone, the father does not communicate with anybody, although he continues to be addressed by his wife and his daughter. The previous two-way communication between the mother and the daughter is now, the arrows indicate, a one-way exchange between Dr. Claire and Gracie, while T.S. continues two-way conversations with his mother and his sister Gracie. What is most striking, however, is that neither before nor after the accident is there any communication whatsoever between the father and T.S., as no lines link the two, irrespective of where at the table T.S. is seated. (We will observe that T.S. takes Layton's place to the left of the father in the second drawing.)

The two drawings not only tell the story of the changes in the family dynamics indicated by the "before" and "after" of the caption, but also of the family's constant: a steady alignment of T.S. with the women in the family and his equally steady lack of contact with the father. This alignment is signaled – but not made much of – in a casual way in the following comment fairly early in the narrative: "Layton, like Father," T.S. tells us, "wasn't interested in anything that had to do with beauty or hygiene and thus never joined us. He belonged with Father in the fields, punching cows and breaking broncs" (9).[6] It is only gradually that the verbal narrative reveals what the drawings visualize: the lack of bonds between the father and the son. A yearning to bridge the gap turns out to be as much an undercurrent of T.S.'s story as is his sense of guilt and responsibility for Layton's death. The journey to Washington D.C. to collect the prize turns out to be also a quest for absolution and for the father's love and recognition.[7]

The point I want to make – once again – is that the images and the verbal narrative tell stories in complex, and intricate ways, sometimes concurrently, most often a-synchronously. Rather than merely illustrating the verbal narrative, the images are woven sometimes in a counterpoint-like manner, sometimes they create disjunctions, excess, or assonance. Such cross-pollinations between word and image are increasingly on the rise in contemporary novels.

It is time to return to my larger claim about the pictorial turn in the contemporary (print) novel. Those familiar with experimental postmodern fiction may object that rather than a shift, we could claim a continuity in the use of images in postmodern novels, such as, say, William Gass's *Willie Masters' Lonesome Wife* (1968) in that they foreground the materiality of the printed page and the physicality of the book, and encourage a discontinuous reading. These are valid observations. But the family resemblances between the look of the early postmodern novels

---

6   The "us" refers to the mother, Gracie, and T.S. This quotation needs little commentary in its employment of the cliché of the West that links the feminine to the domestic and cultural and the masculine to the physical and natural. The "Cowboy Code" and his own place in it is, in fact, one of T.S.'s major concerns.

7   An absolution is achieved as T.S., in a confession-like manner, tells the audience gathered to witness the prize-handing ceremony the story of what happened in the barn, admitting his guilt by saying at the end "I didn't mean to do it. I didn't, I didn't" (314). A short while later he meets his father who has come to the capital to fetch his son and, on seeing him, experiences an epiphany of sorts: "A thousand diagram's of Dr. Ekman's facial units could not capture the relief, the tenderness, the deep, deep love, bound in my father's face. And not just that: I realized that these emotions had *always* been there, they had just been hidden behind the curtains of his silent akimbo" (370). When, the father, in a gesture that resonates with a scene in the 1953 Western movie *Shane*, takes off his cowboy hat and puts it on T.S.'s head (374), the father-son bonding with all its Western overlays is completed and the novel ends. In retrospect, the lack of communication lines between himself and his father in the "Patterns of Cross-Talk" turns out to visualize T.S.'s emotional insecurity, his misreading of family dynamics, and a sense of alienation rather than a lack of fatherly affection.

and *HA!* or *The Selected Works of T.S. Spivet* should not obscure important differences between them.

The novels that are the object of my attention are published under different cultural, technological, and socio-economic conditions. This difference is, obviously, linked to the ubiquitous presence of computer technology and the dramatic impact of World Wide Web and the Internet. To fend off the threat of their extinction, print novels, as N. Katherine Hayles has indefatigably argued, appropriate one of the most salient features of the web – the mixture of word and image. Digital modes of production make the insertion of a variety of images both easier and economically viable; unlike in early postmodernism, pictorial material makes it into mass publications, not only into exclusive and avant-garde ones. Perhaps the most conspicuous difference between the novels written in early postmodernism and today is the fact that while experimental typography in the former was employed (mostly) to impede and even block sense-making processes, to signal the impotence of language, the pictorial in contemporary novels never obstructs reading; the verbal text is seldom – if ever – made illegible. Rather than frustrate, these post-postmodern novels provide delight and evoke wonder and curiosity; rather than deconstruct, they re-mix and re-make. While postmodernism drew upon such popular genres as the detective novel or science fiction, the novels of the "pictorial turn" draw sustenance from the entire spectrum of mass culture, particularly from popular art forms previously deemed to be trivial entertainment, targeting children, such as comics or pop-up books. What we may be witnessing, say some critics, is "a truce in [a] longstanding conflict … between so-called elite and mass cultures" (Michael Saler 3). If so, Johanna Drucker may be right when she says that "the most subversive act that fine art can currently perform may well be to show its own complicity with mainstream culture" (195).

This alignment of (high) culture with mass cultural values of pleasure, delight, joy, wonder, and enchantment signals a remarkable shift in contemporary sensibilities, a shift that makes it urgent to re-think – once again, for our time – the old belief that literary entertainment equates mindless escapism and passive consumption. Lest we dismiss the presence of images in contemporary novels as yet another symptom of our culture going juvenile and sanctioning bad taste, and to put the current trend in a broader historical perspective, we may do well to heed W.J.T. Mitchell's words that "The invention of new means of image production and reproduction, from the stamping of coins to the printing press to lithography, photography, film, video, and digital imagining, is often accompanied by a widespread perception that a 'pictorial turn' is taking place, often with the prediction of disastrous consequences for culture" ("Image" 37).

Works Cited

Drucker, Johanna. *Sweet Dreams: Contemporary Art and Complicity*. Chicago: U of Chicago P, 2005.

Groensteen, Thierry. *The System of Comics*. Transl. Bart Beaty and Nick Nyuyen. Jackson: UP of Mississippi, 2007.

Hayles, N. Katherine. *My Mother Was a Computer: Digital Subjects and Literary Texts*. Chicago: U of Chicago P, 2005.

Homel, David. "Attempting to Explain a Suicide." Rev. of *HA! A Self-Murder Mystery*, by Gordon Sheppard. *The Gazette* 1 November 2003. Web. 5 May 2010.

Larsen, Reif. *The Selected Works of T.S. Spivet*. New York: Penguin, 2009.

McCloud, Scott, writer and artist. *Understanding Comics: The Invisible Art*. Letters by Bob Lappan. New York: Harper Collins, 1993.

Mitchell, W.J.T. *Iconology*. Chicago: U of Chicago P, 1986.

—. "Image." *Critical Terms for Media Studies*. Eds. W.J.T. Mitchell and Mark B.N. Hansen. Chicago: U of Chicago P, 2010. 35-48.

—. *Picture Theory*. Chicago, U of Chicago P, 1994.

Mirzoeff, Nicholas, ed. *The Visual Culture Reader*. London: Routledge, 1998.

Saler, Michael. "Comic Turns: From Book-Burning and Prohibition to Pulitzer Prizes and Prestige; The Cultural Triumph of the 'Graphic Novel.'" Rev. of *The Ten-Cent Plague* by David Hajdu and *Maps and Legends*, by Michael Chabon. *TLS* 6 June 2008: 3-5.

Sheppard, Gordon. *HA! A Self-Murder Mystery*. Montreal: McGill-Queen's UP, 2003.

Stafford, Barbara Maria. *Good Looking: Essays on the Virtue of Images*. Cambridge, Mass.: MIT Press, 1996.

Stephens, Mitchell. *The Rise of the Image and the Fall of the Word*. New York: Oxford UP, 1998.

Byron and Latin-Levantine Europe

Sergio Perosa
University of Venice

> His port lay on the other side o' the isle.
> *Don Juan*, III, 19

1.

Historical circumstances and personal predilections drove Byron to skirt continental Europe: he was attracted by and sought a Mediterranean, peripheral, Latin-Levantine Europe, verging on the East. In his travels and in his poetry he circled round central Europe, from Scotland to the Caucasus, and back; he revelled in sunlit and exotic Mediterranean Europe, constantly seen in opposition to the cold, hypocritical, censorious and oppressive Northern climates.

For his first experience (1809-1811), central Europe was precluded to him: the Napoleonic wars were raging and Europe was under the rule of France, except for Portugal – which was in fact Byron's first stop. *He never visited Madrid, Paris or Berlin*: no traditional Grand Tour was possible for him. (His first wish had been to visit the Islamic world, Persia, India, which he never reached, stopping in Greece, then under the Ottoman Empire, and in Turkey.)

For his second experience, that of his final expatriation (1816-1823), he was refused a passport through France, where the Bourbons had been restored, and he had to cross the Netherlands and Belgium (which he did not like) in order the reach the South by the Rhine. He cuts through central Europe like a knife, as quickly as possible.[1]

Central Europe was then for him the place of war and desolation (as shown by long passages in *Childe Harold's Pilgrimage* Canto III,[2] on Waterloo and the

---

[1] See Andrew Rutherford, '"Samples of the Finest Orientalism": The Turkish Tales Revisited', and John Clubbe, 'By the Emperor Possessed: Byron and Napoleon in Italy and Greece (1816-1824)', both in *Byron and the Mediterranean World*, ed. Marius Byron Raizis, Athens, Hellenic Byron Society, 1995, pp. 13-23 e 105-116, also for what follows.

[2] On the following pages, *Childe Harold* = CH, *Don Juan* = DJ, with references and/or quotations identified by number of Canto and Stanza. No biographical specification is given, as they are available in many current editions. The same applies to quotations from Letters and Journals,

fall of Napoleon), the place of tyranny and oppression, which had spread to England. The centre of Europe known to Byron was that of non-historical Switzerland, whose landscape and scenery he cherished and admired, though he detested the country and its citizens ('Switzerland is a curst selfish, swinish country of brutes, placed in the most romantic region of the world', letter of 19/9/1821 to Thomas Moore), and the Alps, which struck him as the place of transcendence and the sublime (Journal of September 1816 e CH III, 62: 'the Alps, / The palaces of Nature, whose vast walls / Have pinnacled in clouds their snowy scalps, / And throned Eternity in icy halls / Of cold sublimity'), and of titanic rebellion (as for instance in his *Manfred*).

On his first trip Byron celebrates Southern Europe: Portugal and what we could call 'Moorish' Spain (he duly abhors Gibraltar and Malta, two British outposts with all the *cant* of the fatherland), and the deep fascination of the Levant: Albania, with its mingling of peoples, Ottoman Greece and Turkey – a kind of Eurasia, we would say today, the borderline of two worlds. They were the places of the sun, love and classicism, deeply wounded by foreign oppression: a mixture of lights and shadows, of European and Oriental aspects, so deeply attractive also because their beauty and their historical and literary associations are an inducement to writing: 'If I am a poet … the air of Greece has made me one', he confessed to Trelawney. Even in Cephalonia, at the end of his life, he felt 'quieted … enough to be able to write' (Journal of 17/10/1823).[3]

His second trip, too, avoids the historical centre of Europe, leaving France and Spain on one side, Prussia on the other: it cuts through the two blocks of the Holy Alliance (again, abhorred by Byron: 'Spitting in the face of mankind, at Bourbons' restoration', Journal of 19/4/1814). If he feels and sings the flat desolation of Belgium, the romantic quiet of the Rhine, the peace and at the same time the sentimental congestion of Geneva and the Leman, he finds in Italy – and especially in Venice – a glaring and desolate co-existence of East and West, and the stir of revolutionary activities, which would eventually lead him to organise his expedition for the independence of Greece. The places seen as anti-British are now those where the aspirations to political freedom sway the scene.

I must proceed with ruthless exemplifications.

Byron tells us that he wrote in the heat of the moment the first two cantos of *Childe Harold. Harold* '[were] written, for the most part, amidst the scenes

---

which are simply identified with dates. For the readers' convenience, I may refer sometimes to Lord Byron, *Selected Prose*, ed. Peter Gunn, Harmondsworth, Penguin, 1972 (= SP).

3   See Leslie A. Marchand, *Byron's Poetry*, London, John Murray, 1965, p. 124; SP, p. 514 and *Selected Letters and Diaries*, ed. Leslie A. Marchand, Cambridge, The Belknap Press of Harvard U. P., 1982, pp. 299-300.

which it attempts to describe', Preface of 1812, and that he never revised: 'I am like the tyger (in poesy), if I miss my first Spring, I go growling back to my Jungle. There is no second. I can't correct; I can't, and I won't' (letter of 18/11/1820 to John Murray).

As the age did not enjoy the use of telephones, cameras, television, and iPods, but must pre-eminently rely on ocular descriptions, Byron writes of Latin-Levantine Europe in long, splendid letters, in his journals, and almost simultaneously in his poetry. We must take note of this double register: splendid prose expansions on one side, 'live' presentations in poetry on the other, which rarely diverge, and for the most part coincide.

A further characteristic must be kept in mind, even when I do not refer overtly to it. The places which Byron describes and immortalises are not primarily (with a few exceptions) geographic places. They are shaped and *constituted* by historical and literary incrustations, concretions, conglomerations; they bear the burden of the past and of uncanny presences which are almost everywhere.

'Incrustation' is the word used by John Ruskin to characterise Venetian architecture ('The whole architecture of Venice is architecture of incrustation .... the Venetian habitually incrusted his work with nacre; he built his houses, even the meanest, as if he had been a shell-fish' (i.e. roughly inside, mother-of-pearl on the surface).[4] I apply the term advisedly to the places that Byron visited and described as a conglomerate of literary and historical presences ('Ages and realms are crowded in this span', he specifies in CH IV, 109) in a way which I find extremely modern, which would be taken up by great writers and poets after him, and in which an extraordinary *inner* tension or a dialectic of opposites is at work.

Historical events had reduced the Latin-Levantine countries to places of desolation, decay, political oppression, decadence and ruins, strongly appealing to the romantic imagination ('To meditate amongst decay, and stand / A ruin amidst ruins', is Byron's description of it in CH IV, 25). But gleams of past glory and a sublime beauty of landscape shone there, thanks to the thick historical and literary stratifications that writers and poets of all times had deposited on them.

It is an aspect of fundamental importance, and I anticipate two statements which seem conclusive to me:

But am I to be told that the "Nature" of Attica would be *more* poetical without the "art" of the Acropolis? Of the temples of Theseus? And of the still all Greek and glorious monuments of her exquisitely artificial genius? Ask the traveller which strikes him as most poetical, the Parthenon, or the rock on which he stands? The COLUMNS of Cape Colonna, or the Cape itself? (and so forth).

---

4   *The Complete Works of John Ruskin*, ed. E. T. Cook and Alexander Wedderburn, Oxford, George Allen, 1903-12, vol. IX, p. 323.

Nature, exactly, simply, barely, Nature, will make no great artist of any kind, and least of all a poet – the most artificial, perhaps, of all artists in his very essence. With regard to natural imagery, the poets are obliged to take some of their best illustrations from *art*.[5]

Venice can be written about only in so far as Shakespeare and Otway, Schiller and Goethe and others have written of it: their echoes are part of the city itself. The same applies to Greece: Homer and Sappho, poets and playwrights, even more than nature, have created the landscape. Byron evokes and describes those places, their traditional or unusual sights, as a conglomerate of history and literature, imbued with natural, as well as superimposed poetry – adding *his own* literary and poetic incrustations.

He was never a tourist – though he was involved in what we would call today sexual tourism, and according to our laws would have been sent straight to jail on charges of paedophilia abroad. The English Peer, who travelled in state in a Napoleonic coach, considered himself a cosmopolitan, rather than an expatriate, or indeed a citizen of the world: 'I feel myself so much a citizen of the world, that the spot where I can enjoy a delicious climate, and every luxury … will always be a country to me' (letter of 28/1/1811 to his mother).[6] When young, he had claimed with some exaggeration: 'All countries are much the same in my eyes' (letter of 3/5/10 to Henry Drury); towards the end of his life he repeated: 'I am a Citizen of the World – all countries are the same to me!' (letter of 10/12/1819 to Teresa Guiccioli), and later in his life 'as for myself, *I am of no country*' (letter of 22/4/23 to Count Alfred D'Orsay).

2.

I will trace – in a selective way – some of these itineraries and dialectical confrontations.

The first impact in CH (which opens on an invocation to the Hellenic muse and a farewell to his country: 'My native Land – Good Night!', I 13) is with Cintra (I, 18), a kind of 'glorious Eden' among squalor, but writers such as Camoes, Beckford and Southey are immediately recalled. The beauty of Seville is under the shadow of the battle of Talavera. Cadiz is the city of love (I, 65) and

---

5   *Letter … on the Rev. W. L. Bowles's Strictures on the Life and Writings of Pope,* an essay published in 1821, in SP, pp. 399 and 401.

6   See Lesile A. Marchand, *Byron: A Portrait,* Chicago, Chicago U. P., 1970, p. 95, for the exact date, and p. 67.

beautiful women. After Canto 84 Byron meant to insert his song 'The Girl of Cadiz' where we now have 'To Inez' instead:[7]

> Oh never talk again to me
> Of northern climes and British ladies;
> It has not been your lot to see,
> Like me, the lovely Girl of Cadiz.

But all this was already in letters to his mother and to his friends: 'The village of Cintra in Estremadura is the most beautiful, perhaps, in the world' (letter of 16/7/09 to Francis Hodgson); 'Seville is a beautiful town ... Cadiz, sweet Cadiz, is the most delightful town I ever beheld, very different from our English cities in every respect except cleanliness (and it is as clean as London), but still very beautiful, and full of the finest women in Spain, the Cadiz belles being the Lancashire witches of their land' (17/8/09).

In another long letter to his mother (12/11/09) and in CH II 38ff., his description of Albania ('where Iskander rose /.../ thou rugged nurse of savage men') emphasised ethnic hybridization:

> The Turk, the Greek, the Albanian, and the Moor,
> Here mingled in their many-hued array (II 57);

> The wild Albanian kirtled to his knee
> ………………………………..
> The crimson-scarfèd men of Macedon;
> The Delhi with his cap of terror on,
> And crooked glaive; the lively, supple Greek;
> The swarthy Nubia's mutilated son;
> The bearded Turk ... (II 58).

It is a conjunction of East and West, of the picturesque and the romantic. This rough place of strangely-dressed adventurers and warlords reminded Byron of Scotland – which throws a strange light on his anti-British claims and his nostalgia for home. Here, in the Levant, he seems to come full circle with the places of his youth (as will happen in *Don Juan*).[8]

---

7   Marchard, *Byron's Poetry*, cit., p. 43. – Byron's itinerary is carefully described in Simon Cheetham, *Byron in Europe. In Childe Harold's Footsteps*, Oxford, Oxford U. P., 1988.

8   'Albania' comprised 'part of Macedonia, Illyria, Chaonia, and Epiria', Byron specified in a Note. As for the analogy with Scotland: 'The Arnaouts, or Albanese, struck me forcibly by their resemblance to the Highlanders of Scotland, in dress, figure, and manner of living. Their very mountains seemed Caledonia, with a kinder climate'; they wore kilts and their dialect had a 'Celtic' sound; they are slim and robust, wild and bloody, detested and feared by their neighbours. – See Kirsten Daly, 'Nostalgia and *Childe Harold's Pilgrimage*', in *Byron and the Mediterranean World*, cit., pp. 153-66.

Again: Greece bears the painful stigma of Turkish domination: 'Fair Greece! Sad relic of departed worth! / Immortal, though no more; though fallen, great!' (II, 73), but is redeemed by the purity of the landscape and the beauty of its islands and its historical places. Ithaca, Lesbos, Leucadia, Athens, Cape Sunium (a magnificent solitary retreat), the plain of Troy are an uninterrupted hymn to the charm of sunlit regions and to the roots of Europe:

> Where'er we tread 'tis haunted, holy ground
> … one vast realm of wonder spreads around,
> And all the Muses' tales seem truly told,
> Till the sense aches with gazing to behold
> The scenes our earliest dreams have dwelt upon.' (CH II, 88)

Quotations could multiply, and show that the enthusiasm for Greek associations goes hand in hand with a rather perfunctory perception of the Islamic places that Byron had set out to seek. Constantinople, for instance, in CH II and in the letters (e.g. to his mother, 28/6/10), seems more of a touristy discovery than a recognition of the heart – as had been the case, instead, with Greek classical sights.

This is borne out by the fact that Byron's *Turkish Tales* are rather mannered performances, explorations of the merely pictorial: no intertextuality, no historical and literary associations are detectable. It is significant that precisely in these Turkish tales some of the most beautiful evocations of Mediterranean beauty are found in *The Giaour*, Greece is unforgettably presented as a beauty savouring of death, a land of heroes of whom nothing is left; in *The Bride of Abydos*, the land of the sun is evoked with a clear echo of Goethe's famous line 'Kennst du das Land, wo die Zitronen blühen'; *The Corsair* opens with an unforgettable description of a sunset in Greece.[9]

Conversely, here is the centre of desolation of Continental Europe:

> Stop! – for thy tread is on an Empire's dust!
> An Earthquake's spoil is sepulchred below! (CH, III 17)

> And Harold stands upon this place of skulls,
> The grave of France, the deadly Waterloo! (III 18)

---

9   See Marchand, *Byron's Poetry*, p. 66, and p. 60: 'The lyric descriptions of Greece in the Oriental tales are among the "Beauties of Byron" so admired in his own days'. – On Byron's 'Orientalism', Naji B. Oneijan, *A Compendium of Eastern Elements in Byron's Oriental Tales*, New York, Peter Lang, 1999; *Byron and Orientalism,* ed. Peter Cochran, Newcastle, Cambridge Scholar Press, 2006 (a highly articulated and well-balanced study); Nigel Leask, *British Romantic Writers and the East: Anxieties of Empire*, Cambridge, Cambridge U. P., 1992. – In Byron's *Hebrew Melodies*, too, written for music on Old-Testament topics, we find the motif of desolation encroaching on past glory, as for instance in 'The Wild Gazelle' ('The cedars were on Lebanon, / But Judah's statelier maids are gone!'), 'Oh, Weep for Those', 'On Jordan's Banks', 'By the Waters of Babylon', etc.

And thus the heart will break, yet brokenly live on. (III 32)

There is a very life in our despair,
Vitality of poison. (III 34)

Here the motif of Napoleon's grandiose fall is inserted: his presence is endlessly reflected as in a broken mirror (III 33), while the loss of 'revolutionary' hopes becomes a lament of the *sic transit gloria mundi*.[10]

Lake Leman instead lives thanks to its strong literary incrustations. This was already intimated in the 'Epistle to Augusta' (1816: 'Here are the Alpine landscapes which create/A fund for contemplation/.../Here to be lonely is not desolate' (stanza 8), while in 'Sonnet to Lake Leman' (1816) we have:

Rousseau – Voltaire – our Gibbon – and De Staël –
Leman! These names are worthy of thy shore,
Thy shore of names like these! wert thou no more
Their memory thy remembrance would recall.

The shore of the lake, the geographical place itself, would be dead without those literary presences, which make them what they are and immortalize them.

In the 'Alpine Journal' of 1816 and in contemporary letters we find a perfect correspondence: 'Tomorrow we go to Meillerei, and Clarens, and Vevey, with Rousseau in hand, to see his scenery, according to his delineation in his Héloïse, now before me' (letter of 23/6/16 to John Hobhouse); 'I have traversed all Rousseau's ground, with the *Héloïse* before me; and am struck, to a degree, with the force and accuracy of his descriptions and the beauty of the reality. Meillerei, Clarens, and Vevay [*sic*], and the Château de Chillon ... I have finished a third canto of *Childe Harold*' (letter of 27/6/16, to John Murray). Rousseau's descriptions, that is, prevail on the reality of the place, and the *literary* experience of them leads to his own writing.[11]

Similarly, towards the end of CH III, 68-105, Lake Leman is identified with a *literary* rather than geographic landscape: it is primarily the land of that 'self-

---

10 On the Bourbon Restoration and the conditions imposed on Europe by the 'Holy Alliance': 'here we are, retrograding, to the dull, stupid, old system, – balance of Europe – poising straws upon kings' noses, instead of wringing them off! Give me a republic, or a despotism of one .... A republic! ... Rome, Greece, Venice, France, Holland, America, our short (eheu!) Commonwealth' (Journal of 23/11/1913). A violent attack on George III and his ministers, as agents of tyranny and oppression, wais launched in *The Vision of Judgment* (1821).

11 See also in his Journal of 18/9/1816: 'our Guide full of *Rousseau*, whom he is eternally confounding with *St Preux* [in *La Nouvelle Héloïse*], and mixing the man with the book'; soon after, the young paysanne is 'beautiful as Julie herself'... – Of course, Byron warned the reader: 'I by no means intend to identify myself with *Harold*, but to *deny* all connection with him ... I would not be such a fellow as I have made my hero for the world' (letter of 31/10/1811 to Robert Charles Dallas), and in the 1812 Preface he stated that his hero was a fictitious character.

torturing sophist, wild Rousseau' (77), a singer of love and a revolutionary, who remained there as a *constituent* presence:

> Clarens! Sweet Clarens, birthplace of deep Love!
> Thine air is the young breath of passionate thought;
> Thy trees take root in Love; the snows above
> The very Glaciers have his colours caught. (CH, III 99)

> Clarens! By heavenly feet thy paths are trod, –
> Undying Love's ... (100)

Clarens proves the birthplace of *amour-passion*, which has taken root there; Rousseau has coloured the very snows and glaciers. In fact:

> All things are here of *him*
> ....
> Offering him, and his, a populous solitude. (101)

> 'Twas not for fiction chose Rousseau this spot,
> Peopling it with affections; but he found
> It was the scene which Passion must allot
> To the Mind's purified beings. (104)

> Lausanne and Ferney! Ye have been the abodes
> Of names which unto you bequeath'd a name (105, etc.).

Passion and literature are not a fiction: they have imbued and saturated those places.

In Canto IV, to move quickly on, Venice exhibits an alluring mixture of East and West: '[it] has always haunted me the most after the East' (letter of 25/11716 to John Murray); 'it has always been (next to the East) the greenest island of my imagination' (letter of 17/11/16 to Thomas Moore). Like Greece (a connection is established in IV 16), Venice and more generally Italy appear as a commingling of splendour and death, beauty and decay. (As I have written elsewhere at length, Byron opened the way for a long nineteenth-century tradition of 'deaths in Venice'.)

In her 'dying Glory', 'the exhaustless East / Pour'd in her lap all gems in sparkling showers' (CH IV 2); 'In Venice Tasso's echoes are no more /.../ Her palaces are crumbling to the shore /.../ But beauty still is here? (3). The dying city 'Sinks, like a seaweed, into whence she rose!' (13), and an air of utter desolation hovers everywhere: 'her dead Doges are declined to dust /.../ empty halls, / Thin streets /.../ Have flung a desolate cloud o'er Venice' lovely walls' (15). There is beauty in her decay, and attraction in her desolation. ('I have been familiar with ruins too long to dislike desolation', Byron wrote (letter of 17/11/1816 to Thomas Moore)...

The same vision, but with a strong political connotation, would inspire his *Ode on Venice* of 1818, where already the 'marble walls / Are level with the waters' and 'Thirteen hundred years / Of wealth and glory turn'd to dust and tears', I, ll.

1-2, 15-16; there the lament on the loss of Glory, Empire and Liberty (III, ll. 1-2), however, is projected on the hope of republican freedom offered by America, which culminates in the last line: 'One freeman more, America, to thee!'

This is made possible because in Venice, as in Greece, the landscape is imbued with historical reverberations, and the vision is marked by literary recollections. 'It is a poetical place; and classical, to us, from Shakespeare and Otway', Byron had written to Thomas Moore (5/12/ 1816), adding that he had not yet 'sinned against it in verse', but 'sinned' profusely in the poem:

> Shylock and the Moor,
> And Pierre, cannot be swept or worn away –
> The keystones of the arch! though all were o'er,
> For us repeopled were the solitary shore. (IV 4)

> And Otway, Radcliffe, Schiller, Shakespeare's art,
> Had stamp'd her image in me, and even so,
> Although I found her thus, we did not part;
> Perchance even dearer in her days of woe,
> Than when she was a boast, a marvel, and a show. (CH, IV18)

(We have two Venetian characters from Shakespeare and Pierre, the hero of Thomas Otway's *Venice Preserv'd* (1682), while the last-but-one line echoes what had previously been said of Greece: 'And yet how lovely in this age of woe', II 85.)

In Italy, where Byron intends 'To meditate amongst, and stand /A ruin amidst ruins' (IV 25), the mixture of beauty and decay is even stronger:

> thou who hast
> The fatal gift of beauty, which became
> A funeral dower of present woes and past,
> ………………..
> Oh, God, that thou wert in thy nakedness
> Less lovely or more powerful. (IV 42)

Rome is the epitome of such visitations, because there the death-and-splendour oxymoron and historical and literary incrustations are everywhere present. Florence was *shaped* by the triad Dante, Petrarca, Boccaccio, 56-59;[12] Rome, the 'city of the soul' and 'Niobe of nations' (78) 'is as the desert, where we steer / Stumbling o'er recollections' (81). And, as we may well expect,

---

12 The same applies to other places and cities: Sirmione is recalled for the sake of Catullus, who with Claudian and Shakespeare had done more for Verona than she had done for herself (letter of 6/11/1816 to Thomas Moore). – Rather strangely, little is said of Rome in the letters (for fear of Papal censorship? or because, as Byron wrote to sorellastra Augusta on 10/5/1817, 'Of Rome I say nothing – you can read the Guide-book – which is very accurate'.

Alas, for Tully's voice and Virgil's lay,
And Livy's pictured page! – but these shall be
Her resurrection; all beside – decay. (82)

Such examples become a crescendo: 'Ages and realms are crowded in this span' (109, as we already saw). The burden of incrustations and stratifications, of ruins and fascinating decay is overwhelming, and it shapes Byron's vision of Southern Europe. This may be the reason why the poem ends on a typical invocation to the desert: 'Oh! that the Desert were my dwelling-place /.../ That I might all forget the human race' (177); 'There is a pleasure in the pathless woods, / There is a rapture on the lonely shore' (178), and on a prolonged celebration of the Ocean, which sweeps away and cancels all actions and the history of man. (179-84, 182 in particular).[13]

3.

Towards the end of his Venetian visit, however, Byron has been domesticated, 'almost inoculated into a family' (31/8/1820 to Thomas Moore); 'I am in love, and tired of promiscuous concubinage, and have now an opportunity of settling for life' (to John Hobhouse, 6/4/1819: in fact 'strictest adultery' substitutes for his previous 'promiscuous harlotry').[14] To his dismay, he was in danger of becoming a *cavalier servente*: 'I have been an intriguer, a husband, a whoremonger, and now I am a Cavalier Servente – by the holy!' (he recriminated, letter of 3/10/1819 to Hobhouse). Moreover, Ravenna, Pisa and Genoa, where he must follow Teresa Guiccioli, his 'last attachment', are snowy and windy cities, reminding him of London and Northern climates.

Yet his burlesque poems and *Don Juan*, too, which was begun in his Venetian period, present comparable views of Latin-Levantine Europe.

In *Beppo: a Venetian Story* (1818), Venice is a cosmopolitan and multicultural world, in line with a long tradition which in England begins with Thomas Coryat's *Crudities* (1611) and Shakespeare; its Carnival exhibits 'Masks of all times and nations, Turks and Jews, /.../ Greeks, Romans, Yankee-doodles, and Hindoos' (stanza 3). Venice is, above all, the place where East and West meet, where the rite of drinking coffee unites Christians and Turks ('A beverage for Turks and Christians both', 91). Beppo, the husband who is believed to be lost, reappears as a Turk: 'And are you *really, truly*, now a Turk?' (92), and though he

---

13 On this aspect of Byron's poetics, Michael Gassenmeier, 'Lord Byron's Acquatic Experience of the Politics of Acquamania', in *Byron and the Mediterranean World*, cit., pp. 189-200: he totally surrendered to the ocean.

14 See in the catalogue of the exhibition for the 150th anniversary of his death, *Byron on the Continent*, New York, The Carl H. Pforzheimer Library and The New York Public Library, 1974, p. 62.

changes his dress, remains, as it were, suspended between two conditions. National boundaries fade away.[15]

Byron's long, unfinished poem *Don Juan*, equally inspired by a saucy and hilarious Muse ('mine is not a weeping Muse', he warns you, II, 16), is also projected on a Latin-Levantine background and set in a sunlit, amorous South: in the first two cantos, both are relished in opposition to Northern coldness.

Canto I is set in Andalusia, and its heroine (Donna Julia) is said to have some Moorish blood in her veins. Canto II, after a tempest and a shipwreck, presents Eastern Greek islands and, in particular, the Cyclads as a kind of Earthly Paradise of spotless love (Haidée, who is half Moorish; the third heroine we meet, irascible and dominating Gulbeyaz, will be all Turkish). Canto III deals with experiences and recollections of the Levant (Albania, Ali Pasha, etc.); it revels in the fascination of the Orient, but at its centre we find the famous celebration of the 'Isles of Greece', still a mixture of decay and splendour, glory and degradation, as incrusted with literature and history, legend and myth, as is to be expected:

> The Isles of Greece, the Isles of Greece!
>> Where burning Sappho loved and sung,
> Where grew the art of War and Peace,
>> Where Delos rose, and Phoebus sprung!
> Eternal summer gilds them yet,
> But all, except their Sun, I set (inserted after stanza 86),

while at Cape Sunium Byron invokes, in the first person: 'There, swan-like, let me sing and die' (III 16).

In Canto IV we move to Africa and Asia Minor, to the plain of Troy, with Don Juan being made a slave, and to a celebration – much to the point for today's readers – of the mixture or commingling of Europe and Asia, a kind of 'Eurasia', as I intimated before. At Istanbul,

> The European with the Asian shore
>> Sprinkled with palaces
> ....
>> Sophia's Cupola with golden gleam,
> The cypress groves, Olympus high and hoar. (V, 3)

> 'Tis a grand sight from off 'the Giant's Grave'
>> To watch the progress of those rolling seas
> Between the Bosphorus, as they lash and lave
>> Europe and Asia. (V, 5).[16]

---

15 See Malcolm Kelsall, "'Once did she hold the gorgeous east in fee ...'": Byron's Venice and Oriental Empire', in *Byron and the Mediterranean World*, cit., pp. 47-56.

16 Here, too, we find literary incrustations: the details of the panorama 'present the very view / Which charmed the charming Mary Montague' (V, 3: the author of *Turkish Letters*, 1763); and

In Canto VI, overcoming the geographic limits I set myself, the poem reaches as far as the siege of Ismail, then to the Caucasus and the court of Catherine of Russia (IX), where the circle drawn around continental Europe is, as it were, completed. In Canto IX, Byron openly addresses the thorny and for him painful question of political restoration in Europe: 'You have repair'd Legitimacy's crutch' (IX, 3), he rebukes Wellington, and wonders who may really have won at Waterloo, answering that REACTION did: Napoleon *might have* freed Europe from tyrants, but he, too, became one.

Conversely, at one point Byron has Moscow and Madrid almost shake hands ('with the addition of a slight pelisse, / Madrid's and Moscow's climes were of a piece', X, 30), and from a Russia barely sketched as a setting, we fly to the Scotland of his adolescence, now affectionately recognized: 'I am half a Scotch by birth, and bread / A whole one', X, 17; 'And love the land of "mountain and of flood"', X, 18). This final jump to Scotland really closes his circling of continental Europe.[17]

In the final 'English' Cantos a satire of his far-from-sunny and far-from-romantic motherland prevails: 'The English winter – ending in July, / To recommence in August', XIII, 42);

> the shore
> Of white cliffs, white necks, blue eyes, bluer stockings –
> Tithes, taxes, duns – and doors with double knockings (XII, 67),

where political oppression, *cant*, and the literary opportunism of Lake and laureate poets prevails. The only way-out is again into the Ocean ('That Watery Outline of Eternity /.../ Which ministers unto the Soul's delight', XV, 2).

Here Byron becomes more factual and direct, less fanciful: he himself, rather than an 'invented' character (as was the case towards the end of CH), takes over. His Latin-Levantine Europe was an image halfway between fancy and reality; his Great Britain is a place to write about from a distance, with pent-up bitterness and fury. It seems a late confirmation of Byron's idea that his poetry would be

---

here, too, as in the *Turkish Tales*, for the descriptions of Asiatic places Byron relied mainly on book sources, as for instance *A Narrative of Ten Years' Residence at Tripoli in Africa* (1816) by Richard Tully, or *Travels in Various Countries of Europe, Asia and Africa* by Edward Daniel Clark, above all vol. 3 (1817). See *Byron and Orientalism*, cit., pp. 102-07, 123-36, and passim.

17 See Tom Hubbard, 'George Gordon Byron, Scotland and Europe: An Antithetical Mind', in *Alba Literaria. A History of Scottish Literature*, ed. Marco Fazzini, Venezia Mestre, Amos Edizioni, 2005, pp. 313-23, for whom 'Byron's "antithetical mind" creates a rendezvous for Europe's geocultural polarities' (p. 318): in DJ 'all four poles of Europe are brought together', and a North-South, but also East-West synthesis is reached. – In *Mazeppa* (1819) we fly from Poland to Ukraine, from the Caucasus to Tartary. R. L. Stevenson, too, would equate the islands of Polynesia with those of Scotland.

based on facts, rather than on fictions: 'I hate things *all fiction* ... there should always be some foundation of fact for the most airy fabric, and pure invention is but the talent of a liar' (to John Murray, 2/4/1817); 'Almost all *Don Juan* is *real* life, either my own or from people I knew' (23/8/1821, to Murray).[18]

4.

To escape *ennui* and the fear of being 'gentrified', in his last period Byron accentuates the value of political engagement and direct *action*, in preparation for his military expedition in Greece, anticipating Gabrile D'Annunzio's postures a century later at Fiume. 'One hates an author that's *all author*', he had written in *Beppo* (stanza 75), and in his Journal: 'Who would write, who had any thing better to do? .... 'Actions – actions', I say, and not writing, – least of all, rhyme' (24/11/1813, SP. 171); against depression, 'Philosophy would be in vain – let us try action' (20/8/1819, SP 311), while to his physician in Genoa he would claim 'a man ought to do something more for mankind than write verses'.[19]

Under the teasing and mocking tone of *Don Juan* and other poems, under the endless 'licences' he indulges in, a strangely 'moral' note emerges – his exaltation of political liberty, his indignation for, his sympathy and identification with oppressed European countries – Spain, to some extent, but above all Italy and Greece – and his willingness to contribute personally to their liberation would lead him to his early death in Missolonghi.

This is a notable aspect, and I left it for my conclusion.

Let us be very clear. The English Peer in the role of the revolutionary is in the vanguard of a long and often stale tradition of what we would call 'radical chic' today. As he wrote of his hero Lara 'What cared he for the freedom of the crowd? / He raised the humble but to break the proud' (*Lara*, X, 9). The enlightened aristocrat was to lead 'the mob', who would not know what to do without him (his expedition in Greece is a classic example).

Byron proved himself a 'radical' in his first and only speech in The House of Lords (27/2/1812) on the 'Frame-Work Bill', when he spoke against the death penalty which was proposed for workers who destroyed mechanical devices

---

18 Conversely, he had also written: 'I began a comedy, and burnt it because the scene ran into *reality*; a novel, for the same reason. In rhyme, I can keep away from the facts' (see Marchand, *Byron's Poetry*, cit., p. 163).

19 See Marchand, *Byron. A Portrait,* cit., p. 395. – As for Byron's *ante litteram* 'dannunzianesimo', he had designed uniforms, classical crests and helmets for himself, armed a ship of his own, not to mention the violent and untrustworthy followers he chose, though he did more for the cause of liberty in Greece than anybody else.

depriving them of their work, and hated tyrannical rulers: his sympathy and hardly-disguised identification with Napoleon was part of his radicalism.[20] He is a republican: 'give me a republic, or a despotism of one', he wrote (Journal, 23/11/1813). He hates the hypocrisy and *cant* which he finds so rampant in his country; he hates the Bourbons, the Holy Alliance, the so-called balance of Europe, the Pope's oppressive rule, the Turks who humiliate Greece – but like any 'radical chic' he dreams of revolution 'bypassing' the bourgeoisie and political parties. He is all for *individual* and isolated action. He identifies with the uprooted, Promethean, rebel without a country who appears so often in his poetry: Cain, Manfred, the Corsair, Lara, Alpo.

His only positive political leaders, besides Napoleon, who was in any case 'compromised' by his despotic rule, are American leaders: Benjamin Franklin, Bolivar, Washington ('the tyrant-tamer', in *The Age of Bronze,* stanza 10), even 'General' Daniel Boon [sic], 'back-woodsman of Kentucky' and 'happiest amongst mortals anywhere', who features in some stanzas of DJ (VIII, 61ff.). America was for him, as for Goethe, the truest land of liberty (CH IV, 96).

With Italy and Greece, however, Byron was politically engaged, *engagé.* His radicalism becomes a component of his vision. After two centuries, his hymns and paeans for the liberation of oppressed people may ring a hackneyed note. But Byron's Italy is unequivocally linked with his involvement with the Carbonari (he significantly joined the sect of the *Mericani*), who patronized his house, claimed protection and funding, which he awarded with a mixture of superiority and annoyance (he regarded them as sporting revolutionaries).[21] In his letters and Journals of 1820-21, he shows a direct involvement in the cause: 'Naples is revolutionized, and the ferment is among the Romagnuoles, by far the bravest and the most original of the present Italians' (letter of 22/7/1820 to John Murray), and in October 1820 (or possibly 1821) he wrote a proclamation 'Agli insorti napoletani'.

Italy is 'sad' on account of her unsolved political bondage (CH IV, 42-43), and so is Greece, where Byron, however, found factions rather than a nation

---

20 The speech is reprinted in SP, pp. 107-111. For his identification with Napoleon, see Marchand, *Byron's Poetry*, cit., p. 48 and *passim*; Marchand, *Byron's Portrait*, cit., pp. 163-65, 366, and others; also Journal of 18/2/1814, of 9/4/1814, etc.; his ambition, 'if any, would be *aut Caesar aut nihil*' (Journal of 23/11/1813). Napoleon is evoked in CH III and *passim*, in DJ XI and *passim*, and in many other works, from 'Ode to Napoleon' to *Manfred, Mazeppa, The Age of Bronze, The Vision of Judgment,* etc.. Byron travelled in a stately, 'Napoleonic' coach. – On the general subject, Malcolm Kelsall, *Byron's Politics*, Hemel Hampstead, Harvester, 1987.

21 'I suppose that they consider me a depôt, to be sacrificed, in case of accidents. It is no great matter, supposing that Italy could be liberated, who or what is sacrificed. It is a great object – the very *poetry* of politics. Only think – a free Italy!!! Why, there has been nothing like it since the days of Augustus' (Journal, 18/2/1821); also, Marchand, *Byron's Portrait*, cit., p. 341.

(Journal in Cephalonia, 28/9/1823). He had lamented her servitude and expressed a hope for her resurrection, for instance, in CH II, 84: 'Can man its shatter'd spendour renovate, / Recall its virtues back, and vanquish Time and Fate?'. Yet, with all her cultural and historical incrustations and stratifications and her present decay, Greece, even more than Italy, offered a challenge to renovation (as witnessed by his last letters and Journals of 1822-23, and by the expedition which he organized).

In conclusion, I would then submit that if Byron's view and descriptions of Latin-Levantine Europe live to this day as a conglomeration of historical and literary stratifications, of free usages and sunlit beauty, a submerged current runs through them, suggesting a hope for and a possibility of redemption. Paradoxically, it is as if the birth of a new world were envisaged around the grim reality of continental Europe: the peripheral Latin-Levantine countries, which he cherished and evoked so well in his writings, might indeed prove the redemption of Europe itself.

Who Owns Britain? S. T. Coleridge and the National Trust

Klaus Stierstorfer
University of Münster

1. Prologue: The Foundation of the National Trust

The National Trust is one of Britain's most important Charities today, with a membership of more than 3.5 million. According to its programme, it "works to preserve and protect the coastline, countryside and buildings of England, Wales and Northern Ireland".[1] Its birth and baptism date from the late nineteenth century, but its underlying concept can be traced back, I will argue in the following, yet another century, to Samuel Taylor Coleridge. Pursuing this trajectory back to Coleridge and his poetic approach to the question of property can, I hope to show, highlight central issues of the Victorian social, legal and poetic imagination.

The need for an institution like the National Trust became stridently obvious when in 1884 the owner of Sayes Court in Deptford, East London, agreed, after some prodding by social activists, to hand over his manorial gardens to the public. The local situation at this time was remembered by the social activist Frederick Ernest Green (1867-1922) in his book *Surrey Hills* published in 1915:

> The once green "pasture land and orchard" is now a wilderness of brick and mortar, where 100,000 persons inhabit the closely packed, mean streets. 100,000 human beings struggling, fighting, cringing, thieving for their daily bread, packed together within interminable streets without breathing room, without sunlight, without libraries, without recreation grounds, without baths, without the scent of flowers or the perfect perfume of pine woods or the song of birds.[2]

Green claims to have approached W. J. Evelyn, the proprietor of the local manorial grounds and a Victorian descendant of the illustrious 17th-century diarist John Evelyn who had designed the garden. In a letter Green asked Evelyn to present Deptford's last open space, Sayes Court (the manorial house had been pulled down in the eighteenth century), as a recreation ground for the benefit of the

---

1   See http://www.nationaltrust.org.uk/main/w-trust/w-thecharity/w-thecharity_our-present/w-what_we_do.htm; last accessed 1 December 2010.
2   Frederick Ernest Green, *The Surrey Hills* (London: Chatto & Windus, 1915), 122f.

people living in these miserable conditions. The squire eventually agreed, and a green spot of eleven acres has survived on this site to this very day.

This move to create breathing space for the working masses was in a tradition of campaigning, well established by the end of the nineteenth century, for public rights in commons, footpaths and urban spaces. Here, Britain's earliest formally recognized organisation, the Commons Preservation Society, founded in 1865 and still in existence today as the Open Spaces Society,[3] had been active for several decades. The transfer of Sayes Court to the public, which Green claims to have initiated, developed, almost by accident, into a major impact for expanding this movement. For W. J. Evelyn, when finally persuaded to abandon his rights to the grounds, had a caveat, as Green reports from a conversation with Evelyn:[4]

> "Well," he [Evelyn] continued, after pondering for a few moments, "I shall let the people of Deptford have the use of Sayes Court, but I shall not, as you suggest, hand it over to the County Council."

This hesitancy on Evelyn's side triggered a search for an alternative legal solution for this property. The query was referred to Octavia Hill (1838-1912) who, with the help of John Ruskin, had risen to fame as a social reformer by developing a method of providing property for housing the poor.[5] As a member of the Commons Preservation Society, Hill had also campaigned for turning disused London burial grounds and other available sites into playgrounds and recreation areas for the people in her housing projects. The quandary Hill had to face in the case of Sayes Court was the lack of an organisation which had the legal powers to secure the property for preservation. She turned to Sir Robert Hunter (1844-1913), whom, in the partnership of Fawcett, Horne, and Hunter, she had come to know as solicitor to the Commons Preservation Society. The result was the insight that an organization was needed that could hold such rights in permanence, as Hunter wrote in a letter to Octavia Hill: "The central idea of this is that of a Land Company which shall administer its property with a view to the protection of the public interests in open spaces."[6] In search for a name for the project Octavia Hill suggested "the Commons and Garden Trust" in her reply to Hunter arguing:

---

3   See http://www.oss.org.uk/; last accessed 1 December 2010.
4   Green, *The Surrey Hills*, 123-24.
5   See Nancy Boyd, *Josephine Butler, Octavia Hill, Florence Nightingale. Three Victorian Women Who Changed Their World* (London: Macmillan Press, 1982).
6   Quoted in Graham Murphy, *Founders of the National Trust* (London: Christopher Helm, 1987, New Ed. [n.p.]: National Trust Enterprises, 2002), 102.

> I do not know that I am right in thinking that it would be called a Trust. But if it would, I think it might be better than 'Company' – you will do better, I believe to bring forward its benevolent than its commercial character.[7]

At the top of this letter, Hunter then famously noted in pencil "'?National Trust R.H.'", and thus provided the name which was to be adopted for the new association.[8] We can see clearly how the format had moved from the legally less powerful 'society' to the commercial focus of 'company' and eventually to 'trust'. The realisation of this plan turned out to be more complicated than expected, and Evelyn had to give Sayes Court to the County Council after all. But Hunter and Hill were subsequently joined by Canon Hardwicke Rawnley (1851-1920), who had called on them in his campaign against the construction of slate railways in the Lake District, and it was on 12 January 1895 that the three of them eventually founded the National Trust for Places of Historic Interest or National Beauty.

2. Samuel Taylor Coleridge and the National Trust

2.1 Religious Musings

It is not documented whether Robert Hunter was thinking of Coleridge when he pencilled "National Trust" on Octavia Hill's letter as a name for the new organisation, but he certainly was in fact quoting Coleridge verbatim – consciously or not. As far as I have been able to establish, it was actually Coleridge who coined the phrase 'National Trust' in the specific context of the most mature and concise statement of his views on the order of the nation, his frequently underrated treatise *On the Constitution of the Church and State* (1829)[9]. In this late work Coleridge had set out in a systematic way what he had gained in experience from a life's political wanderings in struggle and strife through an age of revolutionary upheaval and social transformation. Throughout his career, one of the problematic social issues that had occupied his mind was the ambiguous quality of property as a source of social deprivation and unrest. What he expounded in the compelling prose of his essay towards the end of his life is, however, already patent in a lyrical version in his early poem "Religious Musings: A Desultory Poem,

---

7   Quoted in Murphy, *Founders of the National Trust*, 102.

8   Murphy, *Founders of the National Trust*, 102.

9   Samuel Taylor Coleridge, *On the Constitution of the Church and State* [1830], ed. John Colmer, *The Collected Works of Samuel Taylor Coleridge* 10 (London: Routledge & Kegan Paul, Princeton: Princeton UP, 1976). Further references to this edition in the text, abbreviated as 'CS'.

Written on the Christmas Eve of 1794", where he traced mankind's fall from the original grace of the pastoral idyll:[10]

> In the primeval age a dateless while
> The vacant Shepherd wander'd with his flock
> Pitching his tent where'er the green grass wav'd.
> But soon Imagination conjur'd up
> An host of new desires: with busy aim,
> Each for himself, Earth's eager children toil'd.
> So PROPERTY began, twy-streaming fount,
> Whence Vice and Virtue flow, honey and gall. (ll.199-205)
> [...]
> From Avarice thus, from Luxury and War
> Sprang heavenly Science; and from Science Freedom
> O'er waken'd realms Philosophers and Bards
> Spread in concentric circles: they whose souls
> Conscious of their high dignities from God
> Brook not Wealth's rivalry; and they who long
> Enamour'd with the charms of order hate
> Th' unseemly disproportion [.] (ll.224-231)

What Coleridge attempts here in a nutshell is nothing less than a poetic rendering of the cultural history of human society. Property, in all its ambiguity, is a central link in this development. The beginning is the idyllic image of the shepherd, who is described as "vacant", that is, in the connotation of the modern usage of 'vacation', without occupation, leisurely, idle. The shepherd's nomadic way of life had no need of ownership, as he freely moved over land shared by all. Interestingly, the fall from this graceful state is induced by imagination, which leads to desire. Desire in turn motivates human toil, a concept that needs brief explanation in its historical context. Thomas More had used it in his *Utopia* (1516) as part of his critique of the exploitation of the poor[11]. In the course of the labour theory of property or appropriation arising from the late seventeenth century onwards, 'toil' became a specific concept to explain the acquisition of private property, of appropriation (from Latin: *ad-propriare*). Thus, John Locke, in his *Second Treatise on Government* of 1690, pursues the central question of how an individual can own a specific part of the world when God has given the world to

---

10   Samuel Taylor Coleridge, "Religious Musings. A Desultory Poem, Written on the Christmas Eve of 1794" in *The Collected Works of Samuel Taylor Coleridge. Poetical Works I: Poems (Reading Text): Part 1*, ed. J. C. C. Mays, Bollingen Series LXXV (Princeton: Princeton UP, 2001), 183-184.

11   More, *Utopia,* Yale Ed. (1964) p.148f (italics K.St.): "I can see nothing else than a conspiracy of the rich. [...] They invent and devise all ways and means by which, first, they may keep without fear of loss that they have amassed by evil practices and, secondly, they may then purchase as cheaply as possible and abuse the *toil* and labour of the poor. These devices become law as soon as the rich have once decreed their observance in the name of the public – that is, the poor also."

humanity at large. The short answer is: toil. The extended argument starts out from the fact that, since, everyone owns himself or herself and hence his or her labour, whatever such labour or 'toil' is applied to becomes private possession. Locke writes in Chapter V §27:[12]

> Though the earth, and all inferior creatures, be common to all men, yet ever man has a property in his own person: this nobody has any right to but himself. The labour of his body, and the work of his hands, we may say, are properly his. Whatsoever then he removes out of the state that nature hath provided, and left it in, he hath mixed his labour with, and joined to it something that is his own, and thereby makes it his property. It being by him removed from the common state nature hath placed it in, it hath by this labour something annexed to it that excludes the common right of other men.

Having thus established the beginnings of property, Coleridge then goes on to describe its ambiguous nature ("twy-streaming fount", "Vice and Virtue", "honey and gall"). On the one hand, Coleridge casts property as the origin of evil outcomes such as avarice, luxury or war, but on the other hand it also produces science and freedom.

Clearly, the poem is more complex in its assessment of property than the blatantly radical position he adopted in his *Lectures* of 1795, when he wrote:[13]

> There is nothing more pernicious than the notion that any one possesses an absolute right to the Soil, which he appropriates – to the system of accumulation which flows from this supposed right we are indebted for nine-tenths of our Vices and Miseries. The Land is no one's – the Produce belongs equally to all, who contribute their due proportion of Labour.

That had been an exclusively negative view of private property, whereas, in the poem, Coleridge's perspective is more complex and, although his ideal remains a communitarian view of property, this aspect is transferred into a utopian, millenarian vision:

> Return pure FAITH! return meek PIETY!
> The kingdoms of the world are your's: each heart
> Self-govern'd, the vast family of Love
> Rais'd from the common earth by common toil
> Enjoy the equal produce. (ll.339-43)

---

12 John Locke, *Of Civil Government. Book II: Second Treatise*, in *Two Treatises of Government and A Letter Concerning Toleration,* ed. Ian Shapiro (New Haven and London: Yale UP, 2003), 100-209, 111f.

13 Samuel Taylor Coleridge, "Lecture 2", *Six Lectures on Revealed Religion its' Corruptions and Political Views* in *The Collected Works of Samuel Taylor Coleridge. Lectures 1795 On Politics and Religion*, ed. Lewis Patton and Peter Mann. Bollingen Series LXXV (Princeton: Princeton UP, 1971), 83-229, 127.

The poem's regulating agency which keeps this imagined ideal alive and links it across the ambiguous realities of the present to the idyll of the "primeval age" are the philosophers and bards. Their main function is the containment of the negative, chaotic effects of property – against which they themselves are immune:

> These [the philosophers and bards] hush'd awhile with patient eye serene
> Shall watch the mad careering of the storm;
> Then o'er the wild and wavy chaos rush
> And tame th' outrageous mass, with plastic might
> Moulding Confusion to such perfect forms,
> As erst were wont, bright visions of the day !
> To float before them […]. (ll. 243-49)

Coleridge clearly saw himself as one of this privileged group, the philosopher and bard, and he can be said to have followed his own advice, trying to mould confusion to perfect form. This "moulding of Confusion to perfect form" can already be observed in his poem where he chose highly regular blank verse to contain his own musings on the subject. His most sustained and systematic effort, however, to square the quagmire of the ambiguities and dangers of property against the poetic vision of utopian social justice was his treatise *On the Constitution of the Church and State*. When he wrote and published it more than three decades later, Coleridge's political outlook had turned around completely from his early radical position to the starkest conservatism. It is all the more surprising, however, that some fundamental lines of thought on property display continuity despite their setting in a profoundly altered political context.

2.2 On the Constitution of the Church and State

What had remained visionary and diffuse in his early poem "Religious Musings" the later Coleridge, true to his perception of his own role as philosopher and bard, began to shape into distinct structures. What seemed to help him immensely in his attempt to bridge the gap between utopian visions of property and the complexities of its social reality was the time-honoured legal concept of trust. As Alastair Hudson explains, the roots of legal trust go back to the age of the Crusades in the 13th century when the question concerning the use of the land during the landlords' absence in the Holy Land had to be addressed. Always a part of equity law, trust quickly developed into "the most significant of the equitable constructs", as Hudson writes:

> The trust grew out of this system of equity as a means of recognising that, in some circumstances, it would not be just if the common law owner of property were able to deny that other people ought to be recognised as also having rights in that property.[14]

Hudson further emphasizes that the trust thus is a product of history, and of English history at that:

> The trust is unique to Anglo-centric legal systems because it is a product of English history. [...] The trust arose by accident of history: other jurisdictions found other legal solutions to identical problems but none of them developed a trust.

The trust as a legal category was, quoting the *Oxford Dictionary of Law*, "recognized originally in Chancery. It is based on confidence and developed from the use, and it has been described as the most important contribution of equity to English jurisprudence":

> [It is] [a]n arrangement in which a settler transfers property to one or more trustees, who will hold it for the benefit of one or more persons (the beneficiaries or *cestuis que trust*, who may include the trustee(s) or the settler) who are entitled to enforce the trust, if necessary by action in court.[15]

Coleridge had an intense interest in legal issues from the start which he retained throughout his career. While poems such as "Religious Musings" show an early interest in questions of property, his attention to the concept of the trust was a preoccupation of his later years. For Coleridge, the concept of the trust helped to define a specific form of ownership which he derived from Biblical precepts. He writes in *Church and State*:

> [T]he proclamation throughout the land, by sound of trumpet, was made to all possessors: "The land is not your's, saith the Lord, the land is mine. To you I lent it." [CS 40-41]

The contingency of ownership which Coleridge points out here has the immediate advantage of giving him a justification for the secularization of Church property in the Reformation under Henry VIII:

> What the state, by law – that is, by the collective will of its functionaries at any one time assembled – can do or suffer to be done; that the state, by law, can undo or inhibit. And in *principle*, such bequests and donations were vitious *ab initio*, implying in the donor an absolute property in land, unknown to the constitution of the realm, and in defeasance of that immutable reason, which in the name of the nation and the national majesty proclaims: – "The land is not yours; it was vested in your *lineage* in trust for the nation." (CS 51; italics in the original)

Coleridge's claim for the power of the state as trustee of the 'propriety' here harks back to Lev. 25:23: "The land shall not be sold in perpetuity, for the land is mine; with me you are but aliens and tenants" (CS 51 n5). As the Israelites are

---

14 Alastair Hudson, *Understanding Equity and Trusts* (London, Sydney: Cavendish Publishing, 2001), 4, 11.

15 *Oxford Dictionary of Law* (Oxford: OUP, 6th ed. 2006), 548.

the aliens and tenants before God, they cannot own property unconditionally, whereas, by an implied twist of the argument, it was only the "tolerated alien" in the Hebrew polity who could own "Property by absolute right":

> And first, let me observe, with the Celtic, Gothic, and Scandinavian, equally as with the Hebrew tribes, Property by absolute right existed only in a tolerated alien; and there was everywhere a prejudice against the occupation expressly directed to its acquirement, viz. the trafficking with the current representatives of wealth. Even in that species of possession, in which the right of the individual was the prominent relative character, the institution of the Jubilee provided against its degeneracy into the merely *personal*; reclaimed it for the state, – that is, for the *line*, the *heritage*, as one of the permanent units, or integral parts, the aggregate of which constitutes the STATE". (CS 39)

Transferring this thought to Britain, he concludes:

> [N]o less intelligibly is it declared by the spirit and history of our laws, that the possession of a property, not connected with especial duties, a property not fiduciary or official, but arbitrary and unconditional, was in the light of our forefathers the brand of a Jew and an alien; not the distinction, not the right, or honour, of an English baron or gentleman. (CS 41)

In his own note to the passage, Coleridge further elaborates:

> A landed estate is a Trust for determinate use – and one of the uses is the existence of *enduring* Families, and of *estates* in a graduated ascent, of magnitude and number in inverse ration. (CS 41 n.4)

In this complex economy of mutual trust in the commonwealth, Coleridge emphasizes the contingency of ownership in his ideal of society, which he always describes as bound to specific social functions and ideas. Possession is never a means for itself, but always bound up in a wider ethic.

The consequences for the organisation of the State are spelt out in *On the Constitution of the Church and State*. The immediate motivation for his last prose work was the Roman Catholic Relief Act of 1829 which allowed Catholics to sit in Parliament. Coleridge, critical of the Act, provides, *ex negativo*, "the absolute disqualifications, the existence of which in any individual, and in any class or order of men, constitutionally incapacitates such individual and class or order from being inducted into the National Trust" (CS 77). What, "in any Order or Incorporation constitutes an *a priori* disqualification for the Trusteeship of the Nationalty"? How can "full, faithfull, and unbiased application of a *National* Trust to its proper and national purposes" (CS 79) be secured? With an eye to Catholic emancipation, "[a]llegiance to a Foreign Power" and "compulsory celibacy in connection with, and in dependence on, a foreign and extra-national head" appear to Coleridge such absolute disqualifications for holding the national trust. But who then is to be trusted with the property of the nation?

True to his calling, Coleridge did not stop with a sceptical position vis-à-vis Catholic Emancipation. He subsequently set out what the concept of a national trust, as he understood it, involved in terms of the organisation of the state as well as the task for himself as "philosopher and bard". In fact, he designed a special group, what he called "the third estate" (CS 83) for himself and his ilk which he called "the National Church, or Clerisy" (CS 83). To this "clerisy of the nation", as he called it in a Table Talk of 1832, belong "its learned men, whether poets, or philosophers, or scholars"; they functioned as "points of relative rest. There could be no order, no harmony of the whole, without them" (CS 46, n.1). In Church and State, membership to this group was even more expansively described, but it is never linked to a specific denomination, and the fact that it is a Christian institution is not a necessary attribute, but, in Britain, "a blessed accident, a providential boon, a grace of God" (CS 55), as Coleridge puts it:

> THE CLERISY of the nation, or national church, in its primary acceptation and original intention comprehended the learned of all denominations; – the sages and professors of the law and jurisprudence; of medicine and physiology; of music; of military and civil architecture; of the physical sciences; with the mathematical as the common *organ* of the preceding; in short, all the so called liberal arts and sciences, the possession and application of which constitute the civilization of a country, as well as the Theological. (CS 46)

The Clerisy is understood in the tradition of the Levites in the Hebrew Biblical polity, and the Hebrew prophets, the Nabim. It is assigned the 'Nationalty', that part of the national property, which it needs to uphold its civilizing function. The major part of the national property, called the 'propriety', is held to be the other two estates, the landed classes and the merchants, so that, and at the risk of some serious oversimplification, the result is the following system as shown in Figure 1.

Figure 1: Coleridge's model of society in *Of the Constitution of Church and State*

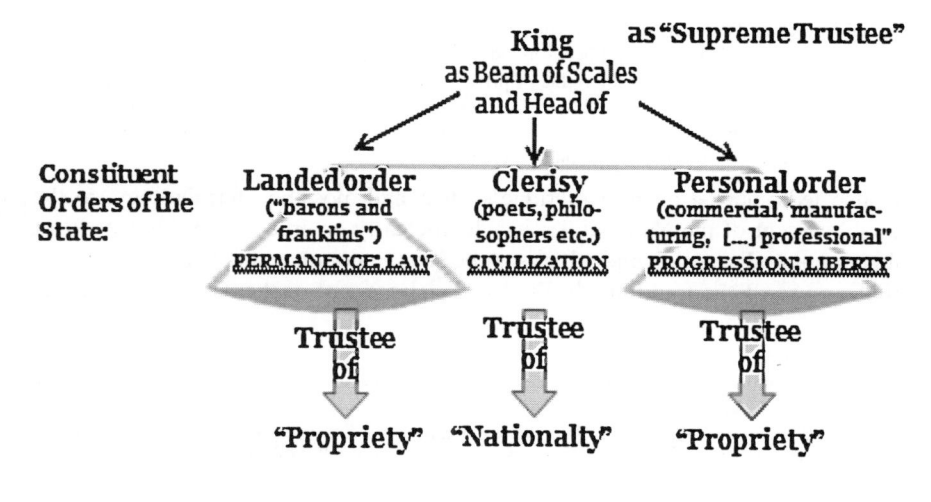

All of the property relations in the system, as we can see, are based on trust, with the king as "supreme trustee", the landed and personal orders in trust of the "propriety", and the clerisy in trust of the "nationalty". Under scrutiny, Coleridge oscillates in his use of the term 'national trust' between making it a synonym of 'nationalty', that is the specific property of the clerisy, and a wider meaning referring to the entire system of property entrusted to various groups in Britain. In this wider meaning, it makes sense in the emphasis of the contingency of ownership in Britain, and as a powerful concept which certainly provided the rationale, and possibly the terminology, for the discussion of national property throughout Victorian Britain.

3. Poetry and the Property

Two main points result in conclusion: First, with his concept of a "National Trust" Coleridge marks an important stage in the perennial discussion about property in Britain. Coleridge would have known by heart John of Gaunt's complaint in his famous speech in Shakespeare's *King Richard II*, which ultimately focuses on King Richard's breach of trust in property:[16]

> This blessed plot, this earth, this realm, this England, […]
> […]
> Is now leas'd out – I die pronouncing it –
> Like to a tenement or pelting farm. (II.i. ll. 50, 57-60)

In Coleridge's own time, the discussion was in full swing, as Anne Janowitz summarizes:[17]

> If we look at the double intention within Romanticism, as part of a literary-historical dialec-
> tic, we can see that the contest between individualism (grounded materially in the supersed-
> ing of customary rights by the rights of private property and its legal apparatus) and com-
> munitarianism (grounded materially in the customary rights of the countryside) yields, in the
> course of the nineteenth century, to both the triumph and the crisis of literal individualism,
> and to the rise of socialist and utopian communitarianism.

It also led, spurred on by Coleridge's ideas and, possibly, terminology, to the establishment of the National Trust, which clearly emerged from the context of this ongoing discussion and which can be seen to continue and specify the Coleridgean use of the traditionally English legal concept of the Trust as an instru-

---

16 Shakespeare, *King Richard II*, ed. Peter Ure, The Arden Shakespeare (London: Methuen, 1956, 5th ed. 1961, repr. 1983), 53.

17 Anne Janowitz, "Land" in *An Oxford Companion to the Romantic Age. British Culture 1776-1832*, ed. Iain McCalman (Oxford, New York: OUP, 1999), 152-161, 160.

ment of equity law, with an aim to protect the interest of the community in the enjoyment and benefits of nature, where "the green grass waved", as Coleridge had put it.

Second, and perhaps more importantly, this tour de force through Coleridge's positioning in the property discussion can provide further evidence that it was also a positioning of the poet and philosopher within British society, and specifically with a view to the law. Three distinct functions for the philosopher and bard, such as Coleridge himself, have emerged in the analysis. Firstly, Coleridge shapes his profile as interpreter of legal texts and contexts, here specifically the Old Testament, which he acknowledged as legal precedent and codex. As poet and scholar Coleridge put forward his interpretative skill, and *On the Constitution of the Church and State* can clearly be read as an essay in legal criticism. Within the system he created in this essay, Coleridge grouped himself and his like as philosopher and bard with the National Clerisy, in charge of the civilization of the country to enable the balance between law and freedom. As could, however, be seen in the reading of "Religious Musings", Coleridge saw, in good Romantic fashion, civilization as profoundly ambiguous because it originated in the ambiguous effects of the rise of property. If civilization was to be secured, property needed to be regulated. Here poets were particularly apt trustees, as they were immune against the attractions of property and hence its negative effects. They were the mediators between the idyllic past and the utopian, communitarian vision of property, from which position they derived the power to create order in the chaos and upheaval raging in between these two visionary states. This establishment of order could, on the one hand, take the form of a prose treatise interpreting legal texts and joining in an argument on legal property; it could also take the poetic form of artfully ordering language in lyrical verse, as in "Religious Musings".

Fresh Light on Christina Rossetti and George Herbert

William Baker
Northern Illinois University

The influence of the great seventeenth-century devotional poet George Herbert (1593-1633) upon the poetry of Christina Rossetti (1930-1894) has not gone unnoticed. Contemporary reviewers of her work noted similarities. For instance a reviewer in the *Eclectic Review*, n.s. 2 in June 1862 reacting to *Goblin Market and Other Poems*, published in March 1862 by Macmillan, drew attention to "the manner of Herbert" in some of Rossetti's' devotional lyrics (p. 494).

Edmund Gosse's influential essay in his *Critical Kit-Kats* published the year of her death when Christina Rossetti's critical reputation was in its ascendancy, referred to her as "a sister" of Herbert and the "poetic inheritor" of Herbert and other seventeenth-century devotional poets (p. 156). Indeed, William Robertson Nicoll in his *Bookman* review for March 1898 of Mackenzie Bell's *Christina Rossetti: A Biographical and Critical Study* placed her "higher" than Donne or Herbert and others in the expression of "religious sentiment" (p. 74).

However, George Saintsbury in his *A Short History of English Literature,* also published in 1898 observes of Herbert: "As a poet he is certainly not the equal of either Crashaw or Vaughan, and in his own quiet fashion he has in the present century been equalled by Keble and surpassed by Miss Christina Rossetti." Saintsbury adding that Herbert "very seldom transports ... his is an equable merit, a soothing and healthful pleasure" – shades of Saintsbury the wine critic – "rather than the dazzling excellence, the contagious rapture, of the great ones."[1]

H.J.C. Grierson's important edition of *Metaphysical Lyrics and Poems of the Seventeenth Century: Donne to Butler* (London: Oxford University Press, 1921: reprints 13 Herbert poems). T.S. Eliot responded to Grierson's introduction and selection in two key essays: in the *TLS*, 20 October 1921, [669]-670; and in *The Spectator*, cxlviii.5411 (12 March 1932), 360-361, in an essay entitled "Studies in Sanctity: VIII George Herbert." Incidentally these Eliot essays became the foundation for Eliot's subsequent British Council pamphlet on Herbert published in 1962. Eliot was much more enthusiastic about Herbert than he perceived

---

1 Cited C.A. Patrides, ed., *George Herbert: The Critical Heritage.* London: Routledge & Kegan Paul, 1983, p. 277.

Grierson's rather limited selection of Herbert poems to be. For Eliot "of all the 'metaphysical' poets Herbert has suffered the most from being read only in anthologies ... his poetry is definitely an *oeuvre*, to be studied entire." Eliot writes: "It is very rare to find a poet of whom one may say, that his poetic gift would have remained dormant or unfulfilled but for his religious vocation" (cited Patrides, pp. 334-335).

Eliot in his 1932 *Spectator* essay discusses the influence of Herbert upon Christina Rossetti and Gerard Manley Hopkins. Christina Rossetti's awareness of Herbert's "The Temple" was for Eliot an early encounter that is seen also in her subsequent poems, especially her four stanza "Up-Hill" beginning "Does the road wind up-hill all the way? Yes, to the very end" and concluding

> Shall I find comfort, travel-sore and weak?
>   Of labour you shall find the sum
> Will there be beds for me and all who seek?
>   Yea, beds for all who come.[2]

In spite of the resemblances between the two in their religious quest and questioning, use of paradox and of internal voice, there are "profound differences" according to Eliot between the two. Eliot writes that "Christina's religious verse suffers, when we read much of it together, from a monotony due to a narrower range of emotion and an inferior intellectual gift. Herbert is an anatomist of feeling and a trained theologian too; his mind is working continually both in the mysteries of faith and the motives of the heart" (cited Patrides, p. 335).

The similarities and differences between Herbert and Christina Rossetti have been explored in the second half of the last century notably by Molly Mahood in "The Two Anglican Poets" in her brilliant *Poetry and Humanism* (New Haven: Yale University Press, 1950, 22-32), and by David A. Kent in his excellent "'By thought, word, and deed': George Herbert and Christina Rossetti" found in the volume he edited *The Achievement of Christina Rossetti* published in 1987 by the Cornell University Press (pp. 250-273). Mahood observes that in Christina Rossetti's religious poetry "anxiety ... takes the place of repose and fear leaves no place for laughter" (p. 27).

Neither had access to Anthony H. Harrison's *The Letters of Christina Rossetti*, 4 vols., 1997-2004 (Charlottesville & London: University of Virginia Press). This contains documentation of Christina's evident admiration for Herbert's life and work. For instance, on 25 July 1888 she writes to the wife of the Swedenborgian poet, and author of mystical prose works, Henry Septimus Sutton, whose "poetic gift" she admires: "may I venture to enquire whether he is descended from our

---

2   All references to the poems of Christina Rossetti are to *Christina Rossetti: The Complete Poems. Text by R.W. Crump. Notes and Introduction by Betty S. Flowers* (London: Penguin Books, 2000).

great and good poet George Herbert?" (4: 83). The response is no. It is clear from other references in her letters that Herbert was Christina's favourite seventeenth-century English poet.

Thanks to the herculean labours of the late William E. Fredeman who died in July 1999, Jan Marsh and others,[3] the veil has lifted slightly on Christina Rossetti's life and work. Fredeman acquired an enormous amount of primary Rossetti materials used for his *The Correspondence of Dante Gabriel Rossetti* (9 vols., London: D.S. Brewer, 2002-2004), and innumerable books and articles on the Rossetti's.[4] Some of these materials recently appeared at auction and in booksellers catalogues. His introduction to *Books from the Library of Christina, Dante Gabriel, and William Michael Rossetti*, Bertram Rota the eminent London book-dealers catalogue 180, appeared in 1973. It does refer to her copy of George Herbert's *The Temple: Sacred Poems and Private Ejaculations* and *The Remains of that Sweet Singer of the Temple George Herbert* published by Pickering in 1844 and 1848. Both volumes contain her signature. The first "Christina G. Rossetti" is dated "5th December 1848" on her eighteenth birthday. The second "to her dear Mother Frances M.L. Rossetti 8th September 1855" (see Kent, p. 257, n. 35).

The whereabouts of the volumes were unknown until they appeared on the shelves of a Dover Kent bookseller last year and were purchased by Richard M. Ford the London dealer. Early in 2010 I acquired them on behalf of Northern Illinois University and they are now in its special collections.

Before describing them and discussing what they reveal about their owners reading of George Herbert, it should be pointed out that there is evidence that Christina was familiar with what her sister Maria described as "that beautiful little poem 'Virtue' by George Herbert" and his "Misery and Virtue" at the age of 14. In December 1844, as Jan Marsh explains in her *Christina Rossetti: A Literary Biography*, William Michael gave her sister Christina as a present *The Sacred Harp* published in Dublin in 1834. Christina copied into a common place book "Virtue." Her imitation "Charity" is included in the verses that her grandfather Gaetano Polidori printed privately in 1847 (p. 46).

Christina too in her Herbert imitation "Charity" laments the passing of time, of the rose and of summer rather than spring. In her final stanza she departs from her model. She speaks of charity and notes Herbert's "virtuous soul." Herbert's poem "Vertue" reads:

---

3 See for instance Jan Marsh, *Christina Rossetti: A Literary Biography*. London: Jonathan Cape, 1994.

4 For some of these, see "Bibliography", Alison Chapman and Joanna Meacock, *A Rossetti Family Chronology* (Houndmills, Basingstoke, and New York: Palgrave Macmillan, 2007, xvi-xxv).

Sweet day, so cool, so calm, so bright,
The bridall of the earth and skie;
The dew shall weep thy fall tonight,
    For thou must die.

Sweet rose, whose hue angrie and brave
Bids the rash gazer wipe his eye:
Thy root is ever in its grave,
    And thou must die.

Sweet spring, full of sweet dayes and roses,
A box where sweets compacted lie;
My musick shows ye have your closes,
    And all must die.

Onely a sweet and vertuous soul,
Like season'd timber, never gives;
But though the whole world turn to coal,
    Then chiefly lives.[5]

Christina Rossetti's imitation reads:

I praised the myrtle and the rose,
    At sunrise in their beauty vying;
I passed them at the short day's close,
    And both were dying.
The summer sun his rays was throwing
    Brightly; yet ere I sought my rest,
His last cold ray, more deeply glowing,
    Died in the west.
After this bleak world's stormy weather,
    All, all, save Love alone, shall die;
For Faith and Hope shall merge together
    In Charity (p. 633).

Her indebtedness is clearly one of technique. As David Kent indicates the key to Herbert's poem is four: the four adjectives in the opening line, the four word refrain in the first three stanzas, the iambic pentameter line (pp. 258-259).

Christina's key however is three not four. There are three key mutability images: the sun, and two flowers (the rose and the myrtle). They embody the encounter with death. In the opening stanza the flowers survive for only a day. In the second stanza the "summer sun" is short-lived. In the final stanza the triad of "Faith and Hope and Charity" represent permanent values – Christina too uses the iambic pentameter line.[6]

---

5   Unless otherwise stated, citations to Herbert's poems are to the great Helen Wilcox edition, *The English Poems of George Herbert* (Cambridge: Cambridge University Press, 2007). "Vertue" is on p. 316.

6   See *Christina Rossetti: The Complete Poems*, pp. 633, 1094.

"Vertue" remains unmarked in Christina's copy of Herbert's *The Temple Sacred Poems and Private Ejaculations*. Her pencilled marginal linings and comments are found throughout both volumes. In the first volume she displays evidence of a close reading of "The Church-porch," a poem, to use Wilcox's words, providing "evidence of five major influences: biblical wisdom literature, the Anglican liturgy, classical teaching, humanist conduct books and proverbial wisdom" (p. 47).

The close of the opening verse of "The Church-porch," a longish 462 line poem, attracts Christina's attention: "A verse may finde him, who a sermon flies/And turn delight into a sacrifice." Technical issues preoccupy her. She omits the comma between "him" and "who," a literal that remains constant in all editions of the poem.

Technical and visual placement are the subject of Christina's observation in her copy: "Throughout this poem, the last 2 lines of each stanza sh^d be on a level with the next." I don't know of an edition which does this. Why she should want this is curious. Although her brother Dante Gabriel Rossetti in his lengthy experimental sonnets "The House of Life" does display considerable attention to visual, to graphic design and form.[7] And in her "Ash Wednesday" beginning, "My God, My God, have mercy on my sin," she uses the contraction techniques in her final four word line "To tell it in" (Crump ed., pp. 429-430).

Herbert's stanza 48, in the middle of "The Church-porch," contains an interesting Christina Rossetti annotation. Herbert's stanza reads:

> If thou be single, all they goods and ground
> Submit to love; but yet not more then all.
> Give one estate, as one life. None is bound
> To work for two, who brought himself to thrall
> God made me one man; love make me no more,
> Till labour come, and make my weakness score.

Wilcox observes "A difficult stanza which even Coleridge could not understand" (76). At the foot of the passage in pencil Christina writes:

> As no less a man than Coleridge in the few notes he has left on Herbert, says that he does "not understand the stanza," it may be permitted to enquire where the obscurity lies. I perceive none unless possibly the form of expression in lines 3, 4, 5 may be considered somewhat curt. "Why" says Herbert "Should I resent his sickness of poverty? for his mistakes also are his misfortune. True in Christian charity I ought to be more concerned at the mistakes wh. are more detrimental to the man than sickness or poverty: but then to resent them angrily is no sign of charity (p. 11).

---

7   Cf. Elizabeth K. Helsinger, *Poetry and the Pre-Raphaelite Arts: Dante Gabriel Rossetti and William Morris*. Yale: Yale University Press, 2008, pp. 313-314 n. 9.

Christina's marginalia shows that she read Herbert as both a poet to be learnt from but also as a Christian model, a source of religious wisdom. Coleridge too writes that the reader of Herbert should be "both a zealous and an orthodox, both a devout and a devotional Christian ... a child of the Church," one who finds the "forms and ordinances" of the Church "acts of religion not sources of formality." This passage from Coleridge is cited in the second volume of the Pickering edition of Herbert read by Christina Rossetti (II: 337). Coleridge's *Biographia Literaria* (1817) and his essays in the *The Friend* (1809-1810) "effected the revival of interest in Herbert single-handedly ... he was the first to commend Herbert primarily on literary grounds" (cited Patrides, p. 166).

In her edition Wilcox refers her readers to her predecessor F.E. Hutchinson's note in his 1941 edition of *The Works of George Herbert* (Oxford: Clarendon Press). What Hutchinson says illuminates the text Christina Rossetti responds to, and reveals her knowledge of Coleridge. Hutchinson locates the source of Coleridge's[8] "I do not understand the stanza" to the second volume of Pickering's *Works of George Herbert*, p. 337, the 1835 edition. Christina annotated the 1848 edition which reproduced the misprint in the second edition of 1838. In this, as Hutchinson points out, the "note was attached to stanza 52" (p. 481). This begins "Be calm in arguing: for fierceness makes/Errour a fault, and truth discourtesie," a stanza that essentially creates few explicatory problems. Hutchinson adds regarding stanza 48 "When Coleridge confessed himself beaten the present editor can hardly hope to succeed" although he does offer an explanation which is hardly pertinent to the present discussion (see Hutchinson: 481). So to clarify, Christina Rossetti's marginalia is attached to the wrong Herbert verse!

Other passages in Herbert's "The Church-porch" too attracted Christina Rossetti's attention. For instance, at the end of verse 56 "A grain of glorie mixt with humbleness/Cures both a fever and lethargicknese," the punctuation of the first line with the word "mixt" produces a pencil line through the letter "t" and in her left hand margin the letters "ed." So she has emended "A grain of glorie mixt with humbleness" to "A grain of glorie mixed with humbleness" (p. 12: line 355). Such an emendation doesn't appear to have been noted by Herbert's editors or to my knowledge other scholarly interpreters.

Stanza 66 of "The Church-porch" concludes with the line "Fast-when thou wilt but then, 'tis gain not losse." The opening two lines of the following stanza read "Though private prayer be a brave designe,/Yet publick hath more promises,

---

8   Hutchinson and Wilcox's edition of Herbert are replete with references to Coleridge. However, a fresh assessment is called for that will take into consideration material in the superb ongoing Bollingen series of Coleridge's *Collected Works* published by Routledge and Princeton University Press (1969–).

more love." At the foot of the page Christina, who has marginally marked these lines, remarks, "I think this must be the right punctuation – not with the semicolon after 'wilt' as in other texts" (p. 14). Wilcox in her 2007 edition uses a semicolon. Hutchinson does not. In the text, both record the alternative punctuation, a comma following "wilt" in the Ms. at Dr. Williams' Library and semi-colon in the Ms. at the Bodleian.

Christina's annotation continues: "The whole stanza requires a little thinking over to see its drift in detail. I wd paraphrase it thus: – 'The due to God [attendance at church] should be paid twice on the Sunday; for He gave thee they food twice [two meals] every week-day. On the Sunday, thy nutriment is improved [from bodily food into spiritual]: neglect not the spiritual food wh. is better, & may perhaps save thee. Thwart not the Almighty God: be not stiff necked. Fast whenever thou wilt, except then on Sunday (when the food be spiritual): for that food is again not detriment" (pp. 14-15).

Wilcox explains "wilt[,] but then 'tis gain" as "Deny yourself food at times, but not when to eat is to gain salvation" (80). Certainly Christina's exegesis in her paraphrase reveals herself too as a sensitive commentator upon the theological implications of Herbert's lines.

Other poems attracting marginalia include "Affliction, I," "The Temper," "The Holy Scriptures, Poem 2," "Employment," "Man," "Providence," "The Collar." Christina's attention is drawn to the fourth stanza of the first "Affliction" poem, a poem regarded by many as amongst Herbert's finest achievements:

> At first thou gav'st me milk and sweetnesses,
>   I had my wish and way:
> My dayes were straw'd with flow'rs and happinesse;
>   There was no moneth but May.
> But with my yeares sorrow did twist and grow,
> And made a partie unawares for wo.

There are no marginal observations, the clear allusion to Canaan, the land "flowing with milke and honey" (*Exodus*, 11:8) or to the Christian baptism. Christina simply marks this verse in her left hand margin: the pencilled lining being suffice (p. 39), no other passage in "Affliction" is accorded this status.

In the first "The Temper" poem, the marginalia is of a different nature. The third word of the opening line of the fourth stanza "Wilt thou meet arms with man, that thou dost stretch," with its echo of *Isaiah* xl:12 and multiple meanings of "meet arms" is scored by Christina with a " ' " above "meet." At the foot of her page (48) she writes "Mete?" spelled "mete" followed by a question mark.

The opening stanza and the third line of the second stanza of "The Holy Scriptures II" are marginally singled out. In the line "Then as dispersed herbs do watch a portion" the word "watch" is underlined. In the right-hand margin she writes "make" and in her left-hand margin "Match" followed by a question (p. 52). As Hutchinson and Wilcox point out, Coleridge suspected "some misprint" for "watch" (Hutchinson: 496; Wilcox: 211) and the line has puzzled commentators who have conjectured "make" and "match" and even "patch" as alternatives.

Christina is attracted to lines in "Employment II" and its wonderful arresting fourth stanza. She draws attention in her left hand margin (76) to:

> O that I were an Orenge-tree
>   That busie plant!
> Then should I ever laden be,
>   And never want
> Some trait for him that dressed me.

Coleridge praised "Man" with its main biblical source in Psalm 8, lines 4 to 6: "What is man, that one art mindful of him" and so on (see Wilcox, p. 84). As Christina Rossetti indicated in her marginalia (90), Coleridge was perplexed by Herbert's seventh stanza:

> Each thing is full of dutie:
> Waters united are our navigation;
>   Distinguished, our habitation;
>   Below, our drink; above, our meat;
> Both are our cleanliness. Hath one such beautie?
>   Then how are all things neat!

The word "cleanliness" is followed by a figure "1" above the line.

At the foot of the page (90) Christina writes: "Coleridge professed to understand this but imperfectly." She adds, "no doubt it is somewhat intricate. I think what Herbert has in mind are waters below the firmament, & waters [heaven] above the firmament." In other words, Herbert evokes *Genesis* 1:7. She glosses: "He [Herbert] says waters united [continuous below the firmament] are what are navigated; divided or distinguished by land, they [i.e. the dividing lands] are what we inhabit. The water below the firmament gives us natural drink & those above the firmament give us no spiritual meal: but these supply our cleansing (natural & spiritual)." Coleridge's problem is with "Distinguished." He writes, "I understand this bit imperfectly. Distinguished – they form an island? And the next lines refer perhaps to this belief that all fruits grow and are nourished by water? But then how is the ascending sap 'our cleanliness'?"

Christina comments that it "seems to refer to waters below firmament & those above that equal 'heaven.'" She also writes "Why not" without a question mark. Her marginal comment reveals her awareness of *Genesis* 1:7. Belief and scriptural knowledge leave her seemingly unperplexed by lines and words that troubled Coleridge.

Another poem attracting Christina's attention is the more lengthy "Providence" with its Biblical source, *Psalm* 104. Christina's attention is not that of a subsequent fine commentator on Herbert's work, Diane Benet who following Hutchinson focuses upon the doubling effect in the stanzas and their relationship to the dual praise of the individual human and the poetic speaker for the total natural universe.[9] Rather Christina singles out for marginal lining the verse:

> How finely doest thou times and seasons spin
> And make a twist checker'd with night and day;
> Which as it lengthens, windes and windes us in,
> As bouls go on, but turning all the way.

Christina is interested in the word "checker'd" following "twist." She erases in pencil the first four letters "check." In her margin (119) she writes, "qu/" and indicates these letters as a replacement. She appears to be reading the word as "chequered." No textual variants are however recorded by Herbert's editors.

It would perhaps be surprising if the well known "The Collar" didn't receive Christina Rossetti's attention. The line, "Of what is fit, and not forsake thy cage" interests Christina. She places a colon following the word "not" in her text, displaying to use Wilcox's words, a sensitivity to the "tangled syntax [that] remains a feature of the poem in both [mss.] versions" (528). The Pickering version Christina is using has no punctuation following "not" (p. 160).

The second volume, *The Remains of that Sweet Singer of the Temple George Herbert* published by Pickering in 1848 contains Christina's factual emendations. For instance, following "George Herbert was born the third day of April, in the year or our Redemption 1593," she adds, "died in 1633" (p. [7]). At the end of the first section containing "Letters of George Herbert" a misprint is corrected. The date "1660" receives the marginal "1590" followed by a question mark alongside "Henry Herbert was the sixth son of *Richard Herbert*, esq. and *Magdalen Newport*, daughter of *Sir Richard Newport*, and born A.D. 1660" (p. [297]). A line on "Jacula Prudentum or Outlandish Proverbs" particularly reverberated receiving underlining and marginal emphasis (p. 277): "God's Mill grinds slow, but sure" (line 747, Hutchinson edition). The line is also written inside the end back cover of the volume.

There is not time to discuss the significance for Christina Rossetti or her mother inserting in volume two what was clearly a cherished artifact, a newspaper illustration of "Old St. Pancreas" Church in the copy (II: 8-9). This is reputed to be one of the oldest sites for Christian worship in England. A New Church was consecrated in 1822 and in 1847 the Old Church that had become derelict began

---

9   See Diane Benet, *Secretary of Praise: The Poetic Vocation of George Herbert*, Columbia: University of Missouri Press, 1984, pp. 159-162.

to be restored. John Polidori, a relative, physician, author of the Gothic tale *The Vampire*, beset by gambling debts, slowly poisoned himself and was buried there in 1821. He had accompanied Shelley and Byron on visits to Geneva (see Marsh: 15).

Clearly then Christina Rossetti's marked up copy of Herbert's poems has reverberations, echoes of which we have only touched the surface. It reveals much about its owners sensibility, her reading, her engagement with Herbert, a poet who left an indelible impact upon his Victorian admirer and fellow devotional poet Christina Rossetti. They reveal Christina's "mind," to utilize T.S. Eliot's words cited earlier, of George Herbert "working continually both on the mysteries of faith and the motives of the heart." Her absorption in Herbert is an additional piece of evidence that the publication of Grierson's edition of *Metaphysical Lyrics* in 1921 rather than beginning pioneering interest in Donne, Herbert and others, consolidated and built upon an interest and admiration whose origins go back before that great nineteenth-century sage S.T. Coleridge, a tradition that "grinds slow but sure."

Bibliography

Benet, Diane. *Secretary of Praise: The Poetic Vocation of George Herbert*, Columbia: University of Missouri Press, 1984.

Coleridge, S.T. *Collected Works, Bollingen Series*. London and Princeton: Routledge and Princeton University Press, 1969-.

Chapman, Alison and Joanna Meacock. "Bibliography", *A Rossetti Family Chronology*. Houndmills, Basingstoke, and New York: Palgrave Macmillan, 2007.

Eliot, T.S. *George Herbert*. London: Longmans, for the British Council, 1962.

–. "Studies in Sanctity: VIII George Herbert." *The Spectator*, cxlviii.5411 (12 March 1932), 360-361.

–. "The Metaphysical Poets," *TLS*, 20 October 1921, [669]-670.

Fredeman, William E. *Books from the Library of Christina, Dante Gabriel, and William Michael Rossetti*, London: Bertram Rota, 1973.

Grierson, H.J.C. *Metaphysical Lyrics and Poems of the Seventeenth Century: Donne to Butler*. London: Oxford University Press, 1921.

Helsinger, Elizabeth K. *Poetry and the Pre-Raphaelite Arts: Dante Gabriel Rossetti and William Morris*. Yale: Yale University Press, 2008.

Herbert, George. *The Temple: Sacred Poems and Private Ejaculations*. London: Pickering, 1844.

–. *The Remains of that Sweet Singer of the Temple George Herbert*. London: Pickering, 1848.

—. *The Works of George Herbert,* edited by F.E. Hutchinson. Oxford: Clarendon Press, 1941.

—. *The English Poems of George Herbert.* Edited by Helen Wilcox. Cambridge: Cambridge University Press, 2007.

Kent, David A. "'By thought, word, and deed': George Herbert and Christina Rossetti" in *The Achievement of Christina Rossetti,* edited David A. Kent. Cornell: Cornell University Press, 1987, pp. 250-273.

Mahood, Molly. *Poetry and Humanism.* New Haven: Yale University Press, 1950.

Marsh, Jan. *Christina Rossetti: A Literary Biography.* London: Jonathan Cape, 1994.

Patrides, C.A., ed. *George Herbert: The Critical Heritage.* London: Routledge & Kegan Paul, 1983.

Rossetti, Christina. *Christina Rossetti: The Complete Poems. Text by R.W. Crump. Notes and Introduction by Betty S. Flowers.* London: Penguin Books, 2000.

—. *The Letters of Christina Rossetti,* Edited by Anthony H. Harrison. 4 vols., Charlottesville & London: University of Virginia Press, 1997-2004.

Rossetti, D.G. *The Correspondence of Dante Gabriel Rossetti,* edited by W.E. Fredeman. 9 vols., London: D.S. Brewer, 2002-2004.

Historical Humanist, American Style

Paul A. Bové
University of Pittsburgh

In 1897, Alfred Thayer Mahan, the so-called "Father of the American Navy," published the most important in a series of his essays in *Harper's Magazine,* entitled, "A 20th-Century Outlook." In this influential and now classical expression of US imperial ambition, Mahan urged that US intellectual and political leaders accept the task of discouraging Americans from any belief that peace is a good. Among the standard means of this sort of vulgarity – self-interest, Manifest Destiny, et cetera. – sits an important variation on a common nationalist topos: the US is the new Rome and must accept its role as the modern hegemon needed to order an advanced world.

In many ways, Mahan met the standards of historical scholarship and derived from European humanism ethically appropriate grounds for a militant geo- and national politics. Bad enough that he theorized US strategy so successfully that we still feel his influence in the US and saw it at work in Japan and elsewhere over the last century; worse that he convinced others that US greatness required that the State order economy and society in and through a science of logistics to support state primacy and national ambition. Perhaps worst of all in his advocacy of war and violence was a direct defense of exterminating entire populations in the name of the civilizing mission – the legitimacy of which he draws from the great German historical humanist, Theodor Mommsen. In 1902, Mommsen won the Nobel Prize for Literature, substantially on the basis of his three-volume *History of Rome* (1854 to 1856) in which he expressed necessary if reluctant admiration for Caesar's embrace of military solutions to otherwise intractable state and civil problems. Mommsen's classical liberalism required a liberal Caesar who like Dante's monarch would lead a Democratic centralist state. Of course no one any longer accepts Mommsen's views and Mahan might have not when 40 years after their expression he nonetheless urged policymakers and intellectuals to accept Mommsen's example of Caesar as an advocate of the truth that the human species' political and cultural achievements (and their defense) depends on arms, preemptive war, and exterminism:

> "When the course of history," says Mommsen, "turns from the miserable monotony of the political selfishness which fought its battles in the Senate house and in the streets of Rome we may be allowed – on the threshold of an event the effects of which still at the present day

influence the destinies of the world – to look round us for a moment, and to indicate the point of view under which the conquest of what is now France by the Romans, and their first contact with the inhabitants of Germany and of Great Britain, are to be regarded in connection with the general history of the world. ... The fact that the great Celtic people were ruined by the transalpine wars of Cesar was not the most important result of that grand enterprise – far more momentous than the negative was the positive result. It hardly admits of a doubt that if the rule of the Senate had prolonged its semblance of life for some generations longer, the migration of the peoples, as it is called, would have occurred four hundred years sooner than it did, and would have occurred at a time when the Italian civilization had not become naturalized either in Gaul or on the Danube or in Africa and Spain. Inasmuch as Cesar with sure glance perceived in the German tribes the rival antagonists of the Romano – Greek world, inasmuch as with firm hand he established the new system of aggressive defense down even to its details, and taught men to protect the frontiers of the empire by rivers or artificial ramparts, to colonize the nearest barbarian tribes along the frontier with the view of warding off the more remote, and to recruit the Roman army by enlistment from the enemy's country, he gained for the Hellenic-Italian culture the interval necessary to civilize the West, just as it had already civilized the East. Centuries elapsed before men understood that Alexander had not merely erected an ephemeral kingdom in the East, but had carried Hellenism to Asia; centuries again elapsed before men understood that Cesar had not merely conquered a new province for the Romans, but had laid the foundation for the Romanizing of the regions of the West. It was only a late posterity that perceived the meaning of those expeditions to England and Germany, so inconsiderate in a military point of view, and so barren of immediate result. ... That there is a bridge connecting the past glory of Hellas and Rome with the prouder fabric of modern history; that western Europe is Romanic, and Germanic Europe classic; that the names of Themistocles and Scipio have to us a very different sound from those of Asoka and Salmanassar; that Homer and Sophocles are not merely like the Vedas and Kalidasa, attractive to the literary botanist, but bloom for us in our own garden – all this is the work of Cesar."[1]

It would perhaps surprise few to know that 100 years after Mahan's article, Paul Wolfowitz embraced his predecessor's position despite his own misleading title, "Managing Our Way to a Peaceful Century." Wolfowitz's now silly seeming embrace of End of History ideology repeated two essential positions of Mahan: peace must not be accepted as a good and state power must acquire and sustain priority over both the economy and over economics as a mode of talk and conceptualization. We might easily imagine intellectuals in this tradition telling us that real humanists are willing to kill, if not to be killed.

Mahan, Mommsen's Caesar, and Wolfowitz at least faintly echo Hegelian and idealist visions of the dialectics of the ethical state, which claims to find in each world historically great power, an Ethical Ideal that advances the species' historical development along a path of emergent cultural perfection that power enhances and defends. State exceptionalism expresses this fact and ideology. Mommsen's historical humanism gave Mahan needed cover for his ambitions:

---

1   Quoted in Mahan p. 528.

Roman Caesar, as well as a putatively analogous liberalized Germany would be examples of state mechanisms in and through which the species invents itself and its own ambitions.

This imperial development of humanism frightened and sickened Henry Adams not only because he was an anti-militant, a man of peace, who opposed particularly the US's war in the Philippines. Adams also loathed the effects such militant and murderous arrogance had upon the Republic, upon the American citizenry, and consequently upon what he called the still experimental American system. At Princeton, the poet critic Richard Palmer Blackmur always taught Adams in the company of Pascal, no doubt because of their common distrust of reason's limits – a point contrasted with Mahanian arrogance. In *The Education of Henry Adams* and elsewhere, Adams insisted that post-Civil War, industrializing America, led by a corrupt and overly influential complex of financial institutions and stocks schemers, produced a regime uninterested in and unable to govern or lead the United States. *The Education* is filled with striking images and among these is one that catches the dangers in Mahan (and Wolfowitz's) programs. He wrote that America had been becoming something new in the world since 1861 and that no one quite understood it or its emerging implications. This is a point shared by the best of Adams' time. Even William James, after all, at times described his projects' goals as helping Americans "to cope" with worlds of new truths and shifting orders.

In Chapter 16, "The Press (1868)," Adams recounts the return of his diplomatic family from London, where his father's success in keeping England out of the American Civil War eased the North's path to victory. The Adamses return to a new world, as unknown to them as the island of Manhattan had first been to the Dutch: "they could hardly have been stranger on the shores of the world," he writes, "how much its [the United States'] character had changed or was changing they could not wholly know, and they could but partly feel." His point, as always, is that none knows any better than they, including the countries' "leaders." He adds this – and here is the image: "America was always trying, almost as blindly as an earthworm, to realize and understand itself; to catch up with its own head, and to twist about in search of its tail." Adams' legendary account of his own failure in American society – a talent left unused because unfit for the new nation – is also an account of competition for effective leadership, for representative ethical status in the new America. Among his as many competitors – from Wall Street magicians who tossed the country into repeated financial crises like ours to advocates of endless commodity consumption – were historical humanists like Mahan and Theodore Roosevelt. Against these militant humanists, Adams posed an aesthetic humanism, as historical and recollective as theirs, but with a different aim of educating the imagination in and through affect to assume responsibility for imagining futures alternative to the tragic repetition Mahan urged on US as its fated obligation.

Mahan adopted the imperial thread in European humanism; he did this to two purposes: first, to establish a policy position that would make the US only the most recent iteration of a European model thematized as world historical; and second to circulate a political rhetoric that would acquire and dispose authority among elites to lead the nation functionally and formally along the line of appropriate great power development he inferred from his own historical studies of warfare, states, and civilizations. He expanded the Baron de Jomini's inventive thinking about logistics as essentially the quarter-mastering of troops to the science of organizing the socio-economy and ideology of the nation in the service of the state's ambition to meet its burdens and opportunities to be a great power. If Mommsen's version of Caesar and Rome illustrated the historical, civil, and perhaps evolutionary necessity of preemptive war and the extermination of populations, Mahan's own studies of English and French imperial competition taught him the advantages of an active state directing national resources to its own competitive glory. English geography created social and cultural skill and ambition that produced sea power unmatched by the continental French – who concentrated normally on land armies and land empire. The single outstanding exception to British naval superiority in French history, Mahan discovered, was the period when Jean-Baptiste Colbert was contrôleur général and supported his mercantilist policy of export driven trade surpluses not only with barriers to imports but the directed construction of a large Navy. In imitation, Mahan urged the structural changes with which we still live – state direction of US economy and culture by a war machine, albeit with variations of scale and success.

We have two different conceptions of humanism and the humanist intellectuals' role in US society. As we know, humanism is not just one thing, but from the same traditions, Adams and Mahan derive different truths, ethical ideals, and conceptions of the human – to say nothing for the moment about their sense of American possibility.

For Mahan, all aesthesis and poesis organize power, influencing affect among the people by, in fact, creating an affective structure that embraces geopolitical state violence as a necessary if fearful fatal obligation and opportunity. For Adams, all human history teaches the necessity of struggling against the exploitation and hardening of affect and imagination – something so easily done! – by educating populations to restore affective responses to human actions, to human possibility, to the record of human achievements, and to the feeling for futural responsibilities.

The Education of Henry Adams is the most famous of his efforts to think this through, but *Mont St. Michel and Chartres,* somewhat earlier and more explicitly historical, aesthetic, and humanistic, dramatizes the sort of difference we see between himself and Mahan while enacting the human virtues of a much differently recollected aesthetic pedagogy. Among others, the chief characteristics of this work are appreciative intellectual humility, – recall the pairing with Pascal – the valuing of quotidian as well as grand creative and restorative efforts of mind and feeling, and education in the affective perceptions of contrapuntal and catechretical developments of cultural and political practices and formations. If time allowed, *Mont Saint Michel and Chartres*, with all its nautical language and concerns for the mapping of cultural, imaginative, and economic political civilizations, would appear as the explicit alternative to Mahan's great thesis of historical scholarship on naval warfare from which he hoped to derive universal principles of state power.

What Adams wanted from humanism was to educate the American population to accept a place not in the conflict but in the imaginative counterpoint of civilizations. There are three elements in *Mont St. Michel* that highlight the potential for this anti-imperialist American pedagogy. First, Adams placed Americans in a continuous relation with Europeans, not with the English per se but with their own conquerors, the Normans. Re-creating a Norman genealogy for Americans simultaneously loosens the old ties between new and old Englanders while shaking the then emerging special US/UK relation. Also contra-Mahan, it attaches the US to a preeminent land power with intellectual and artistic as well as political reach and creativity. Adams' assertion that all Americans have ancestors in Normandy, while certainly racially and socially ignorant and thoughtless, does some good work in opening the US towards racially, religiously, and linguistically complex elements of its origins and formations.

Second, he does this by mapping multi-directional routes of trade, war, and culture. He recollected these as an image of a multipolar world of shifting powers and influences, defined by struggles for and of creativity, struggles often pitched against the ambitions of state and religious empire that would arrest the flows along these roots or reduce them to a controlled logistical system of effective hegemony. At the heart of Adams' recollected mapping are his interests in translation, the circulation of knowledge, and the mixture of styles. A book that looks like a travelogue directed to readers back home with its focus on the corner of an old European state follows movements at least from Baghdad to New England.

And, third, he insists on drawing readers into the experience of aesthetic difference. Adapting Wordsworth, he reverses the trope of America's youth to make Americans old and settled in affect. The narrator persistently points out how affect is alone the only means to feel the value and significance of the art created in the Romanesque and Gothic styles that are, otherwise, unavailable to Americans who come to them numbed by an imperial project that not only lacks sympathy but empathy and curiosity. The narrator is a comparative humanist,

drawing sharp distinctions between times as well as places and, like his predecessor, the great European historical humanist, Giambattista Vico, he would
influence the bases of judgment through aesthetic as well as memorial devices.
Adams' readings of the Cathedral at Chartres, for example, dramatically enact
both the historical circumstances of its creation and the agonistics involved in
bringing Americans into relation with their own affective capacities as the condition
for understanding Chartres and its world as an alternative to theirs. In the comparative aesthetic imagining of a past world, an act that requires and enables the
reactivation of capacities lost to the imperial American, Adams would recreate
the possibility, contra Mahan, for imagining alternative futures the likes of which
offer the more humane possibilities than Mahan's great power ambitions allow.

In the case of China, for example, Adams anticipated the inevitable displacement of US leadership by an ascendant and modernized China. Fearful as
always of war, Adams wrote to Mrs. Cameron from Paris, not long before the
First World War, about the need for the US to win the war of influence in China
over what he called, "Russian inertia." Adams famously influenced George Kennan in the latter's conception of the need for US cultural, ideological, economic,
and diplomatic containment of Russia and the Soviet Union. For Adams, as for
Kennan later, the debate over Russia and China in the US was very much also a
debate over the US and its political experiments. Setting aside for the moment
the arguments over Kennan and the militarization of containment, Adams, as
David Contasta has shown in a study of his politics, always worked for peace, a
goal he believed depended in the US context upon educating the imagination by
developing aesthetically the affective elements of human being – especially the
possibilities of empathy and curiosity.

Always an historical realist in the materialities of power, Adams thought of
the American experiment as a lofty one but uncertain in its democratic outcomes,
that is, uncertain in its ability to persist, to effect transformations in world politics. Unlike Mahan and his allies whose commitment to the opportunities of
power took form in the intellectual arrogance of assured policy decisions, Adams
would hesitate, aware that the right to lead had to reflect the modesty that comes
along with the admiration for an understanding of human accomplishment and
loss. Learned in the comparative values of contrapuntal cultural formations,
Adams escaped the anxieties of a Mahan. Unwilling to murder in an attempt to
assure the world historical status of the American experiment, Adams' humanism would position America as the workings of Norman power had allowed for
contrapuntal creativities that resulted in what Adams remarks is the only known
European example of one dominant power creating two entirely different styles
of life and art.

Between Adams and Mahan, the issue was education and the lessons to be drawn from human historicality. Should all aesthesis and poesis concentrate its powers upon the execution of state power to impact and order the world alone a single line of as yet unsure development, simply because, empowered intellectuals might derive from their histories the apparently universal rules of power? Or, should humanists learn the lessons of multi-polar creativities that tolerantly cross each other, not without human loss and cost? Intellectuals in great powers, or in aspiring great powers, if humanely curious, empathetic, and creative would refuse state demanded service for purposes more responsible to just and balanced futures – purposes that themselves only emerge from populations that served not assaulted, cultivated not coerced, and awakened in their imaginations, not narrowed in their knowledge and sensibilities.

The conflict of American humanisms, drawn from long past European traditions, renewed and repositioned, carry lessons for humanisms in other places and future times. China, for example, would be well served not to repeat the errors of US great power humanists, too committed to nation, too little committed to comparative knowledge and empathy, and too little valuing the cultural and creative products of autonomous human beings, wherever and whenever they might be found.

The Aw(e)ful Spread of Literary Theory

Val Cunningham
Corpus Christi College, Oxford

An aweing phenomenon of our time has been the spread of Literary Theory, its complete canonization as a set of tools for analysis and interpretation – and not just for things literary, but in so many areas of thought and research. *Vicisti*, the literary-critical world has to say, 'Thou hast conquered', as Julian the Apostate is said to have cried, about Jesus the Galilean: 'Thou hast conquered, O pale Galilean', in those words of Swinburne in his 'Hymn to Proserpine'. Theory and theorists have indeed conquered the business of literary study, have completely reshaped reading and interpretative practices, have effected paradigm shift – shifts in fact – across the whole scene of literary hermeneutic. And, in turn, literary theory, or theories, have colonized every interpretative practice there is. Literary theory has leapt over the literary-critical wall; its branches (to use a Biblical metaphor) have spread exuberantly. Derrida famously once said that genres, like texts, transgress all boundaries assigned to them. Literary Theory has wonderfully exhibited such boundlessness. Critique across the board is now thoroughly literary-theorized; often without much, or any, remembrance of its literary-critical roots. So that Literary Theory is often Theory *tout court*. And the extent and interpretative power of modern (Literary) Theory – what's been promoted and promulgated as analytically essential in the wake of the linguistic turn, in our post-Saussurean world, commanded by the two giant masters of modern critique, namely Derrida and Foucault – is indeed awesome.

In his *The Rise of the Novel* (1957) Ian Watt memorably imagined the relationship of the economics story of *Robinson Crusoe* with the religious aspects of that novel as being like that on a newspaper where the economics correspondent might occasionally pop down the corridor to get the views of the religious affairs person. What has happened in the post-Saussurean, post-modern/linguistic turn is that more or less every department of humanistic thinking, analysis, research has gone down the corridor to pick up critical tricks – get the critical 'knowledge' (as London taxi-drivers call their intimates' way of getting around the city) – from the theorized literary colleagues. Historians, art-historians, geographers, psychologists, musicologists, cinematographers, urbanists, sociologists, anthropologists, theologians and Biblicists, even architects have all rekitted, retooled in the English/literature/cultural studies department(s). Stephen D Moore – now the doyen of Queer/Derridean/Foucauldian Bible studies – presents himself in his 2001 book *God's Beauty Parlour: Queer Spaces In and Around the Bible*, as attending the 1994 MLA convention in his one-time standard old-fashioned Bible-historicist persona, mooning about achingly on the fringes of that literary-theory intoxicated event, wishing he were a member of the smart, progressive interpretative guild excitingly busy all around him, strutting their stuff on the Theory front-line. And he lost no time in joining in, going over, down the corridor, keen to genuflect (and as an ex-priest he knew all about genuflecting) in the House of Theory. He soon came out with *Literary Criticism and the Gospels: The Theoretical Challenge* in 1989, followed not all that long after by *Mark and Luke in Poststructuralist Perspective: Jesus Begins to Write* in 1992; and soon after that in 1994 *Poststructuralism and the New Testament: Derrida and Foucault at the Foot of the Cross*; and then *God's Gym: Divine Male Bodies of the Bible* in 1996. The confessional *God's Beauty Parlour* (2001) was followed in turn by *New Testament Masculinities* of 2003. And so on. A dramatic renewal, a repositioning of reading ways and assumptions, rather typical of what has gone on in Biblical studies. A renewal which has likewise gone forward in historical, and geographical and musicological studies, and all the rest *si qua alia*. That epiphanic moment at the MLA is mirrored all over the place. The geographer Derek Gregory, for instance, tells how he left Cambridge University in 1989 for the University of British Columbia with the manuscript of an old-fashioned book called *The Geographical Imagination* in his baggage which he soon threw away at the end of his first term, confronted as he and it were by Canadian multiculturalism, post-colonial awareness and gender anxieties, the going theoretical repertoires exercising his new colleagues – a Theory cast-list named as 'the geographies written into many of Michel Foucault's histories', the 'historical materialism' of Fredric Jameson and Henri Lefebvre, the 'feminism and poststructuralism' of bell hooks and Henri Haraway, the 'cultural studies and postcolonialism' of Edward Said and Gayatri Chakravorty Spivack'. Imagination-stirring encounters – Theory and theorists 'conjur[ing] up a sense of political and intellectual ebullition that is, I think, unprecedented' – which command the (excellent) replacement tome *Geographical Imaginations*.[1] In 1987 the Shakespearian Marjorie Garber brilliantly described Shakespeare as the 'transferential love-object of literary studies'.[2] But what's even truer is how Theory became the transferential love object of literary studies and Literary Theory became the transferential love-object of pretty well all the areas of humanistic inquiry one can think of.

1   Derek Gregory, *Geographical Imaginations* (Blackwell, Cambridge MA & Oxford, 1994), ix, 4.
2   Marjorie Garber, *Shakespeare's Ghost Writers: Literature as Uncanny Causality* (Methuen, NY & London, 1987), xiv.

A kind of gadarene rush down the corridor! Certainly, almost all humanist critique has gotten wedded to the fundamental and fundamentalist post-Saussurean notion that all structures, all systems are textual: are all 'structured like a language', as Lacan put it of the mind, or structured like a made linguistic thing (or things), and are therefore subject to textual, or quasi-textual analysis, using the tools, or angles, of modern textual analytical considerations. So that it has become normal – it is simply normal – for the (very good) art-historian Adrian Rifkin to declare that London is 'an essentially unsatisfactory and even frustrating linguistic structure'. This in a piece entitled 'Benjamin's Paris, Freud's Rome: Whose London?', a stirring combination of history, art-history, urban geography and psychoanalysis; quoted (naturally enough) in an essay by the film-maker and critic Patrick Keiller (the friend and ally of the great London 'psycho-geographer' Iain Sinclair) called 'Imaging', in *Restless Cities*, an *A-Z* (chapters from 'Archiving' to 'Zig-Zagging') about reading the city as if it were a text (and a fictional one at that).[3]

The 'text' in question here is of course a merely analogous item, a metaphor, but still a patently useful one, here as in so many cases. Naturally, not all areas of critique yield to the 'as if' of the textualizing metaphoric as readily as do some others. Biblical studies, for example, involving as they do a Book, or books, are in any case textual studies; so the post-structural assumption sits easily on them. It's a kind of neo-textualizing. By the same sort of token, it's no accident that Neo-Historicist studies should prefer reading historical things via some already textualized form. (I'm thinking of Stephen Greenblatt's foundational illustration of the New Historical project as being all about the circulation of texts, as in the Norman Mailer-Gary Gilmore case: historical work conceived on the New Historicist plan as being all metatextual.[4] Or metahistorical, in Hayden White's so influential way of putting the matter).[5] Plainly, the textual notion has a lot further to travel when applied to (say) the human body, or gender, or the prison system, or colonialism – a point repeatedly brought home in Gregory's *Geographical Imaginations*, which wants clamantly to remind Theorists such as Gayatri Spivack and Homi Bhabha that, though 'India' can profitably be thought of as a hybrid 'discursive site' it is also a real place, comprising real streets and real people really stressed economically and by class and in gender terms (Gregory,

3   Adrian Rifkin, 'Benjamin's Paris, Freud's Rome: Whose London?', *Art History* 22 (1999), 619-32; quoted Patrick Keiller in 'Imaging', *Restless Cities*, edd Matthew Beaumont & Gregory Dart (Verso, London, 2010), 139-154.

4   Stephen Greenblatt, 'Towards a Poetics of Culture', in *The New Historicism*, ed H Aram Veeser (Routledge, NY & London, 1989), 1-14.

5   Hayden V White, *Metahistory: The Historical Imagination in Nineteenth-Century Europe* (Johns Hopkins UP, Baltimore, 1973).

op cit, eg 167ff). But it is arresting – and *Geographical Imaginations* is a fine case in point – that post-modern theorized readings of cities, bodies, prisons, gender, orientalism, and so forth, do work greatly through text, the already textualized, tending to use fictional and non-fictional narratives, aesthetic objects, novels, photographs, films, and so on.

And, of course, there's only one textualizing. Once you, as a musicologist, or geographer, or historian, or whatever, accept the textual assumption, that acceptance (or creed) inevitably lets in – it demands even – that reading, interpretation be done by the current textual, literary, rhetorical means and tropes supplied by Theory. Which means, to take as examples certain very current tropes, that all your now textualized objects of analysis will be conceived of as a site, or a theatre, as play, a performance, as a museum exhibition; that reading and interpretation will be thought of as matters of making, building, construction (or co-construction); that reading will be constrained, or licensed, by what Michel de Certeau calls 'an erotics of knowledge'. Take, for celebratory instance, Michel de Certeau on the rhetoric and poetics of reading the city as a pedestrian (in Chapter 7 of *The Practice of Everyday Life*, 'Walking in the City'), celebrating the 'ecstasy', the erotics, of reading the 'texturology' of New York from the 110th floor of the then-standing World Trade Centre (reminiscent of Roland Barthes gloriously construing the text of Paris from up the Eiffel Tower[6]): a matter of 'pedestrian speech acts', 'pedestrian enunciation', of what de Certeau cites Derrida hailing as 'a wandering of the semantic'; an affair of the rhetorics of space, of movement around the city as the performance of synecdoches and ellipses.[7] It's a wonderful delirium of textualized apprehension, knowledge, interpretation; wonderfully attractive, and convincing, up to a point. As attractive as the historian conceived of and acting as museologist or curator, thinking of the texts of history, of history as text, in terms of museum exhibits, in the museum as a multivalent sign-system.[8]

And, to be sure, there's been massive interpretative pay-off like this from the worldwide interdisciplinarian theorizing which has ensued in literary theory's wake. Literary theory has been a genuine enlivener of so much modern analysis. Modernist/postmodernist Theory has been the password, the access card, the

---

6   Roland Barthes, 'The Eiffel Tower', *The Eiffel Tower and Other Mythologies*, trans Richard Howard (Hill & Wang, NY, 1979), 3-17.

7   Michel de Certeau, 'Spatial Practices', *The Practice of Everyday Life*, trans Steven Rendall (U of California Press, Berkeley & London), Part 3, Ch 7, pp 91-114. Jacques Derrida, *Marges de la philosophie* (Minuit, Paris, 1972), 32 (on metaphor, as it happens).

8   John Urry, 'Postmodern museums' section of 'Gazing on History', in *Representing the Nation, A Reader: Histories, Heritage and Museums*, edd David Boswell & Jessica Evans (Routledge, London & NY, 1999), 226-230.

open-sesame to so much good interpretation. It's opened doors, opened eyes, uncovered what one is persuaded are the actualities of so many systems, so many of the cases which have been so readily swept up into the category of 'discourses'. Especially in analyses driven by real, that is faithful, Derrideanism and by the brilliant historical analyses of Foucault. Think how thinking about power after Foucault has revolutionized perceptions of gender and race (and class). Think how useful the notion of the subordinating *gaze* of power has been in thinking about 'institutions'. (And how analytically useful Foucault's researches have been in their prompting the very model of 'institution'.) No Foucault, in fact – which is to say, at the very least, without Foucault's textualizing of old Marxian concerns – then no new-historicism, no post-colonialism, no third generation feminism or queer studies. And how extraordinarily powerful, how revelatory, has been the genderizing, and queering, of history and art-history, sociology and geography, urban studies, musicology, and so forth. 'Can a flattened third be gay?' someone once asked. Oh yes it can, Q-theorists reply; and musicology has been utterly revolutionized by Q-theory. Nowadays, it is literally unthinkable what humanistic research would do without Theory's analytic repertoires. Characteristically of contemporary humanistic research, the title of historian-of-science Steven Shapin's recent book indicates just how greatly Theory's conceptual and analytic menu has repositioned everything in his subject: *Never Pure: Historical Studies of Science as if It Was Produced by People With Bodies, Situated in Time, Space, Culture, and Society, and Struggling for Credibility and Authority.*[9] Production; Bodies; Time; Space; Authority; Credibility; Struggling for .... (Nicely advertising too the textualized, discursive, metaphorical aspect of these concerns and activities: all *as if.*)

Analytic pay-off, of course. Which comes, though, not without certain perturbations. For my part, I find it hard to take the idea of selving and of ethnicity as matters of mere 'construction' or mere 'performance'[10]; to reckon that gender is a matter merely of theatre, that the self is entirely at the mercy of a kind of personal psychic wardrobe mistress or props manager (the influential Judith Butler assumption, sustained, of course, by the self-fashioning models common in the theorized literary-historical world, exemplified by Stephen Greenblatt's *Renaissance Self-fashioning* [11]). And it does seem to me obvious that too many

---

9   Steven Shapin, *Never Pure: Historical Studies of Science as if it Was Produced by People With Bodies, Situated in Time, Space, Culture, and Society, and Struggling for Credibility and Authority* (John Hopkins UP, Baltimore, 2010).

10   Edward Ball, *Constructing Ethnicity, in Visual Display: Culture Beyond Appearances*, ed Lynne Cooke & Peter Wollen (Bay Press, Seattle, 1995), 143-153.

11   Stephen Greenblatt, *Renaissance Self-fashioning: From More to Shakespeare* (U of Chicago Press, 1980).

of what we have to think of as the Theory converts, the happy neo-textualizers outwith the literary domain, fail to worry enough about the implications of much of what they so greedily borrow. All over the analytical shop there's an awfully unconcerned welcoming of what seem to me some most deeply problematic interpretative and hermeneutic positions: ones utterly intrinsic to the widely borrowed textual assumptions as originally shaped and advocated down the corridor in the literary-theoretical department. In particular, theoretical notions to do with the altogether negativity of text, of text as an always unravellable complex of negativities; a fullness of deceptions, traps, lures; a taunting scene where what's possible is after all only the impossible.

In other words, the utterly aporetic text of Theory. (*Never pure*, as Steven Shapin's title has it.) The complexly unsatisfactory text of Theory. What Adrian Rifkin was drawing on in describing London as 'an essentially and even frustrating linguistic structure'. The there but not-there text – wholly a virtuality, a potentiality, requiring readerly construction, making, building, for its existence: the work brought into being only by reader work (the Barthesian 'work').The apparently overt, but actually covert text; the present, but actually absent text. The forever elusive, deferred, retreating, abysmal text. Beliefs about text, a metaphoricizing, of course based in strong misreading, unbalancing readings, of Derrida's delicately balanced binarism, his central différance, his preoccupation with thresholds, his profound 'two interpretations of interpreting', and so on. All of them difficult enough to grant credence to back at the theory base-camps down the corridor, but characteristically of humanistic research, very difficult indeed to accept as runners when applied to, or assumed in, the concerns of as it were worldly critique. There's real difficulty attendant on supposing that nature, things, city, persons, bodies are altogether, or mainly, merely virtual – blank pages awaiting readerly inscription; no-things, non-presences, until scripted into being.

I take what has happened in Biblical and Religious Studies as a prime case of Literary theory's unstoppable spread, for both good and ill. Recent Biblical and Religious Studies are a clear example of how utterly energizing literary theory has been, and can be, down the corridor. What a magnificent theory-generated *ebullition* there's been in this important area of humanistic research, to use Derek Gregory's word. But here is also an example of how the scepticism-diminishing excitements of converts inevitably go too far.

The initial theoretical hits can be dated exactly: to September 1969, when the French Catholic Association for the Study of the Bible, having got wind of structuralism, got Roland Barthes to do a structuralist job on Acts 10-11, the story of St Peter and Cornelius.[12] Swiftly followed by the Protestants of the Geneva Fa-

---

12 Roland Barthes, 'L'Analyse structurale du récit: apropos Actes X-XI', in *Exégèse et herméneutique: colloque de la Société des exégètes de France, Chantilly, 1969* (Seuil, Paris, 1971).

culty of Theology – not to be outdone – who in February 1971 got Jean Starobinski and Roland Barthes to do a Biblical structuralist double-act, Starobinski
on Mark 5 (the Gadarene demoniac), Barthes on Genesis 32 (Wrestling Jacob).[13]
The effect, especially of Barthes's Wrestling Jacob analysis, could not have been
more momentous – in every direction. Talk about ebullition. As Barthes would
have it, this Biblical text could not have been more ripe for the structuralist and
post-structuralist considerations he liberally anointed it with. This bit of Scripture was, of course, *écriture*, and so a 'literary text'. It was highly *intertextual*
(on the Kristeva plan). Its truths were only textual (Barthes waives the kerygmat-
ic and the Jewish historical, the source in this story of Orthodox taboo on thigh-
bone marrow) – as in his Acts 10-11 reading, this is mere writing about writing,
'as Derrida has said in the *Grammatologie*'. Barthes makes some use of Propp's
Morphology of the Folk Tale – here's a folkloric struggle and branding of the
hero – and of Jakobson's sender-message-receiver model (in which God is both
sender and receiver); but Barthes' interest is already more post-structuralist than
structuralist. So this text is a weave of *differences*, indeterminately bordered (in
the initial doubling by which the Jabok river is crossed twice), a matter of textual
frottement (friction), *grincement* (a grinding of legibility), of *embarass* (ie aporia),
an *embrouillé* text (who exactly are the *he* and the *him* of the story), an affair of
détournement (deviousness: in the antagonist's low winning blow). And the interpretative outcome of this theorizing venture was vast. For Barthes's fellow theorists
and for literary departments in the first place, in the feedback movement often ob-
servable in these leapings over the wall. Wrestling Jacob, as text and exemplum,
was rapidly absorbed as a model for Yale deconstructionists, including Derrida
himself, for J-text obsessive Harold Bloom, for Geoffrey Hartman (modelling midrash as interpretative practice).[14] It was Barthes in the arms of the Geneva Biblicists who set in motion the Biblicization of the Eng Lit professoriate and of the literary syllabus which has been such a phenomenon of contemporary literary study.
The two early massive extenders of Barthes's slim genetic gesture were, of course,
Frank Kermode in *The Genesis of Secrecy* (1979) and Robert Alter in *The Art of
Biblical Narrative* (1981).[15] Kermode offering the Gospel of Mark as a sort of

---

13 Jean Starobinski, 'Le Démoniaque gérasène: analyse littéraire de Marc 5, 1-20'; & Roland
    Barthes, 'La Lutte avec l'ange: analyse textuelle de Genèse 32, 22-32', in *Analyse structurale et
    exégèse biblique* (Labor et Fides, Geneva, 1972).

14 See Geoffrey Hartman, 'The Struggle for the Text', in *Midrash and Literature*, ed Hartman &
    Sanford Budick (Yale UP, New Haven & London, 1986), 1-18; and Harold Bloom, 'Wrestling
    Sigmund: Three Paradigms for Poetic Originality', *The Breaking of the Vessels* (Chicago UP,
    Chicago & London, 1982), 47ff.

15 Frank Kermode, *The Genesis of Secrecy : On the Interpretation of Narrative* (Harvard UP,
    Cambridge MA & London, 1979); Robert Alter, *The Art of Biblical Narrative* (George Allen &
    Unwin, London & Sydney, 1981).

postmodern novel; midrashic, ie intertextual, on Old Testament narratives; offering, but deferring, pleroma; with endless jouissance as its real business, the parables as Freudian dream-texts, and all its 'facts' as figura, or Barthesian 'codes' of history, mere 'illusion of pure reference' (a gloss on Starobinski on the Gerasene demoniac). And Alter doing a lot similar with the Hebrew Bible – its texts read as historicized prose fiction (like Shakespeare's History Plays), or as (post) modernist fiction along the lines of Sterne and Rabelais and their modern avatars, Proust and James, Conrad and Nabokov; texts offering horizons of 'perfect knowledge' which are overtaken according to the Bible's practice of 'contemporary agnosticism about all its meanings'. A 'doing', as Henry James might have put it, of the Bible as a kind of manifesto of (post)modern hermeneutic tropes and opportunities which of course animated the Englit, and plain old Lit, camaraderie in their newly inspired attention to the Bible (eg Gabriel Josipovici, Regina Schwartz, Stephen Prickett, Piero Boitani, Terence Wright, and so on and on[16]), but, even more so, turned on the Biblicists and Religious Studies people as nothing had done since the great arrival of the theory and practice of the Higher Criticism in the 19th century.

Inspired by Barthes's superb avatars Kermode and Alter, Biblicists worldwide hastened to put on the whole armour of Theory. Whole religion departments were converted (at Sheffield university notably). Religion Journals became Theory flagships: *Semeia* notably;*The Sheffield Journal for the Study of the Old Testament* prominently. The Postmodern Bible Collectives swarmed: Theorized bees around the Biblical honeypot. By 1998 André LaCoque and Paul Ricoeur were able to speak confidently for a whole trade in thinking that reading the Bible in a post-structuralist way (stressing the theoretically standard polyvalence, gappiness, multi-dimensionality, midrash upon midrash, reader centrality, and so on) was indeed, as their title of that year has it, *Thinking Biblically.*[17] And to a degree commensurate with experience elsewhere in the freshly theorized humanities, the interpretative payoff hereabouts has been duly immense. Postmodernist feminists led by Mieke Bal undoing the violent patriarchalism of Old Testament stories; angry post-Foucauldian, post-Edward Saidian inspectors of

16   Gabriel Josipovici, *The Book of God: A Response to the Bible* (Yale UP, New Haven & London, 1988); Regina Schwartz, *Remembering and Repeating: Biblical Creation in Paradise Lost* (Cambridge UP, Cambridge, 1988), & ed, *The Book and the Text: The Bible and Literary Theory* (Basil Blackwell, Cambridge MA & Oxford, 1990); Stephen Prickett, *Origins of Narrative: The Romantic Appropriation of the Bible* (Cambridge UP, Cambridge, 1995); Piero Boitani, *The Bible and its Rewritings*, trans Anita Weston (Oxford UP, Oxford, 1999); Terence Wright, *DH Lawrence and the Bible* (Cambridge UP, Cambridge, 2000), & *The Genesis of Fiction: Modern Novelists as Biblical Interpreters* (Ashgate, Aldershot, 2007).

17   André LaCoque & Paul Ricoeur, *Thinking Biblically: Exegetical and Hermeneutical Studies*, trans David Pellauer (Chicago UP, Chicago, 1998).

the politics of Biblical interpretation in terms of class and race; feminist deconstructionists such as Yvonne Sherwood who wonderfully theorizes Hosea's prostitute marriage and undoes the reception history of Jonah; a lot of the group work
of the Postmodern Bible Collectives,[18] and in the continually impressive and
enlightening *Derrida's Bible (Reading a Page of Scripture with a Little Help
from Derrida*: edited by Yvonne Sherwood and including characteristically
strong theorized pieces like Frank Yamada on shibboleths of identity in Judges
12, Mark Brummit on secrets, secretaries and scrolls in Jeremiah, Robert See-
sengood reading the Pastoral Epistles as Derridean post-cards from God, and, of
course, Sherwood's lovely deconstruction of Genesis 23.2, 'And Sarah Died',
structured around the multivalences of Hebrew *waw* with not a little help from Derrida and his obituary of Sarah Kofman and his *Donner la mort* (1999). Critique
could scarcely ask for better.[19] But, horribly too, our theoretically enthused Biblicists too often give us a lot worse.

Lengthily across the shelves of Theology Faculty libraries the worst possible
critical crimes are committed in the name of too uncritically embraced Saussure,
Derrida and Foucault. On those shelves, the parables turn out to be a set of merely arbitrary signifiers; The Book of Revelation is an utterly bottomless pit of
erasure, fissure, ruptured hymen; 'Ponge' Pilate mops up Jesus 'at the stake';
The Gospel of Luke is full of Lacanian lacks; St Paul is penetrated by the rigid
extension of god's phallus, as he organizes a 'chain-gang' of god's buggerees
who groan orgasmically with those 'sighs too deep for words' of the Book of
Romans; Jesus shows he is a masculinist, racist, colonialist, *Birth of the Clinic*
supremacist in assuming to 'heal' the 'demon possessed' Syro-Phoenician woman of the Gospel of Matthew; Jesus is an anti-semite because he wants to overturn Hebraic Law; the apparently oppressive multi-gazings and penetratings of
the Book of Revelation involve not just the Whore of Babylon but the Book's
'effeminized' Lamb; the crucifixion is 'divine child-abuse'.[20] And so on and on.
Chief among the perpetrators of such enthusiastically misguided interpretations
is the eminent Biblicist Stephen Moore – one-time Roman Catholic priest, dabbler
in charismatism, who spent time (of course) in the theorized Sheffield Religion

---

18 See, Bible and Culture Collective, *The Postmodern Bible* (Yale UP, New Haven & London,
    1995), & David Jobling, Tina Pippin and Ronald Schleifer, edd, *The Postmodern Bible Reader*
    (Blackwell, Oxford, 2001).

19 Yvonne Sherwood, ed, *Derrida's Bible (Reading a Page of Scripture with a Little Help from
    Derrida)* (Palgrave Macmillan, NY & Basingstoke, 2004). For fuller detail, see Valentine Cun-
    ningham, 'Bible Reading And/After Theory', *The Oxford Handbook of the Reception History of
    the Bible*, edd Michael Lieb, Emma Mason, Jonathan Roberts (Oxford UP, Oxford, 2011), 649-
    673.

20 Detailed references and grisly more in Cunningham, op cit.

Department, was big in the first Postmodern Bible Collective, he who, inspired by MLA doings, retooled intellectually on heavy doses of poststructuralism. OD'd rather. Moore's Jahwe, for instance, is a body-builder with a body made colossal by the daily intake of animal protein in the Temple's cuisine of sacrifice, but with a body-builder's regular body problems – 'bitch-tits' and shrunken testicles (which is why he shows only his 'back parts' to Moses, embarrassed as he is by his small cojones, but exciting all Israelite males into homosexual lust in the process. Moore's God is a Foucauldian sado-masochist who arranges the cruci-fixion so he can take orgasmic delight in the death of his son.[21] He also takes cruel sexual delight in hurting his Jewish and Christian followers, penetrating the rabbinical scholar with the Torah scroll, which is the phallus of a deity who is turned on by the 'French kissing' of the 'Oral Torah', while the on-looking Bri-degroom of Revelation, another 'she-male', 'all cleft', enjoys 'spiritual cunnilin-gus' from the faithful.[22] Etc, etc, etc. Silly, silly stuff. *Beliebig* critique, John Barton has rightly labelled this sort of thing: the critical folly, crime even, of Saying Absolutely Anything You Like.[23] It's queer reading that's queer in the old common-or-garden sense of queer. It's extreme textual violence, *abusio*, as the old rhetoric books would have it; extreme *katachresis*, *abusio*'s ancient Greek equivalent. Monstrous critique, egged on by the excesses of the literary theorists Moore, and his religionist colleagues, have so cheerfully ingested. All the aweingly awful result of literary theory's uncritical spread – and all too hor-ribly characteristic of Theory's humanist converts.

---

21 Stephen D Moore, *Poststructuralism and the New Testament: Derrida & Foucault at the Foot of the Cross* (Fortress Press, Minneapolis, 1994), 105ff; & God's Gym: *Divine Male Bodies of the Bible* (Routledge, NY & London, 1996), 12.

22 Stephen D Moore, *God's Beauty Parlour and Other Queer Spaces In and Around the Bible* (Stanford UP, Stanford Calif, 2001), 28-35, 405, 222.

23 John Barton, in Postscript in Sherwood, ed, *Derrida's Bible*, 301-3.

The Play and Place of Literary Theory

Jürgen Schlaeger
Humboldt-University of Berlin

„Theories are analytical tools for understanding and explaining a given subject matter." This dictionary definition sounds straightforward and innocuous enough. But theories can be and do many other things as well. The choice of a particular theory always means entering a certain kind of relationship with one's object. Ideally, theories should leave their objects untouched, should look at it, however closely, from the outside, not interfere with it in the act of analysis.

But as we all know, this never happens and is even logically impossible. Theorizing is, after all, also, and in the humanities primarily so, one of the major tools minds have developed to create order in their own complex cognitive and emotional processes and structures. It is basically and fundamentally a self-centred affair and, haven't we all experienced it, turning inward is a very difficult thing to do objectively. So, whatever our analytical minds are up to when they are doing theory, they are definitely not merely concerned with something out there.

This is one of the reasons why the relationships, theoretical endeavours in our fields enter in their effort to analyse and explain, are often so similar to human relationships: theories can thus dominate, efface, suppress, caress, stifle, encourage, foster, exploit or brainwash the objects of their attention. The relationship can be intimate or distanced, symbiotic or parasitical, custodial or consuming.

As far as literary theory is concerned we have seen all of it happening. Literature as a whole or certain bodies of texts have withered away, lost their specificity and identity under too close attention from theoreticians whose interests lay more in the internal consistency of their arguments or in the general moral or political points they wanted to make than in a true and fair dialogue between a theoretical hypothesis and the object under investigation. It usually is not a match between equals. Literature rarely talks back and its readers usually do not care about what the academy is doing with all its theorizing.

Be that as it may, within the academy doing theory has become an indispensible trademark for quality and standing in the profession. Books that do not present their theoretical credentials are few and far between. I have not seen a thesis for quite a while that did not start with a more or less extensive declaration of faith in matters theory. Interpretation, after all one of the universal and central activities of all human cultures, does not seem self-legitimizing any more, at least not among the interpreting professions. Everything we do with a text has to be bolstered up with some theoretical reflection, even when this is not very helpful for unearthing what we think is central to the piece of literature in front of our eyes.

Otherwise, we are afraid, what we want to say, may sound too pedestrian, conservative or out of touch with the latest developments. However, the massive theorizing of the field which we have observed since the fifties of the last century had one real advantage: it replaced the no longer possible consensus on the cannon, on the role of the academy in protecting and expounding it and on the values enshrined in it, by building another apparently more rational, even objective stage for productive debates, for fruitful controversies and, in a more general sense, for some progress in our attempts to understand what literature tells us about our ways of world-making.

But 50 years later we have to admit that theory did not provide the sort of bulwark against the multiplication of interests and the diversification of approaches which we had expected. On the contrary, after a longer period of high hopes theorizing seems to have accelerated the diffusive dynamics of diffusion, so that, today we are in that sense back to square one. Not clear and succinctly argued alternatives govern the debates but an ever growing number of special concerns living peacefully or even oblivious to each other side by side have become typical for the whole field of literary studies.

The battle lines have become confused. The armoury for leading conventional intellectual wars are still there, but if there still is something that looks like a war of minds, it is more of the guerrilla and insurgency type. The generation of my teachers had made literary theory fashionable and we should not be too much surprised that in the process theory has changed its character from being the name for consistent thought-systems with clearly defined methods and solid foundations to mere fashions in which the display of skills in handling a broad range of theoretical concepts counts for more than cognitive substance. Literature is central to our ways of world-making and literary theory used to be the cognitively demanding and logically consistent bird's eye view of that process. Slowly and almost imperceptibly theorizing has lost that distance and has become part of primary world-making. It still claimed and claims the status and weight of an extra academic effort but did and does no longer add to our cognitive grasp of literature's contribution to world-making.

In short, the situation became highly confused, not for the lack of theorizing, but for a surplus of it, particularly for the way it was and is done. Instead of opening spaces for debates about different theoretical approaches it has strengthened the tendency to build coteries and networks of like-minded scholars with similar narrow interests whose basic assumptions are so close to each other that they fail to trigger cognitively stimulating discussions and controversies. If they compete at all it is in the market place for reputations, for the goodies in our profession such as extra sabbaticals and positions in some centre for advanced studies and last, but not least, for remuneration, and not for an advancement of knowledge in the venerable Baconian sense.

Of course, I have no answer to the existing disorientation and fragmentation and I could simply rest satisfied with its richness and plenitude and think of it as the cultural equivalent of biodiversity or, that is to say, as something valuable in itself. But that would obviously be too easy a way out. It would reduce our professional ethos to a mere reproduction of the general cultural state of affairs, if – and that is small comfort – 'on a higher academic level'. And what is more, it would tempt us, I think, to miss the opportunity of drawing highly interesting lessons from our own specific predicaments and shortcomings. What, then, are these lessons?

Literature is, and I hope we can all agree on this, one of the most complex, if not *the* most complex product of human culture and that is of the human mind. To understand how our minds work we need literature, maybe not only literature, but it would clearly be a serious omission if we left it out of the picture. In that sense literature is one of the best and broadest gateways to the working of the breathlessly sophisticated assembly of grey cells we all carry under our skulls.

Confusion in our most serious 'scientific' or scholarly efforts to analyse and understand the basic make-up and development of something that clearly provides us with one of the most fascinating documentary evidence about and insight intohow our minds work, unavoidably spells confusion throughout the professional system. To be wrong about the model of the mind we base all our theorizing on, not to speak of our 'explications de text', means to go massively wrong in the basics.

My, admittedly provocative and somewhat sweeping claim is that the observed confusion is an unmistakable sign of the fact that the mind model entailed in most of the existing theoretical approaches and interpretative practices has definitely past its sell-by date. As a paradigm that had been dominating the field for so very long, it now shows clear signs of exhaustion. Bolstering it up by an ever-expanding range of fashionable agendas and topics is no solution but ultimately aggravates the situation. Replacement by a more adequate model is overdue if we want to regain the edge and the drive we once had.

From this point in my argument I could take off into a number of directions. I could, for instance, present and discuss some of the alternative mind models which promise to get us out of the impasse. But this is not what I am going to do, at least not here and now.

Instead, I have decided to demonstrate my 'exhaustion-thesis' by a particularly telling example. My test case is the late Wolfgang Iser and the reader response theory that came to be associated with his name. He is, to be true, not a particularly good example for the theoretical confusion I have diagnosed as the malaise of our profession today, for the development in his theorizing is characterized by an unusual intellectual discipline, clarity and consistency.

And yet, I have two good reasons for picking him. The first one is personal. He was my teacher and I have had the opportunity of following his theorizing at very close range for many years. The other reason is systematic. The clearly discernible trajectory in the unfolding of his theory allows me to show the productivity but also the limits of the mind model he was working with. And in as far as his mind model is based on assumptions similar to the ones still underlying most of the theorizing today, he is as good a test case as any.

Iser's starting point for launching into theory in the sixties and for the dramatic revision "of the way literature figured in the business of interpretation" was his "encounter with modern literature." Modern literature, so Iser, is a type of writing that exposes and reflects the preconditions of its own production. It forces readers and critics alike to recognize the interim status and tentativeness of all fictional world making. Implicitly and more generally, it also exposes all definitive world views, all attempts at homogenizing and explaining the world, all ideological constructs as predicated on ultimately unwarranted and unwarrantable premises and truth claims.

From this point of view all interpretations which claimed to have unearthed the true meaning of the text fall under this judgment. But this is, of course, not the end of the story nor is it the end of all academic 'explication de text'. For the question arises what is it that comes into view, when readers, in the process of reading a modern literary text, are forced to confront the limitations of their own efforts to see closure or representation of any sort in a at best tentative piece of fictitious world making?

It was this question that drove Iser to develop his theory of reader response and ultimately to his explorations of the anthropological premises and consequences of such an experience:

> [The] conflict of interpretations" manifests itself as competition, with each type trying to assert itself at the expense of others in order to demonstrate its respective importance and the depth and breadth of its insights and range. What the conflict reveals and what makes it interesting, is the inherent limitation of all presuppositions.[1]

Literary theory had been for him not only "a response to the prevailing predicament in literary studies" resulting from the widely practised 'digging-for-meaning-

---

1   Wolfgang Iser, *The Range of Interpretation*, Columbia University Press, New York 2000, p. 3. Iser's major publications are: *The Implied Reader. Patterns of Communication in Prose Fiction from Bunyan to Beckett* (1974); *The Act of Reading. A Theory of Aesthetic Response* (1978); *Prospecting: From Reader Response to Literary Anthropology* (1989); *The Fictive and the Imaginary. Charting Literary Anthropology* (1993); *How to do Theory* (2006).

approach', but also a response to the unacceptable cannibalization of theoretical concepts from other disciplines as an antidote to the rampant subjectivism in the field.

The starting-point of Iser's own search for answers was the conviction that the literary text as an example for the aesthetic had a function radically different from other types of texts and that in the text-reader relationship too much had been taken for granted or not taken into account at all by traditional criticism. Against this background:

> Reception theory was [...] a reaction to what appeared to be a stalemate in literary studies. Of paramount concern for this theory was the impact a piece of literature has on its readers and the responses it elicits. Instead of asking what the text means, I asked what it does to its potential readers. [.....] The message [of the text] that was no longer to be ascertained triggered interest in what has since been called text processing – what happens to the text in reading.[2]

This is the decisive shift in literary theory; it is a shift from 'meaning' to aesthetic processes of constituting it, actually to the mental processes which the literary work triggers:

> Consequently, aesthetic response, as the hallmark of reception theory, is to be conceived in terms of interaction between text and reader. I call it aesthetic response because it stimulates the reader's imagination, which in turn gives life to the intended effect. (311)

As the literary works "brings into the world something that hitherto did not exist and that as best can be qualified as a virtual reality [...] my theory of aesthetic response found itself confronted with the problem of how such emerging virtual reality, which has no equivalent in our empirical world, can be processed and, indeed, understood." (311) Understanding "such an emerging virtual reality" meant for Iser to focus his theoretical interest "not only on the interface between text and reader but also on that between text and context." (311)

How can one conceive of the relationship between the literary work and the way human beings perceive, move in and deal with the world at large? Iser considers it the specific achievement of the work, more precisely of its aesthetic structure, "to refract [...] life's multifariousness" (312)

It is obvious here that Iser radically changed the perspective from which to look at the literary work; but it is equally obvious that he continues to stick to a traditional, basically ontological mind model. For him 'the work' remains a perceptual object, whose effects on a fully conscious, rational mind is at the centre of his concern.

Listen to the following quotation:

> Every literary text normally contains a selection from a variety of social, historical, cultural, and literary systems in which they fulfil their specific functions.This applies both to cultural

---

2   Wolfgang Iser, "Do I Write for an Audience?", in: *PMLA* 115, May 2000, 310-314, p. 311.

norms and to literary allusions, which are incorporated in the literary text in such a way that the structure and the semantics of the systems concerned are decomposed; the systems are rearranged when selected features of them reappear in the text.

These rearrangements move the system into focus, so that they can be discerned as referential fields of the text. [...] The selection disassembles their given order, thereby turning them into objects of observation. (311-12)

In this way literature becomes an indispensible instrument of orientation because it drags into broad daylight what our everyday dealings with the world hide: the limitedness of the available "systems" of explanation and the infiniteness of our imagination.

This basic, almost mechanical model later forms the foundation for his literary anthropology, i.e. for his answers to the question why humans produce and read literature:

What I have since called literary anthropology is thus a direct offshoot of reception theory, and it tries to handle the issues that the latter left dangling, because the function of literature is by no means entirely covered by its interaction with its readers and with its referential realities. Moreover, if a literary text does something to its readers, it simultaneously tells us something about them. Thus literature turns into a divining rod, locating our dispositions, desires, and inclinations and eventually our overall makeup. (313)

With this programme Iser is back to a very important part of his agenda: his fundamental epistemological scepticism, his firm conviction that all attempts to subsume the world under one overarching explanatory system are doomed to failure.

The world is ultimately unknowable, many important things seem to be unsayable, but literature overcomes these "deficiencies" and offers its readers the chance to transcend their limitedness – on one condition only, however: that we are always conscious in the process of reading of the conditionality of everything that takes us beyond ourselves. This is what Iser tried to catch with the notion of negativity.

I am not sure whether his characterization of what people are doing or should do is in anyway close to what actually happens in our dealings with the world out there or with the world as we find it in works of literature, but it is a logical consequence of his initial decision to see the dualism between subject and object as fundamental and to ignore the triangulation between the physical reality of the signs on the page and the complex multi-layered negotiations going on inside our minds. Iser's ontological model takes him to the concept of negation as one of literature's major strategies for shaking off the shackles of existing concepts of the real.

'Negativity' he uses to describe the fundamental anthropological condition which accompanies all our attempts to articulate and understand what is ultimately always unsayable and can never be understood completely. Negativity is the gatekeeper of the other world to which we have only access in the provisionality of fictionalizing. For Iser negativity also drives the permanent urge in human culture to invent ever new strategies for fictionalized self-extensions. Since all these strategies are stigmatized by the conditionality of their own fleeting existence they are intrinsically unstable. This instability is for Iser the main impetus for ever new attempts. We can't help doing it, but we know that it is ultimately at best provisional, in need of a controlling sceptical consciousness and instant repair. This is why we have to continue trying.

It is difficult to underestimate the fascination which this innovative approach and the argumentative force which he bolstered with phenomenological and other theories of perception, could have on his audience. Nobody who heard and saw him teaching and lecturing remained unaffected by the spell he cast, and some central passages in his writings convey that, too.

It has to be noted, however, that his intellectual stringency and inventiveness curiously went hand in hand with what Winfried Fluck once called the "frustrating sameness" of Iser's conclusions.[3] The deeper motivations that seemed to have driven this outstanding theoretician from one evasive move to the next one, from evasion of commitment to any concrete meaning or ideological frame of reference as a practice, to evasion as an anthropological principle, show up clearly in his most sweeping statements about the human condition as such. He was most completely himself in the exercise of the most stringent and rigorous analytical rationality, but at the same time fascinated by everything that lay beyond human reason in the realm of the imaginary.

He made the interplay between the two, and the 'in-between' the centrepiece of his literary anthropology, as if we only and irrevocably have rationality to hold on to and at the same time are tragically tied for ever to its inherent limitations. The mythological figure that comes to mind when thinking about the 'grand theme' in Iser's books, is definitely Sisyphus, and not Apollo, the bringer of light and the guardian of the muses.

One could ask why did he stick so doggedly to what can be called a traditional, if residual, philosophical ontology and with it to a model of the human mind, of human consciousness and its operations, that is heavily predicated on older philosophical thought-systems and their implied model of the workings of the human mind? A convincing answer is difficult because it probably lies in a combination between character, personal experience and the influence of the ruling paradigms in the humanities.

Iser's penchant for spatial metaphors in his attempt to define some of the most dynamic mental processes, speak for themselves. It is 'gaps', 'blanks', 'indeterminacies' and the 'in-between' status of literary texts, it is the dialectics between presences and absences, switch-on and switch-off-effects that structure

---

3   Winfried Fluck, "The Search for Distance: Negation and Negativity in Wolfgang Iser's Literary Theory", in: *New Literary History* 31 (2000), 175-210, p. 191.

his text models and it is 'oscillation' that characterizes the processes between texts and readers.

On the whole one cannot help feeling that Iser, in spite of his often breathtaking sophistication, operated a logo-centric, rather flat and mechanistic model of mind processes. As he went along and as his theories became ever more elaborate and ambitious he must have sensed that he had to extend constantly his theoretical tool kit in order to allow for more complexity and make up for the shortcomings of his basic model of the mind.

So he introduced the cybernetic concepts of feedback loops and recursivity; he fell back on theories of play to counteract the overstretching of his basic assumptions and, by doing it, he very often sorely tested the capacity of his audiences and even expert readers to follow him. No doubt, he was, as always, up to something highly interesting but it appears that the answers he was seeking lay ultimately outside the scope of the theoretical foundations he based his thinking on.

Making sense has been all along a wonderful gift of human evolution, and that long before human cultures developed ever more sophisticated strategies for rational analysis as the proper highway to truth. To posit that literature sits on top of this development feeding on the deficiencies of human reason in its attempts to explain the world, and that its development is driven by the growing consciousness of this human condition, underestimates massively its ability to make use of older, pre-rational and non-rational strata of the human mind which, even in its most conscious and rational operations cannot function properly without, indeed, lives on the multidimensionality of the human brain.

It is somewhat sad to see that Iser was unable to change his cognitive model when it was needed. He obviously preferred the Faustian deal of having to stick to the promises of intellectual control and, and the same time, allowing 'the aesthetic' to break its fetters as a fundamental need of humans. In the end he was facing the consequences in form of endless repetitions and a possible intellectual deadlock. Literary texts build, and train to operate, multidimensional webs of significance. The dynamics of the processes involved are way beyond the simplicities of absences and presences so central to Iser's argument. Nor do I believe, and I hope, my readers are with me here, that literature is being written and read because we as humans have a perverse desire to experience again and again and in ever new ways our own tragic limitations in our attempts to understand the world.[4]

If literary theory wants to move on and if we want to reconstruct some sort of viable intellectual framework for our endeavours to understand the play and

---

4   See also Jürgen Schlaeger, "Wolfgang Iser: Legacies and Lessons", in: *Comparative Critical Studies* 7.2-3 (2010), 311-324.

place of literature in human cultures we have to rethink the mind models on which we base our theorizing.

There is a growing body work inspired by advances in the neurosciences and in cognition studies that can serve as a litmus test for the overdue revision of the models of the mind which still dominate the field. Some of the audacious generalizations which we are bound to find there will strike us rightly as 'over the top', but after reading Mark Turner, Norman Doidge, Merlin Donald, Stephen Pinker and the like, or, closer at home, Alan Palmer, Liza Sunshine, Monika Fludernik and others, who are already using a different mind model, we will realize that the time for some radical revision is ripe. Maybe, the search for a new mind model on a more adequate and less restrictive basis can again provide the field of literary studies with a stage and a benchmark that make possible cognitively productive controversies.

Analyzing the Annotations:
Theories and Practices of Explanatory Notes[1]

Mary Jane Edwards
Carleton University, Ottawa

In April 1993 I attended the Seventh International Interdisciplinary Conference of the Society for Textual Scholarship (STS). This meeting, organized by Trevor Howard-Hill, was more or less dedicated to Fredson Bowers, who had died in 1991 just about the time of this society's previous conference. There were, thus, many sessions on aspects of scholarly editing, including one on "The Multi-Volume Edition." The subject of this session, chaired by Joel Myerson, was four projects, each of which was preparing editions of works by an American author. David R. Chesnutt spoke, thus, on *The Papers of Henry Laurens*, which under his editorship had published in 1992 Volume Thirteen of the letters and other documents of this South Carolina merchant who served from 1777 to 1778 as president of the Continental Congress. Joseph R. McElrath, Jr., who was co-editing with Douglas K. Burgess *The Apprenticeship Writings of Frank Norris 1896-1898* (1996), talked about the journalistic works of this author who, to quote the opening lines of Volume One of this edition, "has long been recognized by cultural historians as a 'touchstone' figure ... of an American school of Literary Naturalism" (xv). Barbara B. Oberg, who was then the editor of *The Papers of Benjamin Franklin*, discussed this longstanding project – it had issued its first volume in 1959 – on this important figure in American culture and history. Herman J. Saatkamp, Jr., the general editor of *The Works of George Santayana*, and the editor with William G. Holzberger of Santayana's *The Last Puritan: A Memoir in the Form of a Novel*, Volume Four of the edition published in 1994, explained some of the challenges involved in preparing the only novel written by this well-known philosopher. These projects represented different kinds of works and various types of editing, but they had all been influenced by the so-called Anglo-American school of scholarly editing, of which Bowers, along with W. W. Greg and G. Thomas Tanselle, were the principal gurus.

---

1   A shorter version of this paper was presented to the section on "Bibliographical, Textual Studies" at the triennial conference of the International Association of University Professors of English held at the University of Malta in July 2010.

I was interested in this session for several reasons. For over a decade I had been involved with the Centre for Editing Early Canadian Texts, or CEECT. Located at Carleton University in Ottawa, Canada, this project, having as its mandate to prepare scholarly editions of major works of early English-Canadian prose, dealt with various kinds of writing from fictionalized autobiography to satirical letters and sketches and followed, for the most part at least, the principles and procedures of Anglo-American editing. By 1993, in fact, I had edited for CEECT Frances Moore Brooke's *The History of Emily Montague* (1985), the work of epistolary fiction originally published in London in 1769 but usually considered the first Canadian novel, and I had been the general editor for eight nineteenth-century works in the CEECT series. For various reasons our pace has slowed since then. Nevertheless, I have been the general editor for two more CEECT volumes, one of them, Thomas Chandler Haliburton's *The Clockmaker, Series One, Two, and Three* (1995), an edition of three discrete works, and I have completed the CEECT edition of *Le Chien d'or / The Golden Dog: A Legend of Quebec*, William Kirby's historical novel first published in 1877 that attempted to provide an heroic past for what was then the new Dominion of Canada.

In 1993 I had already arrived at conclusions, some of them tentative, about many aspects of what, in the fourth edition of *An Introduction to Bibliographical and Textual Studies* published in 2009 by the Modern Language Association of America (MLA), William Proctor Williams and Craig S. Abbott still describe as the two forms of editing; that is, "Documentary (or diplomatic or noncritical) editing" (74), and "Critical editing, the second major form of scholarly editing," which differs from the first because it "constructs a text that may incorporate readings from several documentary texts and may include editorial emendations that establish readings not found in any document" (78).

I wished, therefore, to hear what each editor of the American multi-volume editions had to say about the theories and practices of his or her project.

I was keen, for example, to learn if he or she spoke about preparing "definitive editions." This term seems to have been put into circulation in the late 1940s by the Committee on Definitive Editions established by the MLA's American Literature Group, which may have entertained the notion that one could prepare an edition that never had to be done again. By the early 1990s, however, it was mostly connected with Fredson Bowers, who, according to G. Thomas Tanselle in *The Life and Works of Fredson Bowers*, used the term "in a special sense" to help "emphasize the rigor, discipline, and thoroughness of the bibliographical way," even though he knew very well that such a "product of critical judgment" as a scholarly edition could never be definitive in the usual sense of the word (129). By then I had got my head around Jerome J. McGann's notions about "the social dimension which surrounds the process of literary production" (113), although I still privileged the author. I was beginning to contemplate "the importance of textual evolution and instability" (Tanselle 142), although I still felt that what has come to be called a reading text was necessary. I had long since decided, however, that "a reliable text" was the best that one could hope to create (Brooke liv).

I was particularly curious to hear what each editor had to say in regard to what CEECT called explanatory notes; that is, notes that identified such items as historical events and people in the text or quotations from the works of other writers. I was disappointed, therefore, when this kind of annotation was not even mentioned. And, on the one hand, I was surprised. These four multi-volume editions did have textual apparatus, of course. In the critical edition of George Santayana's *The Last Puritan*, for example, this apparatus, part of the "Editorial Appendix," was called "Textual Record" and included "Textual Commentary," "List of Emendations," "Report of Line-End Hyphenation," and "List of Variants." But these editions all had contextual apparatus as well. Three, in fact, had explanatory notes. In *The Papers of Henry Laurens. Volume Thirteen: March 16, 1778-July 6, 1778* and in *The Papers of Benjamin Franklin. Vol. 28: November 1, 1778, through February 28, 1779* (1990), they appeared, interspersed with textual notes, at the bottom of the page. In *The Last Puritan* these "Notes to the Text," keyed to it by page and line number, took up over fifty pages of the "Editorial Appendix." Only *The Apprenticeship Writings of Frank Norris 1896-1898*, which was dedicated to Joel Myerson, then, lacked explanatory notes, although in the introduction to each of the two volumes that made up this edition there was ample contextual material.

I was disappointed, but, on the other hand, I was not surprised. For, when in the early 1980s we decided that the reliable text of each of our CEECT editions should be placed in its cultural contexts and should, thus, contain among its apparatus explanatory notes, we quickly discovered that there was a paucity of literature on this subject and what there was did not receive much attention. Little has changed since. I have recently read three twenty-first century publications on textual studies, to employ the MLA's term – *Teaching Bibliography, Textual Criticism, and Book History*, the collection of essays edited by Ann R. Hawkins and published by Pickering and Chatto in 2006; *Text Editing, Print and the Digital World*, the collection of essays edited by Marilyn Deegan and Kathryn Sutherland and published by Ashgate in 2009; and *Securing the Past: Conservation in Art, Architecture and Literature* by Paul Eggert published by Cambridge University Press in 2009. Each of these volumes mentions explanatory notes, although they are not always called by that name. In Hawkins, they are referred to in the articles as "annotations" (Hawkins, "Teaching Textual Criticism" 174), "content notes" (Keleman 165), and "explanatory footnotes" (Gadd

71). In the index there is an entry on "annotation" (191), but it only directs the reader to Erick Kelemen's "'Not to pick bad from bad, but by bad mend': What Undergraduates Learn from Bad Editions" and to Hawkins' "Teaching Textual Criticism: Students as Book Detectives and Scholarly Editors." In Deegan and Sutherland they are referred to as "annotations" (Vanhoutte 103), "contextual annotation" (Sutherland 15), and "explanatory notes" (Bree and McLaverty 130, and Eggert, "The Book" 63). The index, however, directs the reader to Sutherland's comments on "contextual annotation" only (199). In Eggert's *Securing the Past*, there is no listing in the index for either "explanatory annotation" (177) or "annotation" (239), although he touches on both in his text. These publications not only disagree on what to call this kind of contextual apparatus, but, with few exceptions, they also avoid giving much detail about it.

The same comments can be made about the MLA's own publications. The entry in the index to "explanatory notes" (405) in *Electronic Textual Editing*, the updated and very useful guide to scholarly editing in the computer age published in 2006, refers to the "Glossary of Terms Used in the Guiding Questions" for those who vet scholarly editions for the Committee on Scholarly Editions to determine if they merit its seal of approval. In this glossary "explanatory notes" are defined as "Notes devoted to explaining what something means or why it is present, rather than textual notes, which are devoted to explaining why the text at a certain point reads in the way it does and not in some other way" (36). The term itself is used in two questions that the vetters are required to answer with respect to "Apparatus and Extratextual Materials" – "Are the explanatory notes appropriate for this kind of edition – for example, in purpose, level of detail, and number?," and "Is there a sound rationale for the explanatory notes, whether or not the rationale is to be made explicit anywhere in the published work?" (31).

In their section on "Documentary Editing" in *An Introduction to Bibliographical and Textual Studies*, Williams and Abbott mention "annotation" that is part of "critical variorum editions ... that is, annotation presenting a record of interpretive, philological, and other commentary on the text (including textual emendations proposed or made by previous editors)" (75), and the "scholarly annotations" supplied in *the complete writings and pictures of Dante Gabriel Rossetti: a hypermedia archive*, the electronic archive edited by Jerome J. McGann (78). They comment on explanatory notes in the penultimate paragraph in their chapter on "Editorial Procedure." "Finally," they write, "depending usually on the publisher's format for the series in which the edition appears and on the supposed audience for the edition, the apparatus may include explanatory notes in which the editors gloss words, trace allusions and sources, and supply historical references" (107). They include two such notes, intermixed with textual notes, on the page from the first volume of Washington Irving's *Journals and Notebooks ... 1803-1806* (1969) edited by Nathalia Wright, their example of documentary editing. They include none, however, in the pages that they reprint from their three examples of critical editing: *The Dramatic Works of Thomas Dekker* (1958), edited by Fredson Bowers; *The Plays and Poems of Philip Massinger* (1976), edited by Philip Edwards and Colin Gibson; and Herman Melville's *Mardi and A Voyage Thither* (1970), edited by Harrison Hayford, Hershel Parker, and G. Thomas Tanselle. And they cite no publications specifically on explanatory notes either in their chapter on "Reference Bibliography" or in their "Works Cited."

Understandably this "Reference Bibliography" is highly selective. I suspect also that it is, consciously or unconsciously, oriented to items about scholarly editions of writers like Shakespeare. In 2001, for example, *English Studies in Canada*, the learned journal I edited from 1998 to 2002, issued a special double issue on *Scholarly Editing in Canada*. This issue, which ran to 250 pages, contained nine articles, eleven reviews, and one review article by such well-known international scholars as A. S. G. Edwards, Juliet McMaster, and David J. Nordloh. Only Paul Werstine's "Copy-Text Editing: The Authorizing of Shakespeare," however, made it into the Williams and Abbott text. Their omission of Lorraine D. Goulden's "Approaches to the Contextual Annotation of Nineteenth-Century Historical Fiction: Constructing an Ideal Reader's Response" was particularly unfortunate for readers interested in explanatory notes, for in this article she provided not only a careful analysis of this apparatus but also complete citations for most of the "very few articles ... of interest to contextual annotation and annotation in general" that had appeared in the second half of the twentieth century (160).

Several reasons have been offered for this lack of interest. In "Some Remarks on Scholarly Editing," a talk given at a public workshop on editorial principles and procedures that CEECT held in 1983, Herbert J. Rosengarten, the editor, or joint editor, of four volumes in the Clarendon edition of the novels of the Brontës, talked about the "purists" who regarded "the addition of explanatory notes glossing allusions and quotations" as "extraneous to the functions of textual editing, since the raison d'être of a scholarly edition [was] the establishment of a good text" (14). One of the most noteworthy of these purists, of course, was Fredson Bowers, who from his edition of Thomas Dekker on generally confined "his introductions and annotations strictly to textual matters" (Tanselle 51).

At the same workshop in a talk entitled "Art and Honesty in Annotation," J. A. W. Gunn, who prepared the explanatory notes for the first two volumes of the *Benjamin Disraeli Letters* (1982), hypothesized that a novel, which was already, in contrast to journals and many letters, "a public document," might not need much annotation. "People who didn't know the author," he maintained, "were expected to be able to make sense of [his or her novel] and hence while one may have to make certain allowances for the passage of time, certainly if one is dealing with an eighteenth-century work of fiction, there should not ... be many places where the editor needs to intervene in order to explain to a modern audience what the author wanted to say" (55). A similar distinction was made more recently by John T. Shawcross. In his article on "The Bibliography and Research Course" in the Hawkins collection, he repeats the commonly-held assumption that "modern literature, particularly prose, is little annotated" (112). He suggests, however, that an "effective exercise for demonstrating annotation or commentary is to edit an unedited personal letter" because this kind of document "can serve to require a general background introduction, identification of people or events alluded to in the letter, possible significance of date, and discussion of basic ideas" (114).

After the session on "The Multi-Volume Edition," Joel Myerson suggested to me that one reason why explanatory notes did not loom large in critical editing in the United States was that they took too long to do. Their achievement, thus, endangered the winning of grants for large editing projects, which depended for their funding at least partly on the speed with which they accomplished their publications. An instance of such financial considerations is apparent in the "Principles of Selection" section of the "Introduction to Volume Thirteen" of *The Papers of Henry Laurens*, which begins, "The increased number of documents for the period of HL's presidency [of the Continental Congress] has led the editors to exercise even greater selectivity than in previous volumes. The increased selectivity is also in part dictated by our continuing concern with rising costs and the threat of dwindling resources" (xviii). Certainly anyone who has had to do with funding agencies can sympathize with such a statement.

At the time I also wondered if the Americans eschewed explanatory notes because they were more certain about the cultural literacy of their fellow citizens than we more self-doubting Canadians. I also meditated on the possibility that the professors who prepared the editions first sponsored by the Center for Editions of American Authors (CEAA), the successor to the MLA's Committee for Definitive Editions, did not wish, on the one hand, to be seen as preparing mere textbooks, but did not dare, on the other, to present their secular texts in ways that resembled many Bibles and other works of what in *The Reading Nation in the Romantic Period* (2004) William St Clair rather peculiarly calls the "official supernatural" (466 et passim).

Seventeen years later, I think that the lack of attention to explanatory notes by many followers of the Greg-Bowers-Tanselle school of Anglo-American editing had more to do with the New Criticism that dominated many English Departments in the 1960s, and that was a reaction to the Historical Criticism that so many of us experienced as undergraduates. Since New Criticism's main interest was the work itself, then what one needed above all else was not only a definitive text of the work but also a text that reflected a kind of Platonic ideal of it, one, therefore, that was removed from time and place, and, thus, from the cultural contexts that marked both the work's birth and its reconstruction as a scholarly edition. In our fallen world of unstable texts, text versioning, and archival and social editing, however, explanatory notes can, and probably should, play more prominent roles in critical editions.

Certainly more critics are coming to their defense. In a long article on "The Aims and Uses of 'Textual Studies'" published in *The Papers of the Bibliographical Society of America* in 2005, Robert D. Hume includes a section in which he asks, "What Should An Edition Provide?" In it he notes that "surprisingly little has ever been published on the principles of annotation in either scholarly or student editions" (214). He insists, however, that "Helpful and conceptually accurate annotation *matters*" (213), and that "explanatory notes that help the reader with conceptual comprehension as well as with historical word meanings and topical allusions" are needed (212). In "Being Critical: Paper-based Editing and the Digital Environment," her article in *Text Editing, Print and the Digital World*, Kathryn Sutherland states that most "serious editors" still "see their proper concern as the establishment of the text, its variants and transmission history" and, thus, consider explanatory notes "a frivolous extra" that is "largely worthless." Yet, she argues, "Contextual annotation … is at the same time the kind of editing most in favour with student readers, general readers and commercially minded publishers" (15). And in "Advice for Scholarly Editors of Australian Literature: 'Just Push On,'" his essay published in *Superior in His Profession: Essays in Memory of Harold Love,* the special issue of *Script & Print* for 2009, Paul Eggert affirms that the "contribution" of explanatory notes to critical editions is to "support the reading text on the one hand while unpacking it into its biographical and cultural contexts on the other" ("Advice" 260). But for whom should these notes be written, what role or roles should they play, how should they be dressed, and when and where should they come on stage? In the rest of this paper I shall consider some of these questions, especially in the light of my experiences as the compiler-in-chief of the explanatory notes in the CEECT editions.

In their comments on this kind of annotation, the author of each of several of the articles that I have cited clearly had a reader in mind. For Herbert J. Rosengarten the "principal readers" of a critical edition were "members of the academic community," but, he cautioned, "that readership is not homogeneous; the professor pursuing his study of Dickens's textual vagaries is in competition for the library copy of *Great Expectations* with the first-year phys. ed. student who has to produce an essay on the maturation of Pip for his English 100 class." Difficult as it was, thus, to satisfy "the differing degrees of knowledge brought to the text by a wide variety of readers," he concluded that it was "important to appeal to an educated but non-specialist audience by giving" critical editions the "extra dimension" of explanatory notes (14). Lorraine D. Goulden, J. A. W. Gunn, Ann R. Hawkins, and Erick Kelemen also imagined students, mostly undergraduates, as their readers. Gunn, however, also introduced "the informed reader," whom he defined as someone who knew "from general knowledge" what the editor also had found out "from the same source," and who could, therefore, "read a document in a relatively straightforward way" without an annotation that was "invitingly easy" to create (49). The truth is, of course, that it is impossible to identify who will read a specific text, including a critical edition, let alone what the reader will be looking for when he or she does take it in hand.

In its *Handbook for Editors* (1985), the CEECT project identified four "categories of material" that "should be considered for annotation": literary quotations; actual events, people, and places; words or phrases in foreign languages; and specialized and erudite diction (51-52). It cautioned, however, that the "rule of thumb" for the CEECT editions "was normally not to annotate anything that appeared in a standard dictionary such as a *Shorter Oxford* or a college edition of *Webster's New World Dictionary*" (52). It then required that for each work the editor, the general editor, and a research assistant – usually, but not always, a graduate student in English – should each compile a list of explanatory notes according to the guidelines outlined for the four categories.

On the whole, these procedures worked well. *Handbook for Editors* reports, for example, that "the list of each of the three annotators coincided almost exactly" for the four works in the CEECT series that were well underway in 1983 (52). The choice of what to annotate even within these frameworks and with relatively little disagreement provoked, nevertheless, lively discussion at the time when the three lists were merged into one, and when the critical text and its apparatus were being prepared. And the wisdom of one of CEECT's decisions, that of not automatically translating words or phrases in French because "French in Canada is not a foreign language" (51), has certainly been questioned. Herbert J. Rosengarten, for example, warned at the 1983 workshop that while French "might not cause concern among the students at Carleton, ... in Brobdingnag on the other side of the Rockies," that is, in British Columbia where he taught, "the natives, even some of the educated ones, look[ed] upon French as a sort of lusus naturae [freak of nature]" (15-16). And while as an Australian nationalist Harold Love sympathized with our privileging the official bilingualism of Canada, at a session on editing at the conference of the International Association of University Professors of English held in Bamberg, Germany, in 2001, he pointed out how strange this stance would seem to his students at Monash University in Melbourne.

There were also decisions to be made about the content, form, and placement of the explanatory notes. In the words of *Handbook for Editors*, our ideal was that they "should represent a minimum level of intervention" (52). Thus, we did not intentionally use them to interpret the work for the reader. We tried to avoid telling all that we had discovered about an event, a person, or a place. When we identified a person, for example, with very few exceptions, we provided neither a birth nor a death date nor a potted biography of the entire life. Rather we concentrated on the particular event in the person's life that illuminated the reference to him or her in the work being edited. When we dealt with a reference to, or quotation from, another work, we concentrated as best we could on the passages from it that were relevant to the lines that we were annotating. When we explained an event or a term, we endeavored to find the specific source or sources that the author had read so that we could suggest what he or she understood or felt about this subject. To ensure their accuracy, we proofread the explanatory notes in the same rigorous way that we verified the edited text; that is, we subjected them to several oral and visual proofreadings and checked each quotation in them against its original source, of which we usually had a photocopy. In each note, furthermore, we provided a section on the works that we had cited. We did this not only because we wished our scholarship to be transparent, but also because critics contradict each other, editions of works vary, and new research can overturn long accepted facts. For ease of reading and understanding, we presented our findings for the most part in sentences. To keep our critically-edited text clear, we did not signal the existence of an explanatory note in its body. And, to preserve a clear page, "Explanatory Notes," introduced by a headnote that outlined the nature of the annotation in the edition, became the first apparatus that we placed in the material that followed the critically-edited text.

Although it does not seem controversial, the placement of explanatory notes has been a topic of discussion for a long time. In *The Footnote: A Curious History* (1997), for example, Anthony Grafton, tracing the role that footnotes have played in historical studies, quotes from J. Y. T. Greig's *The Letters of David Hume* (1932) a letter that this Scottish historian and philosopher wrote on 8 April 1776 to the publisher William Strahan. "Strahan had brought out the first volume" of Edward Gibbon's *The History of the Decline and Fall of the Roman Empire* (1776), and he "was currently printing" a new edition of Hume's *History of England*, which had first appeared in six volumes between 1754 and 1762. After expressing his admiration for "'Mr Gibbon's Roman History,'" Hume "put forward some technical complaints, which he hoped Gibbon might take into account in preparing the second edition of his work." One criticism concerned his "'Notes, according to the present Method of printing the Book.'" Hume explained, "'When a note is announced, you turn to the End of the Volume; and there you often find nothing but the Reference to an Authority: All these Authorities ought only to be printed at the Margin or the Bottom of the Page'" (Grafton 102-03, and Hume 313).

Many recent critics have argued as well that the rightful place for explanatory notes is at the bottom of the page. In "Who Was Benjamin Whichcote? Or, The Myth of Annotation," an article in *Annotation and Its Texts* (1991), a collection edited by Stephen A. Barney, Thomas Mc-Farland expresses his strong belief that this position is the proper one for these annotations, "When notes that constitute a dialogue with the text – we may henceforth call them dialogical notes – are combined with reference notes at the bottom of the page, the maximum harmony in annotation is achieved. When dialogical notes are combined with reference notes at the back of the book, the maximum disharmony obtains." (155). And in "From Printing Type to Blackboard TM: Teaching the History of the Early Modern Book to Literary Undergraduates in a 'New' UK University," his article in the Hawkins' collection, Ian Gadd assumes this location when he writes of the "explanatory footnotes" that form part of "a scholarly edition" (70-71).

I have conflicting views on this subject. I should advise against mixing textual notes and explanatory notes at the bottom of a page as is done in *The Papers of Henry Laurens*. And I should equally advise against mixing textual and explanatory information in the same note at the bottom of the page as is done in *The Papers of Benjamin Franklin*. Vol. 28: *November 1, 1778, through February 28, 1779*. A note about Franklin's "old friend" (28) Daniel Roberdeau, for example, reads, "BF wrote 'Genl' before 'Roberdeau'. It has subsequently been lined through, probably by a later hand. Roberdeau was a brigadier general of the Pennsylvanian Associators: *DAB*" (29). When we were imagining the CEECT editions, however, it took us a long time to decide where to locate their explanatory notes. Because we were dealing mostly with works of creative writing, we finally agreed to place them after the critically-edited text. I still think that we made the right choice. Nevertheless, if I were preparing an edition of letters or of other life documents today, I should most likely prefer to see their explanatory notes at the bottom of the page. I might or might not opt to signal them within the text, however.

The question of the placement of explanatory notes becomes ever more important when one contemplates electronic editions. Because Williams and Abbott cited *the complete writings and pictures of Dante Gabriel Rossetti: a hypermedia archive* as an example of documentary editing in *An Introduction to Bibliographical and Textual Studies*, I used this edition as a test case for the presentation of explanatory notes in an electronic form. And I was not impressed. This archive, in fact, exhibited several problems that I associate with electronic texts in general. One needed Mozilla Firefly in order to view a document, and its print version often contained misplaced data and odd codes that made it tricky to read. The contextual annotation for "On Browning's 'Sordello,'" for example, was layered in such a way that one had to navigate through several portals to find it all. "Editorial glosses and textual notes" were "<u>available</u> in a pop-up window"; there was also contextual information in such sections of the "Scholarly Commentary" as "Introduction" and "Autobiographical." In order to have all this information together, I ended up printing each of the several pages. And I regretted very much that "'revolutionary breakthrough in technology'" called a "BOOK" that Matthew G. Kirschenbaum discusses in "How Things Work: Teaching the Technologies of Literature," his article in the Hawkins collection (156). With this "device … known as Built-in Orderly Organized Knowledge" (Heathorn),[2] I could at least flip back and forth without worrying about overloaded servers and failures of electricity or battery power and, possibly even more relevant in a greening world, without wasting a lot of paper in order to assemble, let alone attempt to make sense of, the contextual notes.

But we not only avoided the trials of electronic editions when we were preparing the CEECT notes; we also skirted many of the pitfalls described by J. A. W. Gunn in "Art and Honesty in Annotation." We did not, therefore, often search for the equivalent of "a Miss Porson" when the text being annotated stated, "'there is no Miss Porson'" (51), and no research assistant ever wandered so far from the work being edited as the one who questioned Gunn "about the processes for preserving fruit in the early nineteenth century" when he was trying to identify the Del Monte mining company in Mexico in which Benjamin Disraeli "managed to lose a great deal of money in 1825" (53). Some of our notes, however, were not as well focused as I think now that they could have been. I shall illustrate one in particular in the CEECT edition of *Roughing It in the Bush or Life in Canada* (1988), Susanna Strickland Moodie's fictionalized autobiography about her life in Upper Canada in the 1830s originally published in London in 1852.

In this instance its editor Carl Ballstadt had recently ascertained that the Tom Wilson of the chapter entitled "Tom Wilson's Emigration" was actually based on an Englishman from Suffolk called Tom Wales. Ballstadt had been preparing, with Elizabeth Hopkins and Michael Peterman, *Letters of a Lifetime* (1985), a documentary edition of the letters of Susanna Strickland Moodie and, therefore, gathering information about their content. He, thus, had collected bits and pieces of data about the Wales family, most of which he included in the explanatory note for "*my friend Wilson*":

---

2   R. J. Heathorn's "Learn with BOOK" was originally published in Punch in May 1962. Kirschenbaum's primary reference to it, however, is to the geocities.com website, where a "complete copy can be found" (160). Alas, when I tried to access this website on 27 October 2010, it was no longer available. The disappearance of data should be yet another worry for those who contemplate electronic editions.

Tom Wales; on 23 May 1852 Agnes Strickland wrote to Susanna that she had seen Lydia and Susan Wales who had "inquired very kindly after" her. She added, "what they will say about Tom Wales, alias Wilson I dont know." A Suffolk family, the Wales were well known to the Stricklands, and in her letters Agnes often reported news of Tom and his relatives. On 23 Apr. 1837 Agnes told Susanna that Tom Wales had "married a very low person. ... His wife sells bedslippers to the great mortification of his poor sisters." On 6 Mar. 1839 Susanna, relating news "from home" to Dunbar, announced, "Tom Wales, has lost his wife and child – and poor Rachel Wales Mrs Wood – died in childbed of twins greatly to the grief of all her friends." (559-60)

The note is factual, it deals only with the Wales, and it further humanizes Tom Wales / Wilson.

To my eye now, however, it is not focused sharply enough on Tom Wales and what happened to him after he returned to England from Upper Canada in 1832. If there were a revised edition of the CEECT text of *Roughing It in the Bush*, therefore, I should recast the contents of this note along these lines:

Tom Wales was a member of a Suffolk family well known to the Stricklands, and Susanna often heard news of him from her family in England. On 23 April 1837 Agnes Strickland told Susanna that Tom had "married a very low person. ... His wife sells bedslippers to the great mortification of his poor sisters." Almost two years later, on 6 March 1839, Susanna, relating news "from home" to John, announced, "Tom Wales, has lost his wife and child." In "Tom Wilson's Emigration," one of her "Canadian Sketches" that appeared in the *Literary Garland* (Montreal) in 1847, Susanna reported that after these deaths, "Tom returned to his brother in New South Wales" (303), where he died sometime before 1846.

This note is not only sharper, but it is also updated in two ways. The first, the spelling out of all the months of the year, was stylistic. After the first few editions in the CEECT series, we abandoned the abbreviation of months of the year. The other, the change of the name of Susanna's husband from "Dunbar" to "John," was substantive. After the publication of both *Roughing It in the Bush* and *Letters of a Lifetime,* a new stash of Moodie letters, which included those that Susanna had written to John Wedderburn Dunbar Moodie during his absence in the late 1830s, was found. In preparing them for publication as *Letters of Love and Duty: The Correspondence of Susanna and John Moodie* (1993), Carl Ballstadt, Elizabeth Hopkins, and Michael Peterman ascertained that Susanna habitually addressed her husband as "John," not "Dunbar." The turning up of previously unlocated or unknown material can affect, thus, the context as well as the text of a critical edition.

Each of the two other changes has a different explanation. The information about Tom Wales' return to, and death in, Australia should have been included in the note from the beginning. On the other hand, Agnes Strickland's comments about Lydia and Susan Wales, Tom's unmarried sisters who were living in Walberswick, Suffolk, in 1852, should more properly form part of the discussion of the reception of *Roughing It in the Bush* in the "Editor's Introduction." There, Agnes' evident concern about the Wales' response to Susanna's publication might usefully have been linked to what in *Susanna Moodie: A Life* (1999) Michael Peterman describes as her own "strong objection to being associated with a book about vulgar people" (144).

If we did not get that note quite right, in our edition of James De Mille's *A Strange Manuscript Found in a Copper Cylinder* (1986), we did manage to trace the nineteenth-century sources of the many "references to scientific discoveries and theories ... in such fields as geology, palaeontology, anthropology, and philology" (271) that he incorporated into this satiric romance about a strange civilization in Antarctica. After a good deal of reading in American, British, and Canadian publications about the War of 1812-14, I succeeded in sorting out what John Richardson was imagining about this event in which he and his brother served when he was composing *The Canadian Brothers or The Prophecy Fulfilled A Tale of the Late American War* (1840), the sequel to *Wacousta or, The Prophecy; A Tale of the Canadas* (1832), his much more famous historical novel. Both are partly based on his family's experiences in the late eighteenth- and early nineteenth-centuries on the borders between Ontario and Michigan, or what had been the northwest frontier of the French Empire in North America. And we did win the approval of Lorraine D. Goulden who in her 2001 article examined the explanatory notes in eight scholarly editions of nineteenth-century historical novels, including two from the project on "The Writings of James Fenimore Cooper," both approved by the MLA's Committee on Scholarly Editions; one from The Academy Editions of Australian Literature; one from the Clarendon edition of the Brontë novels; and two from the CEECT series, one of them *The Canadian Brothers*.

After analyzing notes from each of these publications, Goulden concludes that the "explanatory notes in the CEECT editions" are those that most "clearly demonstrate not only a clarity of purpose, but also a consistency in the application of a rationale for contextual annotation: a rationale that ensures that the historical infrastructure of the text is identified and revealed to the reader without the interference of editorial commentary or interpretation." Readers, therefore, free to explore "the text on their own terms," are encouraged to develop "their own critical and imaginative interpretations" (160). The decision to annotate a particular passage in a critical edition is itself, of course, an act of judgment and, thus, interpretation. Still, Goulden's contention that the aim of an explanatory note is to open, rather than close, a work to a reader is well taken. It is also a contention that has been repeated since by, among others, Robert D. Hume. In "The Aims and Uses of 'Textual Studies,'" he states, for example, "I would not suggest that an editor can legitimately attempt to control textual interpretation on the part of the reader or that explanatory notes should be tilted significantly towards present-day critical preoccupations. A good edition facilitates reading and comprehension; it does not dictate interpretation or even point of view" (215).

To historicize the work being edited; to place it in its cultural contexts; to allow the reader to discover what documents the author read and how he or she might have read them; to stimulate the reader's intellectual curiosity: these are among the roles that explanatory notes play in scholarly editions. They, thus, contribute to various histories, including those of books and readers, not only in the past but also in the present and in the future. For the creators of these editions are also partaking in the production of books and acting as members of reading nations, to echo William St Clair's term. Let us hope, then, that when future readers study the CEECT series of scholarly editions of major works of early English-Canadian prose, they will find their explanatory notes significant signifiers not only of the contexts out of which the works being edited originally developed, but also of the late twentieth and early twenty-first century culture out of which these editions themselves came.

Works Cited

Bree, Linda, and James McLaverty. "The Cambridge Edition of the Works of Jonathan Swift and the Future of the Scholarly Edition." *Text Editing, Print and the Digital World.* Ed. Marilyn Deegan, and Kathryn Sutherland. Farnham, Surrey, and Burlington, Vermont: Ashgate, 2009. 127-36.

Brooke, Frances Moore. *The History of Emily Montague.* Ed. Mary Jane Edwards. Ottawa: Carleton UP, 1985. CEECT Series, No. 1.

Burnard, Lou, Katherine O'Brien O'Keeffe, and John Unsworth, eds. *Electronic Textual Editing.* New York: Modern Language Association of America, 2006.

Deegan, Marilyn, and Kathryn Sutherland, eds. *Text Editing, Print and the Digital World.* Farnham, Surrey, and Burlington, Vermont: Ashgate, 2009.

De Mille, James. *A Strange Manuscript Found in a Copper Cylinder.* Ed. Malcolm Parks. Ottawa: Carleton UP, 1986. CEECT Series, No. 3.

Edwards, Mary Jane. *Handbook for Editors.* Ottawa: Centre for Editing Early CanadianTexts, 1985.

Eggert, Paul. "Advice for Scholarly Editors of Australian Literature: 'Just Push On.'" *Superior in His Profession: Essays in Memory of Harold Love.* Ed. Meredith Sherlock, Brian McMullen, and Wallace Kirsop. *Script & Print* Special Issue 33.1-4 (2009): 251-63.

–. "The Book, the E-text and the 'Work-site.'" *Text Editing, Print and Digital World.* Ed. Marilyn Deegan, and Kathryn Sutherland. Farnham, Surrey, and Burlington, Vermont: Ashgate, 2009. 63-82.

–. *Securing the Past: Conservation in Art, Architecture and Literature*. Cambridge: Cambridge UP, 2009.

Franklin, Benjamin. *The Papers of Benjamin Franklin*. Vol. 28: *November 1, 1778, through February 28, 1779*. Ed. Barbara Oberg. New Haven and London: Yale UP, 1990.

Gadd, Ian. "From Printing Type to Blackboard TM": Teaching the History of the Early Modern Book to Literary Undergraduates in a 'New' UK University." *Teaching Bibliography, Textual Criticism, and Book History*. Ed. Ann R. Hawkins. London: Pickering and Chatto, 2006. 65-71.

Goulden, Lorraine D. "Approaches to the Contextual Annotation of Nineteenth-Century Historical Fiction: Constructing an Ideal Reader's Response." Double Issue: *Scholarly Editing in Canada*. Ed. Mary Jane Edwards. *English Studies in Canada* 27 (2001): 141-63.

Grafton, Anthony. *The Footnote: A Curious History*. Cambridge, Massachusetts: Harvard UP, 1997.

Gunn, J. A. W. "Art and Honesty in Annotation." *Public Workshop on Editorial Principles and Procedures 1983*. Ottawa: Centre for Editing Early Canadian Texts, 1983. 48-57.

Hawkins, Ann R., ed. *Teaching Bibliography, Textual Criticism, and Book History*. London: Pickering and Chatto, 2006.

–. "Teaching Textual Criticism: Students as Book Detectives and Scholarly Editors." *Teaching Bibliography, Textual Criticism, and Book History*. Ed. Ann R. Hawkins. London: Pickering and Chatto, 2006. 174-77.

Heathorn, R. J. "Learn with BOOK." 1962; rpt. http://www.df.lth.se/~cml/BOOK.txt

Hume, David. *The Letters of David Hume*. Vol. 2. Ed. J. Y. T. Greig. Oxford: Clarendon P, 1932.

Hume, Robert D. "The Aims and Uses of 'Textual Studies.'" *Papers of the Bibliographical Society of America* 99 (2005): 197-230.

Kelemen, Erick. "'Not to pick bad from bad, but by bad mend': What Undergraduates Learn from Bad Editions." *Teaching Bibliography, Textual Criticism, and Book History*. Ed. Ann R. Hawkins. London: Pickering and Chatto, 2006. 161-66.

Kirschenbaum, Matthew G. "How Things Work: Teaching the Technologies of Literature." *Teaching Bibliography, Textual Criticism, and Book History*. Ed. Ann R. Hawkins. London: Pickering and Chatto, 2006. 155-60.

Laurens, Henry. *The Papers of Henry Laurens. Volume Thirteen*: *March 16, 1778 – July 6, 1778*. Ed. David R Chesnutt, and C. James Taylor. Columbia, South Carolina: U of South Carolina P, 1992.

McFarland, Thomas. "Who Was Benjamin Whichcote? or, The Myth of Annotation." *Annotation and Its Texts*. Ed. Stephen A. Barney. New York and Oxford: Oxford UP, 1991. 152-77.

McGann, Jerome J. *A Critique of Modern Textual Criticism*. Chicago and London: U of Chicago P, 1983.

Moodie, Susanna Strickland. "Canadian Sketches. No. 4: Tom Wilson's Emigration." *Literary Garland* NS 5 (1847): 283-86, and 293-303.

–. *Roughing It in the Bush or Life in Canada*. Ed. Carl Ballstadt. Ottawa: Carleton UP, 1988. CEECT Series, No. 5.

Norris, Frank. *The Apprenticeship Writings of Frank Norris 1896-1898*. Ed. Joseph R McElrath, Jr., and Douglas K. Burgess. Philadelphia: The American Philosophical Society, 1996.

Peterman, Michael. *Susanna Moodie: A Life*. Toronto: ECW P, 1999.

Rosengarten, Herbert J. "Some Remarks on Scholarly Editing." *Public Workshop on Editorial Principles and Procedures 1983*. Ottawa: Centre for Editing Early Canadian Texts, 1983. 3-18.

Rossetti, Dante Gabriel. *The complete writings and pictures of Dante Gabriel Rossetti: a hypermedia archive*. Ed. Jerome J. McGann. http://www.rossettiarchive.org

Santayana, George. *The Last Puritan: A Memoir In the Form of a Novel*. Ed. William G. Holzberger, and Herman J. Saatkamp, Jr. Cambridge, Massachusetts, and London: MIT P, 1994.

Shawcross, John T. "The Bibliography and Research Course." *Teaching Bibliography, Textual Criticism, and Book History*. Ed. Ann R. Hawkins. London: Pickering and Chatto, 2006. 109-16.

St Clair, William. *The Reading Nation in the Romantic Period*. Cambridge: Cambridge UP, 2004.

Sutherland, Kathryn. "Being Critical: Paper-based Editing and the Digital Environment." *Text Editing, Print and the Digital World*. Ed. Marilyn Deegan, and Kathryn Sutherland. Farnham, Surrey, and Burlington, Vermont: Ashgate, 2009. 13-25.

Tanselle, G. Thomas. *The Life and Work of Fredson Bowers*. Charlottesville: The Bibliographical Society of the University of Virginia, 1993.

Vanhoutte, Edward. "Every Reader his own Bibliographer – An Absurdity?" *Text Editing, Print and the Digital World*. Ed. Marilyn Deegan, and Kathryn Sutherland. Farnham, Surrey, and Burlington, Vermont: Ashgate, 2009. 99-110.

Williams, William Proctor, and Craig S. Abbott. *An Introduction to Bibliographical And Textual Studies*. Fourth Edition. New York: Modern Language Association of America, 2009.

Adam's Two Dreams: Keats on Milton

John Leonard
University of Western Ontario

"The Imagination may be compared to Adam's dream–he awoke and found it truth."[1] Critics have long recognized that Keats was alluding to *Paradise Lost* when he wrote those words, but there has been some doubt as to just which dream he was referring to. Milton's Adam has two dreams that fit Keats's description, but most Romanticists direct us to just one: his dream of the creation of Eve. All of the major editions of Keats's letters, including those by Hyder Edward Rollins and Maurice Buxton Forman, as well as more recent ones, cite this dream and mention no other. Even the eminent Miltonist Douglas Bush, annotating Keats's letters in his Riverside edition, directs us exclusively to Adam's dream of Eve.[2] So far as I am aware, the only edition to mention the fact that Adam has two dreams that come true is (surprisingly) the *Norton Anthology*, which offers this note: "In *Paradise Lost* 8:452-90, Adam dreams that Eve has been created, and awakes to find her real. Adam also describes an earlier prefigurative dream in the same work, 8.283-311."[3] Even this implies that Keats was thinking primarily, if not exclusively, of Adam's dream of Eve. The dismissive phrase "an earlier prefigurative dream" does not have nearly the same emotive force as "awakes to find her real." I find this intriguing for a number of reasons. First, it makes me wonder about the influence annotated editions have in deciding and foreclosing questions of this kind. Second, it makes me all the more curious about Keats's allusion. Was he thinking of one dream or two, and if two, did he think of them as separate events or did he conflate them?

The few critics who have acknowledged that Adam has two dreams have usually conflated them. Lucy Newlyn in *Paradise Lost and the Romantic Reader* compresses both dreams into a single "sequence" that she contrasts with Eve's dream of eating the apple. She summarizes "Milton's position" as follows: "Adam's

---

1 Letter to Benjamin Bailey, 22 November 1817, in *The Letters of John Keats 1814-1821*, ed. Hyder Edward Rollins, 2 vols. (Cambridge, Massachusetts: Harvard University Press, 1956), 1:185. Unless otherwise stated, all citations of Keats's letters are from this edition, hereafter cited as "Rollins."

2 Douglas Bush, ed., *John Keats: Selected Poems and Letters* (Boston: Houghton Mifflin, 1959), 258.

3 *The Norton Anthology of English Literature, The Major Authors*, sixth edition, gen. ed. M. H. Abrams (New York: Norton, 1996), 1816.

unconscious has access to an ideal, Eve's to a fallen world." Newlyn concludes that Eve, like Madeline in *The Eve of St. Agnes*, awakes to find that she has been "cheated by the actual." "Porphyro, by contrast, has all the fulfilment attributed to Adam when he wakes to find his dream come true."[4]

This is an advance from earlier criticism, but it elides some important distinctions. Porphyro is not dreaming when he enters Madeline's dream. One might argue that he is all the more fulfilled for being wide awake, but a man who is not sleeping or dreaming cannot awake to "find his dream come true" and so cannot have "all the fulfilment attributed to Adam." Newlyn also exaggerates Adam's "fulfilment." She must conflate his two dreams and present them as equally happy before she can draw a stable and manifest distinction between fulfilled men and cheated women. I do not deny that Madeline is cheated. Hers is a difficult case and I shall return to it at the end of this essay. My immediate concern is with Adam. My claim is simple and straightforward: we should not conflate his two dreams or lump them together as if they were equally happy, even though Keats's letter encourages us to do just that. Adam's two dreams are quite different from each other and the differences have far-reaching implications for both Milton and Keats. My goal in what follows is to explore these differences and pursue their implications for the oft-repeated claim that the mature Keats rejected Milton.

Let me begin with Adam's first dream—the one that many critics have missed. It occurs soon after Adam has been created, but before God visibly appears to him. Unlike his namesake depicted by Michelangelo in the Sistine chapel, Milton's Adam does not see the face of God as soon as he wakes into life. Where Michelangelo's Adam gazes into the face of his Maker in the moment of his making, Milton's Adam "gazed a while the ample sky" (8.258).[5] God is conspicuous by his absence. Adam deduces the existence of "some great maker" (8.278), but at first he calls for him in vain. "When answer none returned," he falls asleep and dreams:

> soft oppression seized
> My drowsèd sense, untroubled, though I thought
> I then was passing to my former state
> Insensible, and forthwith to dissolve:
> When suddenly stood at my head a dream,
> Whose inward apparition gently moved
> My fancy to believe I yet had being,
> And lived: one came, methought, of shape divine,

---

4   Lucy Newlyn, *"Paradise Lost" and the Romantic Reader* (Oxford: Oxford University Press, 1993), 179.

5   *John Milton: Paradise Lost*, Second Edition, edited by Alastair Fowler (London: Longman, 1998). All citations of *Paradise Lost* are from this edition.

And said, Thy mansion wants thee, Adam, rise,
First man, of men innumerable ordained
First father, called by thee I come thy guide
To the garden of bliss, thy seat prepared.
So saying, by the hand he took me raised,
And over fields and waters, as in air
Smooth sliding without step, last led me up
A woody mountain; whose high top was plain,
A circuit wide, enclosed, with goodliest trees
Planted, with walks, and bowers, that what I saw
Of earth before scarce pleasant seemed. Each tree
Loaden with fairest fruit, that hung to the eye
Tempting, stirred in me sudden appetite
To pluck and eat; whereat I waked, and found
Before mine eyes all real, as the dream
Had lively shadowed. (8.288-311)

Having dreamed of Paradise, Adam awakes to find it truth. A moment later God steps from dream into waking reality:

here had new begun
My wandering, had not he who was my guide
Up hither, from among the trees appeared,
Presence divine. Rejoicing, but with awe
In adoration at his feet I fell
Submiss: he reared me, and Whom thou soughtst I am,
Said mildly. (8.311-17)

A lesser poet would have placed a heavy stop at the end of line 316 so as to bring out the echo of Exodus 3:14 ("I AM THAT I AM. ... Thus shalt thou say unto the children of Israel, I AM hath sent me unto you"). Milton's inversion places just enough stress on "I am" to signal the allusion, but God has no need of self-promotion and his voice becomes still and small as the sense is variously drawn out into the next line: "Whom thou soughtst I am, / Said mildly." "I am" is the complete and ultimate fulfilment of Adam's first dream, but it is all the more fulfilling for being "mildly" understated.

The conclusion of Adam's second dream is very different in tone and feeling:

She disappeared, and left me dark, I waked
To find her, or for ever to deplore
Her loss, and other pleasures all abjure:
When out of hope, behold her, not far off,
Such as I saw her in my dream. ... (8.478-82)

To my mind, Keats's formulation –"he awoke and found it truth" – is closer to Adam's first dream than his second. Both dreams end with "I waked," but only the first dream delivers the word "found" in the indicative mood: "I waked, and found before mine eyes all real." Adam's second dream ends with "find" in the infinitive, not the indicative, and Adam does not at first find what he is looking for: "I waked to find her, or for ever to deplore / Her loss, and other pleasures all abjure...." I admit that there is a corresponding moment of doubt and hesitation after the first dream ("here had new begun / My wandering, had not he who was my guide ..."), but it has none of the anxiety that grips Adam after his second dream. Adam's imagined "wandering" in search of God is a delay rather than an interruption of anticipated joy. The fact that Eve has wandered off is far more desolating for it threatens to deprive Adam of all "other pleasures." Like Madeline in *The Eve of St. Agnes*, Adam experiences a painful change. The parallel is not exact, since Madeline does not fully wake up even when her "eyes were open," but in both cases disappointment infiltrates the dream: "There was a painful change, that nigh expell'd / The blisses of her dream";[6] "She disappeared, and left me dark." Eve disappears while Adam is still dreaming and it is her absence, not her presence, that he awakes to. True, she reappears–miraculously and in person–but even this outcome is less happy than we might expect, for no sooner has she appeared than she disappears again, this time by choice: "seeing me, she turned" (8.507). Although Adam does not say so, we know (from Eve's account in book four) that Eve is turning back to her reflection in the lake. She turns from Adam twice: first in his dream when she wakes into life (presumably she did not even notice him on that occasion) and again, a little later, when the mysterious voice brings her back. She then sees Adam, but does not particularly like what she sees. Adam was "less fair, / Less winning soft, less amiably mild, / Than that smooth watery image; back I turned" (4.478-80). Adam persists and Eve eventually approves his pleaded reason, but their first meeting is not the kind of encounter most people think of when they say "a dream come true." In short, Adam's second awakening (the one to which Keats's editors routinely direct us) is a less happy experience than we might expect from the six words "he awoke and found it truth." Those words are an accurate summary of Adam's first dream, but it is only by an effort of will that they can be applied to the second, where Adam awoke, found that it was not truth, then (miraculously) discovered that it was, but not in quite the way he had hoped.

What are we to make of this? My point is not that editors have got it wrong and that Keats is actually alluding to Adam's first dream. Such an argument could be made, and if I were forced to choose between the two dreams I would indeed cast my vote for the first one. But a particular clause in Keats's letter convinces me that he is thinking of both dreams. Look at his words in context: "I

---

6   *The Eve of St. Agnes*, 300-301. All citations of Keats's poetry are from *The Poetical Works of John Keats*, ed. H. W. Garrod (Oxford: Clarendon Press, 1958).

am certain of nothing but of the holiness of the Heart's affections and the truth of Imagination – What the imagination seizes as Beauty must be truth–whether it existed before or not. ... The Imagination may be compared to Adam's dream – he awoke and found it truth."[7] The words I want to emphasize are "whether it existed before or not." These words encapsulate the difference between Adam's two dreams. God and Paradise already exist when Adam dreams of them in his first dream, but in his second dream he witnesses the creation of beauty that had not "existed before." Eve comes into existence even as Adam dreams of her coming into existence. Keats's phrase "whether it existed before or not" both acknowledges and elides this distinction between the two dreams. I admit that Genesis admits a complication. As John C. Ulreich has pointed out, the relevant biblical verses can be taken to imply that God created Adam before he created Paradise: "And the LORD God formed man of the dust of the ground, and breathed into his nostrils the breath of life; and man became a living soul. And the LORD God planted a garden eastward in Eden; and there he put the man whom he had formed."[8] Citing these verses alongside Keats's letter, Ulreich offers the bold suggestion that God needs Adam's imagination to assist him in the creation of Paradise. Ulreich is the only critic I am aware of to have argued that Keats's letter refers exclusively to Adam's first dream. Commenting on the words "all real, as the dream / Had lively shadowed" (8.310-11), Ulreich writes:

> The assumption that readers naturally make here, I believe, is that Adam's dream merely reflects an external reality: Man awakens to find a place that had already existed independently of his dreaming consciousness. But the situation in Genesis is less clear-cut, since man was created before the Garden. ... And Keats's speculation – "whether it existed before or not" – points to a radically poetic reading of Milton's Eden: Adam's awakening into truth can be understood, not as a passive discovery, but as an active pro- cess of imaginative creation. When Adam enacts his (hitherto unconscious) desire, he brings Eden into being.[9]

This is a fascinating argument and it casts much light on Keats's phrase "whether it existed before or not." Keats conflates Adam's two dreams and makes them equally happy because he wants to make the maximum claim for the creative power of the poetic imagination. But I cannot persuade myself that Milton's Adam "brings Eden into being." It matters that God (not just Paradise) first appears to Adam in a dream. Unless we are willing to deliver an even more "radically poetic reading" and argue that Adam's "dreaming consciousness" dreams God "into being," I think we must conclude that God and Paradise "existed before." Milton does not make so large a claim for the creative power of Adam's imagination as Keats and

---

7 Rollins, 1:184-5.

8 Genesis 2:7-8. All biblical citations are from the King James Version.

9 John C. Ulreich, Jr., "Making Dreams Truths, and Fables Histories: Spenser and Milton on the Nature of Fiction," *Studies in Philology*, Vol. 87, No. 3 (Summer 1990), 363-77 (see pp. 369-70).

Ulreich make. For Milton, creation is God's prerogative and Adam does not encroach upon it.

Adam's limitations are most apparent in his dream of Eve. This second dream is more ominous even than I have intimated, for it makes a poignant allusion to the sonnet Milton had written after the death of his second wife:

> Methought I saw my late espousèd saint
>> Brought to me like Alcestis from the grave,
>> Whom Jove's great son to her glad husband gave,
>> Rescued from death by force though pale and faint.
> Mine as whom washed from spot of childbed taint
>> Purification in the old Law did save,
>> And such, as yet once more I trust to have
>> Full sight of her in Heaven without restraint,
> Came vested all in white, pure as her mind:
>> Her face was veiled, yet to my fancied sight,
>> Love, sweetness, goodness, in her person shined
>> So clear, as in no face with more delight.
> But O as to embrace me she inclined,
> I waked, she fled, and day brought back my night.[10]

The allusion was first noted by the Jonathan Richardsons, father and son, in their *Explanatory Notes and Remarks on Milton's "Paradise Lost"* (1734). Glossing Adam's line "She disappeared, and left me dark, I waked," they write: "Milton had given a Like Image on the Appearance of his Own Wife, Thus Offer'd to him in his Sleep, and Thus Snatch'd Away" (376). The allusion is signalled not just by the sonnet's final line, but by its opening words, "Methought I saw." These three words also appear in Adam's second dream:

> Abstract, as in a trance, methought I saw,
> Though sleeping where I lay, and saw the shape
> Still glorious before whom awake I stood,
> Who, stooping, opened my left side and took
> From thence a rib.... (8.462-66)

"Methought" also appears in Adam's first dream: "one came, methought, of shape divine...." In all three dreams, "methought" introduces a blissful vision, but the outcome is different in each case. In Adam's first dream, there is an easy transition from vision to reality; in the second dream, there is a difficult transition from vision to reality; in the sonnet, Milton awakens to the desolating discovery that his dream was not truth.

---

10 *John Milton: Complete Shorter Poems*, Second Edition, edited by John Carey (London: Longman, 1997).

These distinctions matter because Keats was much concerned with the question of whether it is possible "To unperplex bliss from its neighbour pain" (*Lamia*, 192). Since Jack Stillinger wrote his influential essay on the hoodwinking of Madeline, many critics have come to believe that Keats changed his mind on this question.[11] When he wrote to Bailey in 1817 he believed that bliss and pain could be un-perplexed; by the time he wrote *Lamia*, the great odes and *The Eve of Saint Agnes*, he thought otherwise. The fancy could no longer cheat so well as she was famed to do, and the claim that beauty is truth, truth beauty, was something that a Grecian urn might say, in quotation marks. But if, as I have suggested, the status of "Adam's dream" had always been perplexing, the distinction between the early and the later Keats may be less clear-cut than many critics have imagined. Keats in 1817 may well have wanted to feel "certain" of "the truth of Imagination," but the example he gives – "Adam's dream" – is not unequivocally supportive.

From what I have said so far it may seem that I am arguing against the idea that the younger Keats placed a naive trust in the imagination, and in some ways that is what I am doing. But my argument is a two-way street. If "Adam's dream" is less exalted than is often supposed, some of Keats's later references to Milton might be less disillusioned. Keats was an important figure in the twentieth-century "Milton controversy," for anti-Miltonists presented him as a poet who fell under Milton's bewitching spell and then awoke from enchantment. Anti-Miltonists like T. S. Eliot and John Middleton Murry liked to speak of Milton's "bad influence," and they infused those words with something like the moral opprobrium Milton himself brings to them when he describes Satan's temptation of the angels: "So spake the false Arch-Angel, and infus'd / Bad influence into th' unwarie brest / Of his Associate" (5.694-96). As Eliot (that most influential of critics) tells the story, Milton was the baleful Lucifer who lured a third part of English poets into perdition. Keats's testimony was especially damaging, for he spoke as a convert who had freed himself from Milton's malignant influences. In this version of literary history, Keats, like his own Madeline and Lycius, awoke to find that he had been cheated, but instead of pining for a lost vision he went on to create a genuine beauty of his own.[12]

---

11 Jack Stillinger, "The Hoodwinking of Madeline: Scepticism in 'The Eve of St. Agnes,'" *Studies in Philology* 58:3 (July, 1961), 533-55.

12 See T. S. Eliot, "A Note on the Verse of John Milton," *Essays and Studies* 21 (1935 [misdated 1936]), 32-40. John Middleton Murry invoked Keats as a witness against Milton in several works published in the 1920s and 1930s. See especially *The Problem of Style* (London: Oxford University Press, 1922), 118f. and *Keats and Shakespeare* (London: Oxford University Press, 1925), 189-215.

Keats testifies against Milton in two letters, one addressed to his brother George, the other to John Hamilton Reynolds. He began the letter to George on Friday 17 September 1819, but the passage on Milton is dated Tuesday 21 September –the same day that he wrote Reynolds. The two references to Milton were therefore written on the same day, probably at the same sitting. Addressing Reynolds, Keats rhapsodizes about the beauty of autumn (he had just composed "To Autumn") before turning to Milton:

> I always somehow associate Chatterton with autumn. He is the purest writer in the English Language. He has no French idiom, or particles like Chaucer(s) – 'tis genuine English Idiom in English words. I have given up Hyperion – there were too many Miltonic inversions in it – Miltonic verse cannot be written but in an artful or rather artist's humour. I wish to give myself up to other sensations. English ought to be kept up.[13]

The first thing to note here is the strange way in which Keats uses the word "up." It first appears in the repeated phrase "give up" ("I have given up Hyperion ... I wish to give myself up"), then reappears in the very different locution "keep up" ("English ought to be kept up"). There is something strangely downbeat about those first two "up"s. There is a difference between them. When Keats says "I have given up Hyperion," "given up" means "abandoned"; when he says "I wish to give myself up," "give up" still includes the idea of surrender, but Keats now takes a more positive view of it. Then, just as he is about to give up and lie down, he takes a stand: "English ought to be kept up." It turns out to be Milton, not Keats, who has given up and abandoned his post.

The idea of vigilance–of staying awake and keeping watch–also comes to the fore in the other letter Keats wrote on 21 September. Writing to his brother George, he again contrasts Milton with Chatterton and again has recourse to the verb "keep" and a prescriptive "ought to be." "Paradise lost," he writes,

> though so fine in itself is a curruption of our Language – it should be kept as it is unique–a curiosity – a beautiful and grand Curiosity. The most remarkable Production of the world – A northern dialect accommodating itself to greek and latin inversions and intonations. The purest English I think – or what ought to be the purest – is Chatterton's – The Language had existed long enough to be entirely uncorrupted of Chaucer's gallicisms, and still the old words are used – Chatterton's language is entirely northern – I prefer the native music of it to Milton's cut by feet. I have but lately stood on my guard against Milton. Life to him would be death to me. Miltonic verse cannot be written but i[n] the vein of art – I wish to devote myself to another sensation.[14]

"Devote" literally means to take a vow, which is stronger than the corresponding phrase in the other letter ("give myself up to other sensations"). The singular "sensation" is also more focused than the plural "sensations." Keats had used the

---

13   Rollins, 2:167.
14   Rollins, 2:212.

plural in his letter to Benjamin Bailey two years before, when (immediately after referring to Adam's dream) he declared: "O for a life of Sensations rather than of Thoughts!"[15] In the two passages he wrote in September 1819 we can see Keats struggling to achieve a focused vigilance–not dreaming, but keeping watch. Both of these passages have often been characterized as Keats's "rejection of Milton," and in some ways that is what they are, but we should not exaggerate the degree or misrepresent the nature of Keats's new suspicion. Keats himself does not use the word "reject." He says (guardedly) "I have but lately stood on my guard." Standing on guard is not the same as rejecting. A vigilant guard knows when to bar the way and when to grant access. Keats is quite specific as to what he is guarding against: "too many Miltonic inversions," "greek and latin inversions."

We should entertain the possibility that he meant what he said: no more, no less. Keats had had frequent recourse to "Miltonic inversions" in the poetry he wrote before September 1819. In *Hyperion* adjectives often follow the noun ("palpitations sweet, and pleasures soft," 1.313) or one adjective precedes the noun while another follows it ("Upon the gold clouds metropolitan," 1.129). Both were Miltonic devices familiar from such expressions as "human face divine" (3.44), "dun Air sublime" (3.72), and "dismal Situation waste and wilde" (1.60). Keats still used them in the great odes he wrote in May 1819 ("shadows numberless," "faery lands forlorn," "aching pleasure nigh") but by September he had come to think such inversions "artful." He did not banish them altogether. He uses them sparingly in his last poems, but he does still use them. Even "To Autumn" admits a "treble soft." Keats is on his guard, then, but we should be wary of concluding that his last poems allow no room for Milton. Six days after disparaging "Miltonic inversions," he concluded his letter to George by quoting six lines from the tragedy *Otho the Great* that he had recently written in collaboration with Charles Brown. Maurice Buxton Forman has suggested that one of these lines, "Are shaded in a forest of tall spears" echoes *Paradise Lost*: "A forest huge of spears" (1.547).[16] Keats's adaptation illustrates his ability to stand "guard against Milton" without rejecting him. A vigilant guardsman, he presents arms in regular English fashion ("tall spears" not "forest huge"), but still salutes Milton and lets him pass.

"I look upon fine Phrases like a Lover," Keats had written to Benjamin Bailey in July 1819, right after saying that "Shakespeare and the paradise Lost every day become greater wonders."[17]Although he subsequently repudiated "Miltonic

---

15 Rollins, 1:185.
16 *The Letters of John Keats*, ed. Maurice Buxton Forman, second edition (Oxford: Oxford University Press, 1935), 430.
17 Rollins, 2:139.

inversions," Keats never ceased to appreciate his great predecessor's "fine Phrases," some of which he treasured up to a life beyond life in his own poetry. We should not miss the erotic implications of "like a Lover." As Christopher Ricks has remarked, "it is characteristic of Keats, a man whose imagination was so moved to fine phrases by the thought of a lover looking, that he should have said 'I look upon fine Phrases like a Lover.' He did not just mean that he loved fine phrases.'"[18] That is well seen and I would add only that the erotic implications in Keats's phrase are enhanced by a grammatical ambiguity. "I look upon fine Phrases like a lover" means both "I look upon fine phrases with a lover's eyes" and "I look upon fine phrases as I might look upon a lover." The latter possibility gives a licence to Keats's roving eye, for a lover might welcome and reciprocate his admiring gaze. Keats's simile has special relevance for Porphyro, who both gazes upon Madeline –"Now prepare, / Young Porphyro, for gazing" (196-7) – and wishes to remain "the vision of her sleep" when her "blue affrayed eyes wide open shone" (296).

I shall return to *The Eve of St. Agnes* in a moment, but first I want to attend to the loving attention that Keats bestows upon some of Milton's fine phrases in his heavily marked and annotated copy of <u>Paradise Lost</u>, now at Keats House in Hampstead. We do not know the date of these annotations. Many critics have followed Douglas Bush in dating them to "the early months of 1818," but Nancy Goslee has suggested October 1818 and Robert Gittings has dated them as late as August 1819. Beth Lau suggests that "Keats read and marked his copy of Milton's poem on several different occasions."[19] One annotation has implications for Adam's dreams and Madeline's rude awakening. Keats is commenting on Satan's penetration of the serpent:

> in at his mouth
> The Devil entered, and his brutal sense,
> In heart or head, possessing soon inspired
> With act intelligential; but his sleep
> Disturbed not, waiting close th' approach of morn. (9.187-91)

Keats's note is very rich: "Satan having entered the Serpent, and inform'd his brutal sense–might seem sufficient–but Milton goes on '*but his sleep disturb'd not.*' Whose spirit does not ache at the smothering and confinement–the unwilling stillness–the '*waiting close*'? Whose head is not dizzy at the prosiable spec-

---

18   Christopher Ricks, *Keats and Embarrassment* (Oxford: Oxford University Press, 1974), 17.

19   Beth Lau, *Keats's "Paradise Lost"* (Gainesville: University Press of Florida, 1998), 33. See also Douglas Bush, "The Milton of Keats and Arnold," *Milton Studies* 11 (1978): 99-114 (see p. 100); Nancy M. Goslee, "'Under a Cloud in Prospect': Keats, Milton, and Stationing," *Philological Quarterly* 53 (1974): 205-19 (see p. 213); Robert Gittings, *The Mask of Keats* (Cambridge: Cambridge University Press, 1956), 10.

ulations of satan in this serpent prison – no passage of poetry ever can give a greater pain of suffocation" (153). I have reproduced the note as Keats wrote it, but one textual detail has occasioned some difficulty. "Prosiable" is what Keats wrote, but it is not a word, and so several editors since Harry Buxton Forman in 1883 have emended to "possible." Maurice Buxton Forman prints "possible" in his 1939 Hampstead edition, but adds a footnote in which he conjectures that Keats fused "possible" with "probable" in the heat of composition.[20] Forman's suggestion will seem irrefutable to anyone who recalls "refudiate," the neologism designated "word of the year" by the *Oxford American Dictionary* in 2010 after Sarah Palin had coined it by fusing "refuse" with "repudiate." Without refudiating Forman's prosiable hypothesis, I would add a third element to the textual alchemy: one that is suggested by the *prosaic* fact that Satan does not, on this occasion, melt into anyone's dream. He enters the serpent's mouth, but *"but his sleep disturb'd not."* In part, it is the tedium of Satan's predicament that Keats responds to. Satan neither imparts nor receives any visions, he just lies there, "waiting close." Keats latches onto this phrase, and he is right to do so, for "close" has several suggestive meanings. Most of Milton's editors gloss "close" as "hidden, secret" (*OED* 4), and that sense is certainly present. But Keats brings out additional possibilities with "prison" and "suffocation." "Close" can mean "shut up in prison" (*OED* 3) and "stifling, without free circulation, the opposite of *fresh*" (*OED* 6). The latter sense is now used mostly of the weather, but it was once used of small confined spaces. The serpent is "close" in all three senses: a hiding place, a prison, and a suffocating environment of "bestial slime" (9.165).

Keats recreates something like Milton's effect in *The Eve of St. Agnes* when Angela promises to lead Porphyro "in close secrecy, / Even to Madeline's chamber, and there hide / Him in a closet of such privacy / That he might see her beauty unspied" (163-6). That was a steamy closet if ever there was one, and it is all the more sultry for being hidden and cramped. Porphyro, "Stol'n to this paradise" (244), only has eyes for Madeline, but Keats looks "upon fine Phrases like a Lover" and (if we can tear our own eyes away from Madeline) we may note some of the phrases he has stolen from *Paradise Lost* – and from his own annotations upon it. "Whose spirit does not ache at the smothering and confinement – the unwilling stillness – the *'waiting close'*? Whose head is not dizzy?" Even Angela's head swims: "On such a catering trust my dizzy head. / Wait here, my child" (177-8). Waiting close, "Poryphyro grew faint" (244). Madeline then enters the chamber and, kneeling in the moonlight, unclasps "her warmed jewels

---

20 *The Poetical Works and Other Writings of John Keats*, ed. H. Buxton Forman, revised with additions by Maurice Buxton Forman, (London: Charles Scribner, 1939; repr. New York: Phaeton, 1970), 8 vols., 5:305.

one by one; / Loosens her fragrant bodice," and lets her "rich attire" drop "rustling to her knees" (228-30). "Prosiable speculations"? The possibilities and (since this is a sexual fantasy) probabilities at such a moment are dizzying, but (as so often in Keats's best poems) eager prospects go through a painful change to emerge as the merely prosy: "How changed thou art! how pallid, chill, and drear!" (311).

How fallen, how changed from Adam's dream, when he awoke and found it truth. Or rather, how changed from Adam's first dream. His second dream, as we have seen, has its own moment of disappointment. For me, one of the strangest things about *The Eve of St. Agnes* is the fact that Porphyro should draw encouragement from Madeline's response. Most men upon hearing those baleful words "pallid, chill, and drear" would infer that it was time to make a tactful exit before an already bad situation got any worse. Not Porphyro:

> At these voluptuous accents, he arose,
> Ethereal, flush'd, and like a throbbing star
> Seen mid the sapphire heaven's deep repose;
> Into her dream he melted. ... (317-20)

"Voluptuous accents"? These lines are indeed voluptuous, but the response that inspired them – "how pallid, chill, and drear!"– was anything but. To be fair, I have to admit that I have omitted four lines. The actual sequence goes like this:

> How changed thou art! how pallid, chill, and drear!
> Give me that voice again, my Porphyro,
> Those looks immortal, those complainings dear!
> O leave me not in this eternal woe,
> For if thou diest, my love, I know not where to go.
>
> Beyond a mortal man impassion'd far
> At these voluptuous accents, he arose. ... (311-17)

It is the "Give me" that Porphyro hears as "voluptuous." His hearing is nevertheless selective and I for one still find it hard to believe that he could remain "impassion'd" after Madeline's initial response. This might be Keats's fault as much as Porphyro's. *The Eve of St. Agnes* is a great poem, but it contains one very bad line in "For if thou diest, my love, I know not where to go." In part the line is bad because it makes no sense. Madeline at this moment has no reason to go anywhere and Porphyro is in no imminent danger of dying (unless Madeline's kinsmen discover him, but I do not think that that is what she means). Porphyro does not face imminent death in Madeline's chamber, but he has just had a narrow escape from another peril. He has resisted the temptation to fall asleep. Five stanzas earlier, when he had failed to wake Madeline with the direct address "And now, my love, my seraph fair, awake!" (276), he had briefly contemplated getting into bed with her—not to make love but to "drowse beside thee" (279).

There is something faintly comic about this picture, but I suspect that the poet of *Endymion* really did see sleep as a temptation. For a moment it seems that Porphyro is going to give up *The Eve of St. Agnes*, and give himself up to other sensations, forgetting the more sensational sensation he has come here to devote himself to. But, just in time, "Awakening up, he took her hollow lute" (289) and played "an ancient ditty, long since mute" (291). Milton comes to his rescue, for those words "since mute" are a direct lift from *Paradise Lost*. Satan tempting Eve pulls out all the stops and speaks like "some orator renowned / In Athens or free Rome, where eloquence / Flourished, since mute" (9.670-72). Porphyro is a kind of Satan figure, as critics have long recognized. C. S. Lewis thought that Milton's Satan was "a mere peeping Tom," "a thing that peers in at bedroom or bathroom windows."[21] Many have thought this judgment too harsh, and I too think it a caricature, but caricatures usually have some purchase on the truth (otherwise they would have no point). Both Satan and Porphyro have some of the characteristics of a peeping Tom. But it is Madeline's consciousness that is most fascinating at this moment. Newlyn thinks that Madeline's dream most closely resembles Eve's dream in book five of *Paradise Lost*. She warns us that it is "misleading" to align "Madeline's disappointed awakening" with Adam's "dream sequences" (both of which Newlyn takes to be happy). There are some resemblances between Eve's and Madeline's dreams. The most obvious are the serenade and the offering of fruit. But when Newlyn insists that it is "misleading" to look for parallels between Madeline and Adam it is she who misleads us. As I noted at the beginning of this essay, Newlyn argues for a gender distinction between fulfilled men and cheated women. She aligns Porphyro with Adam and Madeline with Eve. These connections are real, but we can acknowledge them and still see a parallel between Madeline's disappointment and Adam's second dream. Newlyn assumes that both of Adam's awakenings are happy, while Madeline's is not. My own view is that both Madeline and Adam find it difficult to unperplex bliss from its neighbour pain. Adam in his second awakening experiences a bitter-sweet mix of reality and fantasy, disappointment and hope: the full range of prosiable speculations. Madeline's disappointment is different. She is disappointed not because Porphyro has disappeared, but because he is so obtrusively present, and with such a palpable design upon her: "We hate poetry that has a palpable design upon us. Poetry should be great & unobtrusive, a thing which enters into one's soul, and does not startle it or amaze it with itself but with its subject."[22] It is difficult to interpret Madeline's response when she looks upon her uninvited visitor "so dreamingly" and cries "Ah, Porphyro!" Much depends on the tone of

---

21   C. S. Lewis, *A Preface to "Paradise Lost"* (London: Oxford University Press, 1942), 99.
22   Letter to John Hamilton Reynolds (3 February 1818), Rollins, 1:224.

that "Ah." If we hear it as a sigh of yearning, we can read it as Madeline's invitation for Porphyro to enter her soul without startling it, though Porphyro's next act ("Into her dream he melted") is nothing if not startling. But Madeline's "Ah" can also convey disappointment (as in "oh, it's only you"), in which case reality is all too obtrusive and falls woefully short of dreamy vision. However we read "Ah," it is obvious that Porphryo was better in the dream. Madeline awoke and found him a little too true; Adam awoke and found Eve not quite true enough. This difference still has gender implications, but we coarsen them if we reduce them to a simple distinction between fulfilled men and frustrated women. Adam's second dream is deeply troubled and his awakening from it is not nearly so joyful an experience as countless critics (often with their own palpable designs upon us) have imagined. Adam's two dreams are not a single happy sequence in *Paradise Lost*, and it behoves us to stand on our guard against poets and critics who would have us believe that they are. Keats in 1817 was the first of many readers to conflate Adam's two dreams. But even in 1817 he was alert to an important distinction ("whether it existed before or not"), and by 1819 he was fully alive to the ominousness in Adam's second dream and forlorn awakening. Forlorn! The very word is like a bell presaging Adam's fall:

> How can I live without thee, how forgo
> Thy sweet converse and love so dearly joined,
> To live again in these wild woods forlorn? (9.908-10)

These suggestive connections fortify my conviction that Keats never forsook his sweet converse with Milton. He never repudiated or (*horribile dictu*) refudiated the rich prosiabilities that Milton's verse offered him. Keats does not reject Milton; he stands on guard. The elder Jonathan Richardson, the critic who first connected Adam's dream with Milton's sonnet, declared that "the Reader of *Milton* must be Always upon Duty"(cxliv). Keats is often thought of as a poet of imagination and dreams, but when he reads Milton, it is with a wakeful eye: standing on guard, always on duty.

"The hush of the Mediterranean lipping the sand": the libertarian and libidinal politics of Virginia Woolf's Mediterranean discourse

Jane Goldman
University of Glasgow

> How could one sit out another day of speechifying? How could one, above all, face you, our hostess, with the information that your Congress had proved so insupportably exacerbating that one was going back to London by the very first train? The only chance lay in some happy conjuring trick, some change of attitude by which the mist and blankness of the speeches could be turned to blood and bone. Otherwise they remained intolerable. (V. Woolf 1931; 2009: 228)

Virginia Woolf's 1931 account of her uneasy attendance at the Congress of the Co-operative Working Women's Guild in Newcastle in June 1913 may seem an unlikely source for an analysis of her Mediterranean discourse, but it is in fact revealing of her typical deployment of the term, Mediterranean, as an index of the utopian in her discussions of class politics. Woolf wrote this account as part of her prefatory letter for a collection of epistolary memoirs edited by Margaret Llewellyn Davies, *Life As We Have Known It*, by Co-operative Working Women, and published by the Hogarth Press. This 'Introductory Letter to Margaret Llewellyn Davies' had appeared in revised and fictionalised form as an essay in the *Yale Review* (September 1930): 'Memories of a Working Women's Guild'. If she was uneasy in her participation as a middle class woman in the Co-operative Working Women's Guild events in the 1910s, she was equally uneasy seventeen years later writing the epistolary Preface to their letters. In it she records her impressions of the Newcastle Congress in June 1913 and also her impressions of a meeting 'later that summer' at the Guild head office in Hampstead, where Woolf and others were invited by Llewellyn Davies to 'tell [her] how the Congress had impressed us.' (V. Woolf 1931; 2009: 230) An impression of her impressions, Woolf's convoluted recollection of her previous attempt 'to describe the contradictory and complex feelings which beset the middle-class visitor when forced to sit out a Congress of working women in silence' continues with a 'childish game' (V. Woolf 1931; 2009: 228):

> "Let's pretend," one said to oneself, looking at the speaker, "that I am Mrs. Giles of Durham City." A woman of that name had just turned to address us. "I am the wife of a miner. He comes back thick with grime. First he must have his bath. Then he must have his supper. But

there is only a copper. My range is crowded with saucepans. There is no getting on with the work. All my crocks are covered with dust again. Why in the Lord's name have I not hot water and electric light laid on when middle-class women ..." So up I jump and demand passionately "labour saving appliances and housing reform." Up I jump in the person of Mrs. Giles of Durham; in the person of Mrs. Phillips of Bacup; in the person of Mrs. Edwards of Wolverton. But after all the imagination is largely the child of the flesh. One could not be Mrs. Giles of Durham because one's body had never stood at the wash-tub; one's hands had never wrung and scrubbed and chopped up whatever the meat may be that makes a miner's supper. The picture therefore was always letting in irrelevancies. One sat in an armchair or read a book. One saw landscapes and seascapes, perhaps Greece or Italy, where Mrs. Giles or Mrs. Edwards must have seen slag heaps and rows upon rows of slate roofed houses. Something was always creeping in from a world that was not their world and making the picture false and the game too much of a game to be worth playing.

It was true that one could always correct these fancy portraits by taking a look at the ac-tual person – at Mrs. Thomas, or Mrs. Langrish, or Miss Bolt of Hebden Bridge. They were worth looking at. Certainly, there were no armchairs, or electric light, or hot water laid on in their lives; no Greek hills or Mediterranean bays in their dreams. (V. Woolf 1931; 2009: 228)

While it is clear that it is a site accessed by middle class, educated women and higher orders, and that it is a site denied to working class women, the status of the Mediter-ranean here is nevertheless confusing. Is it a geographical location that privileged women actually visit? – or is it more often available to them as photographic, artistic or literary representations of landscapes and seascapes through the books they read, and subsequently in the dreams they dream? Does the Mediterranean stand then for abstract, intellectual and educational privileges and enlightenment values or for Orientalist sensual rustic and aquatic pleasures, relief from the urban and industrial vistas to which British working class women are condemned? Can it really be the case, as Woolf seems to be suggesting, that the Mediterranean did not figure even as a cultural cliché in the collective imaginary of working class women in 1931? Are 'Greek hills [and] Mediterranean bays' coded terms for taboo sexualities? And what are Woolf's own learned and privileged sources for the authority with which she speaks of the Mediterranean?

Woolf's own visits to the Mediterranean are well documented and scrutinised: her juvenile visits with siblings and friends to Greece and Turkey, etc; her later holidays with Leonard Woolf in France, Italy and Spain and with Vita Sackville-West in France; and her stays in the house of her sister in the south of France and of Gerald Brennan in Spain. See Mary Ann Caws' and Sarah Bird Wright's edited collection on *Bloomsbury and France* (2000) and Caroline Patey's excellent essay, in *Anglo-American Modernity and the Mediterranean* (2006), arguing for Bloomsbury's sophisticated dialogue with the Mediterranean culture contra Ro-mantic and Victorian Orientalism. Critics usually identify the authorities for Woolf's Mediterranean discourse either, with reference to Post-Impressionist aesthetics, as her Bloomsbury artist and art historian colleagues, Vanessa Bell, Duncan Grant, Clive Bell and Roger Fry, or, with reference to Classicism and Hellenism, as her mentors and tutors in Greek and Latin, Jane Harrison, Clara Pater and Janet Case. *Jacob's Room* (1922) emerges as a key text for such readings (see for example, Vassiliki Kolocotroni's work on Woolf's Hellenism). Giovanni Cianci's informative essay on 'Jane Harrison's Dionysian Mediterranean' for *Anglo-American Modernity and the Mediterranean* does not mention Woolf but nevertheless provides productive insights into Harrison's particular understanding of Nietzsche, Bergson, vitalism, and unanism that would inform readings of Woolf's Mediterranean as antithetical to Clive Bell's. Pierre Bourdieu's book, *Masculine Domination* (1998), reads Woolf's *To the Lighthouse* through anthropological information about the Kabyle society, a Mediterranean ethnic group. Joanna Grant, in a recent paper, compares Woolf's Levantine Mediterranean with Vita Sackville-West's.

As the Mediterranean as *topos* encompasses such numerous locations, experiences, associations, and allusions in Woolf's oeuvre, I have decided to focus my paper on some of the few instances in her writings, prior to and following her 'Introductory Letter to Margaret Llewellyn Davies', where she uses the word 'Mediterranean' itself. Her letter to Lytton Strachey from Tarragona in Spain in September 1912, for example, serves to illustrate Woolf's orientalist tendency to measure repressed British life against a positively libertine and queer Mediterranean one:

> Just about this moment, you're settling down over the fire, having returned from a brisk walk among the Scotch firs in a Scotch mist, and saying (something I can't spell – it's French) to the effect that life holds nothing but copulation, after which you groan from the profundities of the stomach, [...] . . ., when the bell rings and the sandy haired girl, whom you wish was a boy, says "Dinner on the table". . . whereas I'm just off to walk by the shores of the Mediterranean, by the beams of the dying sun, which is still hot enough to make a cotton dress and a parasol necessary, while the military band plays [...] and the naked boys run like snipe along the beach, balancing their buttocks in the pellucid air. (V. Woolf 1976: 5)

In Woolf's debut novel, *The Voyage Out* (1915), the sight of 'The Mediterranean Fleet' prompts Richard Dalloway to 'raise his hat' and Clarissa Dalloway to exclaim 'Aren't you glad to be English!', but the narrator describes how the 'warships drew past, casting a curious effect of discipline and sadness upon the waters, and it was not until they were again invisible that people spoke to each other naturally. At lunch the talk was all of valour and death, and the magnificent qualities of British admirals.' (V. Woolf 1915: 60) British imperialist martial regime is clearly an unwelcome intrusion on a Mediterranean idyll already tainted by the presence of the Dalloways. Two years later, in 1917, Woolf wrote an admiring review of Norman Douglas's Wildean novel, *South Wind*, identifying its successful narrative strategy to 'Take all the interesting and eccentric people you can think of, put them on an island in the Mediterranean beyond the realms of humdrum but not in those of fantasy' (V. Woolf 1917; 1987: 125). She continues:

> bid them say shamelessly whatever comes into their heads: let them range over every topic and bring forth whatever fancy, fact, or prejudice happens to occur to them: add, whenever the wish moves you, dissertations upon medieval dukes, Christianity, cookery, education, fountains, Greek art, millionaires, morality, the sexes: enclose the whole in an exquisite atmosphere of pumice rocks and deep blue waves, air with the warm and stimulating breath of the South Wind – the prescription begins something in this way. (V. Woolf 1917; 1987: 125-126)

Woolf considers this an escapist, Wildean and Peacockian idyll: 'Upon the Island of Nepenthe, then, "an islet of volcanic stone rising out of the blue Mediterranean", are congregated for various reasons a great many people of marked idiosyncrasy – [...] How often in the coming months will our thoughts seek relief if not repose in the Island of Nepenthe, and with what eagerness shall we await a further and even fuller report of its history!' (V. Woolf 1917; 1987: 126, 127). Writing in 1921 to Roger Fry who was with Vanessa Bell 'on the shores of the Mediterranean' (V. Woolf 1976: 484), clearly a favoured erotic signifier, Woolf again points up the contrasting constraints on sexual freedom imposed in Britain, as well as some mishaps befalling her servants, and dwells on a key term for Bloomsbury's aesthetic formalists – 'civilisation':

> we have been having the devil of a time – the influenza. Leonard refusing to go to bed; Nelly like a hen run over, but unhurt, by a motor car; Lottie [...] an intoxicated Jay: the house ringing with laughter and tears. Do other people go on like this, I sometimes wonder, or have we somehow (this includes you, by the way) slipped the coil of civilisation? I mean, we've jumped the lines. There you are bathing naked with 50 prostitutes; yesterday we had Goldie [Lowes Dickinson] to tea. I do my best to make him jump the rails. He has written a dialogue upon homosexuality which he won't publish, for fear of the effect upon parents who might send their sons to Kings: and he is writing his autobiography which he won't publish for the same reason. So you see what dominates English literature is the parents of the young men who might be sent to Kings. (V. Woolf 1976: 484)

Writing to Vanessa Bell on the same trip, Woolf figures the Mediterranean as a safe receptacle for British scandal: 'Lord! I've just remembered another bit of gossip – but this, on your honour as a Dolphin, you must only whisper to the waves of the Mediterranean, if to them.' (V. Woolf 1976: 493) By 1927, in a love letter to Vita Sackville-West, written while both were in England, the Mediterranean has become Woolf's allegory for Sapphic pleasure:

> My dear Mrs Nicolson,// I cant tell you how I enjoyed myself on Sunday. It was so good of you and your husband to let me come. And what a lovely garden! I cant think how you can ever bear to leave it. But then everything was so delightful. London seemed more commonplace than ever after your delightful Long Barn. And I still have some of your lovely flowers to remind me of the happy time I had with you, and your husband, to whom please give my

best thanks and remembrances, and with much love to you both, I am. There, you ram-
shackle old Corkscrew, is that the kind of thing you like? I suppose so.
   What I think will be so nice next time is the porpoise in my bath – steel blue, ice cold,
and loving hearted. Some prefer dolphins – I dont. I've known one dolphin, the Mediterranean
kind, ravage a whole bedfull of oysters. A lewd sort of brute that. (V. Woolf 1977: 398)

Not surprisingly, in Woolf's tribute to Sackville-West, *Orlando: A Biography*
(1928), Orlando's ship is observed 'in full sail coming with the sun on it proudly
sweeping across the Mediterranean from the South Seas' (V. Woolf 1928: 226).
   Whereas libidinal and racial associations are available in both Post-Impressionist and classical sources for Woolf's Mediterranean discourse and have been
pointed up by critics lingering over her fascination with Gauguin girls and Dionysian rites, the appearance of class politics tends to go unremarked. And so too does
an important Bloomsbury source for Woolf's understanding of the Mediterranean
in wider political and economic terms, Leonard Woolf's *Empire and Commerce in
Africa* (1920), a book his wife helped him research, and then read through a number of times and considered his most important work. Here Leonard Woolf makes
Utopian proposals for 'international government in the interests of the Africans
themselves' and a concomitant 'change in human nature' (L. Woolf 1920: ??), like
those changes in 'human character', in human relations, between master and servant, husband and wife, that Virginia Woolf, in 1924, was to posit had already
begun 'on or about December 1910' (V. Woolf 1924; 1988: 422, 421):

   The "native" is no longer to be regarded as the "livestock" on Europe's African estate [...]
   market for the shoddy of our factories and our cheap gin, or as the "cheap labour" [...] but
   as a human being with a right to his own land and his own life, with a right even to determine his own destiny, to be considered in that fantastic scheme of human government which men
   have woven over the world, an end in himself rather than an instrument to other people's
   ends. [...] These proposals will, of course, appear Utopian, a demand for a change in human
   nature. (L. Woolf 1920: ??)

Leonard Woolf is scathing on the duplicity of earlier apparently egalitarian visions for Africa entertained by rapacious imperialist powers, and translates a case
in point from the French of Émile Banning, who predicted:

   "a great Mediterranean State, open commercially to all nations, and yet withdrawn politically from their competitions. At the same time there have been laid down the bases of an economic legislation applicable to the central zone of the African continent, but destined in fact
   to a wider application. This system, inspired by the most liberal ideas, which removes every
   thought of selfish exploitation, will protect at the same time both the natives and Europeans
   in their relations with the colonizing powers: it provides a sanction for the principles of religious and civil liberty, of loyal and pacific commerce, and openly breaks with the obsolete
   traditions of the old colonial system." Such were men's hopes and visions in 1884: the future was the exact opposite of what they hoped for, and their millennium was shattered by
   their own Messiah. The next generation saw the final act of the Congo Conference become a
   mockery, one more tool of imperialist ambitions (L. Woolf 1920: ??)

I will now turn to a cluster of Virginia Woolf's uses of the word 'Mediterranean' in the 1930s. In August 1930 Woolf was writing from Sussex to her lover Vita Sackville-West who was abroad with her husband, Harold Nicolson:

> Yes, it must be dull, travelling without Virginia – nobody to say Brusque? – oh no Harold would know the word for rough, and so would the boys; but then I daresay at Porto Fino, what with the vineyards and the olive trees, the mediterranean and the old crumbling cliff – […] you've forgotten me, and Potto, and how we crossed the Channel, and how I wept as the white cliffs disappeared. […] Life is so adorably pleasing at the moment […] True it drizzles […] but I dont care; I feel so happy with poor dear Nelly away, and no rows, and no tears, and all my time free; and now Mrs. Walters hints that she wants to come permanently. Lord, what am I to do? Please, as an English lady, tell me. (V. Woolf 1978:197)

Two months later [27? October 1930], she was complaining to her sister, Vanessa Bell, 'Dearest Dolphin,/ Yes I quite agree that it was time you wrote to me – its your duty, being so idiotic as to go to your Mediterranean blue [Cassis].' (V. Woolf 1978: 235) In 1934, Woolf was conceiving 'Phases of Fiction', a precursor to the divided project which became the polemical tract, *Three Guineas* (1938) and the novel *The Years* (1937): 'I have improvised another method for P[hases]. of F[iction]. to be phases of the readers mind: different situations. Part 2. to be in dialogue, in a hotel on the Mediterranean: each chapter to correspond with the period. Thus to rob it of formality.' (V. Woolf 1982: 250) In the 1891 section of the novel, *The Years* (1937), Woolf makes the Mediterranean shorthand allegory for democratic, promiscuous laissez-faire values in contrast to the deadly formal grip of class-ridden British custom as 'the lazy fisher boy […] lying on his back in his boat in the Mediterranean' is set against the cold North where 'Kitty, Lady Lasswade [is] sitting on the terrace beside her husband and his spaniel […] looking at […] the snuffer-shaped monument' (V. Woolf 1937: 89). In her biography of Roger Fry (1940), Woolf quotes his encapsulation on 'civilisation':

> or what it ought to mean. It's apropos of the question of the existence of individuals. It seems to me that nearly the whole Anglo-Saxon race especially of course in America have lost the power to be individuals. They have become social insects like bees and ants. They just are lost to humanity, and the great question for the future is whether that will spread or will be repulsed by the people who still exist, mostly the people round the Mediterranean. We must hope for the complete collapse of Anglo-Saxondom. The Arabs and Turks are still pure. (V. Woolf 1940: 272)

In this bizarre schema, a startlingly un-American Fry reverses White Anglo-Saxon Protestant racial stereotyping so that it is the Anglo-Saxons who are lacking purity, humanity and individualism and are reduced to regimented insects. And Woolf records that 'it was not only the landscape' of Mediterranean Provençal that Fry 'loved; it was the pagan, classless society, where salads were held in common, where every peasant was an individual and the old man who trimmed his olive trees was a more civilized human being than the citizens of Paris, Berlin or London.' (V. Woolf 1940: 282)

Woolf's argument in her 'Introductory Letter to Margaret Llewellyn Davies' concerns the class differences she felt so keenly between herself and working women as somatically marked. Imagination as 'the child of flesh' (V. Woolf 1931; 2009: 228) conjures for her heroic socialist portraits of powerful but long-suffering proletarian women restricted in location and ambition by their service to their husbands (wives are here servants to servants) *and* to middle and upper class women whose bodies are therefore exempt from the physical tolls endured by their servants.

> They did not stroll through the house and say, that cover must go to the wash, or those sheets need changing. They plunged their arms in hot water and scrubbed the clothes themselves. In consequence their bodies were thick-set and muscular, their hands were large, and they had the slow emphatic gestures of people who are often stiff and fall tired in a heap on hard-backed chairs. They touched nothing lightly. [...] Their lips never expressed the lighter and more detached emotions that come into play when the mind is perfectly at ease about the present. No, they were not in the least detached and easy and cosmopolitan. (V. Woolf 1931; 2009: 229)

Alison Light, in *Virginia Woolf and the Servants*, has opened up important and powerful arguments about Woolf's professional and personal relations with, and her depictions of, servants and working-class women, not least regarding the politics of bodily care – issues that remain highly contentious to this day. I am interested in how her Mediterranean discourse functions in Woolf's accounts of the lived bodies of working women. The Mediterranean here seems to stand for the 'detached and easy and cosmopolitan' qualities lacking in the working women whose bodies are powerfully marked and shaped by their harsh regime of labours and whose dreams are bereft of 'Greek hills' and 'Mediterranean bays' just as their homes lack 'armchairs [...] electric light, [and] hot water laid on'. Is the Mediterranean representative of an abstract life of the mind 'at ease' and able to enjoy intellectual freedom precisely because bodily needs have been met, or does it represent a different sense of embodiment? The argument of *A Room of One's Own* (1929) is perhaps being reprised: 'Intellectual freedom depends upon material things' (V. Woolf 1929). Woolf's 'Introductory Letter' attempts to bridge the gap between classes in her account of the visit to the Guild head office, where she draws attention to the labours of two women working there whom she describes in 'symbolical' colours: the office clerk, Harriet Kidd, 'the sombre purple figure who typed as if the weight of the world were on her shoulders' and whose own letter Woolf goes on to quote; and the 'coffee-coloured' Lilian Harris, the Guild's assistant secretary and the lifelong partner of Llewellyn Davies, and who 'was to the Congress what the heart is to the remoter veins.' (V. Woolf 1931; 2009: 231) Woolf now airs the grievances of the silent 'physically uncomfortable' middle class auditors at the Congress:

> We had been humiliated and enraged. To begin with, all their talk, we said, [...] was of matters of fact. They want baths and money. To expect us, whose minds such as they are, fly free at

the end of a short length of capital to tie ourselves down again to that narrow plot of acquisi-
tiveness and desire is impossible. We have baths and we have money. Therefore, however
much we had sympathised our sympathy was largely fictitious. [...] The Guild's women are
magnificent to look at. Ladies in evening dress are lovelier far, but they lack the sculptures-
que quality that these working women have. And though the range of expression is narrower
in working women, their few expressions have a force and an emphasis, of tragedy and humour, which the faces of ladies lack. But, at the same time, it is much better to be a lady; ladies desire Mozart and Einstein [in the *Yale Review* it's 'Mozart' and the Mediterranean
based 'Cézanne' (V. Woolf 1930; 2009: 182)] – that is, they desire things that are ends, not
things that are means. (V. Woolf 1931; 2009: 231)

These progressive ladies, even without the vote, apparently enjoy glimpses of the
right Leonard Woolf looks forward to Africans taking up – to be 'an end in
[themselves] rather than an instrument to other people's ends' (L. Woolf 1920:
??). Woolf's painful self-satire as one of the 'ladies', a term from which she is
everywhere else in her writings energetically distancing herself (see the letter to
the 'lady' Vita Sackville-West), continues by her recalling the lampooning caricatures of 'ladies' performed by some of the working class orators: 'Therefore to
deride ladies and to imitate, as some speakers did, their mincing speech and little
knowledge of what it pleases them to call 'reality' is, so it seems to us, not merely foolish but gives away the whole purpose of the Congress [...]' (V. Woolf
1931; 2009: 231) Given Woolf's recorded fraught and contradictory feelings on
her status as a 'lady' employer of servants and her excruciating experience of
reading and writing character references of servants, whose positions were ad-
vertised in the magazine, *The Lady*, it is little wonder that her 'Introductory Letter' reads in places like a savage conceit on such documents. Her remarks here
must also be considered as in dialogue with or corrective to the article, 'The
Women's Co-operative Guild', signed by Leonard Woolf, and published in a
Suffrage magazine in September 1916, which offers a more benign account of
the Guildswomen's oratory, witnessed by the Woolfs in 1916: 'The most eloquent of orators would not have disdained the applause which some simple
statement of fact called forth, or the rapture of laughter which seized the audience when one speaker imitated the mincing manner of a lady visitor who had
required her to "wash up the pots".' (L. Woolf 1916) Leonard Woolf's account
emphasizes: 'It was laughter, however; not bitterness or indignation. The Congress, despite its eagerness and quickness in taking points, gave one the impression that it was a very broad-minded and tolerant assembly. "We ought not to be
hard on the ladies", one of the delegates observed, and this largeness of view was
shown in the discussion of questions of a less domestic and more broadly political
nature.' (L. Woolf 1916) Leonard Woolf's report of the Congress meeting held
in 1916 is also echoed in Virginia Woolf's later 'Introductory Letter', which
seems to collapse incidents from both 1913 and 1916 Congresses.

The whole passage on class differences, in the 'Introductory Letter', was a point of fierce contention between Virginia Woolf and Llewellyn Davies and it differs from the earlier version of the essay published in the *Yale Review*, as Woolf's side of the correspondence (10 October 1930) shows:

> I am very pleased that Mrs Barton [General Secretary of the Guild] on the whole approves – at the same time I'm amused at the importance attached to the size of the Guilders. Vanity seems to be the same in all classes. But I swear that Mrs Barton shall say exactly what she thinks of the appearance of me and my friends and I wont find *her* unsympathetic. Indeed I wish she would – what fun to hand her a packet of our letters and let her introduce it! What rather appals me [...] is the terrific conventionality of the workers. [...] If they cant face the fact that Lilian [Harris] smokes a pipe and reads detective novels, and cant be told that they weigh on an average 12 stone – which is largely because they scrub so hard and have so many children – and are shocked by the word "impure" how can you say that they face "reality"?, (I never know what "reality" means: but Lilian smoking a pipe to me is real, and Lilian merely coffee coloured and discreet is not nearly so real). What depresses me is that workers seem to have taken on all the middle class respectabilities which we – at any rate if we are any good at writing or painting – have faced and thrown out. Or am I quite wrong? [...] And why, with such a chance to get rid of conventionalities, do they cling to them? However, I must stop. And we must meet and go into the question by word of mouth – if you want me to make them sylphs I will. (V. Woolf 1978: 228)

It surely cannot be the tobacco habit of Llewellyn Davies' companion that was the real 'reality' under dispute. Woolf conceded (in a letter to Llewellyn Davies 1 Feb 1931) to replace the pipe-smoking with a reference to 'a few cigarettes in Lilian's ash-tray' (V. Woolf 1978: 228). Where the 1930 version has the fictional 'Miss Janet Erskine' who 'may have been smoking a pipe – there was one on the table' (V. Woolf 1930; 2009: 181), the 1931 version has the real-life Miss Harris with her 'ash-tray in which many cigarettes had come amiably to an end' (V. Woolf 1931; 2009: 230). Perhaps the change was desired because whereas cigarettes might suggest, in 1913 and in 1930, a woman's possibly suspect progressive morality and hint at feminism, a pipe would perhaps be a more challenging social symbol, and a more robust signifier of Sapphism (despite heterosexual women pipe smokers), a risky narrative strategy in the wake of the *Well of Loneliness* obscenity trial of 1928 (to which Woolf herself elliptically refers in *A Room of One's Own*.) In this context barely spectral lesbians must become or remain invisible. That her interlocutor may have such pressing reason to silence her over such telling detail is again playfully available in the highly possible double entendre of Woolf's closing remarks: 'Have not you and Lilian Harris given your best years – but hush! you will not let me finish that sentence and therefore, with the old messages of friendship and admiration, I will make an end.' (V. Woolf 1931; 2009: 238-239) The end of the sentence may be whispered in a hush 'by word of mouth', but not written in print. Who is speaking or hushing that word 'hush'? Woolf leaves it open (without quote marks) to be read as spoken by herself and/or by Llewellyn Davies and/or by Harris and by the reader silently or out loud.

As it happens, Woolf's 'Introductory Letter' was well received by the Guild women who were 'generous' and 'appreciative' much to her delight (V. Woolf 1978: 341). Perhaps they appreciated that the turning point in Woolf's letter comes when she records the moment she opens and reads the packet of letters by the working women themselves and their own words banish the mutually created antagonisms and stereotypes she has described as arising from the formalities of the Congress: 'The hot June day with its banners and its ceremonies had vanished, and instead one looked back into the past of the women who had stood there; into the four-roomed houses of miners, into the homes of small shopkeepers and agricultural labourers, into the fields and factories of fifty or sixty years ago.' (V. Woolf 1931; 2009: 234) And among numerous instances, Woolf remarks on the account by a mill girl of how 'a chance saying in a book would fire her imagination to dream of future cities where there were to be baths and kitchens and washhouses and art galleries and museums and parks. The minds of working women were humming and their imaginations were awake.' (V. Woolf 1931; 2009: 236)

So does this finally acknowledged energised imagination suggest sufficient detachment and ease and cosmopolitan-ness to allow 'thick-set and muscular' proletarian women access in their dreams at least to the 'Greek hills' and 'Mediterranean bays' that Woolf began by thinking were denied them by the obliterating view of slag heaps and rows and rows of slate-roofed houses? Presumably those already cosmopolitan enough to get hold of a copy of the *Yale Review* would also therefore be able with new found equanimity to read of (and face) the fact that Lilian Harris (albeit in the guise of Janet Erskine) smoked a pipe and read detective stories while at her desk in the Guild head office.

If my paper seems to have drifted off with Woolf on a proletarian tide far from those Mediterranean bays, it is now about to throw an anchor in both directions at once by turning to Woolf's unpublished short story, 'The French Woman in the Train', apparently composed six years later in 1937 as one of a series of 'Portraits'. This is it in its entirety:

> Most garrulous, pendulous, snuffing like a tapir the succulent lower leaves of the cabbages; rootling among the herbage; even in the third class railway carriage avid for some titbit of gossip ... Madame Alphonse said to her cook ... the earrings swinging as in the large lobed ears of some pachydermatous monster. A hiss with a little saliva comes from the front teeth which have been yellowed and blunted, biting at cabbage stalks. And all the time behind her pendulous nid-nodding head and the drip of saliva the grey olives of Provence ray out, come to a point; make a wrinkled background with wry angular branches and peasants stooping.
>
> In London in a third class carriage against black walls pasted with shiny advertisements she would be running through Clapham on her way to Highgate to renew the circle of china

flowers on the grave of her husband. There at the Junction she sits in her corner[,] on her knee a black bag; in the bag a copy of the Mail; a picture of the Princesses – in her bag redolent of cold beef, of pickles, of tented curtains, of church bells on Sunday and the Vicar calling.

Here she bears on her immense and undulating shoulder the tradition; even when her mouth dribbles, when her wild pig eyes glitter one hears the croak of the frog in the wild tulip field; the hush of the Mediterranean lipping the sand; and the language of Molière. Here the bull neck bears baskets of grapes; through the train rattle comes the din of the market; a butting ram, men astride it; ducks in wicker cages; ice cream in cornets; rushes laid over cheese; over butter; men playing boules by a plane tree; a fountain; the acrid smell at the corner where peasants openly obey the dictates of nature. (V.Woolf 1985: 242-243)

Once again the Mediterranean serves as the fantastical measure of British working class lived reality. But what is going on in this story where a respectable, conservative working-class British widow is sandwiched between accounts of a deliciously grotesque and quasi-mythical pig-eyed peasant woman from Provence, a bestial allegory of somatic freedom and of other clichés of peasantry, who shoulders a mysterious 'tradition' in communicating among other things, 'the hush of the Mediterranean lipping the sand'? Is Virginia Woolf's Provençal Mediterranean also 'lipping the sand' of Leonard Woolf's lost African Mediterranean Utopia as well as Roger Fry's WASP-free Levantine Mediterranean? And is the closing yet always and already opening 'hush' of Woolf's 'Introductory Letter', the same possibly Sapphic 'hush' as this 'hush of the Mediterranean lipping the sand'?

Works Cited

Émile Banning (1888; 2010), *Le Partage Politique de L'Afrique D'Après Les Transactions Internationales Les Plus Récentes: 1885 à 1888* (London: Kessinger)

Pierre Bourdieu (1998; 2001), *Masculine Domination*, trans. Richard Nice (Stanford: Stanford University Press)

Mary Ann Caws and Sarah Bird Wright (2000), eds., *Bloomsbury and France: Art and Friends* (Oxford: Oxford University Press)

Giovanni Cianci (2006), 'Jane Harrison's Dionysian Mediterranean', *Anglo-American Modernity and the Mediterranean* (Milano: Cisalpino): 247-62

Norman Douglas (1917), *South Wind* (London: Martin Secker)

Joanna Grant (2006), 'They Came to Baghdad: Woolf and Sackville-West's Levant', *Woolf and the Art of Exploration: Selected Papers from the Fifteenth International Conference on Virginia Woolf*, ed. Helen Southworth and Elisa Kay Sparks (Clemson: Clemson University Digital): 150-58

Vassiliki Kolocotroni (2005),'"This Curious Silent Unrepresented Life": Greek
    Lessons in Virginia Woolf's Early Fiction', *Modern Language Review* 100: 2
    (April): 313-22
Alison Light (2007), *Mrs Woolf and the Servants* (London: Penguin)
Caroline Patey, Giovanni Cianci, and Francesca Cuojati (2006), eds, *Anglo-
    American Modernity and the Mediterranean*, ed. Caroline Patey (Milan:
    Cisalpino)
Leonard Woolf (1916), 'The Women's Co-operative Guild', *Jus Suffragii:
    Monthly Organ of the International Woman Suffrage Alliance* (September)
–. (1920) *Empire and Commerce in Africa* (London: Allen and Unwin)
Virginia Woolf (1915), *The Voyage Out* (London: Duckworth)
–. (1917; 1987), 'South Wind', *The Essays of Virginia Woolf*, vol. 2, ed. Andrew
    McNeillie (London: Hogarth)
–. (1924; 1988) 'Character in Fiction', *The Essays of Virginia Woolf*, vol. 3, ed.
    Andrew McNeillie (London: Hogarth)
–. (1928), *Orlando: A Biography* (London: Hogarth)
–. (1929), *A Room of One's Own* (London: Hogarth)
–. (1930; 2009), 'Memories of a Working Women's Guild', *The Essays of Vir-
    ginia Woolf*, vol. 5, ed. Stuart N. Clarke (London: Hogarth)
–. (1931; 2009), 'Introductory Letter to Margaret Llewellyn Davies', *The Essays
    of Virginia Woolf*, vol. 5, ed. Stuart N. Clarke (London: Hogarth)
–. (1976), *The Letters of Virginia Woolf*, vol. 2, ed. Nigel Nicolson and Joanne
    Trautmann (London: Hogarth)
–. (1977), *The Letters of Virginia Woolf*, vol. 3, ed. Nigel Nicolson and Joanne
    Trautmann (London: Hogarth)
–. (1978), *The Letters of Virginia Woolf*, vol. 4, ed. Nigel Nicolson and Joanne
    Trautmann (London: Hogarth)
–. (1982), *The Diary of Virginia Woolf*, vol. 4, ed. Anne Olivier Bell (London:
    Hogarth)
–. (1985), 'Portraits', *The Complete Shorter Fiction of Virginia Woolf*, ed. Susan
    Dick (London: Hogarth)

Staging the Mediterranean: Developing Views in English Drama

Christopher Innes
York University, Toronto

From the very first, for Renaissance dramatists, the Mediterranean held a fascination because of two factors: first on the historical and cultural level – Rome as the source of Classical heritage, and Troy, for its epic myths. Second: because on the political level, the Mediterranean encapsulated crucial contemporary issues – in particular the influence of Machiavelli and the on-going battles between the Muslim Empire of the Turks and Christian Europe (a defining conflict which is still very much with us).

There were – thanks almost exclusively to Shakespeare – more Elizabethan plays about classical Rome than about any other Mediterranean country or period. However, in general, Rome is seen as part of a common European history, in contrast to the 'Orientalism' of the Levant, Egypt or North Africa. Rome is also represented as specifically male, representing rationality, the bravery of war (a specifically masculine trade), and moral purity – even if this can be taken to excess, as in the figures of Titus Andronicus or Coriolanus: both representing extremes of masculinity in their disastrous actions. Alternatively in Ben Jonson's more sardonic vision, which he promoted as historically accurate, Rome is a site of vicious and corrupt power-politics. Similarly for Shakespeare, as well as other Elizabethan – and particularly for the Jacobean – playwrights, contemporary Italy is presented as a violent and lawless state, where family feuds kill young lovers, a Duchess is terrorized and murdered on the orders of her jealous brother, or an incestuous relationship culminates in a sister's heart being paraded across the stage on the point of her lover-brother's dagger. Or even when the state is presented as stable, it contains plots and deceptions initiated by devious and evil individuals – for instance the bastard Don John, Shylock, or most signally the malcontent Iago. Yet however, motiveless the malignancy of Iago, there is nothing mysterious or 'foreign' about this violence and deception: it is implicitly recognized as an integral part of ourselves – a slightly disguised critique of not just southern European, but by extension of the home audience's English society – and indeed it is associated with over-civilized sophistication.

In contrast, North Africa is presented as either primitive – the home of Aaron the Moor and Othello. Or, still more centrally, as female – through the figure of

Marlowe's Dido, or more iconically, Cleopatra. Notably Marlowe characterizes *Dido Queen of Carthage* in exactly the same terms as Shakespeare describes his Cleopatra twenty years later. Reminded of his destiny by Mercury the Messenger of the Gods, who demands he "leave these unrenowned realms, where nobility abhors to stay," Marlowe's Aeneas describes Dido's power over him: "'Come back, come back,' I hear her cry afar / 'And let me link my body to thy lips…'"[1] – an evocation of physical lust and emotional longing, notably projected through the male gaze, which his Captain, Achates, counters in stereotypical terms:

> Banish that ticing dame…
> And follow your foreseeing stars in all:
> This is no life for men-at-arms to live,
> Where dalliance doth consume a soldier's strength,
> And wanton motions of alluring eyes
> Effeminate our minds inured to war.[2]

A sentiment that immediately makes up Aeneas' mind to leave Dido, exhorting himself:

> I may not dure this female drudgery.
> To sea, Aeneas! Find out Italy![3]

Exactly the same contrasts are expressed in *Antony and Cleopatra* when Antony exclaims "I must from this enchanting queen break off…. Or lose myself in dotage!" – although in sharp contrast to Aeneas, Antony of course proves incapable of leaving Cleopatra.[4] Whatever the risks, as Enobarbus astutely observes, "he will to his Egyptian dish again."[5] And indeed this war/mind/male versus love/body/female opposition forms the frame for Shakespeare's play, with the first speech describing Antony's descent from "Roman virtue":

> … His captain's heart,
> Which in the scuffles of great fights hath burst
> The buckles on his breast, reneges all temper
> And is become the bellows and the fan
> To cool a gypsy's lust.[6]

And the effeminacy created by subjugation to love of a woman, is demonstrated throughout the play: Cleopatra dressing Antony in her clothes, while she "wore

---

1   Christopher Marlowe, *Dido, Queen of Carthage* in *The Complete Plays*. London: Penguin Books, 2003, 4.3.18-19, 27-28.
2   Ibid., 4.3.31-36.
3   Ibid.. 4.3.55-56.
4   William Shakespeare, *Antony and Cleopatra*. London: Arden Shakespeare, 2006, 1.2.135, 124.
5   Ibid., 2.6.128.
6   Ibid., 1.1.6-10.

his sword Philippan;"[7] Antony following Cleopatra's ship out of the sea battle, when she decides to test his love for her. Cleopatra is indeed presented as the eternal feminine: manipulative, mysterious, exotic, sensual, and sexualized. At the same time, the weakness of the female East when faced with the Western male is also symbolized through suicide. Indeed both plays end with multiple suicides in exactly the same configuration: the heroine (Dido / Cleopatra) at least one female attendant (Dido's sister, Anna / Iras and Charmian) and a male who loves the heroine, and is thus drawn into her feminine sphere (Iarbas / Antony).

This corresponds almost too precisely with Edward Saïd's argument, where he goes back to Aeschylus' *The Persians*, arguing that the West has always stereotyped the East. For Saïd, Western writings about the Orient depict it as an irrational, weak, feminised "other," contrasted with the rational, strong, masculine West, a contrast he suggests derives from the need to create "difference" between West and East through presenting mysterious "essences" as immutable.[8]

However, neither Marlowe's nor Shakespeare's perspective on the Southern shore of the Mediterranean has anything to do with imperialist agendas, since it was to be over two centuries more before England as a nation had much contact with the Ottoman Empire, and while just beginning on its colonizing odyssey under Queen Elizabeth, it was only in 1607 that the first colony was established: Virginia, and that was in the New World. Indeed until the arrival of the Moroccan ambassador in London in 1600 about the only knowledge of Africa came from Mandeville's completely invented travels, cited in Othello's description of his homeland. (The very first English ship to sail for north Africa was only in 1551, and the Barbary Trading Company, set up in 1558, only began to prosper after the Moroccan embassy.) European standards may be the norm for Marlowe and Shakespeare, with the southern and eastern Mediterranean seen as an exotic 'Other'; but this portrayal of the feminine has to be complicated by writing under the rule of a very dominant Queen. Of course as the Virgin Queen, who famously claimed 'a man's heart,' Elizabeth shares more with Shakespeare's iron Roman matriarch, Volumnia, than she does with Dido or Cleopatra, both of whom are represented as primarily emotional and sexual beings. And the suicides have to be seen through the classical context, where in such circumstances "Not Caesar's valour hath o'erthrown Antony, but Antony's hath triumphed on itself" as with Cleopatra whose "death is fitting for a princess / Descended of so many royal kings."[9]

A rather different picture is given in Marlowe's *Jew of Malta*, where on the surface the title character – emphasized as one of a trans-Mediterranean network

---

7   Ibid., 2.5.23.
8   Edward Saïd, *Orientalism*, New York: Vintage, 1979, pp. 56-58.
9   Shakespeare, *Antony and Cleopatra*, London: Arden, 2006, 4.15.15-16, 5.2.325-326.

of Jews: aligned with "Kirriah Jairim, the great Jew of Greece, Obed in Bairseth, Nones in Portugal" – is the epitome of treachery and deceit, as well as greed and materialism; crying out (just like Shylock) "My gold, my fortune, my felicity, / Strength to my soul, death to my enemy ... O girl! O gold! O beauty! O my bliss!"[10] Indeed he takes on the clichéd mask of a stage villain by addressing the audience directly at the culmination of his plotting:

> Now, tell me, worldlings, underneath the sun
> If greater falsehood ever has been done?"[11]

Yet all the supposedly 'noble' Europeans, the Governor and Knights who garrison Malta against the Turks, are just as immoral as Barabas, equally fixated on money, no less corrupt and equally treacherous – only not quite so efficient in their plots. Indeed Marlowe introduces Machiavelli as the prologue to his play. And while Machevill claims the Jew as his follower, he is clearly identified as a core part of European civilization. So we get a story of internecine conflict between the defenders of the island, sparked by an unjust and outrageous expropriation of all Barabas' wealth, in which there is nothing to choose morally between defenders of Christianity and the Jewish villain.

This is all the more striking because at the time the play was written, the Great Siege of Malta was being praised as a shining example of heroism that marked an historical turning point, stopping the westward advance of the Ottoman Empire across the Mediterranean. Indeed, in 1565 just 500 Knights and a couple of thousand Maltese citizens defeated an Ottoman army of over 65,000 soldiers. Marlowe of course had a reputation as an atheist and iconoclast, and may well have identified himself with his Machevill's proclamation:

> I count religion but a childish toy,
> And hold there is no sin but ignorance.[12]

In this light, the focus is not on the "foreigner" at all. With the quintessentially Italian Machiavelli as its guiding principle, the play can be read as an attack on the moral standards of Europe civilization, seen here as undermining and discrediting even the most celebrated symbol of European chivalry. Even Marlowe's naming of the Jew as Barabas (the criminal pardoned instead of Jesus) can be interpreted as a way of exposing the equal corruption of his Elizabethan audience, since – with the Barabas-story being the popular source for justifying anti-Semitism – the almost automatic hatred directed at his Barabas-figure aligns

---

10 Marlowe, *The Jew of Malta* in *The Complete Plays*, London: Penguin Books, 2003, 2.1.47-48, 2.1.53.

11 Ibid., 5.5.49-50.

12 Ibid., Prologue 14-15.

the original spectators of the performance with the unjust and exploitive Christian authorities depicted in his play.

Othello can also be seen as reversing the standard Orientalist tropes described by Saïd. Less concerned with topicality, Shakespeare goes back to the war between the Ottoman Empire and Venice, which had lasted from 1480 to 1503 – although the Turks were only to attack Cyprus in 1648, over 40 years after the play (in a siege that lasted over 20 years). In contrast to the Venetians – who, as either racist (Desdemona's father) / alcoholic and manipulable (Cassio and Roderigo) / or malicious and deceptive (Iago), are very much the equivalent of Marlowe's corrupt Europeans – Othello's race, and character, as 'noble savage' are underlined throughout. Even Iago describes him as a "noble nature" – two words that indeed define Othello.[13] But his is a type of 'nobility' that can switch almost instantly to "bloody thoughts with violent pace": the simplicity of pure nobility, which sets him apart from the Venice he serves, and in the end destroys him, being the definition of someone uneducated (as Othello admits himself to be) and close to nature.[14] And because Shakespeare shows racism alive and well in Venice – from Iago's metaphor about "an old black ram ... tupping your white ewe" to Desdemona's father, who excoriates his daughter's preference for "the sooty bosom of such a thing as thou art" – his negritude is slapped in our faces.[15] At the same time, in military terms, in other words in the realm of the physical – another element of the savage – Othello is presented as a truly heroic figure: "brave Othello" who "commands / Like a full soldier."[16]

Shakespeare may have complicated the image of the native "Other" by Othello's position of authority as the general in charge of the war against the Turks. Yet the dualism of Edward Saïd's colonial viewpoint still exists – even if Shakespeare reverses its terms. Othello is by no means the only authority in the play. As Harold Bloom has pointed out, Iago is both director and actor, controlling the action: "Iago is the genius of his time and place, and is all will. His passion for destruction is the only creative passion in the play."[17] But as the embodiment of evil, duplicitous, essentialist in the sense that from him betrayal and hatred for the good is an end in itself, Iago is in fact the equivalent of Aaron the Moor from *Titus Andronicus*, or Barabas from *The Jew of Malta*. Apparently motiveless and ruthlessly malignant, Iago substitutes for the alien 'Other' – the only distinction being that his skin is white: this dualistic inversion being enforced by Shakespeare's choice of a black hero.

---

13   Shakespeare, *Othello,* London: Arden, 2006, 2.1.287 and 3.3.203.
14   Ibid., 3.3.460.
15   Ibid., 1.1.87-88, 1.2.70-71.
16   Ibid., 2.1.38, 2.1.35-36.
17   Harold Bloom, *The Invention of the Human*, New York: Riverhead, 1998, 442.

Of course, our interpretation of these plays is culturally determined: we see them through the lens of the present. Thus when Othello (while nominally at least a convert to Christianity) declares that his murder of Desdemona is not "in hate, but in all honour" – we are inescapably reminded of the contemporary vogue for 'honour killing' among today's Muslim men.[18] In a sense, too, Othello can be viewed as the alien outsider in conflict with the European culture he is paradoxically defending against a Mediterranean invader, while Cyprus could indeed be seen as an imperial outpost.

Through the eighteenth and nineteenth centuries, aside from Dryden's revisionist version of *All for Love*, English playwrights looked further away for exotic settings, to India or the Americas. But with the opening of the modern period, we again find the Mediterranean reappearing on the British stage.

Shaw's *Caesar & Cleopatra*, like *All For Love* a counter-play to *Antony and Cleopatra*, returns us to Egypt. Written in 1898, Shaw's Caesar clearly echoes Wolseley's military takeover of Egypt in 1882 to protect the Suez Canal during a civil war; and the play was an immediate response to the Convention of Constantinople, which in 1888 declared the Canal a neutral zone under the protection of the British. In addition, the first London production of the play, in 1907 may well have been provoked by the notorious Denshawai Incident, just one year earlier 1906, which Shaw refers to in the Preface to *John Bull's Other Island* – a play specifically addressed "for Politicians" and written the same year – where he explicitly discusses the evils of imperialism, citing the Denshawai atrocity.[19]

Undoubtedly his Irish background fuelled Shaw's attack on imperialism, and *Caesar and Cleopatra*, presents its British audience (more used to applauding typically Orientalist plays like *The Green Goddess*, by Shaw's collaborator and the English translator of Ibsen William Archer, which was set in India) with an ironic imperialist reversal in Caesar's colonial secretary Britannus – an ancient Briton, set up as a parody of a Victorian London bureaucrat. But most strikingly, Shaw's Cleopatra does not correspond in any way to Saïd's version of Orientalism. Anti-imperialist, as well as anti-Shakespeare, his Cleopatra is a prepubescent girl, who learns how to rule from Julius Caesar, not how to love. Innocent, even if capable of cruelty, and a stronger personality than her brother, this Cleopatra is in almost every respect the opposite of the Oriental image: trying hard to be mysterious, but constantly deflated by Caesar, whom she addresses as "old gentleman," she matures intellectually during the play, and while represented as having a cat-like sensuality, shows very little emotion.[20] Although loathe to let Caesar leave Egypt, as soon as

---

18 Shakespeare, *Othello*, London: Arden, 2006, 5.2.290.
19 George Bernard Shaw, *John Bull's Other Island*, London: Constable, 1921, p.v.
20 Shaw, *Caesar and Cleopatra* in *The Complete Bernard Shaw Plays*, London: Paul Hamlyn, 1965, p.258.

he promises to send her a young Mark Antony in his place, she happily waves him goodbye.

But in the Edwardian age of empire, Shaw's was a lone voice. More typical is the controversial sensationalism of *Bella Donna*, by a compatriot of Shaw's, James Fagan, which updates the melodramatic Marlovian image of the Mediterranean, without the complexity of *The Jew of Malta* – and which can stand as an image of the standard colonialist attitudes in the drama of the period. Although practically unknown today, Fagan was an important director in London at the beginning of the 20th century. And he was also a highly popular playwright: the first to have three plays running simultaneously on Broadway – and his *Bella Donna* was a major success, both in London and America.

The title figure, who at the beginning of the play already has a notorious reputation, seduces a wealthy idealist who becomes infatuated with her. She marries him for his aristocratic connections, then falls passionately in love with a wealthy Egyptian philanderer; and on a boat trip up the Nile she sets out to kill her husband with poison provided by the Egyptian. Thwarted in her murderous plans by a wise Jewish physician, she is then rejected by the Egyptian. And barred from her husband's villa near the Pyramids, she staggers off alone and desperate into the desert night.... *Bella Donna* was written for Shaw's "Stella", Mrs. Pat Campbell, who performed it to acclaim in 1911 at the West End St James Theatre (Shaw claimed she was "reeking" of the part[21]), while in America the play was produced by Charles Frohman at the Empire Theater in 1912 with the sultry siren Alla Nazimova in the title part, then later (in 1916 and again in 1920) with Pola Negri.

As might be expected, the Edwardian reviewers were simultaneously enthralled and repelled by this image of female evil. But *Bella Donna* also had an impact on serious issues: it provoked a public controversy about the right of doctors to interfere between patient and wife, even when poison was suspected. In that context, it was even more striking that reviewers and audiences so casually accepted the clichéd Egyptian figure: suave, sinisterly handsome with shadowed eyes, slicked-back hair and (of course) dark skin – as well as completely immoral, selfish and corrupt. Indeed there is also a feminine (and thus unnatural) aspect to the Egyptian's character, since his ethics mirror so closely those of the *femme fatale* in the play. This Egyptian philanderer epitomizes some of the basic qualities that Edward Saïd has defined in *Orientalism*, as being at the core of the colonialist view of non-European natives.

In sharp contrast to the kinds of view expressed in drama during the era of Empire, contemporary – postcolonial – dramatists tend to avoid the tropes of exoticism

---

21   Shaw, letter to Ellen Terry, 20 August 1912, in *Bernard Shaw: Collected Letters*, ed. Dan Laurence. Max Reinhardt Ltd, London 1985. Vol III, 111.

and Orientalism by using strongly autobiographical material, when dealing with Mediterranean settings. Two plays from the 1990s illustrate this change.

The first is Christopher Hampton's *White Chameleon* (1991).[22] This portrays the author's own childhood in Egypt, with his younger self appearing as the main character: the lizard of the title, an animal that camouflages itself by mimicking the colours surrounding it. He is also the narrator, looking back on his experience between 1952 (the year of the Egyptian revolution that expelled the Pasha and brought Colonel Nasser to power) and 1956 (the Suez Canal crisis). To young Chris of course, politics seem irrelevant, although events are commented on by the grown-up Christopher. Shuttled back and forth to the supposed safety of England, he is an outsider, regardless of where he is – always trying to blend in (like the white chameleon of the title), a would-be Egyptian, to whom England is more foreign and unwelcoming than Egypt. And while the primary reference is to skin colour (white for the English) fitting in is far more about social context than simple appearance. Foreignness is a difficult burden, costly to overcome, and the main figure in the Egyptian household is Ibrahim, the household servant with a weakness for alcohol and two wives (one of whom supports the British, while the other is a fascist); and it turns out that while the Hampton family can escape the violence by returning to England, there is no escape for Ibrahim, the only figure in the play who cannot make the transition from British-ruled Egypt to national independence.

Here it is the boy, Christopher Hampton himself, who always feels 'Other' while Ibrahim (though wrongly) feels integrated with the family he serves – and the same stance is presented in David Hare's *Via Dolorosa* at the end of the decade (1998), where Hare is (at least at the outset) an objective and uninvolved observer on a fact-finding visit to Israel and Gaza. However, even more autobiographically than Hampton, as the opening stage direction announces: "Via Dolorosa *is a monologue ideally to be performed by its author*."[23] And indeed, Hare himself performed the role both at the Royal Court and in the West End, as well as on Broadway. The journey he undertakes is a search for a country where people "are fighting for what they believe in" – as opposed to "Western civilization … where nobody believes in anything any more."[24] He starts off in Israel, and the interviews in Tel Aviv, Jerusalem and one of the settlements – with a theatre director, with a politician (Menachem Begin's son), with Israeli settlers – frame his onward movement to the Palestinian Territories, where he comes face-to-face with economic destitution imposed by the Israelis, and the brutal corrup-

22   Christopher Hampton, *White Chameleon*, London: Faber, 1991.
23   David Hare, *Via Dolorosa & Where Shall We Live?*, London: Faber, 1998, p. 3.
24   Ibid., p. 4.

tion of Arafat's government which has "stolen" the 'energy' of the Intifada.[25] Just as he has come to recognize that in the settlements the Israelis now "live with no conception of the future"[26] – so, interviewing Palestinian politicians and the only Arab theatre director allowed to stage theatre under the Muslim regime, Hare is told that

"There was a point once, there was a reason. You were fighting for a Palestinian state, and you were willing to die. What on earth would you die for now?"[27]

Neither side proves capable of living the belief that Hare is searching for. And finally he is forced to recognize that there is a third religion in this ancient land: Christianity, and that his journey itself has been a pilgrimage retracing "the Stations of the Cross ... the steps on Christ's journey to his death."[28] With the author directly quoting the words of the people he interacts with, as well as giving his own thoughts, there is a documentary aspect that rules out a superior or colonialist perspective. Indeed he sets out from a position of inferiority, and ends by recognizing that the kind of commitment he has been looking for doesn't exist there either. The Israelis and Palestinians are just as cynical and shallow as the Christians. All have substituted "stones [or possession of land] for ideas."[29] And the play ends with his question:

Are we where we live, or are we what we think?
What matter? Stones or ideas?[30]

Works Cited

Bloom, Harold. *The Invention of the Human*. New York: Riverhead, 1998.
Hampton, Christopher. *White Chameleon*. London: Faber, 1991.
Hare, David. *Via Dolorosa & When Shall We Live?* London: Faber, 1998.
Marlowe, Christopher. *The Complete Plays*. London: Penguin, 2003.
Saïd, Edward. *Orientalism*. New York: Vintage, 1979.
Shakespeare, William. *Antony and Cleopatra*. London: Arden, 2006.
–. *Othello*. London: Arden, 2006.
Shaw, George Bernard. *The Complete Plays*. London: Paul Hamlyn, 1965.
–. *John Bull's Other Island*. London: Constable, 1921.

---

25 Ibid., p. 15, 28.
26 Ibid., p. 23.
27 Ibid., p. 29.
28 Ibid., p. 36.
29 Ibid., p. 42.
30 Ibid., p. 43.

Chaucer, His Boethius, and the Narrator of His *Troilus*

Harold Kaylor
Troy State University, Alabama

> Gret necessite of prowesse and virtu is enc-
> harged and comaunded to yow, yif ye not dissi-
> mulen; syn that ye worken and do [...] beforn
> the eyen of the judge that seeth and demeth alle
> thinges.
>
> *(Boece*, V.p6.305-10)[1]

Introduction

Chaucer produced his translation of Boethius's *Consolatio* about 1380, and he wrote the *Troilus* between about 1382 and 1386. That many verbal and thematic affinities exist between Chaucer's *Boece* and his *Troilus* is unquestioned.[2] However, some of the larger, structural influences of the *Boece* upon the *Troilus* also are worthy of attention. Chaucer certainly employed features of the cosmological model found in the *Consolatio* in his Trojan romance, and he undoubtedly drew upon experiences and insights gained while translating Boethius's Latin work into English as he constructed the *Troilus*. With such structural Boethian influence in mind, readers of the *Troilus* observe a fictional translator working within the universe, or the narrative space and time, of Chaucer's romance, even as that translator himself observes and comments upon events that unfold within the universe of a Latin history, written sometime earlier by a fictional historian, Lollius. The *Troilus* also is a romance in which the readers outside the work and the translator within it participate in semi-authorial foreknowledge of the events that occur in Lollius's history that is contained within the romance.

---

1 *The Riverside Chaucer*. Ed. Larry D. Benson. 3rd ed. New York: Houghton Mifflin, 1987. (All quotations from Chaucer's *Troilus* and his other works are from this source.)
2 See *Chaucer and the Consolation of Philosophy of Boethius*. Bernard L. Jefferson. 1917; rpt. New York: Haskel House, 1965.

The Evidence

Chaucer's narrator is a highly original literary creation. His unusual situation as *translator-narrator* facilitates an objectified presentation of the characters who interact with each other in Lollius's Latin history of Troilus's *aventures in lovynge*. Because Chaucer's nameless narrator also is a character in Chaucer's romance, he is in a position to translate from a third-person point of view and to comment upon that translation from a first-person point of view. He exists in the *Troilus* somewhat as Boethius-in-the-work exists in the *Consolatio,* or as Dante-in-the-work exists in the *Comedia*, or as Chaucer-in-the-work exists in the *Canterbury Tales*. Like all of these characters in relation to their authors, Chaucer's narrator certainly *is* Chaucer, but at the same time he certainly *is not* Chaucer. As a character, he resembles Herry Bailly's depiction of the poet.[3] The narrator is not particularly poppet-like as he sits working at his writing desk; nevertheless, "[h]e semeth elvyssh by his contenaunce / For unto no wight dooth he daliaunce."[4] On the one hand, Chaucer's narrator exists *external* to the narrative space and time constructed by the historian-observer Lollius in his history, and the narrative universe of Lollius's history exists only in a book resting on the writing desk of Chaucer's narrator, within Chaucer's romance. On the other hand, Chaucer's narrator exists, apparently alone, as a translator-observer, *internal* as a character, within the narrative space and time constructed by Chaucer in his romance, and that narrative universe exists only in a book resting on the reading desks of Chaucer's readers, a book that the narrator (or perhaps even Chaucer himself, speaking in his own authorial voice in the closing stanzas of the work) addresses in apostrophe: "Go, litel bok, go litel myn tragedye."[5] It is in this final section of the *Troilus* that Chaucer-the-maker and Chaucer's translator-narrator seem most apparently to converge.

Chaucer's narrator is also a translator-commentator whose work habits probably are modeled on those of Chaucer himself as he somewhat earlier, or perhaps simultaneously, had worked as translator-commentator of Boethius's *Consolatio*.[6] Chaucer's narrator has Lollius's Latin history on his desk, open to the leaf of the manuscript he is trans-lating at the moment. He also seems to have certain reference works on his writing desk. He comments, for example, on information that "I

---

3   Prologue to Sir Topas, 695-704.
4   Prologue to Sir Topas, 703-04.
5   Troilus and Criseyde, 5.1786.
6   See, for example, *The Life of Geoffrey Chaucer*. Derek Pearsall. Oxford: Blackwell, 1992. 160. (Pearsall leaves the question of Chaucer's translating of Boethius prior to or simultaneous with his writing the *Troilus* open, which it is.)

fynde ek in stories elleswhere."[7] When he informs his readers that he does not intend to rehearse the details of the battles of the Trojan War in his own narration, he writes: "But the Troian gestes, as they felle, / In Omer, or in Dares, or in Dite, / Whoso that kan may rede hem as they write."[8] Chaucer himself would not have had the works of Homer directly in the Greek, and he gives Dictys the Cretan somewhat brief attention, but he names Dares the Phrygian twice in the *Troilus*, as an authority on the events of the Trojan War.[9] Apparently, the narrator's work as a translator of Lollius's history is *objective*, so he *does not* influence the *events* that unfold in that history. The narrator's work as a commentator on the events unfolding in Lollius's history is *subjective*, however, in both subtle and less-than-subtle ways, so he *does* influence the readers' *interpretation* of events in the history. At first, he calls upon Thesiphone to help him write down the "woful vers, that wepen as I write."[10] Later, commenting upon Criseyde's pity expressed for the wounds suffered by Diomede in battle, he writes: "Men seyn – I not – that she yaf hym hire herte."[11] Such gratuitous comments do affect readings of the history.

Chaucer's readers also are in an unusual situation: they enjoy a semi-authorial perspective on the shape of the plot. In the first stanza, the narrator-commentator informs the readers of the major turning points of the story: he states, famously, that the events in Troilus's *aventures in lovynge* will fall "[f]ro wo to wele, and after out of joie."[12] A few stanzas thereafter, he initiates his translation by informing the readers that: "ye may the double sorwes here / Of Troilus in lovynge of Criseyde, / And how that she forsook hym er she deyed."[13] Chaucer's readers, existing *external* to the romance, and his narrator, existing *internal* to the romance but *external* to Lollius's history, are somewhat like the *deus*-observer that exists *external* to Boethius's universe. In the *Consolatio*, to illustrate the relationship between this observer and the observed, Boethius gives the example of a human observer of a man sitting. The observer and the man who sits exist in parallel positions, the one simply observing at a distance and the

7   *Troilus and Criseyde*, 5.1044.
8   Troilus and Criseyde, 1.145-47.
9   Homer is mentioned in The Franklin's Tale, l.1443; The House of Fame, 1466 and 1477. *Boece*, 5.m2.1, and 5.m2.2; *Troilus*, 1.146, and 5.1792. Dictys is mentioned in *Troilus*, 1.146; The House of Fame, l.1467 (as Tytus). Dares is mentioned in the Book of the Duchess, 1070; The House of Fame, 1467; *Troilus*, 1.146 and 5.1771.
10 *Troilus and Criseyde*, 1.7.
11 *Troilus and Criseyde*, 5.1050.
12 *Troilus and Criseyde*, 1.4.
13 *Troilus and Criseyde*, 1.54-56.

other simply sitting. They exist in separate spaces – but within the same time-frame – and the observer does not influence the observed.[14]

External to the universe of the romance, Chaucer's readers act as judging observers of the events enacted in the work. They foreknow the shape of the events that will unfold within the romance because that information is presented to them from the opening stanza, and it is reaffirmed or amplified in subsequent stanzas through the romance. In other words, the shape of the history's sequence of events is present in the minds of the readers, all at once, from the beginning, much as all of the universe's events unfolding in space and time are present, all at once, in the mind of Boethius's *deus*-observer. The readers, therefore, from the first stanza onward, observe the specific decisions and resulting actions in the plot of Chaucer's romance as they occur in their linear development, knowing in advance the ends toward which they lead.

The Boethian theme of "foreknowledge necessitating events," or of "events necessitating foreknowledge," also is either explicit or implicit in the thoughts of the principal characters in Lollius's history.[15] It is *explicitly* stated in Troilus's "Boethian" Temple Monologue, which helps to define *him* as a character type. Following the decision made in Troy to hand Criseyde over to the Greeks in exchange for Antenor, Pandarus found Troilus alone in a temple, speaking aloud to himself. "He seyde he nas but lorn, wellaway! / 'For al that comth, comth by necessitee: / Thus to ben lorn, it is my destinee.'"[16] In his rational argument, Troilus decides early-on that because all events are divinely foreknown "they shul comen by predestyne."[17] The example he cites to prove this philosophical position, that events are *predestined*, is the same as that used by Boethius to prove that they are *not predestined*–the example of an observer of a man sitting. Whereas Boethius had stated that if a man is sitting he necessarily sits, and if an observer knows that the man is sitting he necessarily knows this to be true, Troilus reconstructs Boethius's parallel positions in space and time by making Boethius's human observer distinctly divine, and distinctly external, to the space and time universe observed. As Troilus interprets the matter, necessity is enforced upon the sitter to sit because his divine observer exists in a higher, *eternal* realm, while the sitter exists in a subordinate, *temporal* realm. In causing Troilus to view the relationship hierarchically, rather than synchronically, Chaucer exploits a small inconsistency in the reasoning of Boethius, who had used a human-human relationship, with both individuals existing in a space and time universe,

---

14 *Boece,* V.p3.54-82.
15 See Pearsall, 174-175, for a brief, summary discussion of views on the problem of free will and predestination in the *Troilus.*
16 *Troilus and Criseyde,* 4.957-59.
17 *Troilus and Criseyde,* 4.966.

to elucidate a divine-human relationship, with the one entity existing in an eternal realm and the other in a temporal realm. It is by altering the relationships presented in this Boethian example that Troilus apparently obviates the Boethian basis of free will assumed in the original argument of the *Consolatio*. Thus, the monologue affirms Troilus's human predisposition toward a *determinist*'s perspective on his existential situation: it explicitly presents Troilus's rational position that decisions and events are necessitated by divine foreknowledge, which can never err. It also confirms Troilus as an idealist: he *cannot* equivocate his love of Criseyde.

The Boethian theme of "foreknowledge necessitating events," or of "events necessitating foreknowledge," is *implicitly* contained in Criseyde's "un-Boethian" Check Mate Monologue, which helps to define *her* as a character type. Shortly after she first sees Troilus riding with his entourage into the city of Troy from the field of battle, when she is inspired to say, "Who yaf me drynke?"[18] she entertains negative thoughts about entering into a love affair with the young knight. She thinks to herself: "I am myn owene womman, wel at ese" and "Shal noon housband seyn to me 'Chek mat!'"[19] Thus, at the beginning of her extended monologue, Criseyde posits that she can determine the conditions of her existential situation herself, by an act of free will, or free choice. Criseyde's monologue is guided by emotion, even as Troilus's is guided by reason. She gives among the determining factors–those factors that she *wills* to avoid–the jealousy, domineering attitude, and desire for novelty that she ascribes to husbands in general. Thus, the monologue affirms Criseyde's human predisposition toward a *non-determinist*'s perspective on her existential situation: it implicitly presents Criseyde's emotional position that decisions and events are not necessitated by any divine foreknowledge – a philosophical concept that, significantly, she does not address directly in her emotion-driven monologue. It also confirms Criseyde as a pragmatist: she *can* equivocate her love of Troilus.

The Interpretation

Chaucer's use of a translator-commentator as his narrator in the *Troilus* allows the actual "maker" of the romance to insulate himself, or his personality, from the narrated events, which permits at least the appearance of greater objectivity in delivering the narration. Chaucer's use of several hierarchically-arranged narrative realms in the romance distances the readers from Chaucer, Chaucer

---

18 *Troilus and Criseyde*, 2.651.
19 *Troilus and Criseyde*, 2.750 and 754.

from the narrator, the narrator from Lollius, and Lollius from the authors of texts quoted in his history. Thus, the concentric layers of narrative universes within Chaucer's romance conceal the authorial voice or presence of Chaucer, who actually determines the events and the "free-will" actions of the characters. This contrasts markedly, for example, with the strong and apparently direct authorial voice or presence of such romantic narrators as Nathaniel Hawthorne's in *The Scarlet Letter*, a work in which Chaucer is referenced as a custom's agent in London and, therefore, akin to Hawthorne, who served as a custom's agent in Salem, Massachusetts. The readers of Chaucer's romance exist within the same universe that Chaucer-the-maker inhabits; the narrator-translator exists within the same universe that Lollius inhabits; Criseyde and her ladies exist within the same universe that the author of a Theban romance inhabits. Thus, Chaucer constructs his hierarchy of narrative realities in the *Troilus*.

As noted above, *Boethius's divine external observer* of the cosmic universe of space and time (the *deus* in the *Consolatio*) is quite distinct from *Chaucer's human external observers* of the narrative universe of space and time (the readers of Chaucer's romance). Boethius's observer foreknows and judges from the perspective of the divine goodness that defines that particular *deus* as a *deus* type. Chaucer's human reader-observers foreknow and judge from the perspective of the human qualities that define each of them as a reader type. Chaucer never presumes to equate either himself as "maker" of the romance, or his readers as judging observers of characters and events in the romance, with the *deus*-observer in Boethius's external cosmic realm. Chaucer restricts his authorial perspective to the temporal universe inhabited by mankind (and even his idealistic Troilus, who had posited an all-knowing divinity in his Temple Monologue, upon ascending to "the holunesse of the eighthe spere, / In converse letyng everich element,"[20] looks downward through the universe of space and time, to the place of his temporal demise, rather than upward, toward any eternal realm). Some of Chaucer's reader-observers, perhaps a minority, are idealists who are sympathetic toward Troilus's firm commitment in loving Criseyde. Some others, perhaps a majority, are pragmatists who are sympathetic toward Criseyde's sliding commitment in loving Troilus. There is a general tendency among critics to follow the translator-commentator's example and attempt to forgive Criseyde practically anything. The narrator writes toward the end of the work: "That al be that Criseyde was untrewe, / That for that gilt she be nat wroth with me. / Ye may hire gilt in other bokes se."[21] Here, as elsewhere, the narrator-commentator withholds any direct, negative judgment on Criseyde's betrayal of Troilus; the

---

20 *Troilus and Criseyde*, 5.1809-10.
21 *Troilus and Criseyde*, 5.1774-76.

historian Lollius, however, does grant Troilus momentarily a significant ascent to the interface between Boethius's eternal and temporal realms, at the level of the fixed stars, the highest point to which a pagan might rise, to gain a higher understanding of all temporal events—which represents at least an indirect, positive judgment on the "historical" knight.

Conclusion

Boethius constructs only two cosmic realms in his *Consolatio*, the eternal, which lies beyond the universe of space and time, and the temporal, which comprises the universe of space and time. The *deus*-observer exists in the eternal realm, but Boethius-in-the-work exists within the temporal realm. Chaucer, however, constructs a hierarchy of narrative realms in his *Troilus*: the realm of Chaucer's romance, that of Lollius's history, and that of a Theban romance within it. Chaucer's inspiration to create this hierarchy of temporal realms derives, arguably, from his own experience of translating Boethius's *Consolatio*. This is speculation, of course, but it seems probable that Chaucer's reflection upon his experience as translator, vis-à-vis the cosmic universe constructed in the *Consolatio* (the book on his translation desk), is mirrored in the concentric narrative realms (the books-within-books-within-books) that he devises in the temporal universe of his *Troilus*.

Another possible result of Chaucer's reflection upon his experience as translator of the *Consolatio* is discernible in his position as "maker," vis-à-vis the narrative universe that he constructs in the romance. As noted above, he does not presume to equate himself with the divine Boethian observer, but Chaucer's foreknowledge as "maker" is enjoyed within the romance by the translator-commentator of Lollius's history, and that translator-commentator shares his foreknowledge with the readers of his translation, from the beginning. Chaucer's narrator "foreknows" events yet to unfold or betide in Lollius's history because, presumably, he has read the Latin text prior to translating it. Chaucer's readers then "foreknow" events of the history because the narrator presents them strategically in advance of the initiation of the narration of his story of Troilus's love of Criseyde. The structural influence of Boethius's *Consolatio*, upon the romance, and of Chaucer's experience of translating that Latin work into English, thus, is discernible on many levels.

"*Deligite iustitiam, qui iudicatis terram*"[22]

---

22 *The Divine Comedy:* Vol.III: *Paradise*. Dante. Trans. Mark Musa. New York: Viking Penguin, 1986. Canto XVIII.92-93.

Apart from the several temporal observational perspectives that Chaucer constructs in the *Troilus*, he also maintains a subtle observational perspective upon the reader-observers of his romance. Any assumed *divine objectivity* on the part of the readers in observing the characters in the history must collapse quickly into *human subjectivity*, just as any assumed *impartial judgment* in assessing the characters must collapse into *relative judgment*, based upon their particular human predispositions toward idealism or pragmatism. The readers, like Chaucer's characters, seem to fall generally into one or the other of these two philosophical positions, and their human predispositions are reflected in the criticisms they make of the characters Troilus and Criseyde. Such, it would seem, is Chaucer's subtle way of judging the judges "that sen and demen alle thinges" in the romance that he so carefully constructs.

Chaucer is both famous and infamous as a master of ambiguity. The "goddes speken in amphibologies"[23] and so does the "maker" himself. Readers and critics have puzzled over Chaucer's ambiguities for at least six hundred years, and undoubtedly they shall continue to do so. The structuring of the *Troilus* is not always clearly defined, the distinction between the "maker" and his narrator occasionally is obscure, and the correspondences between the various narrative realms are not always precise. Nevertheless, the influence upon the *Troilus* of Chaucer's internalization of the Boethian cosmological model is continuous, and Chaucer's experience of translating and commenting upon the *Consolatio* resonates throughout the romance. The verbal and thematic affinities between the *Boece* and the *Troilus* are extensive, but the structural relationships between the two works are profound.

---

23 *Troilus and Criseyde*, 4.1406.

"Begin, and cease, and then again begin": Rereading Matthew Arnold's "Dover Beach"

William V. Davis
Baylor University

> In an age of disbelief ... it is for the poet to supply the satisfactions of belief.
>
> Wallace Stevens

> The sea's voice worked into my mood....
>
> Robinson Jeffers

"Dover Beach" is one of the most important poems of the nineteenth century and it certainly is one of the most well-known poems of all time. Even so, it has been more admired than analyzed, given lip service to than thoroughly thought through. It deserves to be treated more conscientiously than it has been, both as poem *per se* and as a significant and moving statement of one of the dominant themes of its time – a theme that remains significant and pertinent in our time as well.

Since "Dover Beach" is, and has been, so well known, it perhaps seems unnecessary, or even audacious, to attempt to say anything, or anything new, about it. But I do think that there are things that have not yet been noticed. Therefore, what I want to do here is to provide yet another reading of "Dover Beach" and, by taking into consideration Arnold's theme and craft in the poem, attempt to suggest some things that seem to have been overlooked, things that attest to the abiding significance of the poem.

Arnold felt that poetry ought to voice the contemporary situation and the current circumstances of life. Since "modern problems" had "presented themselves" in his day and since "the dialogue of the mind with itself" had thus "commenced" with respect to those circumstances, poetry, he felt, should address the issues and problems in such a way that readers could "hear ... the [religious] doubts" and "witness the discouragement" that he so clearly saw evidenced in the age (see "Preface" to the First Edition of *Poems* [1853], *Poetical Works* xvii). "Dover Beach" (*Poetical Works* 210-11) is Arnold's classic example and a most apt paradigm of his attempt to deal with such issues and concerns.

Since I want to stress the theological theme in "Dover Beach" the third stanza might seem to be the obvious place to begin – and even perhaps to end. But Arnold carefully prepares for his "Sea of Faith" speech in what leads up to it. Indeed, the opening line of the poem introduces the sea, "calm," and at full tide below the cliffs,

which, like the sea itself, stand "Glimmering and vast, out in the tranquil bay."
The speaker calls his companion to come to the window, to look and to watch with
him. They are both apparently as calm and as untroubled as the sea seems to be. And
here then, in this sea/see pun, Arnold introduces the visionary metaphor that runs
throughout the poem and comes to climax in his "Sea of Faith" stanza. Indeed, the
speaker and his companion simply see the surface of the sea and of the scene before
them. Both are beautiful. They feel that they have nothing to fear from them – at
least not at that moment. They see and then they hear. They "listen." This "Listen!"
(l. 9), spoken by the speaker and directed to his companion, seems simultaneously to
be a self-directed imperative. It thus seems to suggest that a particularly important
avenue for understanding can come through the auditory sense, through listening.
The prescription is simple and accurate: if you listen, you will hear. What they,
the speaker and his companion, here hear (their seeing having made it so) we, as
readers, also hear (and see) – as Arnold's lines so specifically say:

> Listen! you hear the grating roar
> Of pebbles which the waves draw back, and fling,
> At their return, up the high strand,
> Begin, and cease, and then again begin, … (lls. 9-12)

Beyond the beauty and specificity of this description, Arnold not only shows us
what he is watching but he makes us see and hear it as his speaker has – and thus he
makes what he here hears and sees, and what he makes of it, the way he states it,
immediate and memorable to his reader too. Arnold's lines themselves "grate" and
"roar" the way the waves and pebbles do, and the rhythm and meter of his lines duplicate, as they describe, the action of the waves. Line 10 is a pentameter line but the
spondee in its fourth foot both momentarily stops, "draws back," and then "flings"
the line forward again in exactly the same way that the waves work, flinging themselves against the "high strand." The waves, like the onlookers, are momentarily
stopped or stunned, "stranded" in their own actions, just as the spondee has stopped
and momentarily stranded the line itself before it "flings" it on into the next line,
beginning the wavelike rhythm and the "tremulous cadence" that undulates throughout the rest of the stanza. Indeed, the onlookers, the speaker and his companion, seem
to be put into a somewhat helpless position by the description of the rhythm and the
disposition of the waves in these lines. Perhaps they are also even somewhat entan-
gled by what they sense in the "tremulous cadence slow" of this halting, halted, line
which is about to bring an "eternal note of sadness" into their lives.

The magical twelfth line:

> Begin, and cease, and then again begin

is one of the most famous epanaleptic lines in literary history. It begins and then again begins again at the end. Each wave of words, each sound, is the same, yet different, like the sea itself. And, clearly, Arnold didn't want to stress the cessation of the "grating roar," but rather its continuation, its constant beginning – and then its beginning again. It might also be argued that this beginning again, and then again, is indeed *a gain*, as the word itself suggests, a gain in understanding or in knowledge, something which the sea *says*, or seems to say. Thus the "tremulous cadence slow" of the sea's action, relentless and seemingly eternal, creates a like trembling in the observers and "bring[s] / The eternal note of sadness" into the observers' minds. Certainly it brings a note of sadness to the speaker's mind, and to readers' minds as well, since readers experience this same "tremulous cadence" along with the speaker. This first stanza ends on that "eternal note of sadness."[1]

And this "note" – so much like a footnote to what has gone before – reminds the speaker of another sea and another vision or version of the human condition, one likewise filled with "human misery," one that Sophocles saw, one that we hear in his words as well as in Arnold's. And then, almost immediately, this vision, seen visually in the seascape before them and heard auditorally in the sound of the sea as the "sound" of human misery, leads the speaker beyond Sophocles and his literary, scholarly footnote, to his own immediate condition and circumstances. What the reader now hears in the *literal* sound of the sea – what he both hears and sees – is not a natural phenomenon in the movement of the waves but a metaphorical, indeed a theological "wave" which breaks over his consciousness and, having moved over him or through him, leaves him in a deeply melancholic state of mind. The "Sea of Faith," he sees, he has heard (and which he here literally *has* heard), "Was once, too, at the full, and round earth's shore." We cannot but notice how this line halts, as it begins, and how this hesitation suggests a potential reversal as the line describes the "ebb and flow," the coming to crest and the falling back again of the sea, and of the speaker and his companion's potential rising and falling passion, and, perhaps as well, the inevitable and eternal ebb and flow of the "Sea of Faith" – even if, in the now of the poem, this "Sea of Faith," in anything beyond the immediate moment and the personal relationship between the lovers, has already fully ebbed away, as perhaps the speaker's and his companion's faith has as well. "Now" the speaker and his companion only hear "Its melancholy, long, withdrawing roar, / Retreating...." What Arnold and his speaker have seen and heard (and now see that Sophocles in his day and under somewhat different cir-

---

1   Perrine accurately describes the syntactical complexity of the lines 7-14, which he calls "surely of the most eloquent expressions of despair ever written, combining pessimism with imperishable beauty", as "somewhat involved". As he says, "The noun 'roar' (9) is not the direct object of 'hear' but he subject of the infinitives [To] 'Begin,' 'cease,' 'begin,' and 'bring' (12-13). The direct object of 'hear' is the whole infinitive phrase of which 'roar' is the subject" (113-114).

cumstances saw and heard as well) is that Faith is disappearing, and they see that this loss is signaled by the sea's wave's *sound* "retreating." Faith can no longer be "seen" nor even anymore heard. It has disappeared without a trace, as air in air or water into water. This realization, as James Dickey says, is "comfortless knowledge" (236).

Krieger takes a different approach to, and comes to different conclusions with respect to Arnold's visual and auditory effects in these lines but he too notes that with the word "Listen!" "we are transferred from the visual world to the auditory world." He adds, less plausibly I think, that "the shift from the eye to the ear" occurs in each stanza of the poem (75). Other critics have also noticed, and noted, the imagery of sight and sound in "Dover Beach." Holland, for instance, argues that the poem "sees and hears intensely" (118) and that the "images of sight" are "hopeful," while the "images of sound" are "disillusioning," and represent, respectively, "appearance" (or "illusion") and "reality" (116, 119). Similarly, Culler notes that "as the poet descends in imagination into the scene," he "exchanges the flat visual sense for the more penetrating auditory" sensation (39).

The last three lines of the "Sea of Faith" stanza are somewhat confusing – literally, syntactically, and rhythmically. Line 26 ("Retreating, to the breath") consists of two iambs separated by a pyrrhic, perhaps to suggest rhythmically the ebb and flow of the sea with its "withdrawing roar / Retreating." But perhaps there is also, in the curious configuration of these lines, the suggestion of a "retreating" not only "to the breath / Of the night-wind" but also a retreating *of* the breath itself, as Arnold (or the reader) utters the line. Line 28 ("And naked shingles of the world") is a tetrameter line, made up of three iambs and a pyrrhic in its third foot. But line 27 ("Of the night-wind, down the vast edges drear"), enclosed within these two, is both more metrically and semantically irregular and awkward. It begins with a pyrrhic, followed by a spondee, then by a trochee, then another spondee, and it ends with an iamb. (The phrase "down the vast edges drear" might, of course, be scanned as two amphimacers or cretics but either scansion equally stresses the fitfulness of the wind and of Arnold's words in this windy line.) And clearly, Arnold also wants to stress the dreariness or bleakness of his mood, and to stress it in terms of the word "drear." "Drear" is literally rhymed with "hear" in line 24, but it is also a rhyme in which we hear *dear* as well – especially so if we remember that Arnold quite probably wrote "Dover Beach," or an early draft of it in 1851, when he and his wife stayed at Dover on their honeymoon [Hamilton 143], and thus take a "psychological orientation" [Dickey 235] in our reading of the poem. In this passage Arnold emphasizes the way in which he *hears* his realization – drearily, and perhaps with some dread as well – and thus, therefore, and in part at least, the syntax is forced for the sake of the rhyme. The halting of the meter, stopping and starting awkwardly and abruptly, as it does, even though it might be an attempt to duplicate the fitfulness of the wind, especially of a wind near a seashore and beside steep cliffs, might also be an attempt to suggest a "halting," a hesitancy, that may duplicate the speaker's fitful mood, mind, condition, or circumstance. Even so, for all its "vastness" and "edginess," the line remains awkward as well as vague. It is, therefore, all the more surprising that very few critics have paid much attention to Arnold's somewhat devious devices in this line or, indeed, to many of the poetic devices, or to the rhymes and rhythms throughout the whole of the poem, devices and details that Arnold was obviously and overtly concerned with, and struggled with.

Holland is one critic who has helpfully, if generally, commented on the poetic devices in "Dover Beach." He argues that, "[i]n general, strong rhyme seems linked to passages of expectation or trust or acceptance; strong rhythm ... to a sense of reality and solidity." Therefore, "at points where we are strongly aware of the rhythm, the rhyme tends to disappear. ... Conversely, at points of very regular rhyme ... the rhythm becomes irregular and tends to disintegrate. ... Finally, at the close of the poem, not only rhythm, but also rhyme becomes strong ... as the poem comes to its moment of greatest stress and distress in content." He concludes, "[r]hyme, rhythm, and sense all come together at the close to make us experience in ourselves the poems' final rhymed acceptance of a disturbing reality expressed as strongly rhythmic sound" (147-48).

The final nine lines of the poem begin with another imperative, indeed an appeal to the lovers to honor their own sense of fidelity: "Ah, love, let us be true / To one another!" Although this is a rhetorical statement, we might ask, "Why?" Several suggestions of, or elaborations on, what Arnold may have intended have been proposed. Hamilton, for instance, argues that in this line "a deeply felt lament for lost belief gives way to a strained, anxious pledge of faith – or of fidelity" (145). Grob suggests that "Of the saving attributes absent from a world that has 'neither joy, nor love, nor light, / Nor certitude, nor peace, nor help for pain,' the most conspicuous is obviously 'love.'" He adds, "we can only wonder how the speaker's appeal for love and fidelity can ever be made good if the absence of love is a given of human existence" (181). Grob continues: "... critics of Arnold usually slide over the contradiction implicit in this second reference to "love" (though as every teacher of "Dover Beach" knows, students do not), or else they treat this second love as abstract, philosophical, Platonized, a 'universal love,' as J. Hillis Miller calls it, which, if it existed, would 'guarantee particular acts of love ...' [Miller 251]. Indeed, attempting to salvage Arnold's earlier affirmation of love by such arguments runs the risk of trivializing the bleakness [of the poem's] unsparing, final revelation. That revelation ... surely asserts that love is an illusion to be discarded and denied. ... By asserting as an apparently universal maxim the proposition that there is no love, Arnold in effect cancels his original avowal of love, unsays and undoes it" (181-82). Fain, on the other hand, suggests two options for these famous lines: either let "(the two of us) escape into our dream world and enjoy the only consolation still possible," by which he means to describe the meaning which is "derived by those who consider 'Dover Beach' the supreme expression of the Victorian wasteland," or let "(all of us) defy the world in its meaninglessness and be true to one another." He implies that "Arnold may have meant both" of the above, even though the second option "may serve to qualify the characteristic Arnoldian pessimism" (41-42).

The last seven and one half lines of the poem provide Arnold's response to all that has gone before. It is, not surprisingly, not a positive, comfortable, or comforting conclusion. First of all, the world is described as being like "a land of dreams" – that is a figment of the imagination. And this fleeting figuration, although we know that it is something of our own making or imagining, our own imaginative making, is, we also know, something over which we have almost no control. Therefore, in spite of the apparently authentic, if dream-like, qualities that this oneirically imaginative vision seems to set forth, it is not really *real* – even though it has lodged itself in our consciousnesses through our dreams and therefore may seem to be so. Indeed, the reality is that the world "Hath ... neither joy, nor love, nor light, / Nor certitude, nor peace, nor help for pain...." That would seem to leave precious little!²

But even that is not all. Arnold continues:

> And we are here as on a darkling plain
> Swept with confused alarms of struggle and flight,
> Where ignorant armies clash by night. (lls. 35-37)

Dr. Thomas Arnold, Matthew's father, was the legendary headmaster of Rugby. It is well known that one of Dr. Arnold's favorite passages, and a signal text for his teaching, was Thucydides's description of the Battle of Epipolae, during the Peloponnesian War, a battle in which the two sides, fighting "by night," were unable to "distinguish friend from foe," as Hamilton says. He adds that Dr. Arnold "took this as a fitting image of the modern world's confusion and perplexity"

---

2   Bidney (86) has noticed that Arnold borrows four words in this line directly from Milton: "neither joy, nor love," (*Paradise Lost* 4. 509). He goes on to put Arnold's words in Milton's context and to suggest several further, if less obvious, debts to Milton, specifically to *Paradise Lost:* Adam and Eve, "Imparadised in one another's arms" (IV: 506) are separated and self-protected, and thus able to create their own Eden in the midst of a world ruled by chaos. Bidney further suggests that "Arnold implies that the world outside the lovers' window has become Hell," (86) and he argues that "now that the world has become Hell, the embrace of two lovers stranded amid a dark expanse of aimless fury is a very precarious Eden indeed" (89). In Arnold's poem, of course, there is no such embrace, and it is hard to imagine one – in spite of the setting and the speaker's plea – even after the end of it.

(145) but, of course, metaphors of battle have long been compared to mental quarrels, confusions, and self-perplexing considerations. Matthew Arnold must have taken Thucydides in the same way that his father had, since we know that Thucydides was one of his own heroes and a "touchstone" for his test of immortality in literature and history. As Arnold wrote in his "Study of Poetry," "Indeed there can be no more useful help for discovering what poetry belongs to the class of the truly excellent, and can therefore do us most good, than to have always in one's mind lines and expressions of the great masters, and to apply them as a touchstone to other poetry" (*Complete Prose* 9: 168).

In terms of this specific reference, Arnold also seems to see in Thucydides a "fitting image" of his own "confusion and perplexity" and, indeed, he seems to find in the remembrance of that ancient war something that he saw as a "significant spectacle" both for past instruction and for immediate reference. Arnold put his own position forward powerfully along these lines in his inaugural lecture as Professor of Poetry at Oxford in 1857 when he wrote: "[T]he literature of ancient Greece is ... a mighty agent of intellectual deliverance; [and] therefore, an object of indestructible interest." And he added:

> But first let us ask ourselves why the demand for an intellectual deliverance arises in such an age as the present, and in what the deliverance itself consists? The demand arises, because our present age has around it a copious and complex present, and behind it a copious and complex past; it arises, because the present age exhibits to the individual man who contemplates it the spectacle of a vast multitude of facts awaiting and inviting his comprehension. The deliverance consists in man's comprehension of this present and past. It begins when our mind begins to enter into possession of the general ideas which are the law of this vast multitude of facts. It is perfect when we have acquired that harmonious acquiescence of mind which we feel in contemplating a grand spectacle that is intelligible to us. ... This, then, is what distinguishes certain epochs in the history of the human race, and our own amongst the number; – on the one hand, the presence of a significant spectacle to contemplate; on the other hand, the desire to find the true point of view from which to contemplate this spectacle. He who has found that point of view, he who adequately comprehends this spectacle, has risen to the comprehension of his age: he who communicates that point of view to his age, he who interprets to it that spectacle, is one of his age's intellectual deliverers" (*Complete Prose* 1: 20).[3]

Although Arnold does not attribute to himself and to his poem such a "presence" or such an overtly "significant spectacle" for our contemplation, and although he does not suggest that his treatment and "comprehension" of even a much more minor "spectacle," like the one in "Dover Beach," rises to a "comprehension of the age" itself, clearly, as his father had, Arnold felt that Thucydides (like Sophocles) was an "intellectual deliverer" for his age, and he no doubt also felt that he himself had fulfilled, or was fulfilling, such a role in his own age. Of course, many readers

---

3   This lecture was subsequently published as "On the Modern Element in Literature" in 1869 and never reprinted by Arnold.

would agree with Arnold about Thucydides and Sophocles, and they would agree that Arnold, through poems like "Dover Beach," *was* passing down such an intellectual message to subsequent ages.

In the final three lines of the poem the speaker and his companion (and by extension all of us as Arnold's readers as well) are "here," that is *there*, on the cliffs above Dover beach, at dusk or dawning dark, where we witness, or are witness to, some sort of battle or conflict which is both "confused" as well as confusing in its "struggle and flight," a battle carried out by "ignorant armies" during the dark. Indeed, we as readers are here as much "in the dark" as the armies are, or seem to be.

Holland views the final lines of "Dover Beach" from a psychological perspective, arguing that "ordinary explication ... offers little basis for the armies, while psychological explication offers considerable." He finds in Arnold's final lines "a well-nigh universal sexual symbolism" in the "heard-but-not seen, naked fighting at night," in which the sexual roles of a man and a woman in bed are "sublimated" into "a distant, literary, and moral experience, a darkling plain from Thucydides." Indeed, he says that the "metaphorical flight in time and space" at the end of the poem "lets us see two 'true' lovers together with a glimpse of a 'clash by night'" (121, 129). Arnold's armies, of course, are not naked, but only "ignorant."

In thinking of a phrase like "And we are here as on a darkling plain," we might ask, "What does it really mean?" The word "darkling" has drawn considerable blood in the Arnold wars and I have little interest in contributing to the carnage, but I think it worth noting that this fascinating word, which has haunted readers' minds for some centuries now, no doubt haunted Arnold's as well before he used it here. For Arnold, the allusions were no doubt several. In addition to the most obvious references – to Shakespeare's *King Lear* ("So out went the candle, and we were left darkling," 1. 4. 237), (and here we might also remember a passage late in *King Lear* that Arnold may well also have been remembering in terms of his imagery and of the working of the waves upon the shore as he describes them in "Dover Beach," one in which Edgar, not on the Dover cliffs themselves but in "Fields near Dover," and wanting to convince his father that they are literally on the edge of the cliffs, imaginatively describes "The murmuring surge / That on the unnumbered idle pebbles chafes" [4. 6. 19-21]),[4] and to *A Midsummer Night's Dream* ("Oh, wilt thou darkling leave me? Do not so," 2. 2.

---

4   In discussing this passage, Culler notes the mix of the visual and the auditory in the lines, arguing that Shakespeare here "exchanges the flat visual sense for the more penetrating auditory." Culler also mentions that Arnold "was well aware that the Dover cliffs are known as 'Shakespeare's cliffs,'" (39) a fact made clear, for instance, in Arnold's letter to his mother of August 4, 1859, written from Dover, in which he makes specific reference to "Shakespeare's Cliff" (Letters 1: 481-82).

86), or even *Antony and Cleopatra* ("Darkling stand / The varying shore o' the world," 4. 15. 10-11), and to Milton's *Paradise Lost* ("as the wakeful bird / Sings darkling ... [and] in shadiest covert hid / Tunes her nocturnal note," 3. 38-40), or to T. Adams's explication of *2 Peter* 2. 10 ("Our lamps ... at last go out, and leave us darkling"), and to Charlotte Smith's lines in "Written near a Port on a Dark Evening" ("life's long darkling way") (cited in Pitman 128) – I think it is equally likely that Arnold is here also quite possibly remembering Lord Byron's dream poem "Darkness," in which "the stars / Did wander darkling in the eternal space / Rayless, and pathless," where "War ... / Did glut himself again" and "Darkness ... was the universe" (McGann 40-43). (Indeed, it is tempting to consider the possibility that Arnold's line, "Begin, and cease, and then again begin" may owe something of its rhythm to Byron's similarly rhythmic line in "Darkness" – "Morn came, and went – and came, and brought no day.") And certainly Arnold is here clearly remembering Keats's famous lines (lines which surely must have often haunted him) in "Ode to a Nightingale," "Darkling I listen; and, for many a time / I have been half in love with easeful Death" (245). Arnold certainly knew that, as he listened, he was himself "darkling" (as Keats knew he was), and he must have also recognized that he too was often "half in love with easeful Death." (Arnold himself also used the word "darkling" in his "Balder Dead," part 2, entitled "Journey to the Dead" – "And by the darkling forest-paths the Gods / Follow'd, and on their shoulders carried boughs" ll. 63-64. And, of course, this rich word was to occur in later poetry as well, no doubt with Arnold's use of it in "Dover Beach" doubled into the mix of the memories of the other poets mentioned above. Perhaps the most memorable reference in terms of a possible allusion to Arnold's use of "darkling" in "Dover Beach" is to be found in Hardy's "The Darkling Thrush," a poem with an equally pessimistic theme. Hardy's thrush, "aged, frail, gaunt, and small," sings "Upon the growing gloom" (25) at the turn of the twentieth century.)

But there seems to be more to be made of the line "And we are here as on a darkling plain" since, wherever the speaker speaks from here at the end of Arnold's poem, the "here" (with the rhyme and resonance of *hear* in it) is far from specific. Is this "here" a reference to the cliff itself, or to some place near it, a "there" where the speaker and his companion stand, or have taken their, or a, "stand?" Apparently not, since the "here" seems to refer neither to the cliff itself nor to the observation platform spoken from because it is immediately made imaginary by the next word "as"; it cannot, therefore, be literal – unless we imagine that the speaker and his companion are both "here," that is, literally *there*, on the Dover cliffs, and that they are *simultaneously* thinking about being somewhere else, on some *other* "darkling plain."

And what of this "plain?" It is far from clear what Arnold meant, although the various definitions of "plain" are intriguing and, in the context, perhaps instructive.

Apparently Arnold's reference, in essence, is intended to suggest "an extensive area of level" treeless territory, or "a broad unbroken expanse" (Webster's), like that at Dover along the tops of the cliffs, or, indeed, of the expanse of the sea itself. Since it seems certain that, in some ways at least, Arnold does not seem to wish to make his meaning clear, or to put his vision before us in "plain sight" as it were, but rather wants us to see and hear what lies below the surface of his lines and sentences, we perhaps need to look further, or deeper. Is it possible that what is "here," and to be heard by those who can *hear* it, is something deeper than a waking consciousness can see or comprehend, something that can only (or best) be "seen" from within "a land of dreams," something that is "seen" and thereby only understood in an oneiric way? That is, that the "dark" vision and the knowledge known of it – although both might be triggered by external phenomena and particular places – are best known and (only?) understood in a metaphoric or subconscious way; that they are really things internal or interior which, once brought up into consciousness or put forth in the open (in "plain sight" as it were), can only then be understood and applied to a literal, physical time and place?

If this is the case, then one way of reading the enigmatic final lines of Arnold's poem would be: since it is "plain" (clear) that "we" are "here," in "pain," on a "darkling plain" (and simultaneously on a plane, a "level of existence, consciousness, or development," [Webster's] an intellectual plane), caught up in the confusions of our own consciousness (described and defined in the context of Arnold's life-long personal theological "war" within – which wars within us as well, like "ignorant" armies fighting with one another in the dark of our own dreams or imaginings), we have little recourse to any resource of salvation save that which we ourselves can contrive to make or find at hand by being "true to one another," since God, long ago, left us alone and to our own devices, even if we have only recently noticed it. This, I think – and no doubt more than this – is what Arnold was attempting to describe and detail in "Dover Beach." It certainly is a theme whose echoes reverberate (beginning, then seeming to cease, only to begin again) here in the early years of the twenty-first century.

Works Cited

Arnold, Matthew, *The Complete Prose Works of Matthew Arnold.* 11 vols. Ed. R. H. Super. Ann Arbor: U of Michigan P, 1960-77.
–. *The Poetical Works of Matthew Arnold.* Eds. C. B. Tinker and H. F. Lowry. London: Oxford UP, 1950.
Bidney, Martin. "Of the Devil's Party: Undetected Words of Milton's Satan in Arnold's 'Dover Beach.'" *Victorian Poetry* 20 (1982): 85-89.

Culler, A. Dwight. *Imaginative Reason: The Poetry of Matthew Arnold.* New Haven: Yale UP, 1966.

Dickey, James. *Babel to Byzentium: Poets and Poetry Now.* New York: Farrar, Straus and Giroux, 1968.

Fain, John Tyree. "Arnold's 'Dover Beach.'" *The Explicator* 43 (Fall, 1984): 40-42.

Grob, Alan. *A Longing Like Despair: Arnold's Poetry of Pessimism.* Newark: U Delaware P, 2002.

Hamilton, Ian. *Gift Imprisoned: The Poetic Life of Matthew Arnold.* New York: Basic Books, 1999.

Hardy, Thomas. *Selected Poems of Thomas Hardy.* Ed. John Crowe Ransom. New York: Collier Books, 1966.

Holland, Norman N. *The Dynamics of Literary Response.* New York: Oxford UP, 1968.

Jeffers, Robinson. *The Selected Poetry of Robinson Jeffers.* Ed. Tim Hunt: Stanford: Stanford UP, 2001.

Keats, John. *John Keats: Selected Poetry and Letters.* Ed. Richard Harter Fogle. New York: Holt, Rinehart and Winston, 1951.

Krieger, Murray. "'Dover Beach' and the Tragic Sense of Eternal Recurrence." *The University of Kansas City Review* 23 (1956): 73-79.

Lang, Cecil Y., ed. *The Letters of Matthew Arnold.* Vol.1. Charlottesville: UP of Virginia, 1996.

McGann, Jerome J. *Lord Byron: The Complete Poetical Works*, Vol. IV. Oxford: Clarendon P, 1986.

Miller, J. Hillis. *The Disappearance of God: Five Nineteenth-Century Writers.* Urbana: U of Illinois P, 2000.

Perrine, Laurence. "Matthew Arnold's 'Dover Beach.'" In *Instructor's Manual to Accompany Perrine's Sound and Sense: An Introduction to Poetry.* 9th edition. Ed. Thomas R. Arp. Fort Worth: Harcourt Brace College Publishers, 1997.

Pitman, Ruth. "On Dover Beach." *Essays in Criticism* 23: 2 (1973): 109-37.

Shakespeare, William. Ed. G. B. Harrison. *Shakespeare: The Complete Works.* New York: Harcourt, Brace and World, 1952.

Stevens, Wallace. *Opus Posthumous.* New York: Alfred A. Knopf, 1980.

GRAZER BEITRÄGE ZUR ENGLISCHEN PHILOLOGIE

Band 1 Peter Bierbaumer: Der botanische Wortschatz des Altenglischen. 1. Teil: Das Læcebōc. 1975.

Band 2 Peter Bierbaumer: Der botanische Wortschatz des Altenglischen. 2. Teil: Lācnunga, Herbarium Apuleii, Peri Didaxeon. 1976.

Band 3 Peter Bierbaumer: Der botanische Wortschatz des Altenglischen: 3. Teil: Der botanische Wortschatz in altenglischen Glossen. 1979.

Band 4 Gerd Sieper: Fachsprachliche Korpusanalyse und Wortschatzauswahl. 1980.

Band 5 Rüdiger Pfeiffer-Rupp: Studien zu Subkategorisierung und semantischen Relationen. 1977.

Band 6 Bernhard Kettemann: Aspekte der natürlichen generativen Phonologie eines amerikanisch-englischen Dialektes. 1978.

BAMBERGER BEITRÄGE ZUR ENGLISCHEN SPRACHWISSENSCHAFT
BAMBERG STUDIES IN ENGLISH LINGUISTICS
(Die Reihe wird unter neuer Reihenbezeichnung ab Band 7 weitergeführt)

Band 7 Günter Radden: Ein Profil soziolinguistischer Variation in einer amerikanischen Kleinstadt. 1979.

Band 8 Karin Viereck: Englisches Wortgut, seine Häufigkeit und Integration in der österreichischen und bundesdeutschen Pressesprache. 1980.

Band 9 John Oakeshott-Taylor: Acoustic Variability and its Perception. The effects of context on selected acoustic parameters of English words and their perceptual consequences. 1980.

Band 10 Edgar W. Schneider: Morphologische und syntaktische Variablen im amerikanischen *Early Black English*. 1981.

Band 11 Val Jones-Sargent: Tyne Bytes. A Computerised Sociolinguistic Study of Tyneside. 1983.

Band 12 Lee Pederson: East Tennessee Folk Speech. A Synopsis. 1983.

Band 13 Cornelia Zelinsky-Wibbelt: Die semantische Belastung von submorphematischen Einheiten im Englischen. Eine empirisch-strukturelle Untersuchung. 1983.

Band 14 Rolf Bremann: Soziolinguistische Untersuchungen zum Englisch von Cornwall. 1984.

Band 15 Wolf-Dietrich Bald and Horst Weinstock (eds.): Medieval Studies Conference Aachen 1983. Language and Literature. 1984.

Band 16 Clausdirk Pollner: Englisch in Livingston. Ausgewählte sprachliche Erscheinungen in einer schottischen New Town. 1985.

Band 17 Adam Jaworski: A linguistic picture of women's position in society. A Polish-English contrastive study. 1986.

Band 18 Mark Newbrook: Sociolinguistic reflexes of dialect interference in West Wirral. 1986.

Band 19 George Townsend Dorrill: Black and White Speech in the Southern United States. Evidence from the Linguistic Atlas of the Middle and South Atlantic States. 1986.

Band 20 Birgit Meseck: Studien zur konservativ-restaurativen Sprachkritik in Amerika. 1987.

Band 21 Barbara Kryk: On Deixis in English and Polish: The Role of Demonstrative Pronouns. 1987.

Band 22 Sándor Rot: On Crucial Problems of the English Verb. 1988.

Band 48 Gabriele Knappe (Hrsg.): Englische Sprachwissenschaft und Mediävistik: Standpunkte – Perspektiven – Neue Wege. English Linguistics and Medieval Studies: Positions – Perspectives – New Approaches. Proceedings of the Conference in Bamberg, May 21–22, 2004. 2005.

Band 49 Wolfgang Viereck: Selected Writings – Ausgewählte Schriften. English Linguistic and Cultural History – English Dialectology. Englische Sprach- und Kulturgeschichte – Englische Dialektologie. 2005.

Band 50 Wolfgang Viereck: Selected Writings – Ausgewählte Schriften. History of Science, English Surnames, American English, Languages in Contact, Language and School, *Atlas Linguarum Europae*. Wissenschaftsgeschichte, Englische Familiennamen, Amerikanisches Englisch, Sprachen in Kontakt, Sprache und Schule, *Atlas Linguarum Europae*. 2005.

Band 51 Herbert Grabes / Wolfgang Viereck (eds.): The Wider Scope of English. Papers in English Language and Literature from the Bamberg Conference of the International Association of University Professors of English. 2006.

Band 52 Stephanie Barker / Stefankai Spoerlein / Tobias Vetter / Wolfgang Viereck: An Atlas of English Surnames. 2007.

Band 53 Shane Walshe: Irish English as Represented in Film. 2009

Band 54 Barry Heselwood / Clive Upton (eds.): Proceedings of Methods XIII. Papers from the Thirteenth International Conference on Methods in Dialectology, 2008. 2010.

Band 55 Wolfgang Viereck (ed.): English Past and Present. Selected Papers from the IAUPE Malta Conference in 2010. 2012.

www.peterlang.de